Textbooks in Language Sciences

In this series:

1. Müller, Stefan. Grammatical theory: From transformational grammar to constraint-based approaches.
2. Schäfer, Roland. Einführung in die grammatische Beschreibung des Deutschen.
3. Freitas, Maria João & Ana Lúcia Santos (eds.). Aquisição de língua materna e não materna: Questões gerais e dados do português.
4. Roussarie, Laurent. Sémantique formelle: Introduction à la grammaire de Montague.
5. Kroeger, Paul. Analyzing meaning: An introduction to semantics and pragmatics.
6. Ferreira, Marcelo. Curso de semântica formal.
7. Stefanowitsch, Anatol. Corpus linguistics: A guide to the methodology.
8. Müller, Stefan. 语法理论: 从转换语法到基于约束的理论.
9. Hejná, Míša & George Walkden. A history of English.
10. Kahane, Sylvain & Kim Gerdes. Syntaxe théorique et formelle. Vol. 1: Modélisation, unités, structures.
11. Freitas, Maria João, Marisa Lousada & Dina Caetano Alves (eds.). Linguística clínica: Modelos, avaliação e intervenção.
12. Müller, Stefan. Germanic syntax: A constraint-based view.
13. Neacşu, Vlad A. Linguistics Olympiad: Training guide.
14. Glass, Lelia, Markus Dickinson, Chris Brew & Detmar Meurers. Language and computers: 2nd edition.

ISSN: 2364-6209

Language and computers

2nd edition

Lelia Glass

Markus Dickinson

Chris Brew

Detmar Meurers

language
science
press

Lelia Glass, Markus Dickinson, Chris Brew & Detmar Meurers. 2024. *Language and computers: 2nd edition* (Textbooks in Language Sciences 14). Berlin: Language Science Press.

This title can be downloaded at:
http://langsci-press.org/catalog/book/454

ISBN: 978-3-96110-480-2 (Digital)
978-3-98554-109-6 (Softcover)
ISSN: 2364-6209
DOI: 10.5281/zenodo.12730906
Source code available from www.github.com/langsci/454
Errata: paperhive.org/documents/remote?type=langsci&id=454

Cover and concept of design: Ulrike Harbort
Typesetting: Lelia Glass
Proofreading: Amir Ghorbanpour, Annika Schiefner, Ash Price, Brett Reynolds, Caroline Pajančič, Christopher Straughn, Cong Luan Tran, Daniil Bondarenko, Elen Le Foll, Elliott Pearl, Francesco Screti, Harold Somers, Jean Nitzke, Jeroen van de Weijer, Katja Politt, Killian Kiuttu, Lachlan Mackenzie, Mary Ann Walter, Patricia Cabredo, Rebecca Madlener, Sean Stalley, Troy E. Spierer, Wilson Lui
Fonts: Libertinus, Arimo, DejaVu Sans Mono, Source Han Serif ZH
Typesetting software: XƎLaTeX

Language Science Press
xHain
Grünberger Str. 16
10243 Berlin, Germany
http://langsci-press.org

Storage and cataloguing done by FU Berlin

Freie Universität Berlin

Contents

Acknowledgments

The first edition of this book emerged from a course (*Language and Computers*) taught at the Ohio State University beginning in 2004. We are indebted to Peter Culicover and Beth Hume, who were at the time Chair and Director of Undergraduate Studies of the Linguistics Department, for their foresight in recognizing the potential of such a course. We also thank Danielle Descoteaux for encouraging us to turn the course into a book, and Julia Kirk for her work as project editor.

The second edition grew out of a course taught at Georgia Tech beginning in 2018. We thank Kyoko Masuda for proposing the course, and Mark Riedl for helping to cross-list it with a Computer Science number, thus attracting more diverse students. We also thank Sam Bowman, Timothy Dozat, and Yuval Pinter for helpful suggestions about how to structure that course.

We express gratitude to curious and insightful students at Ohio State, Georgia Institute of Technology, Georgetown University, Indiana University, and New York University for feedback as we developed and updated this book to use in their classes.

For generous and helpful feedback on individual chapters, we thank Rebekah Baglini, Jason Baldridge, Stacey Bailey, Lucas Champollion, Anna Feldman, Jon Dehdari, Keelan Evanini, Michael Heilman, D.J. Hovermale, Ross Israel, Sandra Kübler, Xiaofei Lu, Kyle Mahowald, Rajakrishnan Rajkumar, Nathan Schneider, Shane Steinert-Threlkeld, Amber Smith, Michael White, Johannes Widmann, and Amir Zeldes.

We are particularly indebted to Jason Baldridge and Lucas Champollion for encouragement and thoughtful feedback from courses that they taught using drafts of this book.

For examples of diverse writing systems, we thank Tony Meyer and Ayelet Weiss. For assistance with proof-reading, we thank Sheena Phillips, Jason Quinley, Chris Glauder, and Faye Holt. We also gratefully acknowledge the detailed and knowledgeable feedback of the volunteer proof-readers who gave feedback for Language Science Press: Daniil Bondarenko, Patricia Cabredo, Amir Ghorbanpour, Killian Kiuttu, Elen Le Foll, Lachlan Mackenzie, Rebecca Madlener, Jean Nitzke, Caroline Pajanyič, Elliott Pearl, Katja Politt, Ash Price, Brett Reynolds, Annika Schiefner, Francesco Screti, Harold Somers, Troy E. Spier, Sean Stalley,

Christopher Straughn, Cong Luan Tran, Mary Ann Walter, and Jeroen van de Weijer, Harold Somers provided especially detailed comments. Thanks also to Sebastian Nordhoff at Language Science Press for his work to help us to finalize the book.

Speaking individually, Lelia Glass thanks Mark Menzies for companionship and insight, as well as for discussion of Westlaw. Thanks also to baby Lelia Carter Menzies for bringing joy and purpose.

Markus Dickinson expresses gratitude to Stephanie Dickinson for encouragement and support, as well as for dinnertime discussion of the sensitivity and specificity of medical tests. He also wants to thank all the students over the years who have helped make this material what it is, stemming back from 2004, when he had no clue what he was doing, and, in that light, he thanks his co-authors, for being there after he left academia and returned to having no clue.

Chris Brew thanks Sheena Phillips, Matthew and Jamie Brew.

Detmar Meurers thanks his coauthors as well as Walter Meurers for emphasizing the importance of connecting research issues with the real world. He also thanks Kordula De Kuthy, Marius, Dario, and Cora for reminding him that life has a meaning beyond deadlines.

Preface

Much of today's speech and writing is channeled digitally, and computers are increasingly able to disseminate, organize, and produce language along with the information contained therein. Such capabilities make people's lives easier: Now everyone on the internet can correspond instantly with billions of people around the globe, and access information far surpassing even the best research libraries of the past. On the other hand, these tools may trigger a socio-economic transformation with losers as well as winners, and can harm people if used uncritically.

This book takes you on a tour of different real-world tasks and applications where computers deal with language. During this tour, you'll encounter essential concepts relating to language, representation, and processing, so that by the end of the book you will have a good grasp of key concepts in the field of language technology (LT), computational linguistics (CL), and natural language processing (NLP) – essentially names for the same thing, as viewed from the respective perspectives of industry, linguistics, and computer science. The only background you need to read this book is some curiosity about language and some everyday experience with computers.

We explore tools that support writing; foreign language learning; the distillation of information from text for research and business purposes; automatic detection of spam, anti-social content, or emotional sentiment; web search; machine translation; and conversation. We assume that most of you will be familiar with these applications and may wonder how they work or why they don't. What you may not realize is how similar the underlying processing is. For example, there is a lot in common between how your email system filters spam and how a dialog system identifies what you are asking it to do. By seeing these concepts recur – in this case, a machine learning technique called classification – we hope this will reinforce the importance of applying general techniques for new applications.

This book aims to welcome humanities-confident students to learn technical tools, and to invite computing-confident students to appreciate the social richness of language data. From the technical side, we explore the computational underpinnings of language technology; from the humanistic side, we emphasize the nuances of the linguistic data as well as social, economic, and ethical effects of such technology. Whether you feel more confident in humanistic or technical ways of thinking, we hope that this book empowers you to combine both approaches to fully understand the value, limitations, and consequences of language technology.

How to use the book

There are a number of features in this textbook which allow you to structure what you learn, explore more about the topics and to reinforce what you are learning. As a start, relevant keywords are typeset in bold and shown in the margins of each page. You can also look those up in the *Subject index* at the end of the book.

The *Under the Hood* sections included in many of the chapters are intended to give you more detail on selected advanced topics. For those interested in learning more about language and computers, we hope that you find these sections enjoyable and enlightening, though the gist of each chapter can be understood without reading those sections.

At the end of each chapter, there is a *Checklist* indicating what you should have learned in reading the chapter. The *Exercises* found at the end of each chapter review the chapter's material and give you opportunities to go beyond it. Our hope is that the checklist and exercises help you to get a good grasp of each of the topics and the concepts involved. Different exercises will appeal to different students; you are welcome to choose the ones that seem most interesting to you, or challenge yourself to try all of them.

If you enjoy the topic of a particular chapter, we also encourage you to make use of the *Further reading* recommendations. You can also track the *References* at the end of the book.

For more advanced students, we have had success combining this textbook with a reading list of articles about digital humanities, computational social science, and corpus linguistics, such as those discussed in Chapter 4, which students are asked to present in class. (In one of our classes based on this book, the instructor gives a lecture every Tuesday to set up the topic; Thursdays begin with a clicker quiz to test students' understanding, and the rest of Thursday's class is spent on student presentations of articles). The reading list can be updated every year and customized to the interests of the instructor and students, and the presentations give students a chance to learn from one another while practicing valuable humanistic skills in digesting and communicating research findings. Advanced students may also be assigned to pursue a final project, engaging with the literature that they have read throughout the semester.

Finally, on the book's companion website https://osf.io/v7uqm/, we offer an example syllabus and slide decks corresponding to each chapter of this book, which instructors are welcome to use and adapt.

1 Encoding language on computers

1.1 What is language?

This book aims to introduce you to the different ways that computers are able to process natural language. To start off, then, we can ask: What is language? You're using language to read this book, so you have some intuitive idea of what it is, but if you've never studied linguistics before, you might not have a clear definition in mind.

In an attempt to distinguish between language and other animal communication systems, the anthropologist Charles Hockett (1960) proposed some properties that together make language special:

1. Language is produced vocally and understood with the auditory system, or in the case of signed languages, signed with the body and perceived visually.

2. Language is produced intentionally. People intend to say what they say.

3. Language is transitory: Unless you write down what is said, it is ephemeral. As we will explore in detail later, writing – crucially *not* transitory – is distinct from language.

4. Language is interchangeable: Anything that you can hear, you can also say, and vice versa, regardless of its truth or its relation to you. (In contrast, in the realm of animal communication, queen ants produce a chemical signal that other ants cannot produce, meaning that chemical communication for ants is non-interchangeable.)

5. Language involves total feedback: Speakers can hear their own speech, and signers can see their own signing. People know what they are saying.

6. When people speak or sign, the sounds/signs that they produce are specifically intended for communication, not secondary to any other purpose. (In contrast, a dog may indirectly convey that it is hot by panting, but the primary purpose of panting is to cool the dog off, not to communicate.)

7. Specific words/signs are attached to specific meanings.

8. The relation between sounds/signs and meaning is mostly *arbitrary*, chosen by convention. There is no particular reason to call a dog a *dog* except that our community has agreed to it; other communities have chosen other conventions (*perro*, *Hund*, etc.).

9. Even if different people pronounce or sign the same word differently, these variable realizations are mapped to discrete categories (distinct sounds, signs, or words) in the mind.

10. Language can be used to talk about things that are absent, imaginary, or false (in contrast to pointing, for example, which is restricted to entities that are present).

11. Language can be used to lie.

12. Language is made of discrete units: Sentences/ utterances are made of words; words are made of morphemes (pieces of words such as *un-* or *-ing*); morphemes are made of sounds.

13. Language is *productive*: You can use it to say and understand things that have never been said before.

14. Language is learnable: You can learn a (new) language.

15. Language is culturally transmitted: You learn the language(s) surrounding you.

16. Language is reflexive: As we're doing here, you can use language to talk about itself.

Using these distinctive features, you should now be able to explain why music, mathematics, and programming languages – as amazing and useful as they are – do not constitute language in Hockett's sense, even if they share some elements in common with it.

1.2 Language versus writing

Language is perhaps the most amazing technology that humans have ever created: It allows us to teach and learn, explain complicated ideas, build social relationships and societies, create laws and promises, ask and answer questions, make and respond to commands, tell stories, imagine alternate realities, understand what other people believe, recount the past and plan for the future, and collaborate to get things done.

It is important to understand that language is distinct from writing. As Hockett notes, spoken/signed utterances are ephemeral; writing constitutes a further amazing technology which represents speech/signing in a system of lasting physical or digital markings. Distinguishing language from its written representation, language is universal across humans: All human societies use language, and every single human child (except for rare cases of extremely severe neglect or disability) learns language without much formal instruction. In contrast, writing is not universal: Some societies do not use writing. Indeed, of the seven thousand known spoken languages listed in *Ethnologue*[1], only about sixty percent have writing systems; unwritten languages include the Gugu Badhun language of Australia, the Southeastern Pomo language of California, and so on. Writing generally requires formal instruction, and some people do not learn it even if their society uses it. Language is also much older than writing; language emerged around 100,000 to 200,000 years ago while writing arose around five or six thousand years ago. Of course, language is transitory, so its age can only be inferred indirectly, from archaeological artifacts such as decorative beads (Botha & Knight 2009), which indicate a desire to communicate (one's status and appearance) that presumably extends to language. So language is ancient and universal, while writing is new and localized to particular people and societies.

Although it is important to keep language and writing distinct, writing is obviously intimately related to language. Writing allows us to do all the things that language allows us to do – teach, learn, explain, build relationships, organize societies, talk about the past and future, collaborate – across distances and time. With writing, you can learn from people you have never met, from past generations and other continents. You can also keep records of things, such as debts and purchases, that are too complicated to remember; indeed, the first Sumerian writing appears to record commercial transactions, involving both language and numeracy (Glassner 2003). Today, thanks to computers and the internet, digital writing allows us to disseminate language instantly around the globe.

The topics explored in this book involve the word *language* – natural language processing, language technology – but they largely involve writing, because writing is the primary medium through which computers represent and process language. We begin our tour by introducing writing systems and their digital representation, then end the chapter by briefly exploring sound.

[1]https://ethnologue.com, accessed 2024-04-19.

1.3 Writing systems

A *writing system* is "a system of more or less permanent marks used to represent an utterance in such a way that it can be recovered more or less exactly without the intervention of the utterer" (Daniels & Bright 1996: 3). Historically, of course, writing systems consisted of markings on clay, stone, or paper (originally made by hand, later by the printing press); today, these markings are stored and disseminated digitally, allowing for much more text to be written, read, and shared than at any other time in history.

You are reading this book in the Latin alphabet: 26 letters, each of which has an upper-case and a lower-case variant, plus ten numerals and various types of punctuation: In total, a little over a hundred symbols. Simple enough?

But this book is called *Language and computers*, not *English and computers*! So we also have to think about how to represent other languages and other writing systems.

First, going back to the idea that writing systems are distinct from languages, many different languages share the same writing system: The Latin alphabet is used not just for English but also for French, German, Finnish, Vietnamese, Yoruba, and many other languages.

(1) Same writing system, different languages:
   a. English: What is your name?
   b. French: *Comment t'appelles-tu?*

Conversely, the same language can be written in multiple different writing systems. Mandarin Chinese can be written in the traditional characters still used today in Taiwan; in the simplified characters of Mainland China; or transliterated into the Latin alphabet through the Pinyin system.

馬	马	mǎ
Traditional character	Simplified character	Pinyin Latinization

Figure 1.1: 'Horse' (*mǎ*) written in three different writing systems for Mandarin Chinese.

As another example of how languages are distinct from writing systems, Yiddish and German are related to one another and somewhat mutually intelligible, but German is written in the Latin alphabet while Yiddish is written in the Hebrew writing system (which, as we'll discuss below, is not a traditional alphabet because only the consonant sounds are written).

Turkish and Vietnamese are examples of languages currently written in the Latin alphabet but which historically used other systems (for Turkish, Arabic and Greek alphabets; for Vietnamese, an adaption of the Chinese writing system). Japanese is a single language currently written in three different writing systems, all of which can be used for different purposes within the same document.

As discussed above, language comprises a set of mostly arbitrary, memorized pairs of sound and meaning. A writing system can in principle reflect either or both of these elements, sounds or meaning. We will explore three types of writing systems: alphabetic (where each symbol represents one sound), syllabic (each symbol represents a syllable), and logographic (each symbol represents a concept that language refers to). In any such system, some part of the sound/meaning pairing is recorded, but other parts must be independently known to the reader. Reading English in the Latin alphabet, the string of letters *cat* conveys information about pronunciation, but you have to already know the meaning associated with this string of sounds.

Writing systems vary not just in what information is or is not encoded, but also in their direction (the Latin alphabet is conventionally written left to right; the Hebrew and Arabic systems go right to left; Chinese used to be written vertically but is now written left to right); in conventions about capitalization (if it exists) and punctuation; and in whether words or syllables are separated (in the Latin alphabet, by spaces) or contiguous.

1.3.1 Alphabetic systems

We start our tour of writing systems with what should be familiar to any reader of English: *alphabets.* In *alphabetic systems*, a single character typically refers to a single sound (a single articulatory gesture made by the vocal apparatus). In the word *cat*, the three letters represent three sounds: an initial consonant, a vowel, and a final consonant.

But there is not always a perfect one-to-one correspondence between a word's alphabetic spelling and its pronunciation. In English, the orthographic string *ough* can be pronounced at least five different ways: *cough*, *tough*, *through*, *though*, and *hiccough*. Letters are not consistently pronounced, and in fact, sometimes they are not pronounced at all, as in in *knee*, *debt*, *psychology*, and *mortgage*, among others. There are historical reasons for these silent letters, which were by and large pronounced at one time, but the effect is that we now have letters we do not speak.

The idealized one-to-one sound-letter correspondence is also disrupted when single letters represent multiple sounds, such as the *x* in *tax*, which corresponds to a [k] sound followed by an [s] sound. Moreover, multiple letters can consistently be used to represent one sound, as in *sh* in *should* or *ti* in *revolution* – both of which represent a single articulatory gesture in which air is channeled through a narrow passage created by raising the tongue to the roof of the mouth (below, we'll learn that this sound is known as a voiceless post-alveolar fricative).

Finally, we can alternate spellings for the same word, such as *doughnut* and *donut*, and *homophones* show us different words which are spelled differently but spoken the same, such as *colonel* and *kernel.* When the same letter represents multiple distinct sounds, the same string represents multiple distinct words, or the same word/sound represents multiple distinct meanings, we are dealing with *ambiguity* – a recurring issue in dealing with human language that you will see throughout this book.

But while there are exceptions to the idea that each unique articulatory gesture is represented by one unique letter, that is still the organizing principle of alphabetic writing systems.

Looking beyond the familiar Latin alphabet, the Cyrillic alphabet (Table 1.1) is used for Russian and other languages in its geographic region. Although some characters correspond well to Latin alphabetic letters, others are distinctive. The characters within brackets specify how each letter is pronounced; we will return to these in the discussion of phonetic alphabets later on.

Table 1.1: The Cyrillic alphabet used for Russian.

а	б	в	г	д	е	ё	ж	з	и	й
[a]	[b]	[v]	[g]	[d]	[je]	[jo]	[ʒ]	[z]	[i]	[j]
к	л	м	н	о	п	р	с	т	у	ф
[k]	[l]	[m]	[n]	[o]	[p]	[r]	[s]	[t]	[u]	[f]
х	ц	ч	ш	щ	ъ	ы	ь	э	ю	я
[x]	[ts]	[tɕ]	[ʂ]	[ɕɕ]	[-]	[ɨ]	[ʲ]	[e]	[ju]	[ja]

Some alphabets, such as Fraser used for the Lisu language spoken in Myanmar, China, and India also include *diacritics* to indicate properties such as a word's tone (how high or low-pitched a sound is). A diacritic is added to a regular character to indicate more detail about how that sound is supposed to be realized. In the case of Fraser, for example, *M:* refers to an [m] sound (written as *M*), which has a low tone (written as *:*).

You have hopefully noticed the notation used within the brackets ([]). The characters used there are a part of the International Phonetic Alphabet (IPA). Whereas most alphabetic writing systems offer an imperfect correspondence between letters and sound, a *phonetic alphabet* such as the IPA is designed by linguists to capture those correspondences precisely, offering a way to represent the sounds of all spoken languages in a unified and unambiguous framework.

At https://www.ipachart.com,[2] you can view an interactive IPA chart and listen to all the sounds. Most of the English orthographic consonants correspond transparently to the IPA (the IPA symbol [b] represents the sound used in the orthographic word *buy*), but some are non-obvious. For example, [θ] stands for the *th* in *thigh*; [ð] for the *th* in *thy*; and [ʃ] – the post-alveolar fricative previewed above! – for the *sh* in *shy*. Note that the orthographic strings *th* and *sh* correspond to multiple letters in the Latin alphabet, but only one consonant in a phonetic alphabet because they represent only one articulatory gesture.

If you remember the periodic table of the elements from chemistry class, you remember that it is organized left to right by the number of electrons in the atom's outermost shell, and top to bottom by the number of electron shells that orbit its nucleus, so that column-mates and row-mates share important distinctive properties. The IPA consonant chart is similarly organized into meaningful rows and columns: from top to bottom by how much the air expelled by the lungs does or does not stop in the mouth in creating that sound, and from left to right by the position in the mouth, from front to back, where the airflow is constricted.

As seen in Figure 1.2, the top left of the IPA consonant chart represents the sounds [p] and [b] (which basically correspond to their pronunciations in the Latin alphabet), where the air stops fully at the very front of the mouth on the lips. Moving across, the *place of articulation* moves further back in the mouth

[2]Accessed 2024-07-01.

Table 1.2: IPA consonants

	Bilabial	Labiodental	Dental	Alveolar	Postalveolar	Retroflex	Palatal	Velar	Uvular	Pharyngal	Glottal
Plosives	p b			t d		ʈ ɖ	c ɟ	k g	q ɢ		ʔ
Nasals	m	ɱ		n		ɳ	ɲ	ŋ	ɴ		
Vibrants	ʙ			r					ʀ		
Taps and Flaps				ɾ		ɽ					
Fricatives	ɸ β	f v	θ ð	s z	ʃ ʒ	ʂ ʐ	ç ʝ	x ɣ	χ ʁ	ħ ʕ	h ɦ
Lateral fricatives				ɬ ɮ							
Approximants		ʋ		ɹ		ɻ	j	ɰ			
Lateral approximants				l		ɭ	ʎ	ʟ			

(e.g., [k] and [g] are formed by raising the back of the tongue); moving down, the *manner of articulation* involves less and less stoppage of air, with sounds like [f] and [v] allowing air to flow out of the mouth without stopping. The sounds [p] and [b] both share the same place (bilabial, involving both lips) and manner (fully stopping the air) of articulation, differing only in *voicing*: whether the vocal cords are vibrating during the articulation of the sound. Whenever two sounds share the same cell in the IPA consonant chart, the first one is unvoiced and the second is voiced.

The IPA is designed to represent sounds from any human language, and each individual language uses only a subset of the available possible sounds. So some of the IPA sounds are not used in English at all, for example the velar fricative [x] used in the German word for 'book,' *Buch.* (This [x] is distinct from the orthographic letter *x* of the Latin alphabet, used in *tax* and *exit*: in the IPA, the sound represented by the orthographic *x* in *tax* is [ks], and in *exit* can be either [ks] or [gz]! Which version do you use?).

Turning to the vowels, the IPA vowel chart in Figure 1.2 is organized to look like the shape of the mouth, because vowels are distinguished by the place of the tongue in the mouth when the air is expelled. The top left of the vowel chart is the high, front vowel [i], as in the word *bee* – here, the tongue is raised and the air is sent through the upper portion of the mouth. The other sound at the top left of the chart is [y], which is high and front like [i] but also involves *rounding* of the lips. This sound is not used in English; English only allows back vowels (created at the back of the mouth, like the vowel [u] in *boot*), to be rounded. The front rounded vowel [y] is used in French words such as *tu* 'you'.

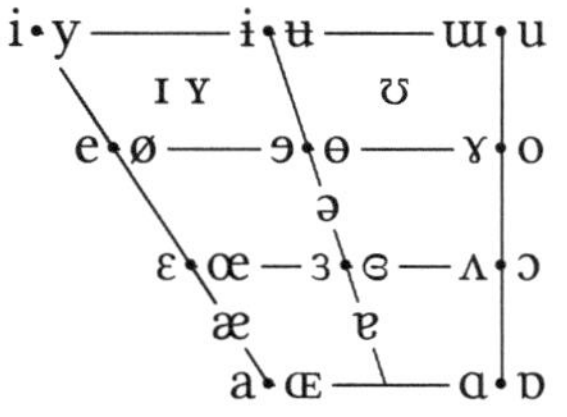

Figure 1.2: IPA vowels.

The IPA coheres perfectly to the idea (roughly true in all alphabetic systems) that each symbol represents exactly one sound. It has the advantage of being unambiguous: A given symbol is pronounced in the same way in all contexts. And yet, despite these major advantages, the IPA is used mainly by linguists to discuss specific sounds; no one actually uses it as a widespread writing system for disseminating text in any language. We will explore why not in Chapter 2.

Returning to writing systems used in the real world, the broad class of alphabetic systems also includes *abjads* (consonant alphabets), which represent consonants only. Some prime examples are Arabic, Aramaic, and Hebrew. In abjads, vowels are typically deduced from context or marked by diacritics, as illustrated by the Hebrew word for *computer* shown on the left-hand side of Figure 1.3.

מחשב	מחשב	מחשב
b š x m	*b š x m*	*b š x m*
[maxʃev]	[mexuʃav]	[mexaʃav]
'computer'	'is digitized'	'with + he thought'

Figure 1.3: Example of Hebrew (abjad) text.

The Hebrew word in its character-by-character transliteration *bšxm* (read right to left) contains no vowels, so the reader must rely on outside knowledge to supply the [a] and [e] vowels shown in the IPA rendering of the word [maxʃev]. (Hebrew is written right to left, so the rightmost *m* in the letter-by-letter transliteration corresponds to the the first sound that is pronounced, matching the leftmost symbol in the IPA. We wrote the letter-by-letter transliteration from right to left to align with the Hebrew letters above.) As shown in the middle and righthand side of Figure 1.3, the same string is also compatible with other pronunciations and meanings: Only the consonants are written, so the vowels have to be supplied by the reader's wider knowledge of the language and the context.

1.3.2 Syllabic systems

Syllabic systems are like alphabetic systems in that they involve a mapping between characters and sounds, but the units of sound are larger, comprising *syllables* made from multiple articulatory gestures.

All human languages have syllables as basic building blocks of speech, but the rules for forming syllables differ from language to language. For example, in Mandarin Chinese, a syllable consists of a single vowel or diphthong (two vowels within the same syllable), optionally preceded by at most one consonant or affricate (two consonants articulated as one), and optionally followed by a nasal ([n] or [ŋ]) or a rhotic sound [ɹ]. Syllables are also distinguished by tone, the contour of pitch throughout the duration of the syllable. This system gives rise to words, transliterated into the Latin alphabet using the Pinyin system, with tones rendered as diacritics above vowels, such as *túshūguǎn* 'library', *Měiguó* 'America', and *xīngqíwǔ* 'Friday' (note that *sh* and *ng* each represent single phonetic consonants, [ʃ] and [ŋ], even though these are spelled with two orthographic consonants in the Latin alphabet).

Most of the world's languages have relatively simple syllables, like Mandarin. This means that the total number of possible syllables in the language is quite small, and that syllabic writing systems work well. In English, Russian, and other languages, however, the beginning or end of the syllable may also include a so-called *consonant cluster*, such as [sp] and [ɹk] in *spark*). This greatly expands the number of possible syllables. You could design a syllabic writing system for English, but it would be unwieldy and difficult to learn, because there are so many different possible syllables.

There are two main variants of syllabic systems, the first being *abugidas*, or *alphasyllabaries*. In these writing systems, the symbols are organized into families. All the members of a family represent the same consonant, but they correspond to different vowels. The members of a family also look similar, but have extra components that are added in order to represent the different vowels. The distinctive thing about an abugida is that this process is systematic, with more or less the same vowel components being used in each family.

To write a syllable consisting of a consonant and a vowel, you go to the family for the relevant consonant, then select the family member corresponding to the vowel that you want. This works best for languages in which almost all syllables consist of exactly one consonant and exactly one vowel. Of course, since writing is a powerful technology, this has not stopped abugidas from being used, with modifications, to represent languages that do not fall into this pattern. One of the earliest abugidas was the Brahmic script, which was in wide use in the third century BCE, and which forms the basis of many writing systems used on the Indian subcontinent.

As an example, let us look at the writing system for Burmese, a Sino-Tibetan language spoken in Myanmar. In Figure 1.4, we see a table displaying the base syllables. Just as in the periodic table of the elements and the IPA of consonants, the rows and columns are meaningful: The top row corresponds to various consonants made by raising the back of the tongue to the velum (soft palate); the leftmost column corresponds largely to voiceless consonants, formed without vibration of the vocal cords.

As you can see in the table, every syllable has a default vowel of [ə̆]. This default vowel can be changed by adding diacritics, as shown in Figure 1.5, for syllables which start with [k].

We can see that the base character remains the same in all cases, while diacritics indicate the vowel change. Even though there is some regularity, the combination of the base character plus a diacritic results in a single character, which

က [ka̰]	ခ [kʰa̰]	ဂ [ga̰]	ဃ [ga̰]	င [ŋa̰]
စ [sa̰]	ဆ [sʰa̰]	ဇ [za̰]	ဈ [za̰]	ည [ɲa̰]
ဋ [ta̰]	ဌ [tʰa̰]	ဍ [da̰]	ဎ [da̰]	ဏ [na̰]
တ [ta̰]	ထ [tʰa̰]	ဒ [da̰]	ဓ [da̰]	န [na̰]
ပ [pa̰]	ဖ [pʰa̰]	ဗ [ba̰]	ဘ [ba̰]	မ [ma̰]
ယ [ya̰]	ရ [ya̰] ([ra̰])	လ [la̰]	ဝ [wa̰]	သ [θa̰]
	ဟ [ha̰]	ဠ [la̰]	အ [a̰]	

Figure 1.4: Base syllables of the Burmese abugida.

က [ka̰]	ကု [kṵ]	ကေး [kéi]	ကို [kò]
ကာ [kà]	ကူ [kù]	ကယ့် [kḛ]	ကိုး [kó]
ကား [ká]	ကူး [kú]	ကယ် [kè]	ကော့ [kɔ̰]
ကိ [kḭ]	ကေ့ [kḛi]	ကဲ [ké]	ကော် [kɔ̀]
ကီ [kì]	ကေ [kèi]	ကို့ [ko̰]	ကော [kɔ́]
ကီး [kí]			

Figure 1.5: Vowel diacritics of the Burmese abugida.

distinguishes abugidas from the alphabets in Section 1.3.1. In this case, characters are written from left to right, but the diacritics appear on any side of the base character.

The second kind of syllabic system is the *syllabary*. These systems use distinct symbols for each syllable of a language. An example syllabary for Vai, a Niger-Congo language spoken in Liberia, is given in Figure 1.6.

Figure 1.6: The Vai syllabary (https://commons.wikimedia.org/wiki/File:Vai.gif, uploaded by user Neal; public domain information with no claim to original authorship).

Whereas the syllables in an abugida are organized into some sort of pattern, the syllables of a general syllabary need not be. For example, in Vai, it is hard to see a connection between the symbols for [pi] and [pa] even though they begin with the same consonant, or any connection between the symbols for [pi] and [di] even though they end with the same vowel.

1.3.3 Logographic writing systems

The final kind of writing system to examine involves *logographs*, or logograms. A logograph is a symbol which represents a unit of meaning, as opposed to a unit of sound. Among writing systems for natural languages, some (such as Chinese) use logographic elements, but cannot be considered purely logographic because they include phonetic information as well.

A purely logographic system is exemplified by the symbols used on signs at United States National Parks shown in Figure 1.7. These are referred to as *pictographs*, or pictograms, because they essentially are pictures of the items they refer to. The upper left symbol, for instance, refers to camping by means of displaying a tent.

Figure 1.7: U.S. National Park Service pictographic symbols (https://commons.wikimedia.org/wiki/File:National_Park_Service_sample_pictographs.svg, uploaded by user Tkgd2007; public domain as the work of the United States government).

Some modern written characters evolved from a more pictographic representation into a more abstract symbol. For example, we can look at the development of the Chinese character for 'horse', pronounced (in the Pinyin romanization) as *mǎ*, as in Figure 1.8. Originally, the character very much resembled a horse, but after evolving over the centuries, the modern character only bears a faint resemblance to anything horse-like.

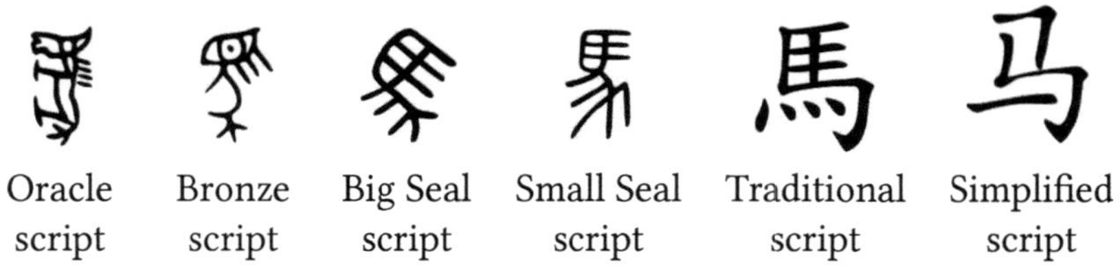

Figure 1.8: Evolution of the Chinese character for 'horse'. (https://commons.wikimedia.org/wiki/Commons:Ancient_Chinese_characters_project, public domain because ancient scripts predate the concept of copyright).

Not only has the logogram for *horse* become less horse-like over time, but it is also used to encode the sound *mǎ* rather than the meaning "horse" in *semantic-phonetic compounds* such as the character for 'mother', pronounced *mā*. The Chinese words for 'horse' and 'mother' are pronounced the same except for their tone, the pitch contour which distinguishes words in some languages: *Mǎ* 'horse' uses a down-up tone, while *mā* 'mother' uses a high flat tone. In writing, the character for *mā* 'mother' has a semantic element on the left, the character for *woman* (phonetically silent here, but pronounced *nü* on its own), and a phonetic element on the right: The character for 'horse', pronounced *mǎ*. The semantic-phonetic compound represents that *mā* 'mother' is semantically woman-like and phonetically horse-like. Both pieces of information are useful, but a Chinese reader still has to memorize the specific sound-meaning correspondence evoked vaguely by these clues.

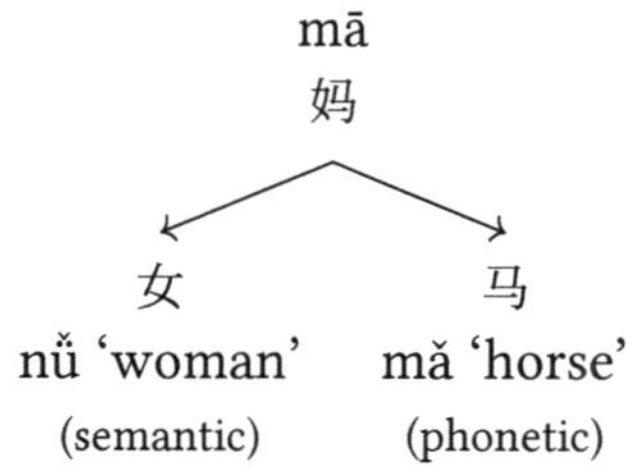

Figure 1.9: Semantic-phonetic compound character *mā* 'mother' in the Chinese writing system.

More broadly, Chinese semantic-phonetic compounds illustrate that the Chinese writing system is not purely logographic; the phonetic portion of the compound still provides information about pronunciation to complement the logographic representation of meaning.

1.3.4 More hybrid systems

You can already see from the Chinese writing system (a blend of syllabic and logographic elements) that the boundaries between alphabetic, syllabic, and logographic writing systems can be blurred. Many systems use a hybrid of these elements.

The writing system for Korean uses both alphabetic and syllabic concepts. This writing system is referred to as *Hangul* (or *Hangeul*) and was developed in 1444 during the reign of King Sejong. The Hangul system contains 24 letter characters, fourteen consonants and ten vowels. These alphabetic elements are grouped into syllabic units. We can see an example in Figure 1.10, which shows how individual alphabetic characters together form the syllabic characters for *han* and *geul*.

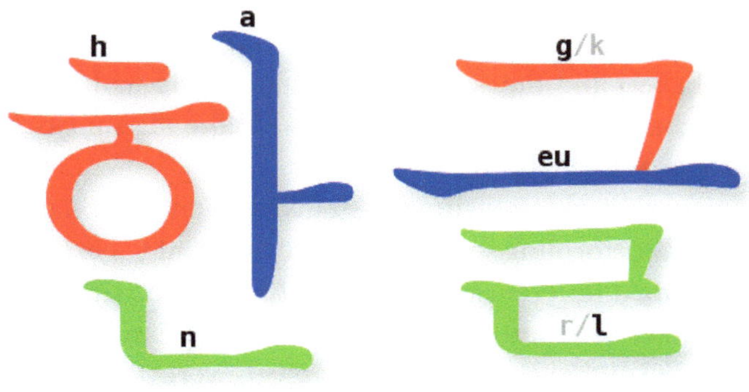

Figure 1.10: Composition of the characters for *Hangeul* (https://commons.wikimedia.org/wiki/File:Hangeul.png, uploaded by user IGEL with CC share-alike license).

Within a syllable block, the alphabetic elements are organized mostly vertically; but the syllables are written left to right. In South Korea, *hanja* (logographic Chinese characters) were historically used too, for a blend of all three (alphabetic, syllabic, and logographic) elements.

Braille is a writing system for people with vision impairments which makes it possible to read through touch. We can see the basic alphabet in Figure 1.11.

The Braille system works by using patterns of raised dots arranged in cells of up to six dots, in a three-by-two configuration. Each pattern represents a char-

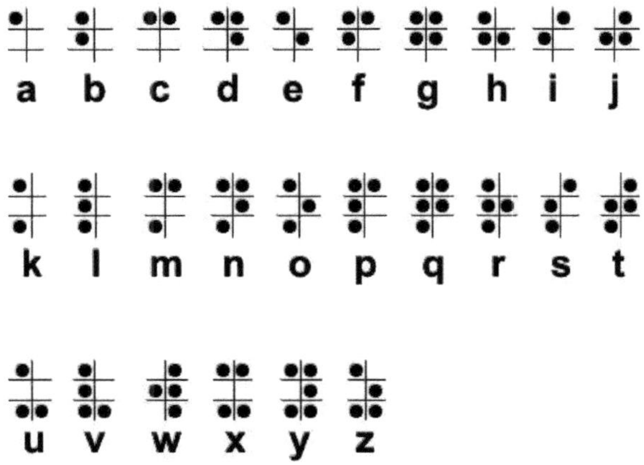

Figure 1.11: The Braille alphabet (https://commons.wikimedia.org/wiki/File:Braille_alfabet.jpg, uploaded by user Maikel Honcoop; public domain information with no claim to original authorship).

acter, but some frequent words and letter combinations have their own pattern. For instance, the pattern for *f* also indicates the number *6* (because it is the sixth letter of the alphabet) and the word *from* (which starts with *f*) – to be disambiguated by the context. So, even though it is at core an alphabet, it has some logographic properties.

As one of the world's oldest writing systems, Ancient Egyptian hieroglyphics seem to record a brainstorming session in all the different ways that language can be recorded in text. At different times, Ancient Egyptians tried writing right to left, left to right, and top to bottom. Some Ancient Egyptian glyphs represented a single sound, as in an alphabetic system; but vowels were usually not represented, as in an abjad. Others represented two or three consonants at once, similar to a syllabic system in that one character reflects multiple sounds. Still others represented a meaning, as in a logographic system; some of these were pronounced as words, but other "mute" logograms/pictograms were meant to clarify the meaning of the text without being pronounced (a pictogram of a boat might be added to clarify the meaning of the alphabetic spelling of the word for *boat*). These ancient pictograms share striking similarities to the non-pronounced *emoji* (see the Under the Hood box) that have become increasingly popular in recent years to enrich the socio-emotional meaning of text.

Under the Hood 1: Emoji

After this discussion of writing systems, you might be wondering about the status of modern digital symbolic systems, such as *emoji*. Emoji appear logographic, in that they depict meaning: A smiley face depicts a cheerful demeanor.

So do emoji constitute a logographic writing system? No, because they are not a writing system! Recall that a writing system is "a system of more or less permanent marks used to represent an utterance in such a way that it can be recovered more or less exactly without the intervention of the utterer" (Daniels & Bright 1996) – by representing some portion(s) of the sound/meaning pairings of a particular language. Emoji do not represent utterances or sound/meaning pairings in any particular language. Instead, many emoji (at least the most common ones, such as the laughing-crying face 😂 and the heart-eyes face 😍) represent the unpronounceable, non-verbalized emotions (conveyed in real life by facial expressions, gestures, and voice quality), which are otherwise absent from writing.

Emoji have historical antecedents in emoticons, such as the smiley face rendered by punctuation :-), and web abbreviations for non-speech communicative acts, such as *LOL*. Emoji were added to some Japanese phones in 1999 by the designer Shigetaka Kurita, and became part of Unicode in 2010 (see Section 1.4.3 for more on Unicode). To this day, the Unicode Consortium manages the set of emoji, vets petitions for new emoji, and records statistics about the most popular ones.

Like traffic-sign pictograms, emoji are relatively universal: Whether you speak English or German, you know the meaning of the heart-eyes emoji 😍. In contrast, written representations of actual languages are not universal; if you only speak English, you will not know the meaning of the German (written) word *Lächeln* 'smile'. Emoji can be universal specifically because they do not represent utterances in any particular language.

Illustrating the limited expressive power of emoji, *Emoji Dick* (Benenson 2010) gathers English-to-emoji "translations" (written by workers on the Amazon Mechanical Turk gig platform, commissioned by the entrepreneur Fred Benenson) of sentences from the classic novel *Moby Dick* by Herman Melville. Imagine trying to read (2b) without the corresponding English sentence! Since emoji do not constitute a writing system for a language, much of the English sentence's information is lost: There is no first-person pronoun and no way of representing the name *Ishmael* in emoji. Instead, the "emoji sentence" (2b) includes information about a boat and a whale, not present in the English original.

(2) a. Call me Ishmael.
    b. ☎🧔⛵🐳👌

In sum, emoji carry important communicative meaning and can be used to represent emotions, non-speech gestures, and some concrete entities such as boats and whales – but they do not constitute a fully expressive writing system for a human language.

Under the Hood 2: Online gig platforms

We just saw that the 2010 book *Emoji Dick* was created by paying gig workers on Amazon's Mechanical Turk platform to "translate" English sentences from the novel into emoji. Mechanical Turk takes its name from a toy created in the 1770s for the Austrian court, a doll dressed in stereotypical Turkish clothing, which was represented as a chess-playing robot but actually concealed a human inside who moved the pieces. The Mechanical Turk doll looked like artificial intelligence, but contained a human at its core. Similarly, Amazon's platform is meant to operate as easily as an automated system – you can post a task online and download your results in just a few hours – but leverages the human intelligence of gig workers. Mechanical Turk is one of several such platforms, including Prolific and CrowdFlower, which are widely used in language research and technology.

In psychology and linguistics research, it is common to conduct text-based experiments. For example, Loftus (1975) played a video of a car driving on a road, and then asked some people, *How fast was the car going on the country road?* while asking others, *How fast was the car going when it passed the barn?*. Later, both groups were asked if they saw a barn. In fact, the video did not show a barn – but the people who had read the sentence mentioning a barn were far more likely to mis-remember one! The study famously shows that the wording of a question can be used to implant a false memory. Although the study was originally run in-person with university students as participants, it serves as an example of a study that could be run online – far more quickly and cheaply. To recruit two hundred university students to come to a physical laboratory to do a pen-and-paper experiment would take thousands of dollars and weeks; to recruit the same number of people to do a study on their own device from home would take a few hundred dollars and an afternoon.

Such web surveys can serve all sorts of purposes. A business might ask people whether they've heard of their product or how much they like it; a political campaign might ask what people think of a candidate or a message. In language technology, one might recruit people to write captions for images (free text), flag comments as hateful or not (labels from a closed class), or provide a rating for the politeness of a request (a continuous scale). These data can provide insight on their own, but can further be used as input for a system that "learns" to handle new data in the same way – for example, learning to label new comments as hateful or not, generalizing the labels provided by humans. Such machine learning tools are discussed further in Chapter 5.

When gathering such data on the web, researchers worry about quality: Are the workers actual humans, or are they bots? If they are humans, are they paying attention or clicking mindlessly through the task? A researcher might add questions to their study specifically to flag poor-quality respondents, but spammers may also find ways around these questions, creating an arms race. Moreover, who are these humans? Is this sample biased in a way that might limit the generalizations that can be drawn from their data?

Gig platforms also raise questions about ethics: Are workers being fairly compensated for their labor? Are they earning minimum wage (in what location?) – hard to count when they may do ten different short tasks in an hour? How many hours do they work on a gig platform, and should they earn overtime or benefits? How should they be credited intellectually for their output or the technologies built from it?

Over time, spammers get more sophisticated and gig-work regulations evolve, so the future of such platforms remains in flux; but they are likely to remain a crucial tool in language technology.

1.4 Digital writing

We have explored how language pairs sounds/signs with meaning, and how writing systems encode some portion of that pairing (sound and/or meaning). Next, we explore how writing systems are in turn encoded digitally, allowing computers to process text.

Before exploring how computers can encode diverse writing systems, we begin with a more basic question: How do computers encode anything?

1.4.1 Bits and bytes

To answer that, we need to know that information on a computer is stored in *bits*. We can think of the memory of a computer as, at its core, a large number of on-off switches. A bit has two possible values, 1 (yes) or 0 (no), allowing us to flip the switches on or off. A single bit on its own does not convey much information, but multiple bits can come together to make meaningful patterns. It is thus often more convenient to speak of a *byte*, or a sequence of 8 bits, e.g., 01001010.

These sequences of bits tell the computer which switches are on and which are off, and – in the context of writing systems – a particular character will have a unique pattern of on-off switches. Before we fully spell that out, though, let us consider a better way to think of sequences of bits, other than just a sequence of mindless 0s and 1s.

Bit sequences are useful because they can represent numbers, in so-called *binary* notation. They are called binary because there are only two digits to work with. The base ten numbers we normally use have columns for ones, tens, hundreds, etc.; likewise, binary numbers have their own columns, for ones, twos, fours, eights, etc. In addition to base two and base ten, you can find encodings such as *hexadecimal*, where there are 16 digits (0-9 and then the letters A-F).

In *Big Endian* notation, the most significant bit is the leftmost one; this is the standard way of encoding and is parallel to decimal (base ten) numbers. The positions in a byte thus encode the top row of Table 1.3. As we can see in the second row, the positions for 64, 8, and 2 are "on," and 64+8+2 equals 74. The binary (base two) number 01001010 therefore corresponds to the decimal number 74.

Table 1.3: The number 74 in Big Endian notation.

128	64	32	16	8	4	2	1
0	1	0	0	1	0	1	0

Little Endian notation is just the opposite, where the most significant bit is the rightmost one, but it is less common. In both cases, the columns are all multiples of two. This is just like with decimal numbers, where the columns are all multiples of ten. As each digit is here limited to either 0 or 1 (two choices), we have to use multiples of two.

1.4.2 Converting decimal numbers to binary

Although many of you are likely already familiar with binary numbers, it is instructive to see how to convert from decimal to binary notation. We will consider the division method of conversion and walk through an example, converting the decimal number 9 into a 4-bit binary number.

The division method is easy to calculate and moves from the least significant to the most significant bit. Because every column has a value which is a multiple of two, we divide by 2 with every step. In Table 1.4, for example, we divide 9 by 2 and find that we have a remainder. A remainder after dividing by 2 means that we started with an odd number. Since 9 is odd, the rightmost bit should be 1.

The trick now is to take the resulting value, in this case 4, and divide it by 2. The same principle is at work here: If there is no remainder, it means that the starting number (4) was even, and this bit needs to be switched off for that to happen. The remaining calculations work the same way, as shown in Table 1.4.

1.4.3 Using bytes to store characters

With 8 bits (a single byte) and each byte storing a separate character, we can represent 256 different characters (= 2^8). This is a sufficient amount for many

Table 1.4: The division method.

Decimal	Remainder?	Binary
9/2 = 4	yes	**1**
4/2 = 2	no	**0**1
2/2 = 1	no	**0**01
1/2 = 0	yes	**1**001

applications and more than enough for anyone wishing to simply type in Latin characters for English. With 256 possible characters, we can store every single letter used in English, plus all the auxiliary characters such as the comma, the space, the percent sign, and so on.

ASCII

One of the first encodings for storing English text used only 7 bits, thus allowing for 128 possible characters. This is the *ASCII* encoding, the American Standard Code for Information Interchange. Figure 1.12 shows most of the ASCII chart.

32		48	0	65	A	82	R	97	a	114	r
33	!	49	1	66	B	83	S	98	b	115	s
34	“	50	2	67	C	84	T	99	c	116	t
35	#	51	3	68	D	85	U	100	d	117	u
36	$	52	4	69	E	86	V	101	e	118	v
37	%	53	5	70	F	87	W	102	f	119	w
38	&	54	6	71	G	88	X	103	g	120	x
39	’	55	7	72	H	89	Y	104	h	121	y
40	(	56	8	73	I	90	Z	105	i	122	z
41	)	57	9	74	J	91	[	106	j	123	{
42	*	58	:	75	K	92	\	107	k	124	—
43	+	59	;	76	L	93	]	108	l	125	}
44	,	60	<	77	M	94	^	109	m	126	~
45	-	61	=	78	N	95	_	110	n	127	DEL
46	.	62	>	79	O	96	‘	111	o		
47	/	63	?	80	P			112	p		
		64	@	81	Q			113	q		

Figure 1.12: The ASCII chart.

Omitted from the chart are codes 1–31 since these are used for control characters, such as a backspace, line feed, or tab. The numeric order reflects alphabetic ordering (e.g., 65 through 90 for uppercase letters), so it is easy to alphabetize the letters by comparing numbers. Although we have written the base ten number, for ease of reading, the binary number is what is used internally by the computer.

You might already be familiar with ASCII or other character encoding systems, as many communications over email and the internet inform you as to different encodings. Emails come with lots of information about themselves. Specifically, Multipurpose Internet Mail Extensions (MIME) provide *meta-information* on the text, or information which is part of the regular message, but tells us something about that message. MIME information tells us, among other things, what the character set is; en example can be seen in (3).

(3)
```
Mime-Version: 1.0
Content-Type: text/plain; charset=US-ASCII
Content-Transfer-Encoding: 7bit
```

Unicode

As you may recall, one of our goals is to be able to encode *any* language. With only 128 possible characters, ASCII clearly is insufficient for encoding the world's writing systems. How, then, do we go about encoding writing systems other than the Latin alphabet?

One approach is to simply extend the ASCII system with various other systems. For example, ISO-8859-1 is an 8 bit encoding that in addition to ASCII includes extra letters needed for French, German, Spanish, and related languages; ISO-8859-7 is for the Greek alphabet; ISO-8859-8 for the Hebrew alphabet; and JIS-X-0208 encodes Japanese characters. While multiple encoding systems make it possible to specify only the writing systems one wants to use, there are potential problems. First, there is always the potential for misidentification. Two different encodings can use the same number for two different characters or, conversely, different numbers for the same character. If an encoding is not clearly identified and needs to be guessed, e.g., by a web browser displaying a web page that does not specify the encoding explicitly, the wrong characters will be displayed. Secondly, it is a hassle to install and maintain many different systems in order to deal with various languages.

Unicode[3] is a system that addresses these problems by having a single representation for every character in any existing writing system. While we have some

[3]https://unicode.org, accessed 2024-05-23.

idea about the variety of writing systems, based on the earlier discussion, we may not have a good feel for how many characters there are to encode in the world. Unicode, version 14.0, has codes for over 144,000 characters from alphabets, syllabaries, and logographic systems. While this sounds like a lot, it should be noted that Unicode uses 32 bits to encode characters. The number of distinct characters a system can encode is equal to 2^n, where n is the number of bits: With 7 bits, we had 2^7 (= 128) possibilities. With 32 bits, we can store $2^{32} = 4,294,967,296$ unique characters.

In other words, Unicode allows for over four billion characters, yet only needs about 150,000. If we use 32 bits to encode every character, that will take up a lot of space. It seems like ASCII is better, at least for English, as it only takes 7 bits to encode a character. Is there any way we can allow for many characters, while at the same time only encoding what we really need to encode?

Unicode's solution is to offer three different versions, which allow for more compact encodings: UTF-32, UTF-16, and UTF-8. UTF-32 uses 32 bits to directly represent each character, so we will face more of a space problem with it. UTF-16, on the other hand, uses 16 bits ($2^{16} = 65,536$), and UTF-8 uses 8 bits ($2^8 = 256$).

This raises the question: How is it possible to encode 2^{32} possibilities in 8 bits, as UTF-8 does? The answer is that UTF-8 can use several bytes to represent a single character if it has to, but it encodes characters with as few bytes as possible by using the highest (leftmost) bit as a flag. If the highest bit is 0, then this is a single character or the final character of a multi-byte character. For example, 01000001 is the single-character code for *A* (i.e., 65). If the highest bit is 1, then it is part of a multi-byte character. In this way, sequences of bytes can unambiguously denote sequences of Unicode characters. One nice consequence of this set-up is that ASCII text is already valid UTF-8.

More details on the encoding mechanism for UTF-8 are given in Table 1.5. An important property here is that the first byte unambiguously tells you how many bytes to expect after it. If the first byte starts with 11110xxx, for example, we know that with four 1's, it has a total of four bytes, i.e., there are three more bytes to expect. Note also that all non-starting bytes start with 10, indicating it is *not* the initial byte.

To take one example, the Greek character α ("alpha") has a Unicode code value of 945, which in binary representation is 11 10110001. With 32 bits, then, it would be represented as: 00000000 00000000 00000011 10110001. The conversion to UTF-8 works as follows: if we look at the second row of Table 1.5, we see that there are 11 slots (represented by the repeated character *x*), and we have 10 binary digits. The ten-digit number 11 10110001 is the same as the 11-digit 011

Table 1.5: UTF-8 encoding scheme.

Byte 1	Byte 2	Byte 3	Byte 4	Byte 5	Byte 6
0xxxxxxx					
110xxxxx	10xxxxxx				
1110xxxx	10xxxxxx	10xxxxxx			
11110xxx	10xxxxxx	10xxxxxx	10xxxxxx		
111110xx	10xxxxxx	10xxxxxx	10xxxxxx	10xxxxxx	
1111110x	10xxxxxx	10xxxxxx	10xxxxxx	10xxxxxx	10xxxxxx

10110001, and we can rearrange this as 01110 110001, so what we can do is insert these numbers into the position held by the *x* characters in the second row: 110**01110** 10**110001**. This is thus the UTF-8 representation.

1.5 Spoken language

To review, we have explored how language pairs sounds/signs with meaning; how different writing systems encode some portions of that pairing (sound and/or meaning); and how writing systems are in turn encoded on computers in bits and bytes. Next, we return to the sounds of spoken language and how these too can be encoded digitally, allowing computers to process and produce speech.

1.5.1 The nature of speech

In order to deal with speech, we have to figure out what it looks like. As we saw above in our tour of writing systems, we can *transcribe* speech into orthographic text or the International Phonetic Alphabet, but first we have to understand the input to such a transcription as a stream of sound.

We segment speech into words and sounds in our minds and write spaces between words orthographically, but speech is actually a *continuous* and undifferentiated stream of sound. Sounds are articulated in quick and overlapping succession, so it is hard for a computer to tell where one sound ends and another begins. Additionally, people have different accents and different vocal tracts and thus say things differently. Two people can say the same word, and it will come out differently.

Furthermore, the way a particular sound is realized is not consistent across utterances, even for one person. What we think of as one sound is not always said the same. For example, there is the phenomenon known as *coarticulation*, in which neighboring sounds affect the way a sound is uttered. The sound for *k* is said differently in *key* and the first sound in *kookaburra*. (If you do not believe this, stick one finger in your mouth when you say *key* and when you say *koo*; for *key* the tongue touches the finger, but not for *koo*.) On the flipside, what we think of as two sounds are not always very different. For instance, the *s* in *see* is acoustically very similar to the *sh* in *shoe*, yet we hear them as different sounds. This becomes clear when learning another language that makes a distinction you find difficult to distinguish. Both articulatory and acoustic properties of speech are thus relevant here; let's now take a closer look at both of these.

1.5.2 Articulatory properties

Before we get into what sounds look like on a computer, we need to know how sounds are produced in the vocal tract. This is studied in a branch of linguistics known as *articulatory phonetics*. As we saw above in introducing the IPA chart, there are three components to a consonant: the place of articulation, the manner of articulation, and the voicing.

The *place of articulation* refers to where in the mouth the sound is uttered. Consider where your tongue makes contact with your mouth when you say [t] (*t* in *tip*) as opposed to when you say [k] (in *key* and *cool*). For [t], the tip of your tongue touches the area of your mouth behind your upper teeth, what is called the alevolar ridge (or a bit closer to the teeth for some dialects), whereas for [k], the back of your tongue rises to the back of the roof of your mouth (i.e., the velum).

While place makes some distinctions, there are sounds said at nearly the same point in the mouth which come out differently, due to the *manner of articulation*. For example, [s] (in *sip* and *nice*), like [t], is an alveolar consonant, uttered with the tongue behind one's upper teeth. However, [t] involves a complete stoppage of air (and thus is commonly called a stop consonant), whereas [s] allows a narrow stream of air to continually pass through the constriction (and is referred to as a fricative).

The final distinction involves *voicing*, or whether or not one's vocal cords vibrate during the utterance. Your vocal cords are in your throat, so you can easily compare sounds by putting a hand on your throat and feeling whether there are vibrations. For example, [s] (in *sip*) and [z] (in *zip*) are both alveolar fricatives, but [s] is unvoiced and [z] is voiced.

1.5.3 Acoustic properties

While studying articulation provides important distinctions, which we will continue to refer to in the following, to represent spoken language on a computer we need speech properties we can quantify, which brings us to *acoustic phonetics*. Acoustic properties of speech refer to the physical characteristics of sound. *Sound waves* that we speak are simply "small variations in air pressure that occur very rapidly one after another" (Ladefoged & Johnson 2014). When these waves hit a recording device, we can measure how often they hit, how loud they are, and other such properties.

As mentioned before, sound is continuous, but computers store data in *discrete* points, as illustrated in Figure 1.13, and thus can only capture the general pattern of the sound. The quality of a recording depends upon the *sampling rate*, or how many times in a given second we extract a moment of sound. The sampling rate is measured in samples per second, commonly referred to as hertz (Hz).

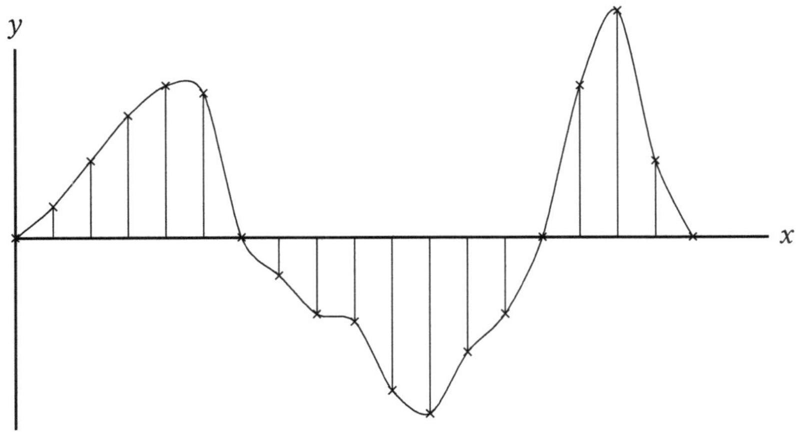

Figure 1.13: A continuous line with evenly-spaced discrete points.

The higher the sampling rate, the better the recording quality, though it takes more space to store. 8,000 samples per second turn out to be adequate for capturing the frequencies of language sounds when using the telephone, and 16,000 or 22,050 Hz is often used when recording speech.

One of the properties of speech we are interested in is the *speech flow*, the rate of speaking and the number and length of pauses. This is easy enough to measure, in units of time (i.e., seconds). Another property is the *loudness*, or *amplitude*, the amount of energy a sound has. Again, we have an intuitive sense of what it means to measure amplitude, and this loudness of sounds is typically measured in decibels.

Most important for classifying sound waves into individual speech sounds are the *freq* [illegible] uency –
or, how [illegible] e to tell
sounds [illegible] d, again
referre [illegible]
To ge [illegible] t with a
wavefo [illegible] *sday*: As
time pa [illegible] oudness,
on the *y* [illegible] Praat, by
Boersm [illegible] t sound,
and the [illegible] nant [d]
which completely stops the air for that instant.

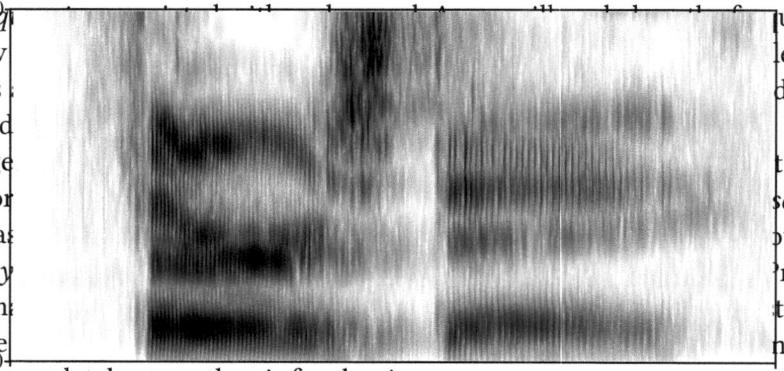

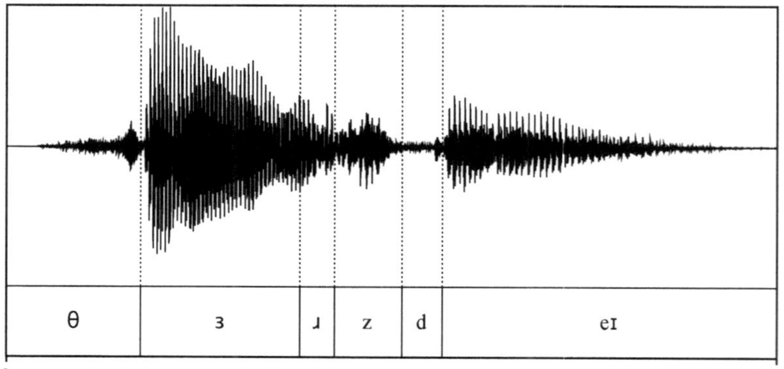

Figure 1.14: A waveform for *Thursday*.

The *pitch* of a sound – how high or low it is – provides additional information, especially for vowels. Speech is composed of different frequencies all at once (due to the way sound reverberates in the vocal tract). The *fundamental frequency* F0 is also known as the pitch. Absolute pitch varies across humans depending on the size of their vocal tract. Relative variations in pitch can distinguishes tones in languages such as Chinese, where the pitch contour of a syllable distinguishes word meaning; rising pitch can indicate yes-no questions in English. On top of pitch, other higher-frequency *overtones*, also known as *formants*, give unique character to each vowel and convey information about the position of the tongue in the mouth as it is articulated. The formant F1 corresponds to tongue height in the mouth, while F2 reflects its front/back position.

Finally, we can analyze spoken language using a *spectrogram*, which is a graph to represent the frequencies of speech (y-axis) over time (x-axis). As we can see in Figure 1.15, each sound is a complex unit made of different frequencies. In fact, what we observe in a spectrogram will help us the most in automatically determining what sound was uttered, which we turn to next.

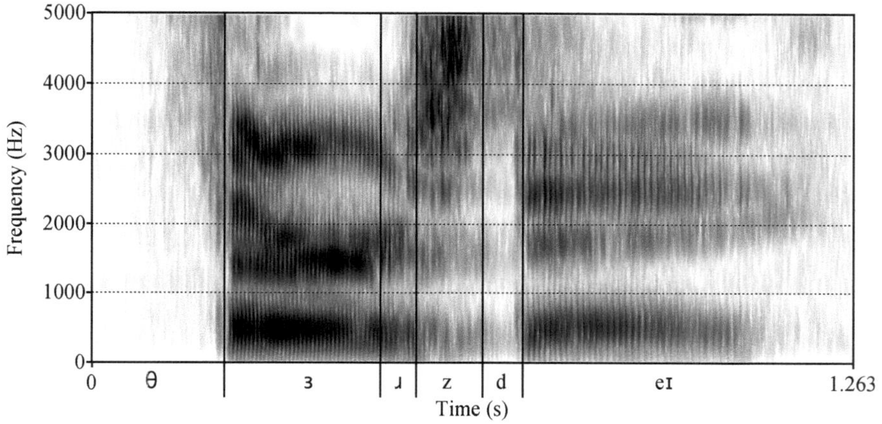

Figure 1.15: A spectrogram for *Thursday*.

1.5.4 Measuring speech

A spectrogram has various measurable properties which tell us what the sounds are. The Under the Hood box on *Reading a spectrogram* provides more details, but we will sketch a few general properties here. When looking at a spectrogram, you should ask:

1. How dark is the picture?

   This tells us how loud each sound is and is measured in decibels. Different sounds differ in their loudness, including some sounds – such as [d] – which involve a moment of complete silence. Compare [θ] and [z] in Figure 1.15 showing that [z] is louder than [θ]. These are both fricative sounds, meaning that the air is channelled through a narrow passage in the mouth without stopping, but [θ] is voiceless (the vocal cords aren't vibrating) whereas [z] is voiced (with vibrating vocal cords) and thus sounds louder.

2. Where are the lines the darkest?

   The darkest lines tell us which frequencies (measured in hertz) are the loudest and the most important for determining the sound. Each vowel has roughly three prominent frequency bands, and the vowels are distinguished by these bands. For voiced sounds, we typically also see a low dark band.

3. How do these dark lines change?

   One last point involves how the frequencies change over time. When we have stop consonants like [t] or [k], there appears to be nothing in the spectrogram by which we can distinguish the sounds, and yet we make the distinction quite easily. It turns out that the transitions of the vowel bands before and after the consonant are unique.

It is these measurements which represent speech on the computer. In other words, to a computer, speech is nothing but a sequence of various numerical measurements. After we discuss reading a spectrogram, we will delve into turning these measurements of speech into text.

Under the Hood 3: Reading a spectrogram

The first thing to note about reading a spectrogram is that the word boundaries are not at all clear-cut. As mentioned before, there are no pauses between words. To know what a word is, what is needed is information about the structure of the language we are looking at. Consider, for example, hearing a string in a foreign language such as *skarandashom.* Can you tell where the word boundary is? If you speak Russian (and understand the transliteration from Cyrillic), you might recognize the break between *s* ('with') and *karandashom* ('(a) pencil'). Otherwise, you probably did not know the boundaries.

But what about the individual sounds? Let us start with the different kinds of consonants. When discussing articulatory properties of speech, we distinguished the manner of articulation – how air is passed through the channel – and it turns out that sounds with similar manners have commonalities in their acoustic properties. We will examine three kinds of consonants: fricatives, nasals, and stops. For each type of consonant, we will give a brief articulatory description and then the acoustic distinctions that make it prominent.

We start our analysis with *fricatives* – in English, these include [f] (*f* in *fist*, *ph* in *photo*), [v] (*v* in *vote*), [s], [z], [θ] (*th* in *thigh*), [ð] (*th* in *thy*), [ʃ] (*sh* in *she*), and [ʒ] (the final sound of *rouge*). All of these involve air passing turbulently through the mouth: The tongue raises close to a point of constriction in the mouth, but it does not completely touch. With this turbulent air, we will see a lot of "noise" in the spectrogram. It is not completely noise, however; you can look at where the shading is darkest in order to tell the fricatives apart. For example, [s] generally has its energy concentrated in the higher frequencies (e.g., close to 5000 Hz), as illustrated in this spectrogram for *fuss* [fʌs]:

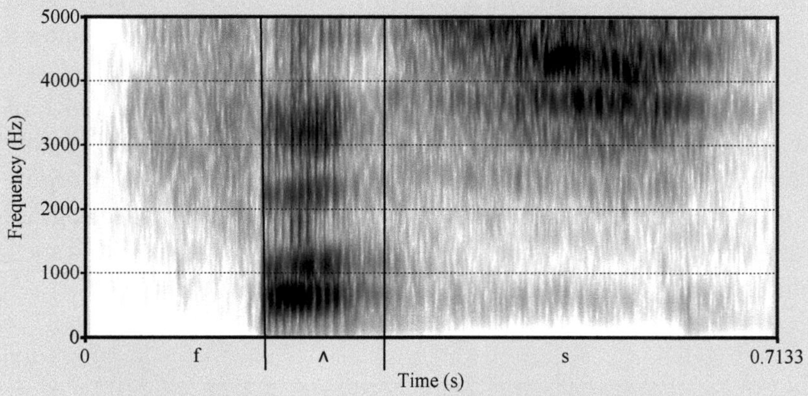

Figure 1.16: A spectrogram for *fuss*.

On the other hand, [ʃ] peaks lower (e.g., around 3500 Hz), and [f] does not really have a prominent peak, as also shown in the figure. The voiced sounds [z], [ʒ], and [v] pattern mostly like [s], [ʃ], and [f], respectively. The main difference is that these sounds are voiced. Voicing, which is the movement of vocal cords, causes there to be low-frequency energy, though it is a bit hard to see precisely in the spectrogram for the word *fuzz* [fʌz]. (Note, however, that the voicing difference co-occurs with a distinct difference in the length of the vowel.)

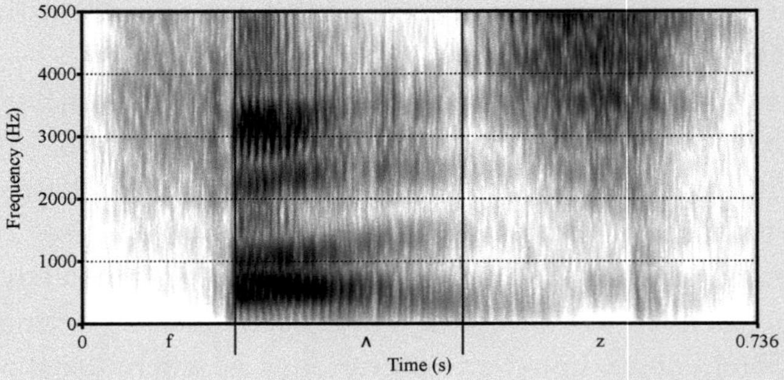

Figure 1.17: A spectrogram for *fuzz*.

The next consonant type to look at is the set of *stop consonants*, also called *plosives*: [p] (*p* in *pad*), [b] (*b* in *boy*), [t], [d], [k], and [g] (*g* in *go*). As with fricatives, there are more stops in other languages. What all of these sounds have in common is that, to make them, the tongue makes a complete closure with part of the mouth.

But if there is a stoppage of air, then stops actually involve a lack of sound. So, how is it that we hear differences? First of all, we should note that stops are often accompanied by a burst of air – what is called *aspiration* – which translates into noise (similar to a fricative) in a spectrogram right after the stoppage. We can see aspiration on the final /t/ in this spectrogram for *deet* [dit].

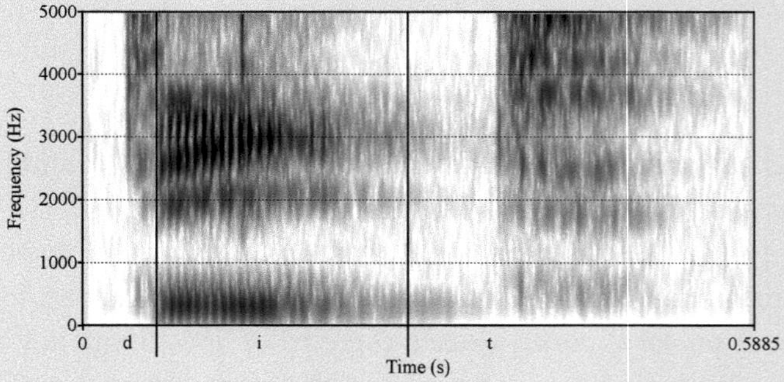

Figure 1.18: A spectrogram for *deet*.

Second, more importantly, the way we hear a distinct stop sound – e.g., [t] vs. [k] – is in the surrounding vowels. The vowels surrounding a consonant transition into the stop and then out of it again, i.e., their formants (see below) move up or down, depending on the consonant.

We can now turn to *vowels*, which can be difficult to tell apart. In articulation, a key aspect of vowels is where in the mouth the tongue is raised: front, middle, or back. We can also talk about vowel height: If the tongue is raised high, low, or somewhere in between. Some of the vowels in English are given in Table 1.6: [i] (*beet*), [ɛ] (*bet*), [æ] (*bat*), [ə] (the *a* in *sofa*), [u] (*boot*), [ow] (*boat*), and [ɑ] (the *a* in *father*).

Table 1.6: Some of the major vowels in English.

	Front	Middle	Back
High	i		u
Mid	ɛ	ə	ow
Low	æ		ɑ

Vowels are generally distinguished by their three bands (stripes) of frequencies: These are the vowel *formants*. We refer to these as F1, F2, and F3. Conveniently, there is a nearly direct correspondence between the formant values and the location of the tongue in the mouth. F1 represents tongue height: The higher the F1 value, the lower the tongue is. F2 represents tongue front/backness: The higher the F2 value, the further forward in the mouth the tongue is. The top (third) band, F3, reflects information about lip rounding and co-articulation of the consonant [ɹ].

In the spectrogram for *deet*, for example, the [i] in *deet* has a low F1 band and a high F2, representing the fact that it is a high, front vowel.

By measuring the formants F1 and F2, it is not just possible to distinguish between different vowels, but also to measure the accents (the position of the tongue in the mouth) of different people who are pronouncing the same vowel. The linguistic subfield of *sociophonetics* uses such measurements to quantify how accents vary across people, regions, and time.

1.5.5 Relating written and spoken language

Having explored how both writing and sounds are represented digitally, we turn to the task of relating one to the other. Automatic speech recognition (ASR) maps speech to text, and text-to-speech synthesis (TTS) maps text into sound.

Automatic speech recognition is the process by which a computer converts a speech signal to text. Such systems are enormously practical, allowing for automatic transcription of podcasts and video calls, real-time dictation of note-taking, spoken conversations with digital assistants, and so on.

In general, ASR systems go through three steps. First, speech is digitally sampled, as was discussed above. As this converts continuous speech into a discrete representation, this will naturally involve *information loss*. Secondly, the speech samples are converted into measurable units, as was also discussed above; this is referred to as *acoustic signal processing*. Here, the digital samples are converted into, among other things, recognizable frequencies, giving the computer a representation of speech to work with. These frequencies are used for the third step, the recognition of sounds, groups of sounds, and words. The frequencies can be used to identify speech sounds, but, as we discussed before, the interpretation of a given frequency is often ambiguous, since different people speak differently. For example, a [t] might sound like a [d]. The system will have to choose the most likely interpretation of an indeterminate sound by leveraging statistics about what people are most likely to say.

Given these basics, there are different kinds of ASR systems. *Speaker-dependent* systems work for a single speaker, whereas *speaker-independent* work for any speaker of a given variety of a language, e.g., American English. Given the range of pronunciations across different people, speaker-dependent systems are clearly more accurate. This is why there are also *speaker-adaptive* systems, which start out as independent systems but adapt over time to a single speaker in order to improve accuracy.

The reverse process of automatic speech recognition is *text-to-speech* (TTS) synthesis, which converts words into speech. This might seem like is a trivial task: Couldn't we simply record a voice saying phrases or words and then play back those words in the appropriate order?

While this might work for talking toy dolls, when we deal with technology such as dialog systems (see Chapter 8), the computer system generates written sentences which need to be synthesized on the fly. Thus, we have to be able to break the text down into smaller units that can be converted into speech. This is challenging, given that writing system representations are often phonetically ambiguous.

The main idea behind speech generation is to adjust the values of the frequencies, the loudness, and other such properties, to produce the correct sounds. Since we know what frequencies correspond to which vowels, for example, we can play those frequencies to make it sound like the right vowel. Of course, as we mentioned before, sounds are always different, across time and across speakers. Historically, one simple way to help in the process of generating speech is to use a database of speech and to use *diphones*, i.e., two-sound segments, to generate new utterances. The contextual information found in diphones is useful because sounds are pronounced differently depending upon the neighboring sounds.

While these technologies are enormously useful and fascinating, they deserve textbooks in their own right. Moving forward, we set speech aside and focus on text.

1.6 Consequences

Spoken/signed language allows us to communicate face-to-face, while written language allows us to communicate across space and time. Digital writing allows us communicate with more people around the world than ever before, and machine-readable text provides data for various applications of language technology to be explored throughout the book.

Foreshadowing some larger themes, this chapter also illustrates how linguistic information (writing, sounds) can be interpreted qualitatively by humans but must be represented quantitatively (in bits, in hertz) on a computer. Throughout the book, we will encounter more ways that computers can quantify language.

Moreover, this chapter shows how text represents some, but not all, of the information conveyed by language. A word is a pairing of sound and meaning, but a phonetic writing system such as our Latin alphabet represents only sounds. While a human knows the meaning independently, what semantic information is available to a computer which has access only to the textual representation of sound? The rest of the book will explore how computers, without access to the outside world or the mental representations available to humans, can approximate meaning.

Checklist

- Describe different types of writing systems (with examples) and how they vary in their use of phonetic and semantic properties.
- Explain the meaning of the rows and columns in the International Phonetics Alphabet for consonants. Explain the organization of the vowel chart.
- Discuss why it is possible for a language to be written in several different writing systems, and what this shows about the relationship between the written and spoken forms of language.
- Recognize that numbers can be represented in different ways, and understand how to convert between representations, especially converting numbers between base 2 and base 10 representations.
- Explain what Unicode is useful for and how the UTF-8 encoding scheme works.
- Sketch how modern technology allows the acoustic properties of speech sounds to be measured, and know how to recognize some speech features by looking at spectrograms.
- Explain the tasks of automatic speech recognition and text-to-speech synthesis, and distinguish between speaker-dependent, speaker-independent, and speaker-adaptive approaches.

Exercises

1. Using the distinctive features of language from the beginning of the chapter, discuss whether music, mathematics, programming lan-

guages, or body language can be considered “language” in Hockett’s sense.

2. Visit Omniglot[a] and pick a syllabary. Take a paragraph from a novel written in English and transliterate it into this syllabary.
   a) What difficulties do you encounter?
   b) Is there any *information loss* in your transliteration? If it were transliterated back into the Latin alphabet, what ambiguities would you find?

3. Assume you’ve been given power to alter the Latin alphabet for the purposes of better writing down English words.
   a) Keeping it as an alphabet, what would you change, add, or remove? Why?
   b) Could you just use the IPA to write down English? What problems might you encounter? Would it be easier or harder for English speakers around the globe to communicate in writing?
   c) Could you convert the alphabet into a system similar to Hangeul for Korean? How would it work?
   d) Assume you have to propose 100 words to be replaced by (logographic) emoji. What types of words would you select for the first 100? Why?

3. As mentioned briefly, *hexadecimal* numbers have 16 digits: 0-9 and then the letters A-F. They are commonly used in computing because they more compactly represent the numbers which are often used for bytes than binary numbers do.
   a) Describe how hexadecimal numbers work, working through the base ten number 46 as an example.
   b) Describe a procedure for converting numbers from a binary (base two) to a hexadecimal (base sixteen) representation.

4. Discuss the optimal way to design UTF-8, in terms of the average number of bytes per character and the number of users of a given writing system.

5. The speech waveforms and spectrograms shown in this chapter were produced using Praat, but there are other useful speech analysis software kits, such as Wavesurfer and VoiceSauce.
   a) Explore one of these software packages and make yourself comfortable with using it.
   b) Pick your favorite book and record yourself reading the first sentence (or 20 words, whichever comes first).
   c) Record a friend saying the same thing.
   d) Compare and contrast spectrograms of your different spoken language examples, describing how what you see corresponds to what you both said and what the differences are.
6. Explain why ASR is an irreversible process. Make reference to the concept of *information loss* in your answer.

[a] https://omniglot.com, accessed 2024-05-23.

Further reading

Hockett's design features of language are pioneered in Hockett (1960).

More information on writing systems, including various nice graphics, can be gleaned from websites such as Omniglot[a]. Additionally, there are books on writing systems, such as Daniels & Bright (1996). Sproat (2000) offers a unique treatment, which focuses on computational properties of writing systems, and Sproat (2011) extends the writing system discussion to language technology and its impact on society. Both are highly recommended. Turning from writing systems to language, a thorough set of information on the world's languages can be found in the Ethnologue (Gordon 2005). For an accessible overview of topics related to language and how language can be studied, check out the *Language Files* (The Ohio State University Department of Linguistics 2022). As a reference book, you can find comprehensive information in David Crystal's Encyclopedia of Language (Crystal 2011).

McCulloch (2020) explores the influence of the internet on language and writing, with detailed discussion of emoji.

For an introductory look at automatic speech recognition and language modeling, the Jurafsky & Martin (2009) textbook is a valuable resource. For a thorough introduction to the field of phonetics, we recommend Ladefoged & Johnson (2014).

[a] https://omniglot.com, accessed 2024-04-19.

2 Writers' aids

2.1 Introduction

English has been written in the Latin alphabet since around the ninth century of the Common Era, first by hand, then via the printing press (starting in the 1470s), the typewriter (1860s), and ASCII (1960s) as discussed in Chapter 1. But English spelling was not standardized until the mid-1600s into the 1700s, influenced by the publication of the King James Bible as well as some of the first dictionaries. In other words, English was written for seven hundred years without standardized spelling. The playwright William Shakespeare (1564-1616) did not use a standard spelling of his own name, writing it in different places as *Willm Shakp, William Shaksper, Wm Shakspe, William Shakspere, Willm Shakspere,* and *William Shakspeare.*

Not only did the most famous English writer not need standardized spelling, but it is also often easy to understand slightly misspelled text: to what extent do the spellling errers in this setnence dirsupt your undertsanding? It's often argued (e.g., White et al. 2008) that readers focus mostly on the first letter and the overall shape of a word rather than processing each character sequentially. So why have standardized spelling at all? What if we let everyone use whatever spelling they want, as in Shakespeare's time? Or, if that sounds too chaotic, what if we replaced the notoriously confusing English orthography with the unambiguous International Phonetic Alphabet introduced in Chapter 1?

On the one hand, if English were written in the IPA, it might be easier to pronounce. We'd no longer have to wonder why *epitome* doesn't rhyme with *tome*, and we'd know from the spelling that *tough* rhymes *cuff* – eliminating the silent letters which might be especially confusing to children or people learning English as a second language.

But on the other hand, imagine a person named Leslie, pronounced by different people as [lɛzli] 'Lez-lee' and [lɛsli] 'Less-lee'. When you want to find Leslie's voter registration, tax documents, or publications, which spelling do you use? How could you search using control-F for Leslie in a long document when their name is spelled inconsistently? When you want to search for a *pen* on Amazon, what if you find different listings under [pɛn] (the pronunciation used in the

Northern United States) versus [pɪn] (used in the Southeastern region)? How would you find the movie *Harry Potter* online if the word *Potter* is listed in some places with the non-rhotic (r-less) British pronunciation and in other places with the rhotic (r-ful) version? As you can see, standardized spelling is useful for record-keeping (which is why dictionaries contributed to spelling standardization) and for communicating across groups who use different pronunciations for the same language.

So whether you find English spelling annoying or fun, it is here to stay. Luckily, for those of us who can never remember how to spell *Massachusetts* or *onomatopoeia*, or who consistently confuse *they're* and *there*, there is technological support in the form of spell checkers, grammar checkers, and predictive autocompletion of words and sentences.

These tools, referred to collectively as *writers' aids*, aim to automate the tedious part of writing, allowing the writer to focus on the ideas. We start our exploration of language technology applications in this book with writers' aids because we assume they are familiar to everybody, and they also provide a platform to introduce many linguistic concepts which recur in the rest of the book.

2.2 Kinds of spelling errors

We begin our tour of writers' aids with spelling correction, in which a computer automatically identifies spelling errors and suggests correctly-spelled replacements. It is always useful in natural language processing (NLP) to start by exploring examples: here, the types of spelling errors that we may encounter.

2.2.1 Nonword errors

So-called *nonword errors* are errors resulting in words which do not exist in the language, for example, when the article *the* is erroneously written as the nonword *hte*.

One can characterize such errors in two ways: on the one hand, we can try to determine why the error happened. On the other hand, we can describe how the word that was written differs from the target word that the writer intended.

Looking first at the *error cause*, nonword errors are usually caused either by mistakes in typing or by spelling confusions. *Typographical errors (typos)* arise when the person knew how to spell the word correctly, but mistyped. Perhaps they accidentally pressed an adjacent key (so the keyboard layout makes certain typos more likely than others); perhaps they pressed the right keys in the wrong order (typing *hte* for *the*); or perhaps they misused the space bar (typing *myphone* for *my phone*). Spacing errors are tricky because they disrupt the default assumption that spaces demarcate word boundaries: rather than just turning a single non-word into a single real word, a spell-checker would have to find a way to split the non-word string at the right place into two different real words.

Spelling confusions occur when the person does not know how to spell the word. A writer might, for example, never have seen the word *onomatopoeia* or might remember that *scissors* has something odd about it, but not be able to recall the details. For the record, *scissors* has at least three odd features: it's unusual for *sc* to represent the [s] sound; for *ss* to represent [z], and for *or* to spell the suffix that is more often written *er*. In English, when you know how to say a word, you may still be a long way from knowing how to spell it correctly.

Spelling confusions based on sound are obviously a major problem; not only do we spell based on analogy with other words, but we often use typical sound-to-letter correspondences when a word is unknown. Thus, spellers may leave out silent letters (*nave* for *knave*), may replace a letter with a similar sounding one (*s* for *c* in *deside* in place of *decide*), or may forget nuances of a rule *recieve*: *i* before *e* except after *c*). In languages with a more *transparent writing system* such as Finnish or Korean, writers face fewer opportunities for such spelling confusions than in a language like English which preserves various spelling irregularities as historical vestiges.

In motivating the need for spell-checkers, it helps to understand why people misspell words. It may also be useful to distinguish typos versus spelling confusions in order to provide the most helpful feedback to a user. But for the practical task of spelling correction, we can often ignore the error cause and focus instead on how the error would need to be fixed. What modifications would we need to turn the misspelled word into the correct spelling? With that perspective, there are four types of operations that we can perform to get to the correctly spelled word:

- *Insertion*: Add a letter.

  aquire → *acquire*

- *Deletion*: Delete a letter.

  arguement → *argument*

- *Substitution*: Replace one letter with another.

  calandar → *calendar*

- *Transposition*: Swap the position of two adjacent letters.

  con<u>cs</u>ious → *con<u>sc</u>ious*

The *edit distance* between two strings quantifies the minimum number of operations that it takes to transform one string into the other. For example, the edit distance between *Catherine* and *Kathryn* is four:

1. Replace *C* with *K* [*Katherine*]
2. Delete the first *e* [*Kathrine*]
3. Delete the second *e* [*Kathrin*]
4. Replace *i* with *y* [*Kathryn*]

Note that the order of these operations often does not matter; we would get the same result if we deleted the first *e* before swapping the initial *C* for a *K*. But the order may matter in the case of transpositions, where two adjacent letters are swapped: whether two letters are adjacent or not may depend on what other operations have come before.

Actually, some people consider a transposition to have a cost of two, involving one substitution and then another. And some give a substitution a cost of two, equivalent to a deletion followed by an insertion. These decisions are arbitrary value judgments based on what works best for a specific purpose.

When the operations used to calculate edit distance are insertion, deletion, and substitution, the edit distance is sometimes called the *Levenshtein distance*, after the Soviet mathematician who proposed it (Levenshtein 1966). This flexible idea has also been used (Sankoff 1992) to quantify the similarity between DNA sequences (represented as strings of letters). It is sometimes specified to refer to the *minimum* number of operations in order to rule out perversely inefficient pathways from one word to another, for example mapping *Catherine* to *Kathryn* by replacing the letter *a* with *x*, then replacing it again with *a*.

We can use edit distance to quantify the steps to turn a misspelled word into the correctly spelled target word, or inversely to quantify how the target word can be turned into the misspelling. The edit distance should be the same in either direction.

2.2.2 Real-word errors

Normally, when the result of an error is a nonword, an automated system can detect the error by trying to look up the word in a dictionary: if the word is not found, it may very well be the result of a spelling error. But this will not work for errors that result in real words, because real words are listed in the dictionary. Here, the error can only be identified by considering the surrounding context of the word. We can distinguish three different kinds of *real-word errors*, each involving context in different ways. As the appeal to context becomes more elaborate, the task of detecting the error becomes progressively more difficult.

First, there are *local syntactic errors*. Generally speaking, syntactic errors are errors in how words are put together in a sentence: different parts-of-speech are used in the wrong places in a sentence or the wrong grammatical forms are used. Local syntactic errors are those where the syntactic violation is detectable by looking within one or two words in the sentence. In 1, for example, a possessive pronoun (*their*) takes the place where a noun phrase (*there*) should be. Normally, we expect a possessive pronoun to be followed by a possessed noun, as in *their book*, but here it is incorrectly followed by the past-tense singular verb *was*.

(1) *Their was a problem yesterday.

To flag that this is an example of an ungrammatical sentence, we mark it with an *asterisk (*)*. This is a common convention in linguistics – and also alerts editors that the error in the example is intended, rather than something to be corrected for publication.

In contrast to local syntactic errors, *long-distance syntactic errors* are those involving syntactic violations spread out over many more words. In 2, *the cabinets are* is a perfectly coherent string of English, but it is incorrect here because *are* corresponds grammatically to the singular subject noun *key*, not to the plural noun *cabinets*, which actually sits within a prepositional phrase. The erroneous agreement with plural *cabinets* is called *agreement attraction* (Bock & Miller 1991), and raises questions for psycholinguists about how people represent sentence structure in their minds.

(2) The key to the cabinets are on the counter.

Finally, there are *semantic errors*. These are errors in meaning: The sentence structure is grammatical, but the problem is that the sentence does not mean what was intended. In 3, *brook* is a singular noun – just like the presumably intended *book* – but it does not make sense in this context.

(3) I checked out a brook from the library.

It is not always easy to decide whether an error is a spelling error or an error in grammar. Example 2, for instance, could be thought of as a real-word spelling error in which the typist simply omitted the *s* of *keys*, or it could be thought of as a problem with subject-verb agreement, which is a grammatical error. Without knowing what is going on in the writer's mind, it is hard to know which explanation is better. In 1, on the other hand, it seems obvious that the writer was trying to produce *There*, so it is safer to classify this as a real-word spelling error. The distinction between spelling errors and grammatical errors is not just philosophical: A writers' aid may be designed to give different feedback to writers depending on the presumed nature of the error.

2.2.3 How common are spelling errors?

When proficient adult English speakers type on a full-size keyboard, they misspell approximately two to three percent of all typed words (Flor et al. 2015). About eighty percent of misspellings are non-word *single-error misspellings*, with an edit distance of 1 from the intended spelling. In most cases, the writer is correct about the first letter of the word and the total number of letters. About twelve percent of spelling errors involve real words (Flor et al. 2015).

On a mobile phone, however, as much as 42 percent of English words are misspelled (according to 2022 blog post by the writers' aid company Grammarly[1]), and the rate is even higher for languages such as French where some letters are accented (*café*), which people often rely on the phone to correct. In general, people rely more heavily on auto-complete and auto-correct when typing on phones. One might, therefore, expect a far greater proportion of *multi-error misspellings* – those that are further in edit distance from the intended spelling. The rate of *real-word errors* may also be higher if auto-complete inserts real words that the author did not intend.

These trends are based on the writing of adults who are proficient in English; but the pattern of errors may look different for children learning to write, people with dyslexia, or people learning English as a second language (see Chapter 3 for more on language learning). Such groups may benefit from writers' aids designed for their specific needs.

[1]https://www.grammarly.com/blog/mobile-communication-study/, accessed 2024-07-01.

2.3 How to build a simple spell-checker

Having explored the sources and types of errors, we can now look at how to automatically detect and correct them. We take inspiration from a classic 2007 blog post (Norvig 2007) by Google Research director Peter Norvig, who presents a spell-checker in 22 lines of Python. For simplicity, we follow Norvig in illustrating the *context-independent* correction of non-word errors (e.g., correcting *hte* to *the*) – setting aside real-word errors and those that can only be corrected with reference to the surrounding context (e.g., *too computers*).

Under the Hood 4: Peter Norvig's spell-checker

Here is Norvig's spell-checker. To run it, you would need a big text file of correctly-spelled English called "big.txt" saved in the same directory as your Python code.

```
import re
from collections import Counter

def words(text):
    return re.findall(r'\w+', text.lower())
    #Split text into words, lower-case all words.

WORDS = Counter(words(open('big.txt').read()))
#Read in a big txt file of correctly-spelled words.

def P(word, N=sum(WORDS.values())):
    #Probability of `word`.
    return WORDS[word] / N

def correction(word):
    #Most probable spelling correction for word.
    return max(candidates(word), key=P)
```

```
def candidates(word):
    #Generate possible spelling corrections for word.
    return (known(
            [word]) or known(
            edits1(word)) or known(
            edits2(word)) or [word])

def known(words):
    #The subset of `words` that appear in the dictionary of
        WORDS.
    return set(w for w in words if w in WORDS)

def edits1(word):
   #All edits that are one edit away from `word`.
   letters    = 'abcdefghijklmnopqrstuvwxyz'
   splits     = [(word[:i], word[i:])
                 for i in range(len(word) + 1)]
   deletes    = [L + R[1:]
                 for L, R in splits if R]
   transposes = [L + R[1] + R[0] + R[2:]
                 for L, R in splits if len(R)>1]
   replaces   = [L + c + R[1:]
                 for L, R in splits if R for c in letters]
   inserts    = [L + c + R
                 for L, R in splits for c in letters]
   return set(deletes + transposes + replaces + inserts)

def edits2(word):
    #All edits that are two edits away from `word`.
    return (e2 for e1 in edits1(word) for e2 in edits1(e1))

### Now try it:

>>> correction('speling')
'spelling'
```

```
>>> correction('korrectud')
'corrected'
```

A simple spell-checker uses three steps: It detects errors; generates candidate corrections; and ranks the candidate corrections to choose the best one.

2.3.1 Detecting errors

To detect a non-word error, we can compare a typed word to a list of correctly spelled words. If the typed word is on the list, it is a real word. If it is not on the list, it is taken as a non-word misspelling.

Where do we get the list of correctly spelled words? We could get it from a dictionary, in which case we might have to generate rules to allow all inflections (*runs, running*) of the word that appears in the dictionary as a *lemma* (*run* – the uninflected form). We'd also have to decide what to do about capitalization: Should *Cat* be considered the same word as *cat* or *CAT*? What about *alex* versus *Alex* versus *ALex*? We could also get our list of correctly spelled words from a *corpus*, a large dataset of (hopefully correctly-spelled) text from sources such as books, news articles, and magazines.

Wherever we get the list of correctly spelled words, people who use the spell-checker might feel that it includes too many or too few. Maybe the corpus contains some typos that should actually be corrected (certainly true of corpora based on Wikipedia, which is not professionally copy-edited). Maybe it includes some words that technically appear in the dictionary but are so rare that they are usually actually typos, such as *teg* (a sheep in its second year, but only sheep farmers know this). Maybe it seems racist for the list of correctly spelled words to include traditional Anglophone names such as *Jane* but not names from other parts of the world such as *Shalini* (exemplifying the larger issue that text data can perpetuate racial biases). And of course, new words are invented all the time (for example, *monoamorous* – antonym to *polyamorous*), so any static word list is inherently incomplete. The dictionary is sometimes invoked as the ultimate authority on language (*look it up in the dictionary!*), but dictionaries have to keep up with the usage and creativity of the wider society.

Once we have curated this list of correctly spelled words, detecting a non-word error is straightforward: If a word appears on the list, then it is a real word and should not necessarily be spell-checked. If it is not on the list, then it is likely a misspelling and so we want to generate candidates for the correct spelling.

2.3.2 Generating candidates

We can generate candidates for the correct spelling using edit distance. In particular, given that most misspellings are single-error misspellings, we can compute all alternative spellings that are within an edit distance of 1 from the misspelled word – restricting our attention to those that actually appear on the list of correctly spelled words. For the misspelling *catt*, our candidate corrections would be *cat, cats, catty, cast, cart*, and perhaps (depending on how we handle capitalization) the names *Cato* or *Matt* or the abbreviation *Capt.* We could also consider alternatives within an edit distance of 2 (for *catt*, we'd entertain possibilities such as *hat* or *sat*) or even 3 (*can't*); but most misspellings are within an edit distance of 1, and the more edits we allow, the more alternatives we have to sort through (to check them against the list of correct spellings).

2.3.3 Ranking candidates

The candidate spellings also have to be ranked so that, depending on the user interface of the spell-checker, the "best" candidate can be chosen automatically or presented as the top suggestion for the writer to approve. Of course, the "best" candidate is what the writer most likely intended. But we can't see inside their mind, so how do we figure out what they intended?

To answer this question, we introduce some ideas that will be important throughout this book, namely the *noisy channel model* inspired by *information theory* and *Bayes' Rule.* We will take a close look at the mathematics in Chapter 5, but for now we will keep the explanation intuitive. The writer has an intended message in their mind (the word they want to write), but this message is sent through a "noisy channel" – typing it imperfectly on a keyboard. As the receiver of this message, we (as readers and spell-checkers) have to make our best guess of what this person meant (the clean message) given what they typed (the distorted message that comes out of the noisy channel). We can use two different pieces of information: The likelihood of a given intended message overall; and the likelihood of typing what they typed given that particular intended message. We combine these two pieces of information to arrive at the most likely intended clean message (the correct spelling) given the noisy typed signal (the misspelling) that we observe.

For example, imagine that someone types the word *Dsvid.* Let's imagine three candidates for what this person intended to type: *Dsvid, Sara,* and *David.* First: did they mean to type *Dsvid*? On the one hand, it is extremely unlikely that anyone would intend to send the message *Dsvid*, as we can infer from the fact that *Dsvid* does not appear on any list of correctly-spelled English words and also is extremely infrequent in corpora of English text: The probability of *Dsvid* being the intended message is quite low. On the other hand, if someone did for some reason want to type the word *Dsvid*, it is very likely that they would indeed type the string *Dsvid* (as reflected by the fact that the edit distance from *Dsvid* to *Dsvid* is 0); the probability of observing the noisy message *Dsvid* given the intended message *Dsvid* is pretty high. But overall, combining these two pieces of information, *Dsvid* is probably not what they meant because *Dsvid* is a very unlikely string for the writer to have intended.

Next, did they mean to type the word *Sara*? On the one hand, *Sara* is a pretty likely string of English: It's in a dictionary and it occurs somewhat frequently in corpora of English text, so the probability of *Sara* being the intended message is quite high. On the other hand, if someone intended to type the word *Sara*, it is extremely unlikely that they would have typed the string *Dsvid* (as reflected by the fact that the edit distance from *Dsvid* to *Sara* is 4): The probability of observing the noisy message *Dsvid* given the intended message *Sara* is very low. So *Sara* is probably not what they meant.

Finally, did they mean to type *David*? On the one hand, *David* is a pretty likely string of English, appearing in dictionaries and corpora: The probability of *David* being the intended message is high. Additionally, if someone intended to type the word *David*, it's quite likely that they would have typed *Dsvid* (as reflected by the fact that the edit distance between them is 1): The probability of observing the noisy message *Dsvid* given the intended message *David* is high. To arrive at *David*, we combined two pieces of information: The probability of the intended message, and the probability of the noisy signal that we observe given that intended message. We choose the intended message that is most probable according to these two combined metrics.

To automate this reasoning process, Norvig's simple spell-checker first considers all correctly-spelled candidates within an edit distance of 1 from the misspelled word, and chooses as the "best" correction the one that is most frequent in a corpus of English text. If there are no correctly-spelled candidates within an edit distance of 1, then Norvig's spell-checker considered all candidates within an edit distance of 2, and again chooses as the "best" correction the one that is most frequent in an English corpus. If there is no word within an edit distance of 2, the spell-checker gives up and just returns the misspelling. Edit distance reflects the probability of the misspelling given the intended message, and corpus frequency reflects the probability of the intended message.

If we wanted to make Norvig's spell-checker more sophisticated, we might note that *s* and *a* are right next to each other on a keyboard, so that *Dsvid* is a particularly likely mistyping of *David*, more likely than *Dbvid* even though they are both equidistant from *David* by edit distance. Another way to improve this spell-checker is to consider the linguistic context of each word, which we explore in Section 2.4.1.

Under the Hood 5: Dynamic programming

The minimum edit distance problem (also referred to as the edit distance problem) is to decide the minimum number of edit operations needed in order to transform a misspelling into a candidate correction. It is an example of an important class of problems that look hard but turn out, when correctly viewed, to have exceedingly efficient solutions. *Dynamic programming* is the technique that makes this possible.

The reason why minimum edit distance looks hard is that there are many different sequences of edit operations that need to be considered. However, by breaking up the problem into smaller sub-problems, it is possible to find enough opportunities for saving time and space that the problem becomes feasible. The key idea is to avoid solving the same sub-problem over and over again. This can be done by solving each sub-problem once, then storing away the answer in case it is needed again. For an in-depth discussion on calculating minimum edit distances, see chapter eight of Mitton (1996), on which we base this discussion.

To set up the problem, we need to ensure that there is a finite number of steps involved. How could we end up with an infinite number of steps? Consider the misspelling *obe* and the correction *oboe*: While we can intuitively see a distance of one between these strings, it is possible to derive *oboe* from *obe* by (i) deleting *o*, (ii) changing *b* to *o*, (iii) inserting *b*, (iv) inserting *a*, and (v) finally changing *a* to *o*. It is pretty obvious that the *a* (step iv) was a pointless diversion, but not immediately obvious how to fix this in a systematic way.

Things are actually far worse than this: We can also do it in six steps. We again start by deleting *o*, then change *b* to *o*, then insert *b*, then insert *a*, change *a* to *b*, then finally *b* to *o*. Or in seven, by converting the *b back* into an *a* before turning it into an *o*. In fact, since you can make the pointless diversion as long as you want, there are an *infinite* number of different ways of doing the conversion. Enumerating all these possibilities is not just inefficient, it is actually impossible. We need to set up the problem to avoid this pointless and infinitely repetitive enumeration of silly possibilities.

Given this, we want the algorithm for edit distance calculation to satisfy two requirements:

1. Letters cannot be changed back and forth a potentially infinite number of times.

2. The number of changes that we consider should be reasonable. In fact, we will show that the total number of changes we need to consider – to find the single best sequence of changes – is proportional to the product of the sizes of the two words being compared. This is definitely efficient enough for spell checking, because words are typically quite short (in English, 40 characters is a really long word). If the sequences were much longer, as happens when comparing strands of DNA in biology, we might need a still cleverer algorithm.

In other words, we never want to deal with a character in either word more than once. With our basic operations, it is obvious that we could get the desired result by deleting each character in the first word and then inserting each character of the second word. This establishes an *upper bound* on the number of edit operations we need. Mathematically, we can state this upper bound as $length(word_1) + length(word_2)$. In other words, if we compare a three-letter word like *tap* to a misspelling like *step*, we know that the edit distance cannot be more than 7. In fact, if you think a little more, you will be able to find a better upper bound on the number of operations needed. We will explain this tighter upper bound at the end of this section.

To calculate minimum edit distance, we set up a *directed, acyclic graph*, where a *graph* – which is a mathematical object that models relationships between items – is represented by a set of nodes (circles) and arcs (arrows). Arcs capture relationships between nodes: *Directed* means that the arcs have a direction to them, pointing from one node to another, and *acyclic* means that there are no loops: We cannot return to a node once we have left it.

We will set up the graph in the following way, as shown. Horizontal arcs correspond to deletions; vertical arcs correspond to insertions; and diagonal arcs correspond to substitutions (including the option that a letter is substituted for itself). We leave out transpositions here, although the graphs can be extended to allow them.

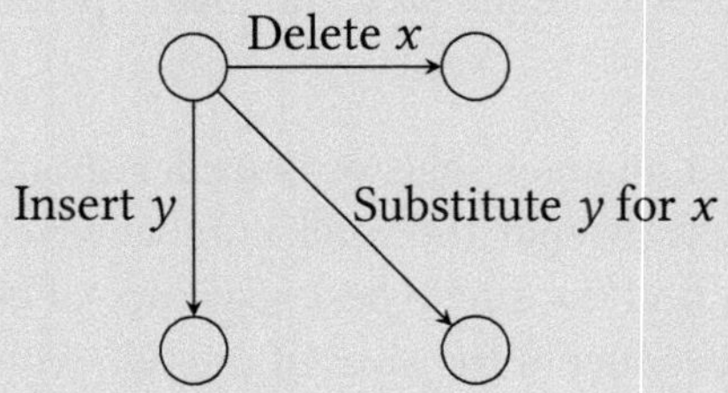

Let us start by assuming that the user types in *fyre*. Given that *fry* is one of the possible corrections, we want to calculate how far away *fry* is. In other words, we want to calculate the minimum edit distance (or minimum edit cost) from *fyre* to *fry*. As the first step, we draw the directed graph:

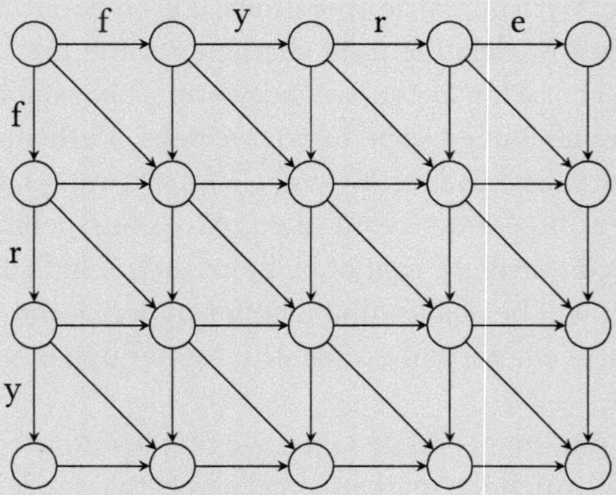

The worst case of first deleting every letter in *fyre* and then inserting every letter of *fry* would be achieved by starting in the upper left, taking every arc across the top, and then following the arcs down the right side.

What is missing from the graph are identifiers for the nodes. If we add an identifier to each state, that will allow us to define a *topological order.*

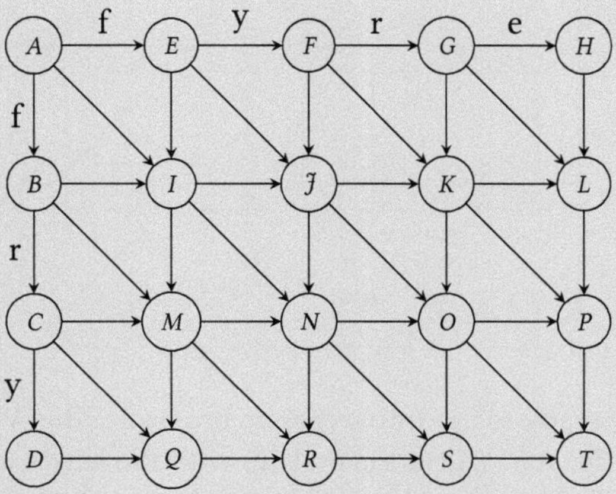

A topological order means that the nodes are loosely ordered, but not completely ordered. Here, for example, node I comes after nodes A, B, and E, but there is no ordering between nodes C and I: There is no way to get from C to I or from I to C. The crucial property of this topological ordering, as we will see below, is that at every node, all the incoming arcs come from nodes prior in the ordering.

In order to actually calculate a distance, we need to add the costs involved to the arcs. In the simplest case, the cost of deletion, insertion, and substitution is 1 each (and substitution with the same character is free), as shown. In other words, there is a distance of one for any non-trivial operation. For example, from node A to node I, we substitute *f* for *f* with a cost of zero, and from I to J, we delete *y* with a cost of one:

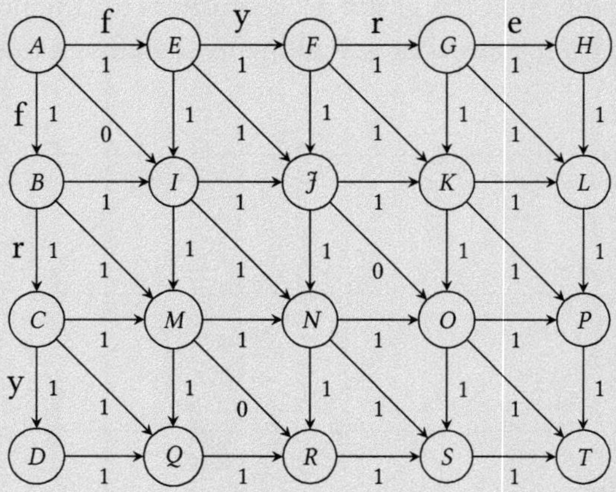

Now, we are ready to get into dynamic programming. We want to find the path from the start (A) to the end (T) with the least cost. How do we do that efficiently?

We will start with a simple but inefficient way of doing it:

1. Follow every path from start (A) to finish (T).
2. See how many changes we have to make for each path.

This is very time-consuming, however. There are too many different paths to check. We would have to check the path A→I→J→O→S→T and then separately check the path A→I→J→O→P→T, and so on.

But note that these paths have a lot in common! In fact, based on this insight, we should instead re-use results, which is exactly what dynamic programming does:

1. Follow the topological ordering.
2. Calculate the *least cost* for each node:
   - Add the cost of an arc to the cost of reaching the node this arc originates from.
   - Take the minimum of the costs calculated for all arcs pointing to a node and store it for that node.

The key point is that we are storing partial results along the way, instead of recalculating everything every time we compute a new path. For example, let's say that we have already processed the nodes A-H and stored the minimum cost at each of those nodes. We are now at node I and need to examine all three incoming arcs (from nodes A, B, and E). Node A has a cost of zero; node E has a minimum cost of one, and node B also has a minimum cost of one. We add the cost of each node to the cost of each incoming arc:

Source to Target	Cost at Source	+	Cost of Arc	=	Total Cost
A to I	0	+	0	=	0
B to I	1	+	1	=	2
E to I	1	+	1	=	2

The least cost of these three incoming arcs is the one from node A, with a cost of 0. So, we store 0 as the minimum cost at node I. This corresponds to the fact that the paths going through nodes B or E are useless for us to arrive at node I: They cost too much, and from this point onwards, we can ignore those paths, keeping only the cheapest one. Now, anytime node I is needed, we give the cost of 0, and we never have to re-calculate its cost.

In this way, the minimum cost at every node is computed, following the ordering from A to T. At node T, we calculate costs in the same way. You can verify that node O has a minimum cost of 1, node P a minimum cost of 2, and node S a minimum cost of 2. Each of the arcs (O→T, P→T, S→T) has a cost of 1, and so the final cost at node T will be 2, taking the path coming from O. Since T is the final node in the graph, this means that 2 is the minimum cost between *fyre* and *fry*.

Dynamic programming avoids infinite repetition, because it looks things up in a table rather than recomputing them. It also satisfies the stronger requirement to avoid all unnecessary repetition, because each intermediate result is entered into the table exactly once. The number of letter-letter comparisons needed is exactly the size of the table, which is the product of the lengths of the source and target string, so we also satisfy the second requirement that the cost of the computation be in reasonable proportion to the size of the problem.

The better upper bound which we mentioned earlier is a simple one. Let us decide to work on transforming the longer word into the shorter word. First we replace all the letters of the shorter word with the corresponding letters of the longer word, then we insert the leftover letters from the longer word. To illustrate this, imagine that the shorter word is *take* and the longer word is *intake*. The old upper bound said that we might need $4 + 6 = 10$ operations. The new upper bound says that we should first replace *take* with *inta*, then insert *ke*, for a total cost of 6. We say that the new upper bound is tighter than the old one. The total number of operations required by the new, tighter upper bound is the length of the longer word.

Obviously, the real minimum cost path for this example is to first insert *in* then match up *take*, for a minimum cost of 2. Dynamic programming will indeed find this path. The upper bound is still useful, because it can be calculated using nothing more than the length of the words. If a node has a cost greater than the upper bound, it cannot possibly contribute to the minimum cost path, so we could design a slightly cleverer version of the minimum cost algorithm that avoids filling in nodes that would cost more than the upper bound. The answer would still be correct, and some time and effort would be saved, at the expense of making the algorithm more complicated. It is usually better to keep algorithms simple, because complicated ones are more likely to have bugs, but in this case, especially if we are dealing with a language with very long words, the extra complexity might be warranted.

2.4 *n*-grams

Imagine that someone types the phrase *You put the catt before the horse*. The word *catt* is misspelled, as we can tell from the fact that it does not appear in a dictionary or corpus. Out of context, the simple spell-checker that we sketched above would consider all candidates that appear on the list of correctly spelled words and are within an edit distance of 1 from *catt*, and then choose the most frequent one: *cat*. But of course, the most likely correction should actually be *cart*, which is less frequent than *cat* but more likely in this particular context.

Intuitively, *put the cart before the horse* is more likely as a string of English than *put the cat before the horse*. We can quantify that intuition using the idea of *n-grams*, which are sequences of elements. The elements can be characters or words (both have their uses, but we use word-level *n*-grams here); and *n* is a number that goes up as high as you want. Unigrams are one-element sequences (for word-level *n*-grams, this means single words: *the*). Bigrams are two-element sequences (*the cat*), trigrams are three-element sequences (*put the cat*), and so on.

If you've ever managed to correctly guess the next word before you turn the page of a book, you are already an expert in reasoning about *n*-gram probabilities. Let's illustrate using bigrams (*the cat*). The idea is that we count all of the two-word strings (bigrams) in a corpus, such as *of the, to be,* and so on. These simple counts are surprisingly useful.

To start, take a look at Tables 2.1–2.3. Here, we've extracted the top twenty most common unigrams, bigrams, and trigrams in two corpora of English text – one million words of comments from January 2018 on the AskReddit web forum (Baumgartner et al. 2020), and the comparably-sized Brown corpus (Francis & Kucera 1979), which gathers data from a balanced blend of sources (newspapers, novels, academic journals, and so on) from the 1960s. By comparing *n*-grams drawn from two different corpora, you can investigate which *n*-gram statistics are common to all English text, and which ones are specific to a particular corpus, genre, or time period.

Consistent across both corpora, we see that the START token (indicating the beginning of a sentence) appears in more of the most frequent *n*-grams than the END token, which shows that the beginnings of English sentences tend to be more predictable than the end. Distinguishing the two corpora, *I* is far more frequent in Reddit than in the Brown Corpus, perhaps reflecting different patterns in personal narratives versus expository writing. Notably, *he* and *his* are among the top 20 unigrams in the 1960s-era Brown corpus, but not among the top 20 unigrams from 2018 Reddit data – perhaps indicating a historical shift in the sociology of gender as well as a difference in genre.

To guess the next word of a book before turning the page, you might take into account the last word on the previous page and then look at the most common bigrams that begin with that word. For example, the most common bigram beginning with *you* is *you are*, so when you see the word *you*, the most likely following word is *are*. The same idea can be used in a simple implementation of auto-complete for texting: The phone can suggest *are* as the next word following *you*.

Table 2.1: Top-20 common unigrams (lower-cased, stripped of punctuation) in two English corpora – one million words of comments from AskReddit, and the one-million-word Brown corpus.

Reddit 1-gram	Count	%	Brown 1-gram	Count	%
the	32404	3.34	the	69971	6.97
i	28940	2.99	of	36412	3.63
to	27629	2.85	and	28853	2.87
a	26724	2.76	to	26158	2.60
and	24795	2.56	a	23308	2.32
of	16106	1.66	in	21341	2.13
in	13649	1.41	that	10594	1.05
that	13636	1.41	is	10109	1.01
it	13281	1.37	was	9815	0.98
my	12412	1.28	he	9548	0.95
you	11404	1.18	for	9489	0.94
for	10350	1.07	it	8760	0.87
is	9790	1.01	with	7289	0.73
was	9541	0.98	as	7259	0.72
but	7313	0.75	his	6996	0.70
have	7295	0.75	on	6741	0.67
on	6588	0.68	be	6377	0.64
with	6446	0.67	at	5372	0.53
not	5912	0.61	by	5306	0.53
they	5794	0.60	i	5180	0.52

2.4.1 Spelling correction in context with *n*-grams

By telling us which strings of English are more or less likely, *n*-grams can also be used to upgrade our simple spell-checker, which will help us identify *cart* as the best correction for *put the catt before the horse.* Specifically, we can use *n*-grams as a simple *language model* – a way of computing the probability of a sequence of words, given a lot of data about the language.

In an *n*-gram language model, the probability of a full sentence is obtained by breaking it down into strings of length *n* and then multiplying the probabilities of each *n*-gram. The probability of *put* given *you* is the percentage of all bigrams starting with *you* that end in *put.* The probability of *the* given *put* is the percentage of all bigrams starting with *put* that end in *the.*

Table 2.2: Top-20 common bigrams (lower-cased, stripped of punctuation) in two English corpora – one million words of comments from AskReddit, and the one-million-word Brown corpus.

Reddit 2-gram	Count	%	Brown 2-gram	Count	%
START i	10917	1.04	of the	9750	0.92
in the	3093	0.30	START the	7055	0.66
i was	2831	0.27	in the	6092	0.57
START the	2529	0.24	to the	3503	0.33
of the	2458	0.23	START he	3040	0.29
START my	2277	0.22	on the	2476	0.23
it END	1939	0.19	and the	2269	0.21
START it	1877	0.18	START it	2122	0.20
and i	1775	0.17	for the	1854	0.17
it was	1694	0.16	START i	1827	0.17
to be	1634	0.16	START in	1795	0.17
START its	1579	0.15	to be	1718	0.16
in a	1566	0.15	at the	1658	0.16
START im	1478	0.14	with the	1541	0.15
START you	1472	0.14	START but	1513	0.14
to the	1464	0.14	of a	1492	0.14
START and	1414	0.14	it is	1475	0.14
when i	1367	0.13	in a	1425	0.13
on the	1326	0.13	from the	1419	0.13
i have	1293	0.12	that the	1399	0.13

In a bigram language model, the probability of *You put the cat before the horse* would be:

(4) $P(\text{you}|\text{START}) \times P(\text{put}|\text{you}) \times P(\text{the}|\text{put}) \times P(\text{cart}|\text{the}) \times P(\text{before}|\text{cart}) \times P(\text{the}|\text{before}) \times P(\text{horse}|\text{the}) \times P(\text{END}|\text{horse})$

And in a trigram language model it would be:

(5) $P(\text{put}|\text{START, you}) \times P(\text{the}|\text{you, put}) \times P(\text{cart}|\text{put, the}) \times P(\text{before}|\text{the, cart}) \times P(\text{the}|\text{cart, before}) \times P(\text{horse}|\text{before, the}) \times P(\text{END}|\text{the, horse})$

According to the trigram language model, the trigrams *the cart before* and *cart before the* should be more likely than *the cat before* and *cat before the*, so the

Table 2.3: Top-20 common trigrams (lower-cased, stripped of punctuation) in two English corpora – one million words of comments from AskReddit, and the one-million-word Brown corpus.

Reddit 3-gram	Count	%	Brown 3-gram	Count	%
a lot of	851	0.09	START it is	604	0.06
START i was	697	0.07	START it was	579	0.06
when i was	602	0.06	START in the	471	0.05
START i dont	538	0.06	one of the	404	0.04
START i have	531	0.05	START he was	367	0.04
START it was	470	0.05	the united states	340	0.03
START i think	456	0.05	START this is	259	0.03
START if you	407	0.04	START there was	258	0.03
START i had	391	0.04	START he had	249	0.02
START when i	381	0.04	as well as	238	0.02
START this is	376	0.04	START there is	204	0.02
i grew up	361	0.04	some of the	179	0.02
one of the	289	0.03	out of the	174	0.02
START i know	275	0.03	the fact that	167	0.02
START i am	251	0.03	START but the	166	0.02
to go to	245	0.03	START on the	156	0.02
i was a	244	0.03	the end of	149	0.01
START i grew	244	0.03	part of the	145	0.01
i have a	242	0.02	START at the	145	0.01
START i just	234	0.02	it was a	143	0.01

language model should give the sentence *You put the cart before the horse* a higher probability than *You put the cat before the horse.* Such a language model therefore would allow our spell-checker to take the context into account and choose the desired correction, *cart.*

Now that you understand the idea of *n*-grams, you can see how it encompasses even our simple context-free spell-checker from above. There, we computed the frequency of each single word in a corpus and used it to decide which candidate word is most likely. In the terminology of *n*-grams, we considered unigram frequency and used it to estimate the probability of the writer's intended message. Here, we are using bigram or trigram frequency to do the same thing, but the larger *n* incorporates information about the linguistic context of the misspelling.

But is a larger *n* always better? Not necessarily: The larger the *n*, the fewer examples of each *n*-gram will appear in a corpus, so that many 5-grams or 6-grams (*Samantha works as a party juggler*) are totally unique and thus absent from corpus statistics. You can see this yourself by considering the counts in Tables 2.1–2.3 (unigrams are more frequent than bigrams, which are more frequent than trigrams), or by searching the web in quotation marks for various two-word string of English (*Samantha works*, *works as*) versus various six-word strings (*Samantha works as a party juggler*), and comparing the number of hits. Language is fascinating in part because it is *productive*: We can use it to generate and understand infinite new utterances that we have never heard before. These utterances will include *n*-grams that don't appear in any corpus.

The productive power of language leads to *data sparsity*: No matter how much data we use, there will always be something we have never seen before. Data sparsity is a core problem in much of statistical NLP, where the behavior is guided by the data one has seen. Part of the solution to data sparsity is to look at more data, from a larger corpus; but even then, you're guaranteed to encounter new *n*-grams that you've never seen before. Another solution is to pretend you've seen more data than you really have, for example using *plus-one-smoothing* – adding 1 to the count of every single possible *n*-gram, pretending that you've seen any novel *n*-grams once in the past instead of never. This way, you can avoid multiplying by zero, or trying to take the log of zero (undefined), both of which could cause problems for the calculation of a language model. A third solution is to *back off* to $n - 1$ if you have never seen a particular *n*-gram of length *n*: If you've never seen the trigram *my glamorous elephant*, you can at least estimate its probability in your language model by taking the probability of the bigrams *my glamorous* and *glamorous elephant*.

Stepping back, *n*-gram techniques are a simple form of *machine learning*, where a computer is able to generalize knowledge (*n*-gram counts from a corpus) to solve a new problem (deciding the probability of a sentence it has not seen before). We will see much more of machine learning in Chapter 5.

We can also use *n*-grams to correct real-word errors. For example, encountering a sentence such as *You put the cat before the horse*, we could calculate the *n*-gram probability of this original sentence and compare it to alternative versions where we alter each word by an edit distance of 1 (restricting our attention to edits that also appear on a word-list of correct spellings). This way, *You put the cart before the horse* would be identified as a string with higher probability than *You put the cat before the horse*.

Instead of using sets of candidates based only on spelling differences, these techniques often use *confusion sets* consisting of words that are potentially confounded with one another in any relevant property. For example, a set could contain the words *there*, *they're*, and *their*, so that the task of the system is to figure out which of the words was meant in a given context. The advantage of such confusion sets is that the words do not have to be similar-looking: *amount* and *number*, for instance, can make up a set of words which are commonly confused. The disadvantage of these confusion sets is that someone usually has to define them in advance.

2.4.2 *n*-grams as a generative language model

So far, we have used *n*-grams to create a language model that represents the probability of different strings, for example capturing the fact that *put the cart before* is a more likely string of English than *put the cat before*. But we can also use *n*-grams as the basis for a very simple *generative* language model which creates probable strings of text. The term *language model* is used in both senses.

To create a generative language model using bigrams, we would store all the bigrams in our corpus along with their frequency. To generate a new sentence, we begin with the START token. Next we choose a word *w* to complete the bigram ⟨START, *w*⟩. We could choose the word that appears in the most frequent bigram beginning with START, which would be *The* in the Brown Corpus (there are 6544 instances of ⟨START, *the*⟩ in Brown). But if we always chose the most likely word, then our language model would generate the same sentence repeatedly, beginning every sentence with *The*. If we want a bit more novelty, we can choose a random bigram beginning with START, such as ⟨START, But⟩. We have seen this bigram 1271 times in the corpus, so it's a plausible way to a sentence, but it's not the most frequent one, so our language model will generate more interesting and less predictable text. Next, we choose a new word *w* to complete the bigram ⟨START, But⟩. Again, we could choose the most frequent bigram beginning with *But* (which is *the*), or a random one for more creative text (such as *there*). And so on. We keep generating text until we reach a final punctuation mark; then the sentence ends.

Here is an example of some text generated by this bigram language model:

(6) But there should always particularly when finally convinced that nobody else?

Here, the individual bigrams are reasonable (*but there, there should, should always*, and so on), but the full sentence is not very coherent.

When we use trigrams instead of bigrams in our language model, we generate text like this:

(7) But with the increasing complexity of markets and their importance in the north, where no one had been allowed to go.

Here, individual pieces of the sentence make sense (*increasing complexity of markets and their importance*), but again the full sentence seems to lose track of itself partway through.

Already, we have created a very simple example of a generative language model, which distills insights from a corpus to produce new sentences. We have also seen that the sentences are more interesting if we add some randomness to the process. These insights persist in modern generative language models, to be introduced below.

2.5 Grammar checkers

When our context-sensitive spell-checker replaces *their* with *there*, we are moving from spell-checking into *grammar checking* – automatically identifying errors in sentence structure. Before we investigate how to correct grammatical errors, we first must unpack the idea of grammar.

2.5.1 What is grammar?

Linguists view *grammar* as the implicit set of rules that speakers use to create and understand sentences in their language. For linguists, grammar is *descriptive*: The rules describe how people *actually* use language, not how they *should* use it. Thus, for linguists, *I ain't got no books* is a perfectly grammatical sentence in some varieties of English, because people use it and understand it, whereas **book the read student* is ungrammatical (indicated by the asterisk) because no one would ever use it.

In contrast, educators and editors view grammar as a *prescriptive* set of rules for how people should create sentences in a way judged by some authority to be clear and correct. Educators and editors may argue that *I ain't got no books* does not follow the prescriptive rules of standardized English, likely because this pattern is not used by the people who have historically had the power to declare their usage conventions as the correct ones. **Book the read student* would in some sense be prescriptively incorrect too, but prescriptive grammarians might not even think to prescribe against a sentence that no one would ever use.

While linguists focus on descriptive rules, in reality, commercially available grammar checkers correct text according to both descriptive and prescriptive rules, as writers generally want to adhere to both. To understand how such rules can be represented on a computer, we need to take a long look at how linguists analyze grammar. In linguistics, grammar – as we have been using the term – is studied largely within the subfield of *syntax*, where the goal is to identify rules and representations that explain how speakers create and understand new sentences.

Sentences are interesting because on the one hand, words are ordered linearly: They are written from left to right (in the Latin alphabet used to write English), and spoken one after another over time. But on the other hand, words are represented in the mind in a hierarchical structure, as we're going to see: Groups of words form chunks called *constituents*, and words are mentally and structurally "closer" to their constituent-mates than to other words that may be equidistant linearly. Such hierarchical structure is not directly reflected in speech or writing, but is important for understanding the meaning of a sentence, so a syntactic theory must find a way to represent it.

In (8), for example, it seems like *most of the reindeer* forms a unit, and this intuition is backed up by the fact that we can replace it with other, similar phrases, like *the children* or *two of the students*. We can also ask questions about this sentence for which *most of the reindeer* is the answer, such as: Who plays extremely fun games? And we can conjoin *most of the reindeer* with other constituents using *and*: *Most of the reindeer and some of the dogs play extremely fun games.* So, according to these *constituency tests* (replacement, answering of a question, conjoining), *most of the reindeer* forms a constituent.

(8) Most of the reindeer play extremely fun games.

Large constituents are made up of smaller constituents. *The reindeer* is a constituent too: We can replace it with other noun phrases (*the puppies, my students*). It might be hard to phrase a question about (8) such that *the reindeer* is the answer, but we can conjoin *the reindeer* with other similar constituents: *Most of the reindeer and the puppies play extremely fun games.* So *the reindeer* is a constituent.

Just like *most of the reindeer*, *reindeer play extremely fun* is a four-word string of the same sentence, but this one does not behave like a meaningful unit. It cannot serve as the answer to a question, nor can it be conjoined with or replaced by any other constituent.

In syntax, one of the goals is to articulate a set of rules for how to assemble words into constituents and constituents into sentences. Starting at the word level, the way a given word fits into constituents and sentences is determined by its *part of speech* (also known as its *lexical category*). The main parts of speech are verbs (*play*, *run*, *believe*, *throw*), nouns (*reindeer*, *game*, *government*, *basketball*), adjectives (*fun, beautiful, potential, brown*), adverbs (*heavily, well, later*), prepositions (*on, at, into*), articles (also known as determiners: *a, the, this, some*), and conjunctions (*and, or, since*).

To identify a word's part of speech, the clearest evidence comes from its *distribution*: Where does it typically appear in a sentence? For instance, nouns like *reindeer* can appear after articles, like *some* or *the*, while a verb like *eat* cannot. The second criterion is the word's morphology, the kinds of prefixes or suffixes a word can have. For example, verbs like *play* can take an *-ed* ending to mark them as past tense; but a noun like *reindeer* cannot. Words that share a similar distribution and similar morphological patterns are put into the same lexical category. Linguists use categories that are finer-grained than the familiar parts-of-speech, but they still talk about nouns, verbs, adjectives and so on, meaning roughly the same thing as an educated non-linguist does.

Turning to a word's meaning, there is some truth to the common intuition that nouns (*reindeer*) prototypically describe people, places, and things, while verbs (*play*) describe actions and events, and adjectives (*cute*) describe properties. But there are also exceptions: *Earthquake* is a noun but seems to describe an event almost like a verb, and *beauty* is a noun but describes a property almost like an adjective. Therefore, a word's distribution distinguishes its part-of-speech more clearly than its meaning.

In any case, a word's part-of-speech determines the syntactic behavior of the constituents built from it. Constituents are built by assembling words according to their part-of-speech. *The reindeer* is a constituent because it follows a general English rule of combining an article (*the*) with a noun (*reindeer*). *Play games* is a constituent because it follows a general English rule of combining a transitive verb (*play*) with a noun phrase (*games*). Just as words combine according to their lexical category, constituents combine with other constituents according to their *phrasal category*: A *noun phrase* (*the reindeer*) can combine with a *verb phrase* (*run, play extremely fun games, eat lunch*) to create a sentence.

When we know a word's part of speech, we know that we can substitute other words from the same part of speech into a sentence in such a way that – even if its meaning changes or even becomes nonsensical – the sentence still follows the rules of English. Similarly, when we know the phrasal category of a constituent, we can substitute any other constituent from the same category. (Try it!)

Chomsky (1957) observed that the sentence *Colorless green ideas sleep furiously* is nonsense in terms of its meaning and contains very unlikely *n*-grams such as *colorless green*, but still grammatical as a sentence of English because all of the lexical and phrasal categories are combined correctly. From his perspective, this example shows that the rules for building grammatical sentences are based on the sentence's structure rather than its meaning.

All of this prose discussion of syntax can be more explicitly formalized and visualized in a particular syntactic framework. We introduce two such frameworks, phrase structure grammar (influential in American formal linguistics) and dependency grammar (widely used in NLP).

2.5.2 Phrase structure grammar

If you have taken a linguistics class, you have most likely encountered phrase structure grammar, introduced by Noam Chomsky in the 1960s. Phrase structure grammar is a set of rules for breaking down a sentence into its constituents. For this, we need two things – a lexicon of words categorized by their parts-of-speech; and a set of syntactic rules for how to assemble or decompose constituents according to the parts-of-speech of the words therein.

Of course, the lexicon is huge and new words are added all the time, so we can't write down all the words in every lexical category. And there are lots of different syntactic rules for handling complex structures such as relative clauses, questions, and so on. But we don't necessarily need to engage with all of that complexity to get started on a phrase structure grammar. Instead, we can start with a *grammar fragment*, a toy grammar that includes just a few words and a few syntactic rules, which serves as a *model* for how we think grammar works more generally.

In our grammar fragment, we keep it simple with just a few words and phrase structure rules:

"S → NP VP" is a rule meaning that a sentence (S) can be broken into a Noun Phrase constituent and a Verb Phrase constituent. "NP → Det N" means that a Noun Phrase constituent can be broken into a determiner followed by a noun. "Det → *the, a, some, many*" means that a Determiner constituent can be instantiated by these words. "N → *reindeer, dragon, lunch, game*" means that a Noun node can be instantiated by these nouns. When a constituent is manifested by an individual word, we call that constituent a *terminal node*, because it doesn't contain any further constituents.

"NP → Det (A*) N" means that a Noun Phrase can consist of a determiner; an optional (indicated by parentheses) and unlimited (indicated by the asterisk) number of adjectives; and a noun. This rule parsimoniously captures Noun Phrases with and without adjectives, such as *the reindeer, the beautiful reindeer, the beautiful interesting reindeer*, and so on.

Table 2.4: An English grammar fragment, including rules for words.

Lexicon:
N → *reindeer, dragon, lunch, game, evening, morning*
V(trans) → *play, eat*
V(intrans) → *run, swim, dance*
Adj → *fun, beautiful, interesting*
Det → *the, a, some, many*
P → *for, in, to, at*

Phrase structure rules:
S → NP VP
VP → V(trans) NP
VP → V(intrans)
NP → Det (A*) N
NP → N(plural)
NP → NP PP
PP → P NP

We can use these phrase structure rules to draw a *phrase structure tree* (Figure 2.1) for our sentence. These rules are meant to indicate both syntactic hierarchy and linear order. Concerning hierarchical structure, the idea is that if a given string of words is a constituent, that string of words will share a so-called *parent* node not shared by other words (e.g., *the reindeer* with its parent NP, *played games* with its parent VP). If a string of words is not a constituent (e.g., *reindeer played*), then these words will not share a parent node to the exclusion of other words. As for linear order, the terminal nodes can be read from left to right to arrive at the word order of the sentence.

In a formal sense, each phrase structure rule must have a left-hand side, which is a single *non-terminal* element; non-terminals are defined as (phrasal and lexical) categories. So, *NP* is an acceptable left-hand side, while *reindeer* is not. Secondly, each rule must have a right-hand side, which is a mixture of non-terminal and terminal nodes – *terminal* because they are the final nodes in a tree. So, *Det Noun* or *Noun and Noun* or *Preposition NP* are acceptable right-hand sides.

Note one other property of phrase structure rules: the label of the parent (i.e., the left-hand side) reflects the lexical category of the word within it that is in some sense the most important for determining its distribution. This most important word is called the *head*. So, a Noun Phrase is headed by a noun, a Verb Phrase is headed by a verb, and so on.

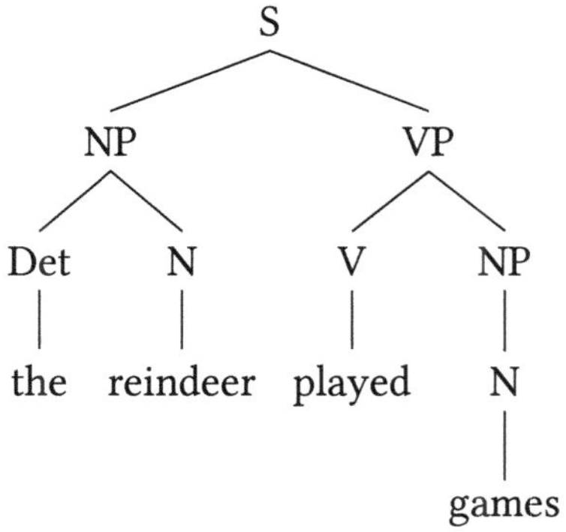

Figure 2.1: Phrase structure tree for *The reindeer played games.*

A grammar built on phrase structure rules is called a *context-free grammar*, which means that each rule is designed to be independent of the others. These rules can be used wherever the category on their left-hand side occurs. Rules cannot be further restricted to only apply in some places but not others. So, for example, you cannot have a rule which specifies that "PP → P NP" is applicable only when there is a verb phrase (VP) above the PP. The real reason for this is complexity: by having simple rules that apply everywhere, you can reason in a modular fashion about what is going on inside a particular constituent. (For more information on this topic, see the Under the Hood box on *complexity of languages*.)

The larger idea is that a phrase structure grammar represents an attempt to write down the implicit rules that explain how speakers create and understand new sentences, and thus to represent the infinite possibilities of language using a finite set of rules.

Note that these rules are *one-to-many*, meaning that the same left-hand side can correspond to multiple right-hand sides of a rule. "VP → V NP" captures the behavior of transitive (object-taking) verbs such as *throw* (*throw the ball*), while "VP → V" captures intransitive (object-less) verbs (*swam*). "NP → Det N" captures *the reindeer*; "NP → N" captures bare (determiner-less) noun phrases such as *reindeer*; and "NP → Det A N" handles *the beautiful reindeer*. One-to-many rules give phrase structure this important flexibility.

Phrase structure rules are also *recursive*, meaning that a rule can be used in building its own sub-structure. In (9), for instance, NP is reapplied within itself, thus allowing for phrases such as [[*the dog*] [*on* [*the porch*]]]: the whole thing is an NP, with smaller NPs (*the dog, the porch*) inside it.

(9) a. NP → NP PP
b. PP → P NP
c. NP → Det N

Similarly, the top S node can be embedded within a larger S node, for example to deal with sentence-level conjunction (*I ran and I swam*) as well as embedded clauses (*They know that you won*). Recursion is another way that phrase structure rules capture the infinite possibilities of language.

Finally, phrase structure rules are *language-specific*, meaning that each language has not just its own lexicon but also its own grammar. The English rule "S → NP VP" will not work for Irish, which uses *VSO* word order – meaning that the verb comes first, the subject second, and the object last (*Threw Alice the ball*).

With phrase structure grammar, it is not obvious how to deal with sentences where there is a *long-distance dependency* between words, meaning that the linear position of a word and its structural role seem to come apart. In (10), the word *what* is far away from the word *eat*, and yet there is a sense in which *what* is extremely closely related to *eat*, asking a question about the syntactic object of the eating. Different syntactic theories handle long-distance dependencies in different ways. Phrase structure grammar uses additional rules known as *transformations* or *movement*, which allow a word to essentially be in two places at once (one reflecting its linear order, another reflecting its structure); other theories add special rules for words like *what*. Such rules are interesting for linguists, but tricky for practitioners because things get more complicated when the structure and the form of the sentence don't match up.

(10) What did you eat?

In sum, phrase structure grammar is a hugely influential idea in linguistics, and it can help build systems for grammar checking. However, in many NLP applications, the grammar of a sentence is actually represented in a different framework: dependency grammar.

2.5.3 Dependency grammar

Dependency grammar, introduced by the French linguist Lucien Tesnière (Tesnière 2015 [1929]), inspired by ideas dating back to the ancient Indian linguist Panini, provides a way of representing the syntactic relations between words in a sentence as a series of *binary*, *asymmetric* relations between pairs of words, a *head* and a *dependent*.

For example, Figure 2.2 shows a dependency representation for *The reindeer played games.* Each word is labeled for its part of speech (*the* is labeled as DT, which refers to determiners; *reindeer* is NN, which refers to a singular common noun) and is linked to another word via a dependency relation. Here, *the* is the dependent of the head word *reindeer.* The relation between these words is asymmetric, in that *the* is the dependent of *reindeer* (and not vice versa), as represented by the unidirectional arrow from *reindeer* to *the.* Each relation is also *typed,* meaning that it has a specific label: here, the determiner relation (labeled *det*). In turn, *reindeer* is the dependent of the head *played* (a past-tense verb, with the part of speech VBD); in particular, the dependency relation between *reindeer* and *played* is labeled with the *nsubj* relation type, which indicates a subject noun. Finally, *games* (a plural common noun, with the part-of-speech tag NNS) is also the dependent of the head *played,* related through the *obj* relation (for the syntactic objects of transitive verbs). The verb *played* is the *root* of the sentence because it does not depend on anything else.

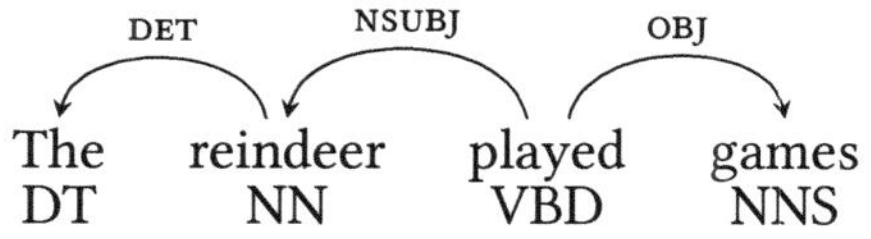

Figure 2.2: Dependency graph for *The reindeer played games.*

One big advantage of dependency grammar is that the same set of dependencies can be used for any language, regardless of the word order. In a language such as Irish where the verb comes first, the Irish equivalent of the verb *played* could come at the beginning of the sentence, with both its *nsubj* dependency and its *obj* dependency coming afterward. Indeed, dependency grammar was inspired in part by Lucien Tesnière's work on Slavic languages such as Russian, which allow many different word order options and use word endings known as *case markings* rather than word order to indicate the relations between words in a sentence. As a result, dependency grammar can be used to generate consistent representations for sentences in a multilingual corpus. The *Universal Dependencies* project (Nivre et al. 2016), based at Stanford, offers a corpus of sentences in over 100 languages, all annotated for their dependency relations in a consistent framework. Such a corpus helps linguists to study *language typology* – the ways in which different languages are similar or different – and empowers technologists to build robustly multilingual language technologies.

Because dependency grammar can reflect dependencies between non-adjacent words, it also offers a more transparent representation of long-distance syntactic dependencies. Whereas a phrase structure grammar needs special rules to handle sentences like *What did you eat?*, a dependency grammar can just allow a long-distance dependency, with an *obj* relation between *what* and *eat* (Figure 2.3). Moreover, because dependency grammars are based on words (*eat*) rather than phrases (*VP*), these representations invoke fewer invisible abstractions and stay closer to what you see in the text.

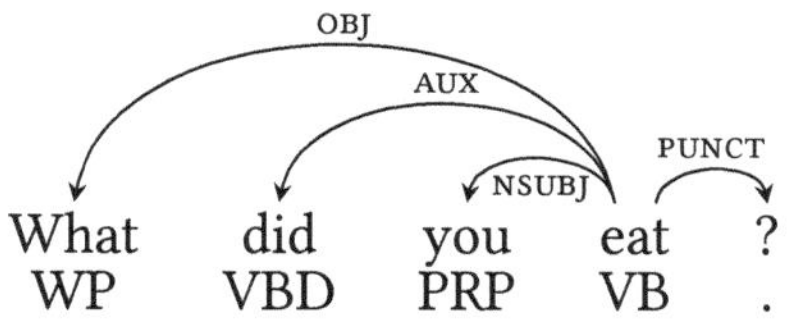

Figure 2.3: Dependency graph for *What did you eat?*

In dependency grammar, the root of a sentence is generally a verb, reflecting the idea that verbs are very important. The main verb of a sentence determines many elements of its syntax: if it is a transitive verb such as *throw*, the sentence will contain at least two noun phrases (the subject and the object of the verb), whereas if it is an intransitive verb such as *swim*, it can contain only one (the subject). The main verb is also important for understanding the event that the sentence describes, which all other elements of the sentence are related to. The syntactic relations between a verb and its dependent nouns (for example, the *nsubj* relation between a verb and its noun subject) correspond roughly to semantic relations between this event and its participants. For example, the syntactic *nsubj* relation often corresponds to the semantic relation of agency: in the sentence *Alice swam*, Alice is not just the subject but also the agent, the doer, of the swimming event. And in languages such as English, the main verb is also marked for tense, placing this event in time. So by building the sentence around the verb, dependency grammar aims to highlight information relevant to the sentence's meaning.

In comparing phrase structure grammar to dependency grammar, it is important to understand that each framework has different goals. Phrase structure is aimed at capturing how speakers of a particular language can generate infinite sentences from a finite set of words and rules; dependency grammar tries to capture the syntactic and semantic relations between words in a sentence in any language. If you go on to study syntax within linguistics, you should know that there is no single true theory of sentence structure; different theories capture different pieces of the puzzle.

In practice, for all the reasons described above, dependency grammar is widely used in NLP. Tools are available to automatically generate a structural representation for a new sentence, a task known as *parsing*. To parse a sentence, the words are first tagged with their parts of speech (noun, verb, adjective, determiner); then the parser reads the sentence one word at a time, and at each word has to decide whether to assign a dependency relation (choosing the direction, the head, the dependent, and the type of the relation) between that word and a previous word. Parsers are built using huge datasets of sentences already annotated for their dependency structure, and are trained using machine learning to generalize this information to assign the right parse to new sentences. Two of the most widely used dependency parsers are the Stanford Parser (available in Java and Python; de Marneffe et al. 2006) and SpaCy (Python; Honnibal & Johnson 2015). Both of these also offer web demos to visualize what is going on.

2.5.4 Fun with ambiguity

After this somewhat technical introduction to phrase structure grammar and dependency grammar, we can pause to appreciate one of the insights that we gain from a syntactic theory: it helps us to understand *syntactic ambiguity*. Syntactic ambiguity arises when the same string of words could be assigned to multiple distinct syntactic representations, each with a different meaning. Syntactic ambiguity is possible because, as we have seen, sentences have structure above and beyond the linear order of words.

In (11), for instance, we might understand the sentence to mean that the person whom I saw had a telescope (in which case *with the telescope* modifies the noun phrase *the person*); or we might understand it to mean that I used the telescope to see this person (in which case *with the telescope* modifies the verb phrase *saw the person*). This ambiguity is known as a *prepositional phrase attachment ambiguity* because it involves the position of the prepositional phrase *with the telescope*. Using phrase structure or dependency grammar, we could draw two different structures to reflect these two different meanings.

(11) I saw the person with the telescope.

Sometimes the effects of ambiguity are amusing. In (12), a *Time* headline from 2013, the author intends the headline as a noun phrase: the article describes the incremental steps (plural noun) that the Pope has taken on LGBT issues. The amusing alternative interpretation takes *steps* as a present-tense verb, meaning that the non-existent *Pope's baby* has stepped on some gay people. The ambiguity begins with the part-of-speech of the word *steps* (plural noun or present-tense verb), with consequences for the structure of the whole sentence.

(12) Pope's baby steps on gays.

Using the same thought process, you should be able to identify the source of the ambiguity in (13a)–(13c):

(13) a. MBA studies mushroom.
b. Complaints about referees growing ugly.
c. Hospitals are sued by 7 foot doctors.

It is worth noting, though, that not all ambiguity comes from syntax. There are also cases where the structure of the sentence is clear, but it is still compatible with multiple distinct meanings. In (14), the intended meaning is presumably that the leader of Iraq is seeking military equipment; the amusing alternative is that there is a disembodied Iraqi body part in search of additional body parts. Here, the ambiguity stems not from the structure, but a *lexical ambiguity*: the multiple (distantly related) meanings available to the words *head* and *arms*.

(14) Iraqi head seeks arms.

Another non-syntactic source of ambiguity is illustrated in (15a)–(15b). Here, the structure of the sentence is clear, but what's unclear is exactly what role is played by the participants in the event. One way to *replace* a pillar is to purchase a new one; another way is to physically stand in its place. A pleasant way to *include* children in baking is to let them participate; a macabre way is to use them as ingredients. Here, the ambiguity arises from multiple ways that individuals can participate in the real-world event described by the sentence.

(15) a. Pillars replaced by alumni.
b. Include your children when baking cookies.

We hope that this exploration of syntax has given you the tools to explain not just syntactic ambiguity, but also its cause. We also hope that you see the importance of structure, above and beyond linear word order, in interpreting sentences.

Under the Hood 6: Complexity of languages

We discussed context-free grammars earlier, which can be used to process natural languages and to assist in error detection. But what we did not justify was that context-free grammars are: a) all we need (we call this being *sufficient*) and b) nothing more than we need (*necessary*). In other words, maybe there are simpler ways of analyzing language? On the other hand, maybe context-free grammars are incapable of capturing all natural language phenomena?

What we are discussing is linguistic *complexity*, or the limits of what a particular type of grammar can do. Intuitively, the idea is that the phenomenon under discussion might be too complex to fit into the framework that we have for characterizing it. But what exactly do we mean by being too complex? To answer this, we need to sketch some *formal language theory*. In formal language theory, we *define* a language as a set of acceptable sentences (albeit, an infinite set). This is a technical use of the word *language*, not the everyday one, but it turns out that there is a close parallel between the mathematical reasoning that we can do about formal languages and the scientific reasoning that we want to do about natural, human languages. In the same way, there is a formal definition of what a grammar is, and a mathematical description of exactly what it means for a language to be characterized by a grammar.

Formal grammars, such as context-free grammars, differ in terms of which formal languages they can and cannot describe. Loosely, what we are going to say is that a formal grammar is more powerful than another if it can draw finer distinctions among formal languages. Instead of relying on informal intuitions about power and complexity, we can use mathematics. The point of the move to mathematics is to gain clarity by learning to view our scientific questions in an abstract way. For many of us, this is a scary thing to do. Fortunately, in the case of formal language theory, the results of doing the abstract thinking are so valuable, and so obviously relevant to language, that overcoming the initial discomfort is worthwhile.

Formal grammars and languages are therefore useful tools in coming to grips with the issues around the complexity of natural languages. You should think of formal language theory – with its precise definitions for what a grammar is, what a language is and what mathematical operations are allowed – as a working model of aspects of the way that natural language behaves. Real languages are obviously messier than this, but the models are still useful.

For example, we can write a context-free grammar to capture the following kinds of *center-embedded structures* in English:

(16) a. The frog is happy.
b. The frog *that the princess saw* is happy.
c. The frog *that the princess that the prince liked* saw is happy.

At some point, these sentences become difficult to understand, but in theory we can have an arbitrary number of sentences embedded within other sentences in English. (As a side point, we can also remove *that* and get a valid sentence.) The relevant context-free rules might look as in (17).

(17) a. S → NP VP
b. NP → NP S

It turns out that context-free grammars are more powerful than regular grammars, such as those used to write regular expressions, as in Chapter 6. (Note that in regular grammar and regular expression we are using *regular* in a technical sense.) There is no way to write a regular expression which can capture an arbitrary number of center embeddings. Thus, it seems like we need to at least use context-free grammars for natural language syntax.

We have said that context-free grammars are more powerful than regular grammars. This is not the end of the matter: there are even more powerful grammar formalisms, capable of describing yet more complex formal languages. namely *context-sensitive grammars.* It turns out that context-free grammars cannot capture what are called *cross-serial dependencies.* With center embeddings, as shown above, we have a noun phrase subject which is associated with a verb phrase; in all three sentences, *the frog* and *is happy* go together. When we look at it this way, we see that the last sentence has a structure akin to *abccba*, as shown in (18), a repeat of (16c).

(This tells us that we can use context-free grammars to write palindromes, too!)

(18) The frog$_a$ that the princess$_b$ that the prince$_c$ liked$_c$ saw$_b$ is happy$_a$.

Cross-serial dependencies, on the other hand, are of the form *abcabc*. They are called *cross-serial* because, if we draw a dependency between the two *a*'s, it has to cross over the dependency between the two *b*'s. If we imagined English to have cross-serial dependencies, we would expect (16b) to be rewritten as in (19).

(19) The frog$_a$ the princess$_b$ is happy$_b$ saw$_a$.

This clearly does not happen in English, but does it happen in other languages? Perhaps surprisingly, the answer is yes. In Swiss German, for example, verbs and their direct objects cross. We can see this in (20), from Shieber (1985), where *em Hans* ('Hans') is the object of *hälfed* ('helped'), and *huus* ('house') is the object of *aastriiche* ('paint'). At least some languages, then, need more powerful grammars than context-free grammars.

(20) ... mer em Hans es Huus hälfed aastriiche.
... we DATIVE Hans the house-ACC helped paint
'... we helped Hans paint the house'

2.5.5 From grammar to grammar checkers

After this long detour into syntax and the nature of grammar, we are finally ready to explore how these ideas can be applied to grammar checking. And it turns out that we've already done the heavy lifting by figuring out how to assign structures to sentences!

To begin, a grammar checker can first try to assign a dependency parse to a sentence. If the grammar checker cannot parse the sentence at all, it should probably be flagged as erroneous. If the grammar checker can assign a dependency parse, it can check this parse against a set of hand-written grammatical rules (a *rule-based* technique) corresponding to common errors: for example, it could check that if a verb's *nsubj* dependent is part-of-speech-tagged as a singular noun (with the tag NN), the verb should also be part-of-speech-tagged as the singular third-person form (with the tag VBZ). Such a grammar checker would flag *The dog swim* and perhaps suggest that it should be corrected to *The dog swims.*

As an aside, it's important to note that there are some varieties of English (including Norfolk English and African American English) where *The dog swim* is perfectly acceptable. So by treating it as an error to be corrected, our grammar checker already blends together prescriptive grammar with descriptive grammar.

A grammar checker could also combine error detection and error correction. For example, a grammar checker could automatically consider all alternative spellings for common confusion sets (*there, their,* and *they're*) and then suggest the one that has the highest *n*-gram probability or yields the most probable dependency parse. To build such a grammar checker, you would need a fast and accurate dependency parser plus a (potentially hand-written) set of rules and confusion sets corresponding to common errors. A grammar checker could also be crafted not just to flag errors, but also to explain what grammatical rule is violated, along with suggested corrections.

2.6 Style checkers

Moving further into prescriptive ideas about language, most modern grammar checkers also incorporate suggestions for rephrasing a sentence to align with prescriptive rules of writing style. Functionally, a style checker works just like the grammar checker described above, checking a (dependency) parse against a set of potentially hand-written rules; the only difference is the nature of these rules.

For example, a style checker might suggest avoiding split infinitives, where an adverb falls between *to* and a verb (*to go boldly* might be suggested as a correction for *to boldly go*). A style checker might propose more socially inclusive language, for example suggesting *server* as a replacement for *waitress.* A style checker could also suggest that very big noun phrases (*the refusal of the advisors to consider the downsides*) should be replaced by sentences (*the advisors refused to consider the downsides*), thought to be easier for readers to understand.

Sometimes, a style checker enforces subjective rules that a writer might disagree with, such as the idea that the passive voice (*The law was passed*) should be replaced by the active form (*Congress passed the law*). The popular Grammarly tool even flags *hedges* such as *I think that* and *somewhat,* suggesting that "strong, confident" writing is preferable. But there may be situations where it is actually advisable to hedge one's claims.

Some stylistic norms would be easy to automate and yet are not commonly flagged by modern grammar checkers: a writer should vary the length and structure of their sentences; the same adjective should not be used too often within the same paragraph (unless it is a technical term).

Other stylistic norms would be very difficult to check automatically, at least without a much richer representation of textual meaning: the idea that the syntactic subject of a sentence should be a previously established discourse topic (a preference which sometimes conflicts with the avoidance of the passive voice!); that parallel ideas should be discussed using parallel sentence/paragraph structure; that the end of a sentence is a place of structural emphasis and should be used to introduce new information or to advance one's point. Modern grammar checkers do not have a way of knowing what a writer's point is, much less whether it is a convincing one, and are therefore limited in their capacity to effectively style-check writing. Grammarly's advertisements have suggested that it can help you to write a concise, heart-warming, and hilarious speech for your best friend's wedding, but in reality it will not help you with the content.

2.7 Auto-complete and beyond

So far, we have focused on writers' aids that correct already-written text. But some newer writers' aids also help to generate text, suggesting completions for words or sentences that the writer has begun to type.

Auto-complete suggests ways to type the current or subsequent word. A simple auto-complete program could be written using an *n*-gram language model, for example suggesting the word *the* after the word *of* because *of the* is a common bigram. In an email client, a fancier version of auto-complete can identify the name of the email recipient and auto-complete their name in the salutation, to help avoid embarrassing mis-spellings of the addressee's name.

In Google's email client, the *SmartReply* feature "reads" an incoming email (*You're invited to a birthday party*) and suggests a variety of short replies (*See you there!, Sorry, we won't be able to make it*). *SmartCompose* suggests ways of completing an entire sentence: when you type *I ho...*, it will suggest *pe you are doing well.* SmartCompose also suggests subject lines for emails that you've drafted, such as *Happy Birthday* in an email containing birthday greetings. These tools are built by using various machine learning techniques (discussed further in Chapter 5–Chapter 7) to generalize from all of the email data that Google has available. To suggest ways of replying to an email, SmartReply looks for common replies to similar emails in a humongous email corpus; to suggest a subject line, SmartCompose looks for common subject lines of similar emails. Of course, the architects of such tools had to take care not to violate the privacy of the people who use Gmail, so the researchers did not read or have access to any of the email data themselves, and made sure that people's private information such as names and addresses would not be suggested. These modern writers' aids blend together error correction with *language generation*: automatically generating text, so that the computer itself is in some sense taking advantage of the productive power of language.

More recent *generative language models* do not just assist a human writer, but to some extent replace them by generating full paragraphs of text. *ChatGPT*, released in 2022 by the company OpenAI (Ouyang et al. 2022), is a tool trained to guess the next word in a string of text – checking whether it was correct, and updating its representations to get closer to the right answer next time, so that it has learned to distill a massive amount of information about language. ChatGPT works like a much fancier version of predictive text on your phone: given a string of words (*How are ...*), it guesses possible next words along with the probability of each one (the most probable one is *you*, then *your*, then *we*, and so on). Just as previewed in our generative *n*-gram language model above (Section 2.4.2), ChatGPT is designed to sometimes randomly choose slightly less probable next words rather than always choosing the top-ranked one, because this strategy leads to more contentful text. In your own text messages, you probably sometimes choose a word other than the top-ranked one, for example when you write the slightly less probable, information-richer string *How are your kids?* rather than the highly probable, emptier *How are you doing?*. ChatGPT does the same thing to generate more realistic prose.

ChatGPT is trained on over 300 billion words of text. For comparison, a typical novel is about 100,000 words long, so if you read a novel a day for 80 years, you would read 2.92 billion words (100,000 * 365 * 80) in your lifetime – less than one percent of what ChatGPT has read! Moreover, the creators of ChatGPT further trained the model to write text evaluated as "better" according to human gig workers. Just like a human writer, ChatGPT learns from both practice (writing probable sentences word by word) and feedback (human evaluations of its output).

Using sophisticated techniques for distilling such information, when a human prompts ChatGPT with a few words to get it started, this tool is able to generate extremely lucid text: grammatical sentences of English that flow into a cohesive narrative, far more sophisticated than the *n*-gram examples above.

Can such *large language models (LLMs)* replace a human writer? The consequences of generative LLMs are still unfolding, but it probably depends on what the human writer wants to say. If they want to generate a few comprehensible paragraphs about *Romeo and Juliet* for a school assignment, or some pleasant holiday wishes for a mass email, then a generative LLM may do the trick more efficiently than a human – raising concerns about cheating in school! But if they want to write a legal brief describing the facts of a particular case, or a news story reporting a detailed investigation of a particular scandal, the LLM is unlikely to be much help, because its vast general knowledge about text does not include specific fact patterns from the outside world. For some tasks requiring a mix of rote formality and situation-specific details, such as writing a cover letter for a job, perhaps the LLM could generate a usable first draft to be tailored by a human, leveraging the complementary abilities of humans and computers. As such tools improve, digital writers' aids may take over more and more pieces of the writing process.

2.8 Consequences

Stepping back, this chapter has foreshadowed some larger themes of the book.

Edit distance quantifies the distance between two words, but because our writing system reflects sound rather than meaning as discussed in Chapter 1, two words that are close by edit distance are unlikely to be close in meaning. When we explore text as data in Chapter 4, we come back to the idea of quantifying distance between words, but in a way that captures meaning rather than sound. In spelling correction, candidate correct spellings are generated and then ranked; in Chapter 6, the same process of generating and ranking candidates is applied to relevant results for a given search term. Spelling correction can be seen as one instantiation of the noisy channel model, whereby we reason about the most likely intended message as well as the likelihood of the observed noisy signal given that message; the same idea can also be applied to speech recognition in Chapter 1 and to machine translation in Chapter 7. We have used n-grams to create a simple language model, a representation of likely sentences learned in a bottom-up manner from data, which comes back in Chapter 5.

Our discussion of grammar emphasizes that a sentence is not just a list of undifferentiated words, but a structured grouping thereof. In future chapters such as Chapter 5 on text classification, we will sometimes use the simpler unstructured view as a starting point, but it is important to realize what information is lost when we ignore structure.

Moreover, recurring concerns about ethics and representation are raised when we consider that spell-checkers may favor majority cultural groups or that grammar-checkers may privilege the language variety spoken by people with power.

Writers' aids also have consequences for education. (Chapter 3 comes back to education in the context of second-language learning). Would you consider it a waste of time to memorize correct spellings when a computer can fix misspellings for you? (If you didn't spend time learning to spell, what would you study instead?) Would you spend less time studying grammar if you knew that you would always have access to a grammar checker? Would you learn to write and type more easily with the assistance of writers' aids? Should children should spend more time learning to type than learning to write by hand? Would you worry that they might over-rely on digital tools in such a way that they fail to learn important skills?

On a more philosophical note, if writers' aids can to some extent produce language, what does this mean for the idea that language usage indicates intelligence? To what extent do writers' aids automate tedious tasks versus threaten to make skilled human labor redundant? We will keep coming back to the question of whether humans versus computers compete or complement one another.

Checklist

- Give two reasons why standardized spelling is useful.
- Give examples of various types of spelling errors and explain why they occur.
- Calculate the edit distance between a misspelling and a correct spelling.
- Explain some methods for generating and ranking spelling corrections.
- Give examples of common unigrams, bigrams, and trigrams in English.
- Explain how *n*-grams can be used in a simple generative language model.
- Give an example where a simple *n*-gram language model can help to correct spelling errors in context.

- Compare and contrast phrase structure grammar with dependency grammar.
- Give an example of a syntactic ambiguity – a string of words that can be assigned two different grammatical structures, each with a different meaning – and use phrase structure grammar or dependency grammar to distinguish these two structures.
- Give an example of how a dependency parse could be used to automatically correct grammar.
- State the difference between descriptive and prescriptive grammar, and explain why grammar checkers use both.
- Sketch some affordances and limitations of language-generation tools such as ChatGPT.
- Explain why dynamic programming methods are efficient.
- Provide an example of how context-free grammars are insufficient as mathematical descriptions of human languages.

Exercises

1. Phrase structure grammar is built on the idea that the grammatical behavior of a word is not unique to that word, but can be generalized across all members of a lexical category. For example, the noun phrase *the reindeer* manifests the more general rule that any determiner can be combined with any noun to make a Noun Phrase, a rule which applies equally to *some games*. You can try out this exercise with a partner, inspired by the children's game of Mad Libs. One partner begins with a sentence, which they keep secret from the other partner. For each word in the sentence, the first partner asks the second partner for a word of the same lexical category (de-

terminer, adjective, noun, transitive verb, intransitive verb, and so on), replacing the sentence word by word until it's a totally new sentence. Is this new sentence a grammatical sentence of English? Does it make any sense?

2. Please draw a phrase structure tree and a dependency graph to represent multiple interpretations of some humorously ambiguous strings such as *Pope's Baby Steps On Gays.*

3. Explore a web demo for a dependency parser, such as the Stanford Parser or SpaCy. Try out some sentences and see how it visualizes their dependencies. How does it handle *Pope's Baby Steps On Gays*? (Does it matter how you capitalize that string?) What happens if you give it a sentence containing a grammatical error, such as *The key to the cabinets are on the counter*?

4. Please write some pseudo-code sketching how you would identify a subject-verb agreement error in sentences such as *The dog swim* using a dependency parse such as (21). Next, please write some pseudo-code sketching how you could do the same thing using a phrase-structure parse (22). Please assume that in both cases, *dog* is part-of-speech-tagged as *NN* (for singular nouns) and *swim* is part-of-speech-tagged as *VB* (the bare form of a verb) when the correct subject-verb agreement would use *swims*, tagged as *VBZ* (3rd-person present singular).

(21)
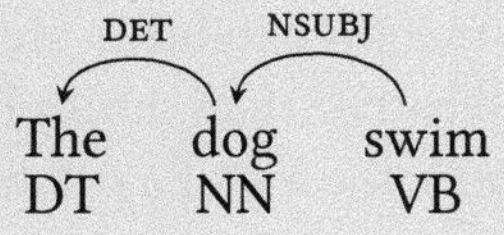

(22)
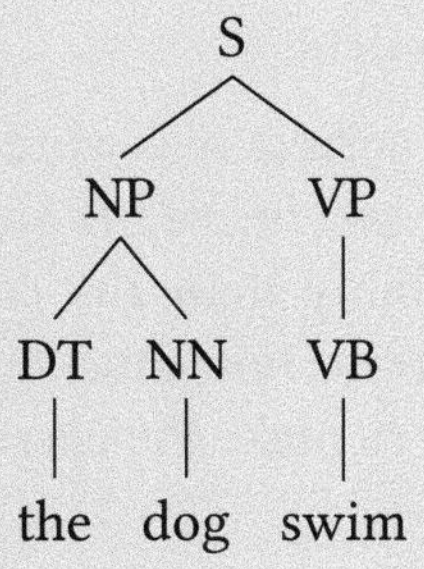

5. Explore the Google N-grams tool.[a] For example, search for *cheese and **, which gives the most common trigrams beginning with *cheese and.* Are you able to correctly guess the most common next word? How does the frequency of this trigram change over time (in data from historical books)?

6. To get a firmer grasp on how *n*-grams work, write a program which takes a large text file as input and stores all its unigrams and bigrams as well as their counts.

   a) Write a program that takes in a starting word w_0 and then generates the next 19 words $w_1 \ldots w_{19}$, in each case choosing the word w_{n+1} with the highest bigram probability given w_n.

   b) How sensible is the text generated by your word-prediction program?

7. In our exploration of *n*-gram models, we discussed how these models rely on probability. To gain a more thorough understanding of *n*-grams, try out the below problems.

   a) Can you estimate the unigram probability for the sentence *You put the {cat/cart} before the horse* using the Maximum Likelihood Estimate equation below?

$$P(w_i|w_{i-1}) = \frac{\text{count}(w_{i-1}, w_i)}{\text{count}(w_{i-1})}$$

   b) In actual implementation, the probabilities are usually log-transformed and then added rather than multiplied; these operations are equivalent because the log of a product is the sum of the logs. Replicate the above calculation using logs to see how these operations are equivalent.

   c) We discussed using *n*-grams to correct real-word errors, as in the example where *You put the cart before the horse* would result in a higher *n*-gram probability than *You put the cat before the horse.* As a thought exercise, how much higher do you think the probability should be to make the correction?

8. Select your favorite spell checker and evaluate its effectiveness by designing a *test suite* of sentences with spelling errors. A test suite is simply a list of cases which are used to test the effectiveness of a system. Include 10-20 errors and include some non-errors, too.
    a) What is the purpose of each error? In other words, what is each type of error attempting to test about the spell checker's capabilities?
    b) Of the number of words flagged by the checker as errors, how many (what percentage) are actually errors? (This measures *error detection precision.*)
    c) Of the errors you introduced, how many (what percentage) does the spell checker flag? (This measures *error detection recall*; precision and recall are discussed more in Chapter 6.1.3.)
    d) Of the suggestions the checker makes, how often (what percentage of the time) is the first correction the correct, intended word? (This measures *error correction precision.*)
9. Select your favorite spell checker and type in a number of misspellings.
    a) In terms of edit distance, how far off can your misspellings be and still have the correct spelling suggested?
    b) Select your second favorite spell checker and perform a comparison of their performances. For each of your misspellings, which spell checker has a better ranking? Can the misspellings be more or less farther off?
    c) For each system, does it provide helpful feedback? Does it make a correction for you automatically or just suggest it as an option? Compare and contrast the user experience of both systems.
10. Compare and contrast several different writers' aids (grammar and style checkers), including Grammarly, LanguageTool, and Ludwig Guru (search online). Which one would be most useful for a person who is not fully confident in English? Which one would be best for

a person with dyslexia? What about an adolescent learning to write on the computer?

11. Imagine that you're interviewing for a job at Grammarly. They ask you what new feature you'd propose. What is your response?

12. Examine the predictive text suggestions on your mobile device. To what extent are these suggestions customized to your own specific language usage? How can you tell?

13. A user types in *folg* when they meant to type *frog*. Draw the directed graph and describe how minimum edit distance is calculated, using only deletions and insertions.

14. Describe how such a graph could be redrawn to allow for transpositions and substitutions.

15. We discussed edit distance techniques for generating correction candidates (Section 2.3.2) and also discussed using confusion sets (Section 2.4.1). But these aren't the only methods for finding possible corrections. For example, the Soundex algorithm – developed over 100 years ago for census data by Robert C. Russell and Margaret King Odell (Russell 1918) – is another way to generate candidates, based on phonetic properties of words. To take one example, the word *nub* would be assigned the code N2: an N for the first letter, a 0 (zero) (which is later eliminated) for the vowel, and a 2 for a bilabial (*b*, *p*, *f*, *v*). The words *nob*, *nap*, and so on would thus be put into the same bucket.

    a) Read more about Soundex by searching online.

    b) What is the point of Soundex and why is it different from edit distance?

    c) Why would Soundex be useful for analyzing (early twentieth-century) census data in particular?

    d) With computing techniques becoming faster, why not compare a misspelling to every single word in the dictionary?

   e) We would argue that it's better to have a handful of possible corrections than just a single candidate: why is that? And how many candidate corrections do you think is ideal?
   f) Soundex doesn't take into account anything like edit distance, while edit distance is based on orthography and not phonetics: can you think of ways to combine these techniques?

16. Let's further explore the Soundex system for generating candidates for correction.
   a) Develop your own Soundex-like system for grouping similar words into buckets by working out what rules you need to map a word to the appropriate bucket. Can your rules handle transposition errors?
   b) If you're a programmer, implement your Soundex rules. Make sure that each of the following sets of words all get mapped to the same bucket:
      i. Catherine, Kathryn, Katherine
      ii. principal, principle
      iii. eye, I, aye

[a]https://books.google.com/ngrams, accessed 2024-07-01.

Further reading

Peter Norvig's blog post *How to write a spelling corrector* (Norvig 2007) is a classic.

Universal Dependencies, dependency representations for over 100 languages, is presented in Nivre et al. (2016).

For background on the types of spelling errors and their causes, Damerau (1964), Kukich (1992) and Mitton (1996) are classic references; Flor et al. (2015) discusses errors made by English learners. As for grammar correction, classic references include Wilcox-O'Hearn et al. (2008), Hirst & Budanitsky (2005), and Leacock et al. (2010). For rule-based grammar checking, Naber (2003) originally used 56 rules to achieve good performance. This later developed into the open-source software Language Tool.[a]

For more on formal language theory and complexity, see Chapter 16 of Jurafsky & Martin (2009). A comprehensive formal treatment of the topic can be found in Hopcroft et al. (2007). For a deeper understanding of dynamic programming, see Chapter 6 of Kleinberg & Tardos (2006).

To delve further into the privacy measures Google took for SmartReply and SmartCompose, see Carlini et al. (2019) on machine learning and security measures.

Lingard (2023) evaluates the opportunities and limitations of using large language models such as ChatGPT as writers' aids.

[a]https://www.languagetool.org/, accessed 2024-04-17.

3 Computer-assisted language learning

3.1 Introduction

At the intersection of language and educational technology, the field of *computer-assisted language learning (CALL)* develops tools that help you learn a second language. In this chapter, we explore how people learn languages, how digital tools can support them, and what such tools need to know about language.

3.2 Learning language

You already picked up your first language (*L1*) as a baby. Later on, you probably encountered a second language (*L2*) in a classroom or when you visited another country. When we speak here of first and second language, we should not take this literally. If you grew up bilingually, in a context where multiple languages were spoken, you can have more than one L1; and L2 typically is used to refer to all languages that you learned after your L1 was in place, even if this actually was the third or fourth language you learned.

This chapter focuses on computer-assisted tools for learning an L2, but it is informative to first compare and contrast how people learn an L1 versus an L2 in general.

3.2.1 Similarities between L1 and L2 learning

Learning any language involves many different aspects. You have to learn how to articulate the sounds with your mouth (*articulatory phonetics*), or, for signed languages, how to form the signs with your body; how sounds can combine (*phonology*), how to form words (*morphology*) and sentences (*syntax*), and what they mean (*semantics*). You might not be able to state these rules explicitly unless you have training in linguistics, but you know them implicitly as part of your ability to speak a language.

You also have to learn a lot of *vocabulary* – thousands of sound/meaning pairs, memorized so well that it feels subconscious – as well as statistics about what words are likely to appear in sequence in which context. You have to learn social skills such as how to have a conversation, how to model someone else's beliefs and goals, and what you should say in different situations (competence in *turn-taking*, *pragmatics*, and *discourse*). And you have to learn about the culture of the people you talk to in this language – the history, politicians, holidays, music, etiquette, and foods that people take for granted (*cultural competence*). Moreover, to function in a literate society, you have to learn to read and write, and how to write for different purposes, in different genres.

Whether you are learning an L1 or an L2, there are some similarities. Comprehension precedes production: At each stage of learning, you can understand more complicated vocabulary and sentences than you can produce yourself. Simple sentences are learned before complex sentences, and frequent words are (mostly) learned before infrequent ones. People learning their L1 or their L2 also make similar types of "errors", saying things that a full-grown L1 speaker would not say. To use an example from articulatory phonetics, when learning English as an L1 or an L2, people struggle to pronounce the [ð] fricative in the word *the* – sometimes pronouncing it as the stop [d], which shares the same general tongue placement and voicing. Interestingly, most languages do not use the sound [ð] in their system of phonemes – and, indeed, it is often the case that the harder something is to learn, the more rare it is across different languages. As for grammatical errors, both L1 and L2 learners of English may *over-regularize*, for example applying the rule for marking past tense even on irregular verbs (e.g., producing **I goed*).

Turning to vocabulary, both L1 and L2 learners may make errors involving *over-extension* of word meanings, for example using the word *car* to describe trucks or golf carts. They might also struggle with *under-extension*, for example, using *car* for road vehicles while not realizing this word can also apply to the chunks of a train. Of course, under-extension may not give rise to obvious errors the way over-extension can, which points to a deeper methodological question in the study of language learning: even if a language learner appears to understand a word or to use it sensibly, how do you know if they understand it the same way as another speaker?

3.2.2 Unique elements of L1 learning

Even though L1 and L2 learning involve similar steps and error patterns, there are also many differences between acquiring an L1 and learning an L2 in different contexts. For their L1, a child understands and produces speech (or signs) long before they learn to read and write. The child has to pick up a lot of non-linguistic information at the same time: They have to develop concepts of themselves, other people, and of physical and mental events and entities.

As their first steps towards vocalizing and communicating, babies can cry at birth and smile at around six weeks. They explore more complex vocalizations soon after, and by about six months, babies typically begin using sequences of consonants and vowels such as *bababa*, a stage referred to as *babbling*. Next, their first words tend to be names for people and physical objects (*Dada, doggie*), with other words – abstract nouns such as *happiness*, verbs such as *walk*, grammatical markers such as *the* – coming later on. Children quickly start learning words by their first birthday and can form simple two-word utterances by the time they turn two. Children then make use of more and more of the language structure, so that by the age of three they can already voice and understand sentences of surprising complexity. In the following years of childhood, more and more words and complex language structures are acquired, with some structures such as passive sentences being added relatively late, around nine or ten years of age. When learning their L1, the child has no other language experience to *transfer*, neither to help them nor to confuse them.

Children learn their L1 from the *input* provided by their caregivers, which takes the form of *child-directed speech*. Across many different cultures, adults speak differently to children than to other adults: They use simple words, repetitive sentences, and highly variable pitch to capture the child's attention; they narrate daily activities, point at objects to name them, and rephrase the child's utterances in more adult terms.

Children all start learning their L1 in infancy. There are a few extremely tragic cases where children were not exposed to any L1 until later in life and seemed to struggle to learn it. These situations are confounded by other traumatic elements, so it is hard to draw clear conclusions and unethical to run studies, but they are sometimes taken as evidence that L1 learning must occur in a *critical period* of a child's life, before adolescence, to be fully successful.

A child learning their L1 gets quite a few hours of input and practice each day, and – even if they can't reflect on it – has an extremely strong incentive to succeed, because they need to learn language to participate in society. As a result, excluding cases of extremely serious disabilities, all children achieve "success" at learning their L1 (at least in speaking and listening, if not reading and writing), in the sense that they all become L1 speakers of it and can use it to say anything they want.

Although children have a strong incentive to learn their L1 and get lots of practice, they do not receive much formal instruction. All children achieve essentially the same level of "success" in learning their L1 even when the input that they receive varies widely across families and cultures. In this sense (as proposed by Lenneberg 1967), learning an L1 is like learning to walk rather than learning to play the piano or dance ballet: All children learn language just like all children (with working legs) learn to walk, regardless of how explicitly their family tries to teach them, whereas children only learn to play the piano through dedicated instruction. Like walking, therefore, L1 success is sometimes analyzed as an *innate* human capacity rather than one that *emerges* from one's experience. That is why it is sometimes referred to as *L1 acquisition* rather than *L1 learning*, based on the idea that acquisition is innate and automatic while learning requires explicit instruction. But the idea of innateness is controversial, since it ties into a huge debate (pervasive across social sciences) about *nature versus nurture*. If children are said to be born with certain knowledge that helps them acquire language, it is very difficult and contentious to spell out exactly what that knowledge would be, and how it complements the input that they experience. Whether it is true or not, the idea of innateness is inspired by the striking fact that children all learn their L1 successfully and essentially automatically.

3.2.3 Unique elements of L2 learning

Whereas everyone learns their L1 as a child from their caregivers, people learn L2s in different contexts, for example in a classroom or upon immigrating to a new place. When learning an L2, a person may learn to read and write at the same time as they learn to speak and understand. The L2 learner already knows quite a lot of general information (how the world works, how conversations work, the idea that words refer to things) which is not obvious to a child learning an L1. And while everyone learns their L1 as a child, people encounter L2s at all ages after they've learned their L1.

Like L1 learners, L2 learners go through different stages and levels of sophistication, but they can learn verbs, abstract nouns, and grammar from day one, depending on the input that they receive. While a child's first words might be *Dada* and *doggie*, an L2 learner might start with *hello* and *my name is*.

Whereas children learn their L1 from the spoken input of caregivers, people learn their L2 from all sorts of input – conversations, media, signage, and educational resources. The L2 learner may also transfer some knowledge of their L1 to their L2, which can both help and hurt them. L1-to-L2 transfer is useful in the case of *cognates*, which are words that are similar in both languages (due to a common historical origin or borrowing from the same source); for example, 'coffee' is *kāfēi* in Mandarin and *café* in French. L1-to-L2 transfer can also help with some grammatical rules: If your L1 is English and you are learning French or Chinese, you can carry over the Subject-Verb-Object rule of word order. But L1-to-L2 transfer can also cause errors if you transfer something that is not shared between the L1 and the L2, for example incorrectly transferring the Subject-Verb-Object word order to Irish, where the verb comes first.

A person learning an L2 in a classroom might get about five hours of practice per week, and their incentive is most likely determined by their commitment to the class. A person learning an L2 as an immigrant will get more or less practice depending on their job and social network, and their incentive may derive from how much they need the L2 to function. Because the incentives and the amount of practice vary so widely across L2 learners, it is perhaps no surprise that people achieve wildly different levels of "success". Some people teach classes and write award-winning books in their L2, while other people can barely check in to a hotel after years of schooling.

3.2.4 Defining and achieving L2 success

What does it mean to succeed at learning an L2? Ultimately, success is defined by your own priorities. It could mean that you can function professionally and socially in the L2, that you can produce the L2 without "errors", or that you can translate accurately in both directions. (Which of these would you consider most important?) Most people would not say that L2 success requires the learner's speech to be completely indistinguishable from that of an L1 speaker; even highly proficient learners may still have an accent influenced by their L1.

Various language-teaching organizations have put forward scales of L2 success. The American Council on the Teaching of Foreign Languages (ACTFL) ranks speakers as Novice, Intermediate, Advanced, Superior, or Distinguished (with some levels further subdivided into Low, Mid, and High). According to the 2024 ACTFL guidelines (with example interview videos at each level on their website), speakers at the Novice level "can express basic personal information and satisfy a limited number of personal needs using formulaic and rote utterances, lists, and phrases" (American Council on the Teaching of Foreign Language 2024). Their "limited language control may require a sympathetic audience to be understood". At the other end of the spectrum, speakers at the Distinguished level "can negotiate, use persuasive and hypothetical discourse, comment thoughtfully on a range of general topics, and tailor language to a variety of audiences".

Similarly, the Common European Framework of Reference for Languages (CEFR; Council of Europe 2001) uses three levels (A=Basic, B=Independent, C=Proficient), each subdivided into a higher and lower portion (A1, A2, B1, B2, and so on). The lowest level A1 "can introduce him/herself and others and can ask and answer questions about personal details such as where he/ she lives, people he/she knows and things he/she has"[1]. The highest level C2 "can understand with ease virtually everything heard or read [and] can summarise information from different spoken and written sources, reconstructing arguments and accounts in a coherent presentation".

These functional *can-do statements* are designed to capture the vastly different levels language learners have in making use of a foreign language. Among Anglophone American high schoolers, even students who get the top score (5/5) on an Advanced Placement foreign language exam only get to about an Advanced Low ACTFL level ("able to participate in most informal and some formal conversations on topics related to school, home, and leisure activities [...] can also speak about some topics related to employment, current events, and matters of public and community interest"). Among other Anglophones who don't get a 5 on the exam, the level of proficiency is lower. After high school, a student's L2 level may decline sharply when they stop taking classes; only a few dedicated Anglophone L2 learners will go on to the Superior/Distinguished levels by seeking opportunities to practice the language beyond the classroom. But across the globe, it is very common for L2 learners to achieve "Distinguished" proficiency in a language that they learn through immigration or in school to use as a *lingua franca* (a language of commerce or higher learning).

Given that different people achieve such different levels of success, what factors contribute to it? The researcher Stephen Krashen (Krashen 1982) argues that an L2 learner achieves greater success when they receive more "comprehensible input" at the *i*+1 level, meaning input that goes just a bit beyond (+1) their current level of understanding (*i*). This idea echoes the *zone of proximal development*, an idea from the Soviet psychologist Lev Vygotsky (1978) used in education theory. The idea is that the *i*+1-level input provides a built-in review of what the learner already knows while also exposing them to new words and structures that they can figure out from what they already understand. This theory is meant to explain, for example, why a person who already took two years of Spanish might improve greatly after a summer in Mexico, because they receive a lot of language exposure at their intermediate *i+1* level from commercial transactions, friendships, and so on. In contrast, a person with no Spanish experience might not learn much, because most of this Spanish exposure lies far beyond their basic *i*+1 level and thus goes over their head. Krashen's theory therefore predicts that a classroom environment is especially important for the early stages of learning, because it is one of the only places where a student will encounter input tailored

[1]https://www.coe.int/en/web/common-european-framework-reference-languages/table-1-cefr-3.3-common-reference-levels-global-scale, accessed 2024-07-01.

to their low *i*+1 level. While Krashen's theory has been critiqued for focusing on comprehension rather than production, it is certainly the case that students learn best (in all areas) when they encounter surmountable challenges in their zone of proximal development.

Another important factor is the learner's attitude. L2 learners achieve greater success when they are more motivated; when they have a positive attitude towards the L2 and its culture; and when they are willing to make mistakes, using a *growth mindset* (the belief that one's mind is a muscle strengthened by exercise, an idea proposed by the psychologist Carol Dweck and colleagues; Blackwell et al. 2007). Of course, these attitudes are all intertwined, not just with each other but with the amount of input at the *i*+1 level that the learner will seek out, as well as their incentive for learning the L2.

The effect of the learner's age remains controversial. On the one hand, one might think that it would help to learn an L2 as a child during the pre-adolescent "critical period", the way people learn their L1, and the fact that adult L2 learners usually retain a foreign accent suggests that there may be a critical period for articulatory phonetics. On the other hand, mature learners have better study skills, and people can learn grammar and vocabulary at all ages. In any case, the effect of age is hard to isolate from all the other factors that correlate with it, such as the amount of practice the learner receives and their incentive for learning the language.

Researchers in L2 teaching evaluate various teaching techniques by exploring the extent to which they advance L2 success by providing more *i*+1 input and/or by sparking the learner's motivation. Such techniques include tools in computer-assisted language learning.

3.3 Why does CALL need to be "intelligent"?

In a broad sense, CALL encompasses all the ways in which computers pervade education and society. As a general medium for information, computers are used by L2 learners to find and present information – as a multimedia textbook, a dictionary, a tool for writing and consuming media content, and a way to connect socially with speakers of the L2.

More narrowly, CALL describes tools used to present sequenced exercises for language learners, along with feedback on the learner's responses. The task of CALL is to design these exercises and feedback in the most efficient and helpful ways.

At a simple rote level, one could design a CALL system consisting of dozens of handwritten *fill-in-the-blank* questions (also known as *cloze* or *gap-fill* exercises), which ask whether the learner understands a sentence well enough to complete it sensibly. If these questions have multiple-choice answers as in (1), it might take work for the CALL designer to write the *distractors* (the wrong answers) as well as the correct answer (*on*), but at least it is easy for the CALL system to grade the correct response from among these constrained options. Alternatively, if the question offers a free-text box (2), then the CALL designer has even more work to do: Instead of writing three distractors, they have to write a longer list of potential right answers – *on, near, by* and so on – to assess the learner's answer.

(1) The detective lives ___________ Baker Street.

   a. at
   b. on
   c. in
   d. with

(2) The detective lives ___________ Baker Street.

In a *frame-based CALL system*, a student's answers are matched against a set of correct and incorrect answers which are explicitly specified by an instructor in a so-called frame such as (1)–(2). In addition to judging the answer as correct or incorrect, the frame can be designed to include more elaborate pre-written feedback for each of the choices, also known as *canned text*. If the learner incorrectly chooses *in* for (1), one could specify the feedback *Incorrect: While the preposition "in" can be used for cities, it cannot be used for streets as in this example.* The system might also need a *fallback case* if it receives totally unexpected input: If the user types *Help!* in (2), the system could reply: *You entered Help!, which is not a preposition of English. Please enter a preposition of English.*

The person designing these exercises will use their own metalinguistic insights to organize the exercises at escalating levels of difficulty, for example placing simple sentences (*The girl eats the apple*) before complex ones (*The boss didn't realize that the employees were unhappy*) and choosing plausible distractors of the same lexical category as the target answer (as in (1), where all the choices are prepositions). They will also use their knowledge of language to write metalinguistic feedback as canned text. But so far, the simple frame-based CALL system that we have described does not itself distill any insights about language. As a result, such a system is very brittle and laborious. Without any deeper representation of language, it just matches the characters entered by the learner against strings stored as potential answers for the exercise. If the response matches an expected answer, whether right or wrong, the system can trot out the prescribed action.

But if the response is unexpected, the system will have to fall back on default responses, which are unlikely to be very helpful. This simple system also does not represent any information about the learner; it would just give all learners the same exercises in the same order, which different people might find too easy or too difficult.

In contrast to this hypothetical rote system, modern CALL tools aim to be "intelligent" in that they represent information about both the structure of the specific language and the progress of the specific learner. That way, they can be designed efficiently to offer more exercises, handle more diverse input, and give more helpful feedback that extends even to new or unexpected input. Such systems also aim to customize the exercises and feedback for each specific learner, so that it's neither too difficult nor too easy. Next, we will explore how intelligent CALL systems represent both language and learners.

3.4 Modeling language

Now that we have seen why it is useful to capture generalizations about language instead of hand-specifying answers for individual questions, we explore what is involved in realizing this idea. The application of CALL takes us on a tour of many different tasks involved in text processing more generally.

3.4.1 Parts of speech

For starters, the words of the target L2 can be automatically labeled for their part of speech (noun, verb, adjective, preposition, and so on), and such labels can be used to give metalinguistic feedback that can be generalized across many exercises.

In English, the transitive verb *buy* requires a direct object (*I bought groceries*) while the intransitive verb *shop* cannot take a direct object (*I shopped*). If the intelligent CALL system represents the allowable *argument structures* (subject/object configurations) for each verb, then if the learner chooses *shop* in question (3a), the system could reply: *"Shop" is an intransitive verb, so it cannot combine with an object. Please try again.*

(3) Maya went to the store to __________ flowers for Juan.

a. Fill in the blank: *Buy, shop.*

b. Who is going shopping?: *Maya, Juan.*

In English, some verbs work like *shop* in that they cannot have a direct object; others work like *buy* in that they need one; while others work like *eat* in that they can go either way: *I ate; I ate lunch.* Researchers in lexical semantics have worked to explain which verbs go which way. For example, why can we say *I ate* but not **I devoured*? Whatever the reason, a CALL system could record the *argument structure* (syntactic potential) of each verb and use it to explain errors identified from a dependency parse. Such feedback could be recycled any time a learner tries to give a direct object to any verb that doesn't take one (*swim, run, laugh, sleep*, and so on). If a learner's free-text answer is part-of-speech tagged, this information could also be used to provide general, widely re-usable feedback such as *The sentence you entered is missing a verb.*

In contrast, other feedback would depend on information explicitly specified in a given exercise; (3b) hinges on the content of this specific example, where it is stated that Maya rather than Juan went to the store, rather than any general fact about English grammar. If the designer of an intelligent CALL system is writing questions along with feedback for incorrect answers, it is probably more strategic for them to design the questions so that the metalinguistic feedback is general, and thus can be used for other questions in the same system.

Expanding on ideas introduced in Chapter 2, parts of speech are labels for classes of words which behave alike. There are three dimensions of what it means to behave alike. The first is *distribution*, by which we refer to the linear order with respect to the other tokens, i.e., the slot a word appears in. For example, in the sequence *Maya gave him* ____ *ball*, the slot between *him* and *ball* is the distributional slot of a determiner such as *the* or *a*.

When designing automatic part-of-speech taggers, distributional information is typically collected in the form of statistics about which POS sequences are how likely to occur, parallel to the *n*-gram statistics we saw in the discussion of language models in Chapter 2. To be able to observe possible part-of-speech sequences, one naturally needs a corpus that is already annotated with part-of-speech tags. Such corpora with so-called *gold-standard annotation* are generally created using significant manual effort to annotate or correct the annotation. Such corpora are used to train a computer to automatically label parts of speech in new data. To obtain gold-standard corpora of the size needed to train current POS taggers (and supervised machine learning approaches in general – see Chapter 5) thus requires large, long-term projects. Correspondingly, they so far only exist for less than ten percent of the roughly six thousand human languages; it is much more difficult to find good training data for lower-resourced languages such as Navajo, making it harder to develop CALL tools for such languages.

The second type of evidence is the one you use every time you look up a word in a dictionary. For some words, *lexical stem lookup* provides an unambiguous part-of-speech category. For example, *claustrophobic* is only listed as an adjective. Yet, many words are ambiguous and belong to more than one part-of-speech class. For example, the word *can* occurs as an auxiliary in *The baby can walk*, as a full verb in *I can tuna for a living*, and as a noun in *Pass me that can of beer, please!* Even a word like *some*, where at first glance one might think that it unambiguously is a determiner (e.g., *some cars*), it can also be used as an adverb (e.g., *the cut bled some, you need to work on it some*) or a pronoun (e.g., *Some like it hot*).

Another problem of lexical lookup arises from the fact that there are words we do not find in the lexicon. Even if we tried very hard and got the world's best dictionary resource, there still would be words not listed there since new words are added to the language all the time; words such as *googling* or *facebooked* clearly did not occur in texts from the eighties (as mentioned in Section 2.3.1). But even with such limitations, lexical information is useful for an automatic part-of-speech tagger.

The third type of evidence for part-of-speech classification presents itself when we take a closer look at the form of words, their morphology. Certain markings, such as *suffixes* added to the end of stems, encode information that is only appropriate for particular parts of speech. For example, *-ed* is a suffix indicating a past-tense marking of words as, e.g., in *walked* or *displayed*. Thus, if we find a word such as *brachiated* in a sentence, even if we know nothing about this word or its context, we can infer based on the *-ed* suffix, that it is likely to be a past-tense verb.

Apart from such *inflectional suffixes* indicating information such as the tense or agreement markers (e.g., the *-s* found on verbs in the third person singular), other potential sources of information include *derivational affixes*, such as, for example, *-er* which is used to turn verbs into nouns (e.g., *walk – walker, catch – catcher, love – lover*). In automatic POS-taggers, such *suffix analysis* is often included in a *fallback step*. Whenever a word has not been seen before in the training data, so that no lexical or distributional information is available for that word, handwritten suffix analysis rules are used to determine the most likely part of speech. If none of the suffix rules apply, then as a last resort, part-of-speech taggers generally assign the most common option, usually a noun tag.

While we already discussed parts of speech in Chapter 2, these concepts encounter new challenges in the context of CALL. Here, learners do not write like the text (newspapers, books, and so on) used to train part-of-speech taggers; instead, they make "errors" as they use a so-called *interlanguage* derived from their nascent L2 along with the influence of their L1. Consider the following two sentences written by Spanish learners of English (from the NOCE corpus, Díaz Negrillo et al. 2010):

(4) a. ... to be *choiced* for a job ...
 b. RED helped him *during* he was in the prison.

In (4a), the word *choiced* distributionally appears in a verbal slot, and morphologically it carries verbal inflection (*-ed*), whereas lexically the stem *choice* is a noun (or adjective). And in (4b), the meaning of the sentence is fine, but *during* distributionally is a preposition, which cannot appear in the distributional slot of a conjunction. To apply part-of-speech tags to L2 writing, our system must account for potentially mismatching evidence.

3.4.2 Tokenization

Of course, to represent a word's part of speech, the first step is to identify the words – a task known as *tokenization* or *word segmentation*. Here, we describe the complexity of this task and its relevance for CALL.

In English, tokenization may seem easy: We might think that a word is just any string between spaces. But some writing systems do not use spaces. As we saw in Chapter 1, Chinese uses characters (called *zi*, each one representing a syllable along with some logographic information about its meaning) which are written without spaces. Thus, the same string of characters will have different meanings depending on how one groups the characters together into words.

Take for example the two-character string 要害 *yào hài*. If we segment it as two words of one character each (*yào hài*), it means 'will hurt'; if we segment it as a single word consisting of two characters (*yàohài*), it means 'vitals'. Which tokenization is chosen depends on the context – much like the context determines whether an occurrence of the English word *bank* refers to a financial institution or a river bank. Such a segmentation problem, where two or more characters may be combined to form one word or not, is referred to as a *covering ambiguity*.

A second kind of tokenization problem is *overlapping ambiguity*, which refers to cases where a given character may either combine with the previous or with the next word. Lu (2007: 72) illustrates this ambiguity with the string 布什在谈话中指出 *Bùshí zài jiǎnghuà zhōng zhǐchū / zhōngzhǐ chū*.

Depending on whether the second-to-last character 指 *zhǐ* is part of the last word or the word before that – *zhōngzhǐ chū* 'middle-finger out' or *zhōng zhǐchū* 'in the middle (of the talk) point out' – the meaning of the sentence changes significantly, as illustrated by (5) (even though in Chinese only the second segmentation option is a grammatical sentence).

(5) A potential overlapping ambiguity in Chinese.

a. * 布什 在 谈话 中指 出
Bush at talk middle-finger out

b. 布什 在 谈话 中 指出
Bush at talk middle point-out
'Bush pointed out in his talk'

You may consider yourself lucky that the writing system used for English makes it so much easier to determine what the words are by simply starting a new word whenever there is a space. But even for English, life is not that simple. After all, *inasmuch as* and *insofar as* would then be split into two tokens and *in spite of* into three – but to process them further or even just to look them up in a dictionary, clearly identifying them as a single token would be most useful! For an even more common case, let's start with a simple sentence such as (6a), where starting a new token for every word is straightforward.

(6) a. I got my car fixed yesterday.
b. I got my flu shot yesterday.
c. I got my jacket yesterday.

If we hear (6a), we assume the speaker hired someone to fix their car. But if we see (6b) on the lapel sticker of someone in the street, we do not think that they hired someone to shoot their flu! We immediately interpret *flu shot* as a single token, parallel to occurrence of *jacket* in (6c), even though it contains a space. Naturally, this is very much language-dependent, as a *compound noun* such as *flu shot* is written without spaces as *Grippeimpfung* in German. So spaces should presumably be allowed in some English tokens, which immediately raises the question of when exactly a tokenizer should identify words that include spaces and when not.

The opposite problem is posed by strings such as *I'm*, *cannot*, or *gonna*. None of these tokens contains a space, but we know that *I'm* is nothing but a short form, a so-called *contraction*, of *I am*. Similarly, *gonna* occurs in the same places and is interpreted in the same way as *going to*. And a word such as *dunno* (which might well appear in an English text to be processed even if some prescriptive writing instructors would say not to use it) seems to be equivalent to *do not know*. So, does it make sense to treat them as one token in the contracted form and as two or three tokens in the form including a space? Clearly, treating the two variants in such radically different ways would complicate all later processing, which would not be necessary if we, e.g., tokenized *I'm* as two tokens *I* and *'m*. This naturally raises the general question of when exactly a tokenizer should split up English strings that do not contain spaces into multiple tokens.

In sum, processing text requires us to separate it into word tokens. This task may seem straightforward in writing systems that use spaces; but even in English, there are challenging cases such as *flu shot* (which contains a space but functions grammatically as a single noun) and *dunno* (which contains no spaces but functions grammatically as three words, *do not know*). The challenges are even greater in writing systems that do not use spaces, such as Chinese, and in lower-resourced languages for which we can find less data to train an automatic tokenizer.

Returning to CALL as an application, an intelligent CALL system needs to tokenize the L2 text in order to provide metalinguistic feedback on it. Depending on the language and the writing system, that task might be more or less difficult. Tokenization might also be harder in the free-text writings of L2 learners, who are still figuring out how to use the target language's conventions for spelling and spacing.

3.4.3 Grammar and syntax

Once we have tokenized and part-of-speech-tagged the words of a language, it can also be helpful for an intelligent CALL system to create a syntactic representation for each sentence, using a dependency parser as introduced in Chapter 2. Then, just as with the writers' aids discussed in Chapter 2, this representation could be used to provide metalinguistic feedback leveraging general insights about the grammar of the language.

A syntactic representation could be used in a CALL system to offer helpful explanations of spelling errors (Chapter 2), for example correcting **la casa rojo* in Spanish to *la casa roja* 'the red house,' making sure that the adjective *roja* 'red' *agrees* in gender and number with the noun *casa* 'house' that it modifies. *Rojo* is a real Spanish word, so the only way to identify it as an error is to recognize that its gendered suffix *-o* mismatches with the gender of the noun *casa* that it modifies. A dependency parse of this sentence could be used by the CALL system to flag the error and explain why *roja* is the correct form.

The gendered adjective endings in Spanish represent one type of *inflectional morphology* – the way that a word changes form depending on its grammatical context. Inflectional morphology also extends to verbs, which inflect in English for tense as well as agreement with their subjects, as in *Holly swims*; a CALL system could use a dependency representation to explain why **Holly swim* uses the prescriptively incorrect inflection. Similarly, a dependency representation could be used to explain why **Me love pizza* is incorrect: English pronouns take different forms (called *case*) depending on their grammatical role in the sentence; *I* is the *nominative* form used for grammatical subjects, while *me* is the *accusative* form used for objects. The structure and functions of such word forms are investigated in *morphology*, a subfield of linguistics.

Beyond the form of individual words, a dependency representation could also be used in a CALL system to flag and explain errors in how the words are organized into a sentence. As mentioned above, if the learner writes **Maya shopped flowers for Juan*, an intelligent CALL system could explain that *shop* does not combine with a direct object such as *flowers*; if the learner writes **Maya bought*, it could explain that *buy* does need a direct object.

Of course, to give such metalinguistic feedback, the CALL system would have to map a past-tense inflected form such as *shopped* to the *lemma* (also known as the *citation form*) *shop*, the form given in a dictionary or a list of intransitive English verbs.

The grammar of a language is in some ways rigid (*Me love pizza* is rigidly ungrammatical in standard English), but also flexible in that it allows many options. For example, the fill-in-the-blank exercise (7) should allow the particle *down* to appear right after the verb as well as at the end of the sentence. An intelligent CALL system should allow such options not just for this exercise and this phrasal verb (*turn down*), but for all exercises using any phrasal verb (*set up, put in*, and so on).

(7) Maya, the radio is much too loud. Please ________________!

  a. turn down the radio.
  b. turn the radio down.
  c. *down turn the radio.

While phrasal verbs allow multiple grammatical options, the syntax of English is generally quite rigid: Sentences follow a strict Subject-Verb-Object word order (*Maya bought flowers*, not **Bought flowers Maya*). But other languages such as Russian and Latin allow *free word order*, using case-marking suffixes on nouns rather than word order to indicate their grammatical role. In (8), we know that *puella* 'girl' is the grammatical subject of the sentence, no matter where it occurs, because it uses the nominative case marking. *Canem* 'dog' is the object because it uses the accusative case. A CALL system for Latin should allow all these options in the learner's writing.

(8) a. Canem puella amat
dog-ACC girl-NOM love-3SG
'The girl loves the dog.'

b. Puella amat canem
girl-NOM love-3SG dog-ACC
'The girl loves the dog.'

c. Puella canem amat
girl-NOM dog-ACC love-3SG
'The girl loves the dog.'

The sentences in (8) are *glossed*, meaning that they are written in three lines such that the top line reflects the target Latin orthography; the second line offers a literal word-by-word translation space-aligned with the top line, including an analysis of case marking and inflection (*nominative, accusative, third singular*); and the third line provides an ordinary English translation. This format is used whenever linguists represent data from other languages.

All three options in (8) are grammatical, but one might be preferred over another depending on the larger context. Generally (Clark & Clark 1977), people prefer to follow the *given-before-new* principle, placing information earlier in the sentence when it is already related to the prior conversation, and later in the sentence when it introduces new individuals or ideas. For a human or a computer to implement that constraint, one would need a rich representation of the discourse above and beyond the syntax of a particular sentence.

Returning to the value of syntactic representations for CALL, such tools could also help the CALL designer to design further exercises efficiently. For example, if the CALL system already uses the sentence *The girl eats the apple* in its question bank, it could automatically suggest further sentences by swapping out the noun phrase *the girl* for any other noun phrase denoting an animate (living) entity – *my dog, your brother*, and so on; or replacing *the apple* with other vocabulary words from a unit on food (*pizza, breakfast,* and so on). Multiple-choice distractors could be automatically suggested from among other words in the same part-of-speech category as the target answer; perhaps the system could even use a language model (a fancier version of the *n*-gram probability model sketched in Chapter 2) to ensure that the distractors would result in a markedly less probable sentence than the correct answer, thus automatically recognizing *pizza* as a better completion than *phone* for *Your brother eats the....* Leveraging such insights, an instructional designer could automatically generate a suite of questions and example sentences rather than writing each one by hand.

Expanding on the utility of language models, a generative language model could also be prompted to offer metalinguistic feedback automatically, or to write further questions and example sentences. For well-resourced languages such as English, such tools hold great promise for CALL because they are able to distill information about grammar from large-scale data even without making direct reference to explicit representations such as dependency parses. For lower-resourced languages without generative language models, CALL designers may need to use more traditional handwritten exercises and feedback. But in either case, distilling insights about the language helps an intelligent CALL system to give more general, flexible feedback across more diverse, unexpected input from the learner.

3.4.4 Representations of meaning

So far, we have explored how a CALL system can provide metalinguistic feedback about grammar. As another way that CALL tools can represent language, we introduce some simple tools aiming to capture not just structure, but meaning.

We saw above that a CALL system should allow multiple different word orders (*turn down the radio, turn the radio down*) as correct answers, because English word order is flexible for phrasal verbs. Similarly, a CALL system should allow many different answers to a question such as (9), because all of these different formats (9a)–(9f) refer to the same date. (Americans prefer to write months before days, as in 11/6, whereas Europeans prefer the opposite order 6/11).

(9) Today is November 5. So tomorrow is ________________.

  a. November 6.

  b. the sixth.

  c. November the sixth.

  d. 6/11.

  e. 11.6.

  f. 6 November.

Of course, if (9) were framed as a multiple-choice question, then the predetermined answer choices could be hand-labeled as correct or incorrect; but if it is a free-text fill-in-the-blank question, then the CALL system would have to handle all the different possible formats for dates. In language processing, dates are one example of *named entities*; they refer to specific real-world entities such as dates on a digital calendar. Other examples of named entities include names of people, companies, countries, addresses, and so-called *deictic* words such as *today, tomorrow*, and so on, whose reference depends on the context in which they are used. The task of *named entity recognition* aims to identify such phrases in text, for example to help extract structured information (discussed further in Chapter 6) from text, or to use digital assistants for scheduling purposes (Chapter 8). For CALL, named entity recognition would allow many different formats for a date to be understood as *synonyms*.

At this point, one might object that the different ways of formatting dates is not a particularly interesting aspect of language learning. But the goal of representing meaning is much more broadly useful. For example, consider fill-in-the-blank exercise (10), modeled on a German exercise in the E-Tutor system of Heift (2010).

(10) John works in New York City, but his family lives in Boston. On the weekend, he drives home. Fortunately, John has a new ____________.

The possible correct answers go far beyond different formatting for dates. For one thing, the possible correct answers include synonyms such as *car* and *automobile*. And as we discuss in the context of machine translation in Chapter 7, there are various other *lexical semantic relations* between words. In our context, another relevant lexical semantic relation is hyponymy; this is the option of picking a more specific term, a so-called *hyponym*, such as *pick-up*, *SUV*, or *Volkswagen* in place of the more general term *car*, the *hypernym*. Finally, though the people designing exercises generally try to avoid this, there may also be multiple different meanings that make sense for a slot in a given exercise; in (10) the context would also be compatible with inserting *helicopter* or even *audiobook* (to listen to in the car!) – and for each one of them, various semantically related words could be used.

Rather than simply trying to brainstorm all possible answers for (10), an intelligent CALL system could count any vehicle-related words as correct, either by using a hand-built resource such as WordNet (Fellbaum 1998), which represents hypernym and hyponym relations, for example specicifying that trucks and cars are vehicles; or a representation learned bottom-up from text in ways to be explored further in Chapter 4.

3.4.5 Types of CALL exercises

Having explored some text-processing tools used in CALL, we turn to the types of questions typically used in CALL systems. For each one, it is useful to consider: How would a CALL system automatically recognize the learner's answer as correct? What sorts of metalinguistic feedback could be given for incorrect answers? How could text-processing tools or generative language models be used to create further questions? Finally, how difficult is each type of question – for a CALL designer to write, for a CALL system to grade; or for a learner to complete correctly? Turning from the language to the learner, which questions will be most useful, fun, or frustrating for them?

- Matching a (spoken or written) word in the L2 to an image or a translation in the learner's L1, or vice versa.
- Fill-in-the-blank exercises where a learner has to complete a sentence with an appropriate missing word or provide the correct form/conjugation of a given lemma. These could take the form of multiple-choice or free-text-box exercises.
- Given a set of options, choosing the one that constitutes the most sensible reply to a previous conversational turn.
- Testing the comprehension of spoken or written material through true-false or multiple-choice questions.
- Dictation exercises, where the learner is asked to transcribe a sound clip – using a word bank or a free-text box.
- Pronunciation exercises, where the learner is asked to say something into a microphone, graded for accuracy via a speech-to-text system.
- Translation exercises, where the learner is asked to translate from the L2 to the L1 or vice versa – with a word bank or a free-text box.
- Correct-the-error exercises, where a learner is asked to select an erroneous word in a sentence that they are given.
- Open-ended free-text or free-speech questions, like *Hello, welcome to our café, what would you like to order?* or *What was your favorite part of this story?* – to be graded for length, grammatical correctness, and whether the learner's answer makes sense in context.

3.5 Modeling the learner

CALL systems aim to model not just language, but also learners and learning. Here, we explore how CALL tools can represent exercises and learners to offer the most motivating and helpful curriculum for each learner.

3.5.1 Sequencing of material

At the most rudimentary level, a *linear CALL system* would give all students the same exercises in the same order. Even here, we face design choices: If a student gets a question wrong, should they still just move to the next question, or should they get another chance to get it right before proceeding? Either way, a linear CALL system runs the risk that advanced students may get bored, and struggling students may feel overwhelmed.

In contrast, in *branching CALL systems*, the sequencing of the exercises depends on what the student does. If a student answers one question right, the system offers a slightly harder question; if the student gets it wrong, the system reverts to a simpler question and might provide additional feedback or practice related to the student's mistake. Like giving each student their own one-on-one tutor, a CALL system could offer instruction precisely tailored to learners' individual needs.

This type of *dynamic sequencing* is also used in *computer adaptive testing*, such as the GRE (Graduate Record Examination, offered by the Educational Testing Service). Here too, the sequence of questions depends on the test-taker's previous answers. But this time, the goal is different: If the system can make sure that strong students do not spend time on questions that are much too easy for them, and weak students do not spend time on questions that are much too hard, then it will be able to assess each student's ability accurately using fewer questions and less time. This adaptive strategy is only feasible if the test is delivered electronically.

To sequence questions dynamically by difficulty, a CALL system would have to associate each question with a difficulty level – perhaps the level that it targets according to a metric of L2 success such as the ACTFL or CEFR scales mentioned above; a unit in the course curriculum (Level 3 Spanish); or – leveraging the CALL system's own usage data rather than a human-assigned label – the percentage of learners (overall or at a given level) who get it right.

3.5.2 Characteristics of individual learners

In addition to modeling the target language and the difficulty of each exercise, it is also useful for a CALL system to represent information about the individual learner. This endeavor is known as *learner modeling*.

For one thing, a given learner is associated with more or less stable properties such as their L1 and their motivation for learning the L2 (school, travel, immigration, and so on). Other relatively stable properties might include their technical setup (whether they use a desktop or a mobile phone; whether they avoid talking out loud because they are doing their CALL exercises in a silent library); their preferred learning style (whether they want to focus on speaking or writing, whether they enjoy longer stories or quick flashcards). Some of these learner traits might be inferred from how the learner interacts with the CALL system, but others could be gathered through a survey when they sign up.

Then a CALL system could customize itself to these traits, for example focusing on travel vocabulary for future travelers, or avoiding speech-to-text exercises for people who don't have a sound setup. More importantly, the L1 of the learner strongly influences the mistakes that they might make when learning an L2. For example, languages such as Chinese and Czech do not use determiners (also called articles; *the, a*), so English learners from those L1 backgrounds may need more feedback and exercises related to determiners. For an English learner from a determiner-using L1 such as German, though, the absence of a determiner might be a minor typo, so perhaps it should not be emphasized as much by the CALL system. In other words, tutoring systems are often designed to focus on the learner's most important errors rather than overwhelming them with dozens of corrections at once (*prioritization of feedback*).

Of course, L1 transfer can also be helpful, as when learners can take advantage of cognates shared across languages (English *coffee*, French *café*). Thus, modeling each learner's L1 can be used to tailor the CALL curriculum to their strengths as well as their areas for improvement.

Beyond the learner's stable personal traits, a CALL system might also analyze their dynamic interactions with the CALL system – the questions they get right and wrong; the number of days and minutes per day they have spent learning; and the words and structures they seem to know versus the ones they struggle with. To draw inferences about a learner's knowledge of structure, a CALL system has to abstract away from specific questions/answers to distill information about both the learner and the structure of the language.

For example, one might want to assess whether a learner knows present-tense subject-verb agreement (in English, *I swim* versus *Maya swims*). If so, the CALL sequence could move on to more advanced topics; if not, it could offer further instruction. If they have clearly mastered subject-verb agreement but seem to get it wrong unexpectedly, perhaps the CALL system should take this error as a typo rather than a true confusion (echoing the discussion of spelling errors in Chapter 2).

But it is not trivial to infer from a learner's behavior whether they have learned a target pattern such as subject-verb agreement. To draw such an inference, each question would have to be labeled (perhaps automatically) for the patterns that it tests. For intelligent tutoring as well as *language testing*, instructional designers have to be wary of *construct under-representation* – drawing incorrect inferences when the learner has not answered enough questions to assess what they truly know, for example inferring that they know subject-verb agreement when they just made a lucky guess in a multiple-choice question. This problem can only be avoided by giving the learner more questions pinpointing the target knowledge.

To ensure valid inferences, it also is not enough to consider the learner's answers themselves. Instead, we also need to include information on the exercise the learner was completing and the strategies learners may employ to succeed in such a task. For example, a particular learner answer may simply have been copied from the context of the question, which is known as *lifting*. A student who responds with (11b) might not be truly confident in creating relative clauses (*places I've visited*) if they are just lifting that phrase from the question.

(11) a. What is your favorite place you've visited?
 b. I like many places I've visited.

To be able to interpret learner answers in terms of what they allow us to infer about the learner's abilities, an intelligent tutoring system thus also needs to take into account *learner strategies* such as lifting or avoiding structures that the learner is unsure about.

Such inferences constitute one example of learner modeling. More broadly, by amassing data on what the learner gets right and wrong, a tutoring system can draw inferences about the words or grammatical structures they can understand; the words or grammatical structures they can produce spontaneously; the probability of them answering a given question correctly; the maximum length or difficulty level of a sentence that they can write/translate correctly; the probability of them quitting or persevering; the amount of time they will choose to spend learning; and so on. The tutoring system could customize the curriculum to these traits, for example offering exercises to each learner that they have about an 80 percent chance of getting right. Of course, harder exercises can be both instructive and discouraging, and easy exercises can be both boring and affirming, so CALL researchers analyze learner data to strike the right balance.

In sum, in modeling both language and learners, intelligent CALL systems also have to model both general and specific facts. CALL systems model general facts about the structure of the language as well as how those facts are manifested in specific exercises to be sequenced, tagged with the words/structures that they test, and associated with metalinguistic feedback. They also represent general facts about how L2 learning progresses along with specific inferences about the progress, preferences, strengths, and weaknesses of individual learners drawn from the history of their interaction with the CALL system. The key to success lies in synthesizing all this information to create the most effective and enjoyable system.

3.6 Example: FeedBook

To illustrate how CALL systems actually work, we explore the example of FeedBook, an *intelligent language tutoring system (ILTS)* developed at the University of Tübingen (Rudzewitz et al. 2017, Meurers et al. 2019), based on an official textbook for seventh-grade English in Germany. It is called FeedBook because it augments the textbook with intelligent, individualized metalinguistic feedback.

The exercises are inspired by *task-based language learning* – the idea that students should learn to use the L2 to accomplish authentic tasks in context, such as booking travel or stating one's opinion about a news article, rather than simply drilling words and rules in the abstract. But the exercises also target specific grammatical forms of the L2. Therefore, FeedBook is built to provide feedback on both form and meaning.

Looking first at feedback on form, in Figure 3.1, the learner sees information about two options for a flight to Greece. Which flight would they choose, and why? In a free-text box (parallel to a written response on a paper homework assignment), the learner has written (12a). Here, a pop-up box responds with (12b).

(12) a. *The tickets at Air-Con are expensiver than at Midair.
b. When an adjective has three or more syllables, we form the *comparative* with "more" and the *superlative* with "most."

The student has an opportunity to rate this feedback as *hilfreich* 'helpful' or not; then they have a chance to revise their answer. Here, the feedback does not just say that something is wrong, nor does it provide the full solution (which might be optimal for a grammar checker for native speakers, as discussed in Chapter 2). Instead, FeedBook gives a hint by explaining the general pattern that the learner is missing, which the learner can then apply to the specific word *expensive*, so that the learner has to consider the pattern and apply it themselves.

As for feedback on meaning, in Figure 3.2, the learner sees a multi-paragraph autobiographical narrative about a kayaker, and is asked an open-ended comprehension question (13). The learner has written (13a); FeedBook has replied with (13b).

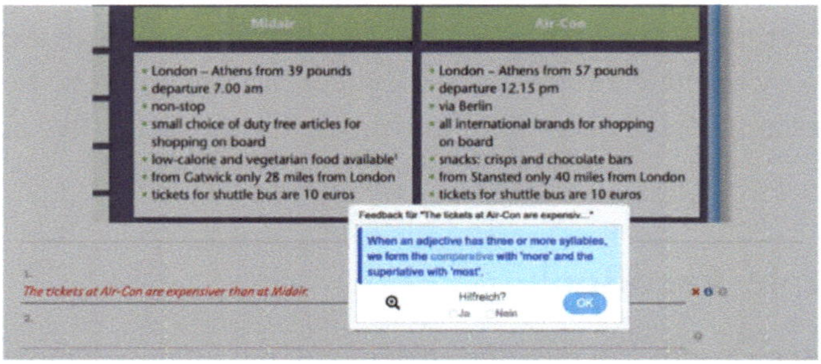

Figure 3.1: FeedBook: "Focus on form" feedback.

(13) How did James feel when he first came to St David's?

  a. James was a student.

  b. There seems to be important information missing in your answer. Please have a look at the highlighted passage in the text.

The beginning of the narrative is highlighted in green, including the sentence *I wasn't very confident when I first arrived.* Again, FeedBook does not just say that the answer is wrong, nor does it give the correct answer; instead, it gives a hint by narrowing down the long text to the portion containing the answer. The student still has to figure out for themselves that *when I first arrived* aligns with *when he first came to St David's*, and that *I wasn't very confident* answers the question *How did James feel?* The exercise becomes more manageable, but the learner still has to use their brain.

FeedBook aims to supplement rather than replace an in-person class with a live teacher. Whereas teachers historically had to correct students' work by hand and then return it to them days later, FeedBook provides immediate grading and feedback at scale, so that the teacher can focus on preparing the in-person class sessions. FeedBook also functions as a *learning management system* such as Canvas or Blackboard (used in schools as a platform for course material, homework, grading, discussions, and so on), in that it sends reminders about missing homework to students and compiles statistics for the teacher on what students know and don't know. Whereas the earliest such *intelligent tutoring systems* were built for math instruction, where students' answers are more constrained (i.e., to numerals), FeedBook leverages language technology to handle the unconstrained domain of language.

Figure 3.2: FeedBook: "Focus on meaning" feedback.

3.7 Example: Duolingo

As an example of a very popular language tutoring system, we turn to Duolingo, which offers online language lessons.

3.7.1 Duolingo as a business

Duolingo was founded in 2009 and released to the public in 2012 by Luis von Ahn, a Guatemalan-American computer science professor, and Severin Hacker, a Swiss graduate student, both at Carnegie Mellon University. Luis von Ahn had previously founded ReCAPTCHA, a web verification tool for distinguishing humans from bots by asking them to transcribe a few characters of text from an image, which – in an attempt to kill two birds with one stone – was used to digitize portions of old books and newspapers that were too illegible to be processed automatically. Duolingo was originally designed around the same two-birds-one-stone idea, aiming to teach people L2s while also gathering translations for the web, but the translation portion was eventually abandoned to focus on L2 teaching alone.

As of 2023, Duolingo claims to have been downloaded over 500 million times, with 4.2 million paid premium users and 54 million monthly active users. Duolingo offers 43 different languages in over 100 different L1/L2 pairings. Courses for lower-resourced languages are shorter and not as fully developed, but Duolingo advertises as a point of pride that they teach minority languages such as Navajo, Hawaiian, and Irish. They even offer *constructed languages*, those consciously crafted as part of a fictional world-building exercise: Klingon (created for the television show *Star Trek*), High Valyrian (from *Game of Thrones*), and Esperanto (invented with the goal of fostering global understanding and peace). Globally, the most popular language on Duolingo is English, followed by Spanish and French; in the United States, it is Spanish followed by French or, in some states with high immigration rates, English.

Duolingo uses a *freemium* business model. The free basic version cuts the learner off after they make five mistakes in a session and makes them watch ads, while the paid premium version allows unlimited mistakes, no ads, and offline lessons. Duolingo can be considered a form of *edutainment* because it tries to *gamify* language learning. Learners can follow friends, congratulate one another on their progress, jockey for positions on a leaderboard, maintain their "streak" (number of consecutive learning days), earn points to spend in an online store (to buy an additional lesson on flirting, or to miss a day without losing their streak), and win badges to be shared on social media. Duolingo is also notorious for sending persistent push notifications and emails (sent at the time of day when each learner usually logs on!) to keep learners coming back every day. In other words, Duolingo is optimized not just for language learning, but equally for *user retention.*

3.7.2 How does Duolingo teach language?

Duolingo is organized into five-minute lessons of about 17 questions each. Each lesson automatically self-extends to give the learner another chance at what they got wrong, and the lesson is only complete when all questions have been answered correctly. Lessons are organized into topics (content topics such as greetings, travel, clothing, and current events; and grammar topics such as pronouns, future, past, and so on) and difficulty levels. In the L1-English-to-L2-Spanish course, for example, the first level of a lesson on clothing might focus on matching words to pictures of clothing, and translating sentences from Spanish to English with a word bank, while further levels of that lesson would emphasize translating the same sentences from English to Spanish, first with a word bank and later into a free text box. In addition to matching and translation, the questions also involve multiple choice, comprehension questions for text and audio, fill-in-the-blank, dictation, and repeating sentences out loud. Even for exercises involving text rather than speech, the app plays text in the L2 out loud (leveraging text-to-speech tools) so the learner sees and hears it at the same time. To move to the next level of a lesson, the last portion of each level requires the student to review their previous mistakes until they can answer them all correctly. If a learner makes no mistakes on an early level of a lesson, the premium version of Duolingo allows them to skip to the next level.

The lessons are organized into units, each one ending with a test that the learner must pass to unlock the next unit. For learners who already have some experience with the L2, Duolingo offers a placement test so that they can skip the units that they already know. Early units focus on greetings, basic vocabulary, and simple grammar such as the present tense, while more advanced units use sentences about politics, religion, and complex grammar such as the subjunctive and *not only ...but also*. Some lessons start with an optional section of grammar tips, where a grammatical rule is stated explicitly and illustrated with examples. Leveraging language-aware generalizations, the same grammar tips recur as feedback if a learner makes a mistake on that grammatical pattern.

Within a lesson, the variety of question types (matching, fill-in-the-blank, multiple choice, dictation, saying a sentence out loud, different types of translation exercises) are chosen to keep learners engaged, and sequenced so that the hardest exercises come at the end of the lesson when a learner is least likely to give up. If a learner makes multiple mistakes in a row, Duolingo fosters a growth mindset with encouraging messages about how making mistakes is part of learning. The lessons feature cute animations of Duolingo's characters, each associated with their own voice, and correct answers are rewarded with a pleasant chiming sound plus an animation of one of the characters dancing or celebrating. In all these ways, Duolingo is designed around the idea that a learner's attitude matters.

In contrast to the long text-comprehension questions used by FeedBook, Duolingo's exercises are much shorter and simpler, constrained by the size of a phone screen. Because FeedBook is assigned by schools while Duolingo requires self-motivation, perhaps Duolingo's users are more likely to give up and thus prefer their work to be bite-sized.

Duolingo is also structured around the fact that comprehension precedes production. Exercises are sequenced to move from comprehending L2 sentences (translating L2-to-L1, with a word bank) to eventually producing the same sentence freely (L1-to-L2 in a free text box). In the same way, Duolingo's "story" exercises first ask learners to answer comprehension questions from material

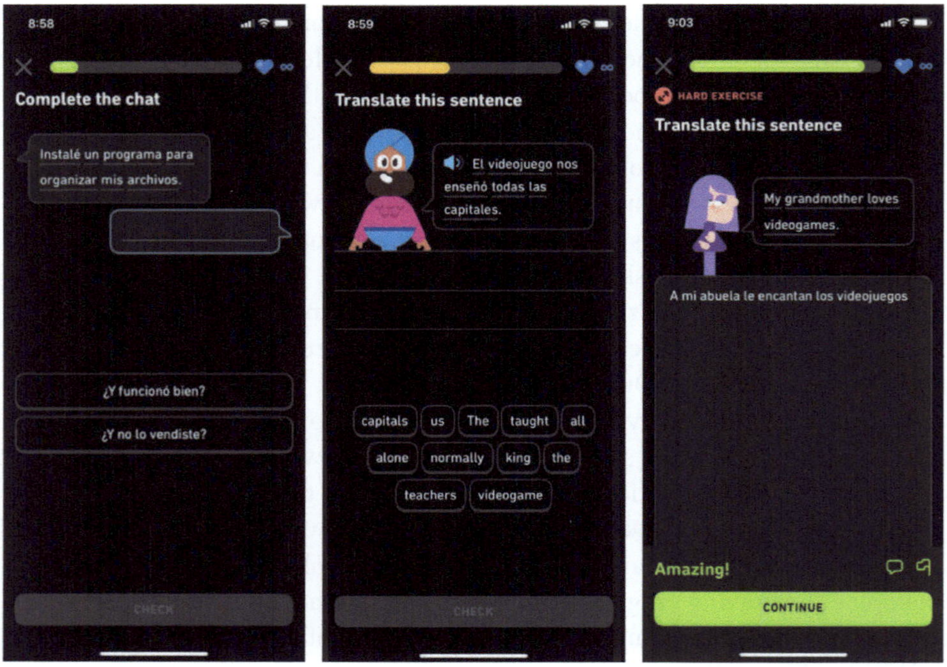

Figure 3.3: Screenshots from the Duolingo Spanish course: A multiple-choice comprehension question; a translation question from the L2 to the L1, with a word bank; and a translation question from the L2 to the L1, with a free text box. As indicated by the progress bar, the questions get harder as the lesson progresses.

that is both spoken and written, and then at the next level uses only spoken material with no transcript, leveraging the fact that it is easier to understand paired speech and text compared to speech alone.

The sentences used in Duolingo exercises (such as *My grandmother loves videogames*) are constructed carefully – originally by hand, now presumably also leveraging language-generation tools (which may result in a trade-off between quality and quantity, especially for less-resourced languages). Each sentence is designed to be cheerful, inoffensive, consistent with the brand's identity, and sensible out of context. (When Duolingo's creators abandoned the idea of translating text from the web, perhaps part of the reason was that the out-of-the-blue sentences from web text – *wow this is quite the analysis*; *That's one way to reach midlife crisis!* – don't fit into clear lesson topics, might create a scattered brand identity, and often do not make sense out of context.) Using a blend of human labor and automatic tools, each sentence is also associated with a topic (for example, travel), various grammatical structures (past tense), a set of vocabulary words, and a difficulty level. With different types of questions and directions of translation, the same sentence can also be recycled at escalating levels of difficulty.

The recycling of material uses *spaced repetition* – the idea, rooted in the work of the 19th-century German psychologist Hermann Ebbinghaus and central to Duolingo, that learners forget information over time but are more likely to remember it if they keep reviewing it. By reusing different versions of the same questions and recycling old vocabulary in new lessons, Duolingo is designed to mix review with new material.

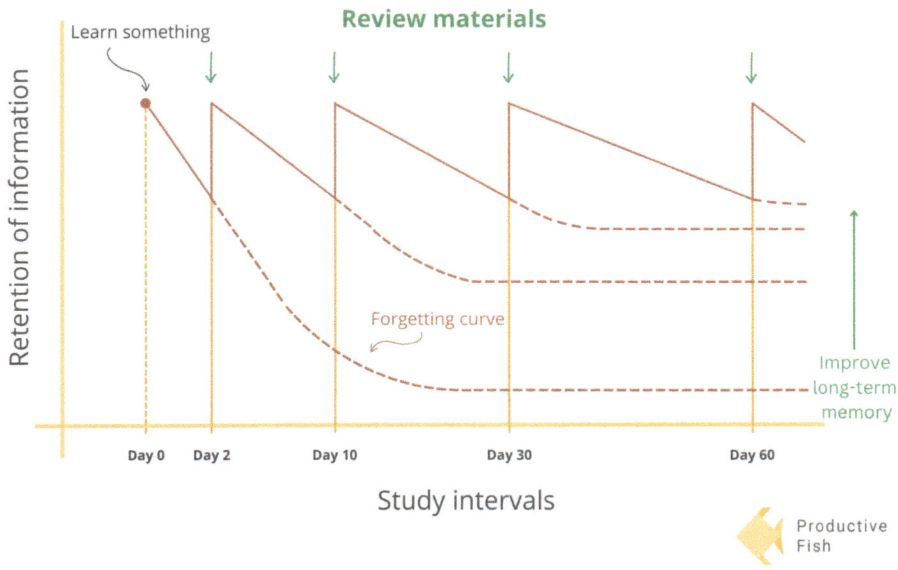

Figure 3.4: Spaced repetition: Memory declines over time, but a learner is more likely to remember something if they review it across multiple days (https://commons.wikimedia.org/wiki/File:Forgetting_curve_and_work_of_Ebbinghaus.png, uploaded and dedicated to the universal public domain by user Productive.Fish).

3.7.3 Evaluating Duolingo

Like any popular product, Duolingo has critics as well as devoted fans. Critics of Duolingo would note that it can only get learners to an Advanced Beginner or Low Intermediate ACTFL level ("able to handle successfully a limited number of uncomplicated communicative tasks by creating with the language in straightforward social situations"). Courses on less-resourced languages are shorter and must promise an even lower proficiency level. Learners may find it frustrating for a translation to be marked as wrong when the gist is correct or when only one word is mis-typed. Moreover, translating pre-written sentences on Duolingo is arguably not as useful as learning to make oneself understood in a spontaneous conversation. According to *Forbes*[2], the Chief Revenue Officer of Duolingo could not respond to the spoken question *¿Hablas español?* 'Do you speak Spanish?' after six months of Duolingo Spanish.

Finally, like many other online courses, Duolingo struggles with attrition. Exact numbers are elusive and depend on the length of the course, but course completion rates fall far below one percent. (After 1277 consecutive days of studying Spanish, one of the authors of this textbook is working through "Intermediate Spanish, part 1," so completing a course requires an extremely sustained commitment).

On the other hand, fans of Duolingo would argue that Duolingo is better than nothing and teaches as much as can be expected in one or two five-minute lessons per day. The app is user-friendly, fun, and always improving as researchers analyze data from millions of users. Spontaneous production is the hardest, but Duolingo certainly improves passive spoken and written comprehension and can serve as a valuable complement or stepping stone to other exposure through schooling, work, travel, socializing, or consuming media (including Duolingo's own associated podcast) in the L2. Through Duolingo for Schools, teachers can assign Duolingo exercises as homework and track their students' progress. But should language teachers be grateful for Duolingo as a supplementary tool, or should they feel threatened that it may replace them? This question – about whether humans and language technologies compete or complement one another – will keep coming back.

3.8 Evaluation

Stepping back to CALL systems as a whole, how good are they? They are surely better than nothing, but how do they compare to a traditional classroom? Taking inspiration from the still timely discussion of Meskill (2002), such systems have advantages and disadvantages compared to in-person instruction. Looking first at the advantages, CALL tools can provide self-paced, dynamically sequenced,

[2]"Game of tongues: How Duolingo built a $700 million business with its addictive language-learning app," 16 July 2019, by Susan Adams, *Forbes*.

automatically graded exercises to any number of students across regions and time zones at scale, making L2 learning accessible. CALL tools can judge predetermined right-or-wrong answers and provide immediate feedback in the form of pre-written hints or corrections matched to the student's input. Such tools can record detailed information about the learner's progress, providing data to both learners and researchers of L2 learning and allowing for learner modeling and dynamic sequencing. CALL tools can provide authentic multimedia language usage and can motivate the student's persistence through encouraging canned text, push notifications, integration with "likes" on social media, and other digital rewards.

As for the disadvantages, CALL tools still struggle to evaluate unexpected input. In an in-person introductory language class, students learn to introduce themselves and to describe their own biography and opinions, but such exercises are harder to automate in a CALL system because there is no single correct answer. CALL tools therefore do not offer as many opportunities for a learner to practice producing language extemporaneously. Finally, the social element of language learning is missing: The learner cannot engage in the process – arguably the end goal of L2 learning – of trying to make themselves understood in a real-life conversation.

To give learners greater opportunities for extemporaneous production, some language instructors have leveraged the dialog capabilities (discussed in Chapter 8) of generative language models so that students can practice open-ended conversation in the target language, via speech or writing. The dialog system could in principle be prompted to adjust its output to the student's L2 level. Dialog systems allow the student to practice producing language at any time and frequency, without the logistical challenges or potential social anxiety of a human interlocutor. But dialog systems do not currently grade the student's output for correctness, so they cannot model the learner's strengths and weaknesses as more structured CALL systems can. It remains an open question how dialog systems will be integrated with other CALL tools.

The more people who use a CALL system, the more its designers can use large-scale usage data to improve. User-experience researchers use *A/B testing*, an experiment where learners are assigned randomly to one of two conditions (A or B) which are compared with respect to some outcome variable (for example, probability of passing a certain test, number of minutes spent learning, probability of continuing or giving up, and so on) that the researcher wants to maximize. One condition serves as the control group, where the system is kept as-is, while the other condition pilots a new feature. If the people who encounter the new feature have a better outcome, the feature might be deemed successful and implemented for all learners. A/B testing is a type of *between-subjects experiment*, meaning that the experiment compares the outcome across different groups of people, each assigned to a different condition. Between-subjects experiments contrast with *within-subjects experiments*, where the same person encounters multiple different conditions at different times. A/B testing is used widely beyond CALL, in any context where a company wants to use evidence to decide whether a new feature would improve users' experience, but in a CALL context it could be used to choose the exact exercises and feedback that are most instructive or motivating.

In a similar spirit, education researchers might conduct a *randomized controlled field trial*. Here, students – or entire classrooms – are randomly assigned to one teaching method or another. For example, perhaps one classroom uses CALL tools as additional homework, while the other classroom does not; or perhaps some students are given a simpler CALL system, while others get a fancier version. Then researchers might test whether the two groups differ meaningfully in their performance on a year-end exam. The students or classrooms must be assigned randomly to each condition, to control for confounding variables such as the students' starting level, socioeconomic status, and so on; that way, any difference that is found can be attributed to the intervention (the instruction method) rather than underlying differences between the learners. (A careful researcher will also gather data on such variables to make sure that they are controlled across the randomized groups.) The trial will also be more robust if it includes many students or many classrooms, so that the results are not skewed by, for example, one classroom having a particularly good teacher.

Such trials take inspiration from medicine, where it is common to assign patients randomly to take a drug or a placebo to then test whether the drug-taking patients heal faster or live longer than the placebo group (in a randomized controlled clinical trial). The phrase *field trial* indicates that the trial takes place in a real-world setting such as a classroom, rather than a clinical medical setting such as a hospital. A/B testing is a type of randomized (field) trial because users are randomly assigned to one condition or the other, and then compared with respect to some outcome. The phrase *A/B testing* tends to be used more often in a corporate context, while *randomized trials* are discussed by academics, but they are essentially the same idea – using data to quantify the effectiveness of different teaching strategies.

Across both in-person learning and CALL tools, one of the biggest challenges in L2 instruction is motivating the learners to continue learning. Therefore, designers of CALL tools focus on creating a friendly *user experience*. Error-correction messages are written to be encouraging as well as metalinguistically illuminating; push notifications are piloted via A/B testing to find the one most likely to get the learner to open a CALL app; learners are modeled and exercises are sequenced to optimize perseverance. Example sentences are designed to be socially inclusive and appropriate for children, and might describe interesting characters, stories, or cultural knowledge to keep learners engaged.

In sum, designing a good CALL system requires insight from many different areas, including the study of how people learn and what motivates them (drawing on education, psychology, and behavioral economics) as well as human-computer interaction, applied linguistics, and language technology.

3.9 Consequences

By exploring all the things you learn when you learn a new language, we hope to illuminate the richness of language both in its own right and as a domain to be tackled computationally. We might suggest reading this chapter in tandem with Chapter 7 on machine translation to compare what it means, for a human versus a computer, to be multilingual. As machine translation improves, do you think humans have less incentive to learn a new language?

Computer-assisted language learning also evokes larger debates in education technology more generally. On the one hand, web platforms have made education more accessible than ever. Whatever you want to learn, you can most likely find a helpful video tutorial about it. There are platforms that teach programming languages and music using the same principles that underlie CALL, offering progressively difficult bite-sized exercises in the learner's zone of proximal development to be checked for objective correctness. These tools are cheap and can be accessed by millions of people around the world.

On the other hand, online learners often give up, and the people who learn online most successfully are often those who were already highly motivated and self-sufficient at the outset. It remains difficult to retain learners who have less commitment or confidence. Moreover, to the extent that education provides socialization as well as information transmission, that element is diluted online.

Education technology took on new significance when some schools were closed during the coronavirus pandemic. Some students adapted to online learning, but others suffered tragically. What tools could have helped those students, and what tools can help them improve now? As education evolves, to what extent should education technology be seen as a complement or a competitor to in-person schooling? Moreover, as artificial tools get better at integrating language with the larger visual and social context, will robots ever take over the role of in-person language teachers?

Each form of education has distinct pros and cons. Whereas a single teacher may struggle to teach multiple levels at once, education technology can offer self-paced exercises customized to the zone of proximal development of each learner. And while a generalist teacher may not know every topic deeply, high-budget educational technology tools can leverage the knowledge of specialized content experts as well as the insights from large-scale A/B testing. In contrast, online learning can be notoriously isolating and depressing, while an in-person classroom can offer a socio-intellectual community where students can feel welcome, motivated, connected, and understood through person-to-person conversations. It remains an open question how the pros and cons of education technology should be balanced with those of in-person schooling.

Checklist

- Compare and contrast L1 and L2 learning.
- Discuss metrics for measuring L2 success, and whether such metrics are applicable to L1 learning.
- Identify the factors that contribute to success in L2 learning.
- Explain why learning is advanced by input pitched to one's zone of proximal development.
- Explain the idea of spaced repetition and how it is used in Duolingo.
- Give examples of the types of questions used by language tutoring systems.
- Give examples of ways that a tutoring system can use learner modeling to teach more effectively.
- Compare and contrast the capabilities of intelligent CALL systems versus dialog systems for L2 learning.
- Discuss the pros and cons of Duolingo and explain whether you see it as a supplement or a threat to L2 learning in a classroom.

- Discuss the affordances and limitations of practicing an L2 by conversing with a dialog system.
- Give examples of A/B testing and why it might be useful in education as well as business.

Exercises

1. Search online to find videos from ACTFL at each proficiency level. Can a partner correctly guess a speaker's ACTFL level from a video that you play them?
2. Explore www.wordbank.stanford.edu[a] for data and visualizations of the words that children learn at various ages around the world. Can you find an example of a word that is learned much earlier in one language/culture than another? (Can you propose an explanation?) What factors are predictive of a child's productive vocabulary size (the number of unique words that they produce) at each age?
3. A friend comes to you with a business idea: They want to make a Duolingo-like app to help babies learn their L1. Do you think there is a market for such an app? How would it compare or contrast to tutoring systems designed for an L2?
4. Read online about some of Duolingo's competitors, Babbel and Rosetta Stone. What are the pros and cons of each compared to Duolingo?
5. Choose a grammatical construction of English that L2 learners might struggle to learn (talk to a linguistics student for ideas!). Write a multiple-choice question with plausible distractor items to test this construction. Ask a friend or classmate to answer the question and offer feedback.

[a] Accessed 2024-04-26.

Futher reading

A general overview of the use of NLP in the context of language learning is provided in Meurers (2020). A detailed discussion of ICALL projects, including a historical overview and a characterization of the techniques used, can be found in Heift & Schulze (2007).

Munday (2016) describes Duolingo and argues that is a useful complement to classroom instruction.

Huang et al. (2022) review the literature about dialog systems for language learning.

On tutoring systems more generally, some classic references include Swartz & Yazdani (1992) and Holland et al. (2013), as well as Heift (2010) and Amaral & Meurers (2011) for language in particular.

4 Text as data

So far, our tour of language technology has incorporated a great deal of linguistic theory and representations. We used the International Phonetic Alphabet when we introduced writing systems in Chapter 1; we invoked theories about syntax when we discussed writers' aids in Chapter 2; and we leveraged research in L1 and L2 learning when we explored CALL in Chapter 3. So you might be getting the impression that language technology always builds on constructs created by linguists. But actually, there is also a lot to be gained from letting the language data itself tell us about language, independent of any particular theory.

And there is a wealth of language data out there to learn from! Every day, humans produce billions of words of electronic text – social media content, emails, journalism, schoolwork, scholarly papers, lawsuits, Wikipedia pages, books, television scripts, product reviews, doctors' notes, and more. Such text contains a wealth of information about society, politics, economics, science, and language itself. *Text as data* describes a cross-disciplinary endeavor to extract this information and distill its insights.

In other words, this chapter pivots from more top-down *knowledge-driven* applications, like writers' aids (Chapter 2) and CALL (Chapter 3), to the use of more bottom-up *data-driven* technology. There is rarely a clean split between using knowledge and using information from data, but focusing on language data as an object of study can help us when we explore applications in later chapters that often use language as a means to an end – and that often seek to extract some kind of meaning automatically from the text. That meaning will be used to conduct searches, classify texts, translate between languages, and build systems that can engage in dialog.

4.1 Introduction

We begin with a tour of examples of questions answered using text in various scholarly and practical fields – digital humanities, corpus linguistics, computational social science, and author profiling (overlapping domains with no strict boundaries). A question might be as simple as "Do people still use the abbreviation *lol* (laughing out loud)?" or much more elaborate, such as "How do journalists for different kinds of publications reveal their ideological orientation through word choice?" Of course, our examples (focused on English-language text) represent only a tiny portion of these massive and growing domains.

For each example in this brief tour, please consider the type of text that is used, which is often referred to as a *corpus* (see Section 2.3.1). How large is the corpus? How large does it need to be for the task at hand? Does the corpus include *annotations* – additional information on top of the text itself, such as part-of-speech tags or grammatical structure? What *metadata* are required to answer the question – data about the data itself, such as dates, locations, authors/speakers and their attributes, or the intended readers of the text? What methodology is used to extract information from the text and what statistics are used to draw inferences from it? In other words, think about how different kinds of textual data present both opportunities and challenges for answering such real-world questions.

4.1.1 Digital humanities

Digital humanities describes the study of humanities – literature, culture, and history – using digital tools. Here are some examples:

- Moretti (2013) observes that any one scholar of literature can only read a very small portion of the books ever published, and an even smaller portion in close detail. As a complement to traditional *close reading*, he proposes *distant reading* – seeking a macro-level view of literature through digitally-generated "graphs, maps, and trees", such as a map of all the places mentioned in various novels; a diagram of which characters in a play talk to each other and how much; a graph of the number of novels published in each genre in each year; or a table of the books purchased by libraries in each year. Note that the last two examples are strictly questions about metadata and not about the text itself. It remains an open debate how such quantitative findings might or might not be useful to scholars of literature.

- Underwood et al. (2018) explore gender in fiction from the 1800s to the 2000s. They use a program that automatically recognizes named entities (characters) in digitized books along with their gender, then they gather all of the nouns (*doctor*), verbs (*smiled*), and adjectives (*young*) predicated of each character, and use that information to try to predict the character's gender. Interestingly, the words *smile* and *laugh* are associated with women, while *grin* and *chuckle* are associated with men! Over time, they find that it becomes harder to predict a character's gender from the words predicated of that character, showing that character descriptions have become less gender-stereotyped over time. They observe that the percentage of women authors declines between the mid-1800s and the mid-1900s – perhaps because fiction became more prestigious and started to attract more men during that period, or because intellectual women began to enjoy career opportunities beyond fiction-writing. They also report that male and female characters are equally represented in works written by women, while male characters predominate in works written by men.

- Klein (2013) explores a digital archive of the papers of the American president Thomas Jefferson (author of the Declaration of Independence, and owner of enslaved people). She finds that the archive provides rich, searchable metadata about the people who exchanged letters with Jefferson, but very little about the enslaved people mentioned therein. Klein uncovers all mentions of the enslaved cook James Hemings in Jefferson's papers (including all irregular renderings of his names, such as *Jim* and *Jimmy*) to recover a picture of his life. She argues that digital archives must confront the question of whose stories are structurally privileged or erased, and work to avoid reproducing historical inequities.

Essentially any computer-aided study of text (literature, newspapers, archives) can be considered part of the digital humanities if the research question is framed as a humanistic one.

4.1.2 Computational social science

Computational social science, as the name implies, is the use of large datasets (often text) to study some area of the social sciences. Some examples:

- Danescu-Niculescu-Mizil et al. (2013) gather a corpus of requests (*Do you have any code that we can look at?*) from Stack Exchange question-answer forums and Wikipedia talk pages. They pay workers on Amazon's Mechanical Turk gig platform to rate the requests for politeness, and then train an automatic system to generalize those ratings to new data. As predicted by linguistic theories of politeness (Brown & Levinson 1987), they find that requests using greetings (*hey*) and apologies (*sorry*) are rated as more polite. They also find that Wikipedia editors become less polite after being elected to positions of power on the site.

- Demszky et al. (2019) study tweets about mass shootings in the United States. They classify tweeters as Republicans or Democrats based on the politicians that they follow on Twitter, finding (among other things) that Republican tweeters prefer the word *crazy* for white mass shooters and the word *terrorist* for mass shooters of color, while Democratic tweeters show the opposite preference. They also find that Democrats tend to tweet about gun laws in response to mass shootings more than Republicans do. The study confirms several intuitive hypotheses about the public's polarized response to mass shootings.

- Jurafsky et al. (2018) use a corpus of restaurant menus (with the type of food and dollar-sign price range taken from Yelp) to explore differences between cheap and expensive menus motivated by theories of social class. They find that cheap menus highlight what they call "traditional" authenticity (*Grandma's recipe* – touting a connection with the past) while expensive restaurants focus on "natural" authenticity (*wild-caught salmon* – emphasizing a connection to the environment). Moreover, cheap menus use more words, more frequent words, and more adjectives emphasizing quality (*juicy burger with real cheese*), while expensive menus use fewer words, less frequent words, and constructions that presume the quality of their food goes without saying (*Oceanaire burger*).

Computational social scientists also might visualize what topics get the most attention from which news outlets; explore how ideas spread through social networks using social media; study which people fit in or stick out in online communities; or quantify anti-social internet behavior such as trolling and fake news.

4.1.3 Author profiling and identification

Author profiling describes the attempt to draw inferences about a person using text that they wrote – their likely gender, age, mental health status, personality traits, political ideology, or native language. Often, one begins with a dataset of documents (for example, tweets) correctly labeled for certain properties of their author and then learns to generalize these labels to new data – a problem known as *text classification* (to be introduced in Chapter 5). In tweets, women are more likely than men to use first- and second-person pronouns (*I, you*; Bamman et al. 2014); older people may use more standardized spelling than younger people; people with depression may use fewer *we*-pronouns than people without depression; and so on. Perhaps a person who leaves out determiners (*the, a*) in their English writing may be a native speaker of a language that lacks determiners.

These findings are intriguing, and systems trained on such data can achieve good results. But author profiling also raises questions about data privacy: Where did these data come from? How do you gather a corpus of tweets labeled for the author's age/gender while respecting their privacy and perhaps getting their consent? Researchers engaged in author profiling should also think critically about the nature of the labels that they assign. What is gender? If a person's gender can be inferred from their tweets, why might that be? If certain people are "outliers" – diverging from the behavior of the majority of those who share a label with them, as when a younger person tweets more like a older person, or a "man" tweets more like a "woman" – these outliers should be considered carefully for what they can tell us about the assumptions underlying these labels, the boundaries between the labels, and the hypothesized causal relation (if any) between a person's label and the text they might author. Moreover, if a person's demographic traits can be predicted from their tweets, how could this information be used? What if a company wants to sell certain products or advertise certain job opportunities to people whose tweets suggest that they possess certain demographic traits? How worried would you be about the potential for intentional or accidental discrimination?

Author profiling is also used in *forensic linguistics* to infer properties of a criminal from a text they authored. The celebrity pilot Charles Lindbergh's baby was kidnapped in the 1930s and murdered by someone who wrote in a ransom note that the baby would be in "gut [good] care" – bolstering suspicion of a German immigrant carpenter, because *gut* means 'good' in German. The Unabomber terrorist, who sent bombs in the mail from 1978–1995, was identified through a manifesto that he sent to a newspaper, which indicated his high level of education and used distinctive phrasings (*cool-headed logicians*) recognized by his relatives.

When the author of a text is unknown, *author identification* is the attempt to infer who wrote it – usually from a closed set of candidates, each of whom already has other writings attributed to them. Most famously, Mosteller & Wallace (1963) analyzed some of the *Federalist Papers*, which might have been written by the American "founding fathers" Alexander Hamilton or James Madison. They found that the papers in question patterned with Madison's writing style rather than Hamilton's: Madison preferred the word *whilst* but Hamilton favored *while*; Madison used the word *for* far more often than Hamilton did. Similar techniques[1] were used to substantiate a tip that *Harry Potter* author J.K. Rowling had written a crime novel under a pen name.

[1] *Scientific American*, 20 August 2013, by Patrick Juola: "How a computer program helped show J.K. Rowling wrote *A Cuckoo's Calling*".

Even when the author of a text is known, the same techniques can be used to quantify elements of their style – taking us back to the digital humanities. What are the most common unigrams, bigrams, and trigrams in an author's work? What verbs, adjectives, or nouns do they use more often than other authors do? How diverse is their vocabulary, i.e., what ratio of word types (unique words) to word tokens (total words including repetitions) do they use? How long are their sentences, on average, and what words do they like to use to start one? These facts – which you can compute yourself, if you have some machine-readable text and a working knowledge of a programming language – can shed light on an author's literary voice, which can also lead to the identification of further texts that they wrote. In 2020[2], the historian Scott Sandage found a previously unknown article written by the 19-century American anti-slavery activist Frederick Douglass by searching historical newspapers for a rare adjective, *couchant*, that the historian knew Douglass uniquely favored.

4.1.4 Corpus linguistics

So far, we have seen examples of how information is distilled from text to illuminate society and culture. *Corpus linguistics*, on the other hand, uses repositories of attested language use in order to study the nature of the language itself.

Often, such studies explore not just the corpus itself but also *annotations* – additional information – added on top. Chapter 2 already introduced the annotated Universal Dependencies project of Nivre et al. (2016), which provides cross-linguistic corpora (from news, books, and so on) in which each word is annotated for its part-of-speech tag and each sentence is annotated for its grammatical dependency structure. Nivre et al. (2016) present detailed *annotation guidelines* – rules and examples – to standardize the annotations gathered from different annotators and across different languages. We also already mentioned the study by Danescu-Niculescu-Mizil et al. (2013) which gathered annotations of the politeness of requests.

Who are these annotators? In the case of Universal Dependencies, the annotators are human experts – people (often, paid graduate students) who speak and read the language that they are annotating, and are trained to implement the detailed annotation guidelines for a sentence's dependency structure. Other studies, such as the one on politeness of requests (Danescu-Niculescu-Mizil et al. 2013), may gather annotations from novices on paid gig platforms such as Mechanical Turk or Prolific, requiring short, simple instructions. The fastest and

[2] *The Guardian*, July 5, 2020: "Discovery of Frederick Douglass letter sheds light on contested Lincoln statue" by Martin Pengelly.

cheapest annotations come from automatic tools, such as part-of-speech taggers and dependency parsers that can be applied to any sentence you want. Leveraging the ability of computers to generalize patterns, such tools are trained to extend human annotations (such as those provided in Universal Dependencies) to new data.

Annotated corpora empower researchers to test predictions of various linguistic theories, and/or build tools to extract meaning from language computationally. Here are some examples of studies using annotated corpora to illuminate linguistic theory:

- Futrell et al. (2015) show that words are generally closer to their syntactic dependents in the Universal Dependencies corpus than in computer-generated sentences with randomly scrambled words. For example, in the real sentence *The manager ran the company*, the verb *ran* is one word away from its subject (*manager*) and two words away from its object (*company*). In the computer-generated scrambled sentence **Ran the the company manager*, the verb *ran* is four words away from its subject (*manager*) and three words away from its object (*company*). Across many languages and many sentences, real sentences show shorter dependencies than scrambled ones. This study demonstrates a robust quantitative pattern in the structure of sentences across many languages.

- Rosenbach (2005) explores the choice between the two English genitive (possessive) constructions, *'s* (*the baby's legs*) and *of* (*the legs of the chair*). In both a fill-in-the-blank experiment and a corpus study of 6000 genitive constructions taken from transcribed speech, she finds that people prefer the *'s* genitive when the possessor is annotated as animate (a sentient being – *the baby's legs*), and the *of* genitive when the possessor is annotated as inanimate (*the legs of the chair*) – even controlling for other factors such as the number of words describing the possessor and whether it has already been mentioned in the prior discourse.

- Levin et al. (2019) consider the relation between the two words in a compound noun, such as *water jug* (used to hold water) and *water spinach* (spinach that grows in wet conditions). They gather over 1500 attested compound nouns from the domains of edible plants and cooking as well as gemstones and jewelry, taken from the websites of online retailers, and then recruit graduate students to annotate the relation between the two words in the compound according to detailed annotation guidelines. In compounds referring to artifacts (things made by humans for a purpose), the relation tends to involve an event in which the artifact is used (a *water jug* is used to hold water), whereas in compounds referring to natural kinds, the relation tends to involve essential properties of the kind such as its appearance, habitat, or place of origin (*water spinach* grows in wet conditions). Humans interact with artifacts and natural kinds in different ways, and these differences are reflected in the interpretation of the compounds used to name them.

- Potts (2010) shows in a corpus of Internet Movie Database reviews that the negation marker *not* is most prevalent in reviews with low star ratings – perhaps surprising for a word with a purely logical meaning. He finds in the Switchboard Dialog Act Corpus (a corpus of conversations with each turn annotated for its discourse function, such as apology, thanking, agreeing) that *not* is over-represented in face-threatening *rejecting* turns (disagreeing with people's opinions, declining offers), perhaps explaining why *not* is associated with negative sentiment.

In the simplest case, a corpus can be used just to show that a certain grammatical construction exists and is attested (not just as a typo), with no specific claims about its frequency, which is especially interesting if other literature has claimed it to be impossible. For example, White (2021: 12) shows that *think* actually can appear with the complementizer *whether* in corpus examples such as (1).

(1) And it does cause you to *think whether* or not it makes sense for us to be there.

But a prototypical quantitative corpus study involves making and testing a prediction about frequency – that one construction should be more frequent than another, or more frequent in one sort of text compared to another, as when Potts (2010) shows that negation appears more frequently in negative movie reviews.

To sketch just a few more examples, corpus linguists also study how language has changed over time: For example, the word *gay* used to appear in contexts similar to *happy*, now it appears in contexts similar to *lesbian* (Hamilton et al. 2016). Corpus linguistics explores differences between writing and speaking and different genres thereof (also known as *stylistics* – the study of genre, register, and grammatical style across contexts). One can also investigate what distinctive patterns are used in the writings of people learning a second language at different levels of proficiency. Furthermore, a corpus can be used to uncover how language usage varies across different people (of different genders, ages, socio-economic status), across locations, or over time, shedding light on *sociolinguistic variation.*

Turning to its real-world applications, corpus linguistics can be applied in the legal field to offer evidence about the meaning of laws. The *United States v. Costello* court case (2012) involved a federal statute which made it a crime to *harbor* undocumented immigrants. A woman picked up her undocumented boyfriend at a bus stop and let him stay with her for several months until he was later arrested on drug charges. Did she *harbor* him? The verb *harbor* is derived from the noun denoting a place to dock boats; which elements of a marine harbor are extended to the metaphorical meaning of the verb derived from it? Does *harbor* mean hosting someone (as she did), or does it require actively shielding them from pursuing authorities (which she did not do)? In his opinion for the Seventh Circuit, Judge Richard Posner did a simple corpus study, finding that most of the Google hits for the string *harbor friends* describe cases of helping Quakers (Friends) hide from persecution, not just providing lodging for friends, so he determined that the woman did not criminally *harbor* her boyfriend. Of course, a corpus study cannot substitute for legal judgment, because one must exercise judgment in designing the study and interpreting the results – an important caveat for any inference drawn from the use of text as data.

4.1.5 And more!

In proportion to the amount of text available, the exploration of text as data is massive and growing. Other areas include *bibliometrics* – the study of what scholarly papers get cited and why, in turn illuminating how ideas spread across disciplines and through time; automatically extracting information from scholarly articles; attempting to predict the stock market based on news articles or tweets taken to reflect economic sentiment; automatically finding incriminating statements in documents turned over as part of a legal proceeding (*legal document review*); flagging abusive language (*content moderation*); updating dictionaries based on current language usage (*computational lexicography*); predicting a patient's prognosis from the text of their medical records (*NLP for healthcare*); and much more.

Under the Hood 7: The Voynich Manuscript

The mysterious, undeciphered Voynich Manuscript illustrates that one can explore quantitative patterns in text even without knowing what language or writing system the text might be written in. This manuscript, housed at Yale University and handwritten on animal skin carbon-dated to the 1400s, remains undeciphered. Because it uses a totally unknown writing system, it is not clear whether the text represents a particular human language (which one?), some sort of code, or perhaps nonsense.

Figure 4.1: A page from the Voynich Manuscript (https://commons.wikimedia.org/wiki/File:Voynich_Manuscript_(32).jpg, uploaded by user JovanCormac; public domain because the creator has been deceased for over a century).

The manuscript features colorful paintings of plants, stars, and nude women in pipes (it looks as odd as it sounds). A page is shown in Figure 4.1. The imagery would suggest that the book might discuss recipes, potions, astrology, and medicine. As shown in Figure 4.2, the text appears to be written from left to right without punctuation. Groups of characters are separated by spaces, just like words in the Latin alphabet, but it is not clear whether these groupings can be considered meaningful words.

Researchers have struggled with the Voynich Manuscript for centuries. Some people have claimed to have deciphered it, but only by telling stories after the fact. If the manuscript has a meaning at all, then it can only be truly deciphered by a specific, reproducible process for mapping the text to a particular human language and back again.

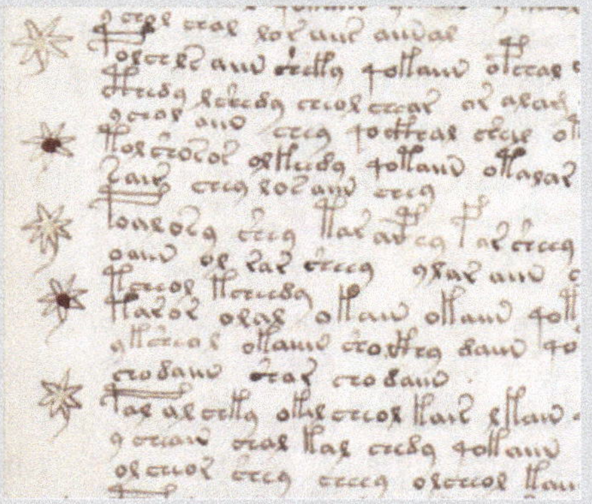

Figure 4.2: A close-up of some writing in the Voynich Manuscript (https://commons.wikimedia.org/wiki/File:Voynich_manuscript_recipe_example_107r_crop.jpg, uploaded by user Tomhannen; public domain because the creator has been deceased for over a century).

One way to make progress on the Voynich Manuscript is to study it as a historical artifact – who owned it, who wrote about it in the past, who would have had access to the materials used to produce it, how it compares to other historical manuscripts, and so on. From such investigations, it appears that the Voynich Manuscript originated in Europe in the 1400s, perhaps in the Alpine region, although it is still an open question who produced it and why. As we will see, the Voynich Manuscript is full of contradictions from every angle: Here, it is puzzling that the manuscript is physically clearly European while the content appears alien.

Another way forward is to start from the illustrations, assuming that some "word" (space-separated string) on the page may refer to the picture

– perhaps one of the first words, one that appears frequently on that page, or one written near the illustration. Just as children learn early words from pointing and naming physical objects, this strategy would leverage the fact that language refers to entities in the world. But without knowing which words to associate with the picture, it is not easy for this strategy to get off the ground. Among the illustrations, more contradictions emerge: The paintings use expensive material but also look slapdash, and the depicted plants are a mix of real and fantastical.

Most relevant for our purposes here, a third strategy is to explore the manuscript as a (digitized) text, asking to what extent it resembles other texts. This strategy builds on the idea that we can identify quantitative patterns within text even without reading it or knowing how it relates to the outside world. That is, techniques employed to treat text as worthy of research in and of itself can be used to help decipher the nature of mysterious texts.

There is no Unicode mapping for the unusual handwritten character system used in the Voynich Manuscript, so in order to digitize the text, each Voynich character has been mapped to an ASCII version – involving difficult judgment calls about whether multiple subtly distinct markings should be grouped as one character or two. The Voynich writing system uses about 22 different characters, suggesting that the writing system is an alphabet or an abjad rather than a syllabary or a logographic system (which require more distinct characters).

From the standpoint of textual statistics, we find even more contradictions. Just like in text of known languages such as English, some characters are much more frequent than others, and some tend to appear in pairs or in certain positions of a word. A few words appear very frequently, and many words appear very infrequently (Zipf's power law; see Section 4.3.1). A relatively infrequent word may appear quite frequently on a given page, which occurs in known-language text with words relevant to a particular topic. But unlike text of known languages, there are also characters with a striking tendency to appear at the beginning or end of a line, which is highly unusual in prose, where line breaks are generally not meaningful. And while text in known languages tends to include highly frequent bigrams (e.g., *of the*, *it is*), the Voynich Manuscript surprisingly lacks such predictable bigrams. Instead, the same word is often repeated twice or three times in a row, or repeated with a difference of only one character, which is highly unusual.

In other words, the Voynich text does not pattern like text in any known language, but has enough in common with known-language texts that it is unlikely to be gibberish. It remains mysterious whether it is a hoax, a cipher, or a meaningful document. If you explore this mystery further (which we recommend!), you will learn more about language, writing, history, and digital humanities.

4.2 Available (English) corpora

Here are some of examples of English-language corpora that you can explore. For each one, it is useful to consider who built it and why, and thus what kinds of questions the corpus can help to answer.

- The million-word Brown Corpus (Francis & Kucera 1979) is the earliest machine-readable corpus of American English. It is a *balanced corpus*, meaning that it aims to represent a balance of different genres – news, editorials, religious texts, fiction, magazines, academic articles, and so on. If you know Python, you can access this corpus through Python's Natural Language Toolkit (Loper & Bird 2002).

- Project Gutenberg digitizes various books old enough to be in the public domain. Some of these texts are available through the Natural Language Toolkit in Python (Loper & Bird 2002).

- The British National Corpus (Bunard & Aston 1998) comprises one hundred million words of British English from the late 20th century. Ninety percent of the data comes from a balance of different written sources and ten percent comes from transcribed speech. The corpus can be browsed through a web interface, or downloaded in XML format.

- CHILDES (MacWhinney 2000) is a suite of corpora offering transcripts, audio, and video of interactions between children and their care-givers in several languages. This corpus, which can be browsed and downloaded from the CHILDES website, is used to study the language exposure and development of children.

- The website English-Corpora.org houses dozens of different English corpora, many of them spearheaded by Mark Davies. Most of these corpora can be browsed through a free web interface, but require a paid license to download all the data. The corpora include:
  - The Corpus of Contemporary American English (Davies 2009) – a billion words from a balance of both written and spoken genres from 1990 until the present. This is a *monitor corpus*, meaning that it is updated each year.
  - The Corpus of Historical American English (Davies 2012) – four hundred million words, balanced across genres, from 1810 to the present. All texts in this corpus are annotated with dates, allowing historical comparisons.
  - The Coronavirus Corpus – comprising media text annotated by date throughout the pandemic – recording the frequency over time of phrases such as *anti-mask*, *reopen*, and *social distancing*.
- Social media data (from Reddit, Yelp, Stack Exchange, and so on) is often already available in a user-friendly format online; search online before you try to scrape such data yourself. But some such repositories were taken down around 2023 after large language models were trained on them without compensation.

You can explore further publicly available corpora at repositories hosted by Lancaster University (https://cqpweb.lancs.ac.uk/) and Georgetown University (https://gucorpling.org/cqp/). This chapter focuses on text, but there are also audio and video corpora, which are important, for example, in the study of pronunciation and the relation of language to embodied action.

As you can guess, choosing a corpus begins with one's research question. What data do you need? Are you doing *exploratory research* – looking for interesting patterns, getting a sense of the data, trying to generate hypotheses? Are you doing *confirmatory research* – testing a falsifiable claim? What corpus data would verify or falsify that claim? What numbers will you collect, what other numbers will you compare them to, and how will you analyze them statistically? To what extent will your findings generalize beyond your particular corpus?

Imagine that you are looking for an extremely low-frequency phenomenon, such as the bigram *think whether* explored by White (2021). In this case, you might simply use a web search as a corpus: One can search for a phrase online to see if people use it, or compare the number of hits for two alternative phrases.

The web is massive, which is good for finding low-frequency phenomena. It may also, however, contain typos, duplicates, and gibberish, which are less likely to be found in a curated corpus.

Your research question might also require certain metadata or annotations: Above, we encountered corpora of sentences annotated for their dependency structure, requests annotated for their politeness, compound words annotated for the relation between the two words, and menus from cheap versus expensive restaurants. Usually, a corpus with such features tends to be smaller than one without.

If you need metadata or annotations that are not already available, you might have to construct the corpus yourself. How will you gather annotations – from whom, at what rate of pay, with what annotation guidelines? If you gather annotations from multiple people, how do you ensure that they are consistent with one another? As the researcher, it might be quickest to annotate data yourself, but will your annotations be biased by your hypothesis? You may have to consider privacy concerns (whose data are you using, and what have these people consented to?) alongside principles of open science, and weigh these factors to decide whether you will make your data available to the community.

You will also have to consider how you need to access the corpus. If you are new to working with data, it may seem like clicking around on a free web-interface tool is sufficient – and for many tasks, it is – but for some questions, you may need to write code to process the data yourself.

In choosing or creating a corpus, it is also important to consider how the corpus may be biased. How were the data selected? Whose data does it represent? Many corpora favor the standardized form of a language over varieties spoken by people who have less power. Our discussion has also been biased towards English; in general, the more geo-politically powerful a language is, the more corpora are available in that language. *Low-resource languages* by definition do not have large corpora, which makes it harder to study them and to build language technologies for their speakers. Like any other data, corpora reproduce the inequalities of the society in which they were created.

4.3 How are words distributed in text?

Investigating text as data often involves counting words in the text. But what are words, how do we count them, and how are words distributed in text?

A "word" may seem obvious to you, but, from a theoretical standpoint, it is not easy to define. Should *mother-in-law* count as one word or three? What about *flu shot*, mentioned in Section 3.4.2? What about languages such as Chinese, where bisyllabic "words" consist of two meaningful morphemes, each of which acts word-like itself (similar to the English compound verb *kickstart*)? But from a practical standpoint, it is simple enough to define a Latin-alphabet "word" as the text between spaces – the process of *word tokenization* mentioned in Chapter 3 (recognizing that tokenization is harder in writing systems that do not use spaces). Then you have to decide if you want to *lemmatize* the words by removing grammatical inflection (e.g., standardizing *running* and *ran* into basic verb form *run*), or whether you might want to *stem* the words by removing morphological markers that determine its part-of-speech (standardizing *democracy* and *democratic* into *democra-*).

Some words are extremely frequent across all English texts (*the, a, for*), while other words (*horse, dance, stoic*) are infrequent or vary widely in frequency depending on the particular text. These two types of words map onto the distinction proposed in linguistics between *function words* and *content words*.

Function words (determiners such as *the, a,* and *every*; prepositions such as *for, to,* and *with*) are difficult to paraphrase, very rarely admit borrowings or neologisms (thus are said to be a *closed class*), and provide information about the grammatical structure of a sentence. Function words comprise the *stop words* that are sometimes filtered out of text on the grounds that they do not make relevant distinctions between documents. On the other hand, function words can be crucial for tasks such as author profiling and author identification.

Content words (nouns, verbs, adjectives, and adverbs – *unicorn, run, pretty, slowly*) are much easier to paraphrase, allow endless borrowings and neologisms such as *quaranteam* (thus, they constitute an *open class*), and supply the content of a sentence. The boundary between function words and content words is fuzzy – with borderline cases such as *have* in *have eaten* or *take* in *take a shower* – but the prototypical examples on each side are clear.

Having introduced these qualitative concepts of what a word is, let us turn to counting words, and to the principles underlying the quantitative distribution of words in text.

4.3.1 Zipf's laws

The American linguist George Kingsley Zipf (1902-1950; Zipf 1932) formulated two fundamental observations about word frequencies: *Zipf's power law* and *Zipf's brevity law* (each of which, confusingly, is sometimes just called "Zipf's law").

Zipf's power law observes that the frequency of a word is inversely proportional to its frequency rank. To step back, one must first understand the *type-token distinction*: A word type is a unique word, no matter how many times it is repeated, while a word token is a specific usage of a word, counting all iterations thereof. For example, *a rose is a rose is a rose* (a poem fragment by the American modernist poet Gertrude Stein) contains three word types (*a, rose, is*) and eight word tokens. The type-token distinction allows us to explore how various word types differ in their token frequency.

Instantiating Zipf's power law, the first-ranked English word by frequency in the Brown Corpus is *the*, and this word type accounts for about six percent of all word tokens. *The* is about twice as frequent as the second-ranked word, *of*, which accounts for about three percent of word tokens. *The* is roughly three times as frequent as the third-ranked word, *and*, which comprises 2.6 percent of tokens. *The* is about four times as frequent as the fourth-ranked word, *in*, which comprises 1.8 percent of tokens. And so on. This pattern is observed across all texts and languages, for reasons that are still not fully understood.

When we plot a word's frequency rank on the x-axis and its frequency on the y-axis (Figure 4.3), we observe that the frequency of words falls steeply from the top few very frequent (function) words to the *long tail* of very many infrequent (content) words. This graph represents a *power law distribution*, generated by a mathematical function where y is a function of x raised to some power α (usually, a negative value).

While first observed in the domain of words, Zipf's power law extends to many other phenomena. The distribution of wealth, social media followers, citations of articles, the populations of cities, the number of workers at companies, and other phenomena involving the unequal distribution of scarce resources follow a similar pattern: A few individuals have an enormous amount (of wealth, followers, citations, population, workers, etc.), and most have very little.

In contrast, other phenomena follow the familiar *normal distribution*: Most people are of about average height/weight, with a few very small and very large people at the edges of a *bell curve*. The lengths of words, in characters, roughly follow a bell curve, albeit an asymmetrical one, with a defined lower bound of one character and an upper bound which is unlimited in principle, given that new words are created all the time and can be lengthened by adding productive morphemes such as *un-*, *anti-*, or *-able*. In reality, most English words are between four and ten characters, with a few very short and very long words at the edges of the curve, as in Figure 4.4.

As a consequence of Zipf's power law, a few word types represent a plurality of word tokens, and many word types appear once or never in a given text, as can

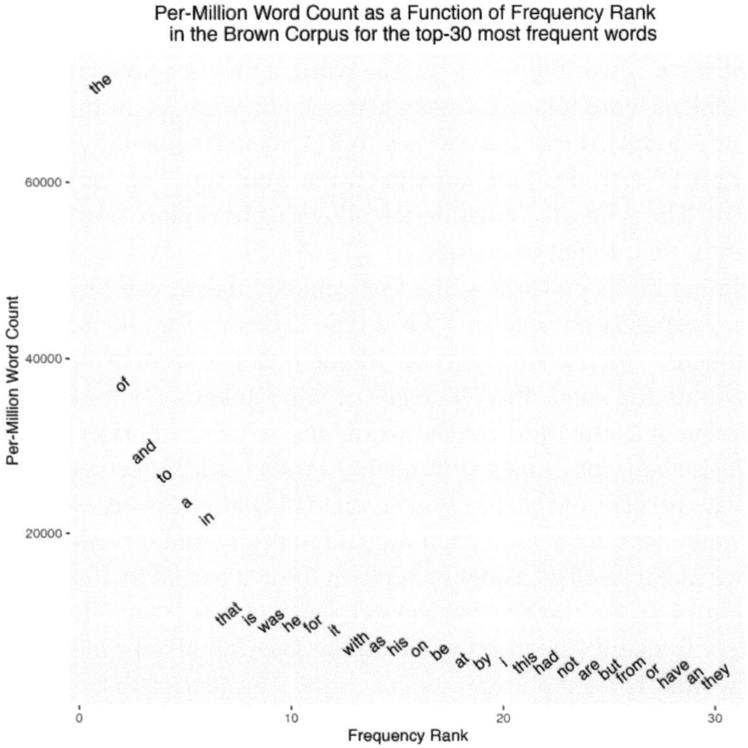

Figure 4.3: Per-million-word frequency of words in the Brown Corpus as a function of their frequency rank (ordered from left to right as the first most frequent word, the second most frequent, and so on).

be seen by the trailing long tail in Figure 4.3. *Heap's Law* (Heaps 1978) predicts the number of distinct word types appearing at least once in a document as a function of its length: That is, the longer the document, the more word types it will contain, but, as a document gets longer, the marginal likelihood of encountering a new word type diminishes. Researchers use techniques such as *Laplace (add-one) smoothing* – pretending you have seen a word type once rather than zero times, to avoid dividing by zero in various equations – to account for the reality that any NLP technique will encounter new word types in new data. A *hapax legomenon* ('said once' in Greek) is a word that occurs only once in a document. About 38 percent of words in the Brown Corpus (such as *mirthless* and *pastels*) are *hapax legomena*, and another 14 percent are *dis legomena* (such as *syndicated* and *lamentations*), occurring only twice.

The second of Zipf's laws, Zipf's brevity law, observes that across all languages and texts, more frequent words tend to be shorter (in characters or syllables)

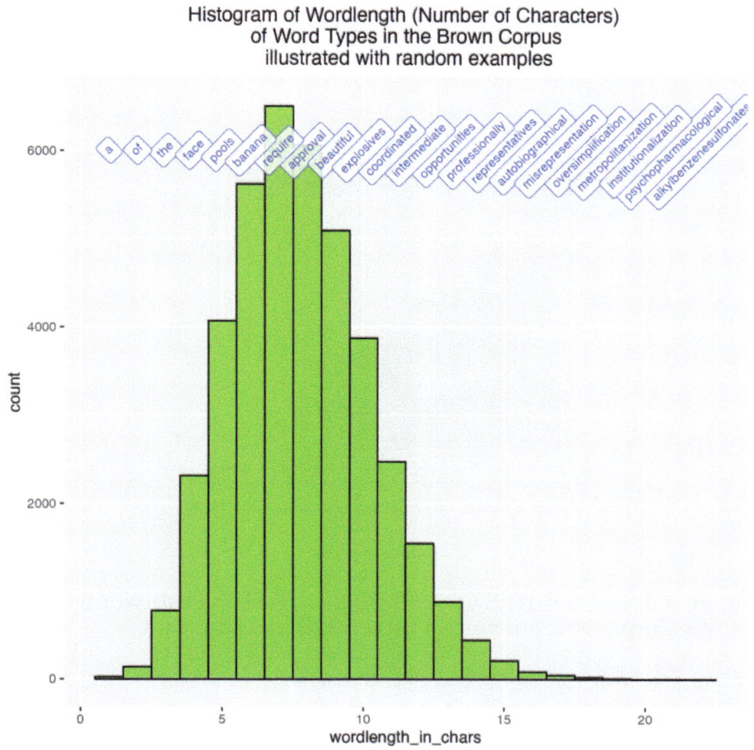

Figure 4.4: Histogram of the length (number of characters) of all word types in the Brown Corpus.

than less frequent words. Figure 4.5 shows that the shortest words are most frequent, while longer words are less frequent. For example, the top ten most frequent words in the Brown Corpus (*the, of, and, a, in, to, is, was, I, for*) are all one syllable, three letters or less – lower than the most common length of four to ten characters – while the hapax legomena (*mirthless, pastels*) are longer. The precise mechanisms are debated, but intuitively Zipf's brevity law suggests that languages evolve for efficiency: When the most frequent words are short, communication takes less effort. Imagine how onerous it would be if the meanings for the words *the* and *therefore* were swapped!

4.3.2 Topic models

So far, we have considered the distribution of words at a large scale. But how are words distributed across smaller documents, such as individual paragraphs,

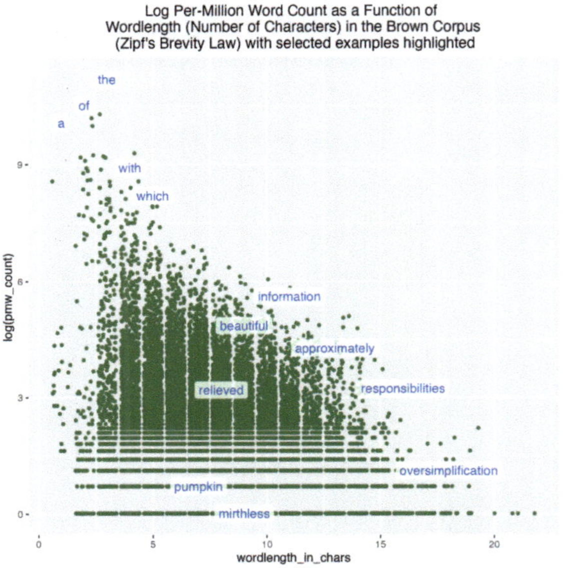

Figure 4.5: Log per-million-word frequency of English words in the Brown Corpus as a function of their length in characters.

chapters, articles, tweets, or product reviews? Documents can differ by *genre* (e.g., personal anecdotes versus news articles versus fiction) and by *topic* (e.g., text about pets versus politics versus travel); of course, there is some interaction between genre and topic, as different genres favor different topics. Crucially, texts about different topics are likely to differ in the distribution of content words: A text about animals will contain words like *cat, dog,* and *fish,* while a text about politics will mention words like *election, poll,* and *candidate.*

Topic modeling is a technique used to discover how different documents and words reflect these different topics. A topic, on this view, is a probability distribution of words associated with that topic: In the "pets" topic, for instance, the words *cat* and *dog* are quite likely to appear. A document is also a probability distribution over the topics that it discusses, as conveyed by the words therein and the topics that they evoke. A tweet about dogs and cats is most probably associated with the topic of pets, less probably associated with politics.

Topic modeling is generally used as an exploratory technique when you have a lot of documents, with no topic labels assigned to them at the outset, and you do not know in advance which different topics they discuss. For example, maybe you are an attorney reviewing a thousand emails turned over as part of a court proceeding, looking for emails about a particular project which may have involved fraud. Instead of reading all the emails by hand, you might use topic modeling to cluster the emails into different topics (office-wide announcements, hiring, projects) to get a bird's-eye view of the data before you dive in, and to target your attention to emails discussing the most relevant topics. As for other applications, perhaps you have surveyed customers asking them for open-ended feedback about your product, and you want to gauge the different topics discussed; or perhaps you want to show users more social media posts about the topics that seem to interest them.

One of the classic topic modeling techniques is called *Latent Dirichlet Allocation*, LDA for short (Blei et al. 2003). *Latent* (which means 'hidden') refers to the idea that a document's topic, in many cases, is implicitly inferred rather than explicitly labeled. *Dirichlet*, named after a German mathematician, is a type of probability distribution; as we'll see, the idea is to associate: (i) each topic with a probability distribution over the words associated with it, and (ii) each document with a probability distribution over the topics it discusses. *Allocation* refers to the fact that we allocate each word and each document to the topic(s) most strongly associated with it. LDA is a type of *unsupervised learning*, because we never provide any labels or "right answers" for the algorithm to generalize; instead we just give it some data and ask it to find the meaningful topic groupings therein. We will see more examples of both supervised and unsupervised learning in Chapter 5.

LDA works as follows: We begin with a set of documents – for example, emails turned over during legal proceedings. Next, we choose the number of topics we want to find. When you are using topic modeling for exploratory purposes, it is common to try different numbers of topics, settling on the one that yields the most intuitive results; for our purposes, let us imagine that we want two topics. Then we randomly assign every word token in every document to one of those topics. With two topics, we essentially assign each word token to a topic by a coin flip. As is common in topic modeling, we lemmatize all words and filter out stop words.

Next, we build a matrix, as in Table 4.1, where the rows are word types, the columns are topics, and the values are the number of tokens of that word type assigned to that topic. The columns (topics) are labeled with numerals; any descriptive label (*pets, politics*, etc) must be provided by a human who interprets the output of the topic model once it is complete.

After we have gone through this process of assigning words to topics at random, we iterate through each word token in each document, meaning that we just look at each word individually rather than any grammatical or semantic re-

Table 4.1: Topic modeling with two topics, stage one: Random assignment of words to topics.

	Topic1	Topic2
dog	5	4
cat	8	7
election	7	8
candidate	2	4
walk	5	5
weekend	10	14
pet	2	3

lations between them. Each word token has already been assigned a topic by a coin flip, represented by the parenthetical numbers in (2).

(2) dog(2) walk(1) weekend(2) pet(1)

We begin with the token *dog* in (2). This token of *dog* has previously been randomly assigned to Topic 2; we now un-assign the topic of this word token. We update our term-by-topic matrix to reflect this change (decrementing the first row, second column of our matrix to 3 instead of 4). Next, we re-assign a topic to this token of *dog* token by considering two factors: (i) the topics most prevalent in this particular document; and (ii) the topics most commonly associated with the particular word type *dog*. To quantify the topics most prevalent in this document, we observe that two of the remaining three words (*walk* and *pet*) have been assigned to Topic 1, so Topic 1 is twice as prevalent in this document as Topic 2. To quantify the topics most commonly associated with *dog*, we observe that *dog* is used five times in Topic 1 and three times in Topic 2 (which we read from the first row of our matrix, with the 4 decremented to a 3, as we have un-assigned the topic of the current token of *dog*). Both this document and the word type *dog* favor the assignment of Topic 1 to this token of *dog*. So we update the assignment of *dog*, and update our term-by-topic matrix, as in Table 4.2.

(3) dog(1) walk(1) weekend(2) pet(1)

We keep going through each word token in each document, and then go through it all again as many times as we want (perhaps 50 or 100 times). Eventually, the words that tend to co-occur within the same document will end up being assigned to the same topic, perhaps something like in Table 4.3.

Table 4.2: Topic modeling with two topics, stage two: New values based on data-driven reassignments.

	Topic1	Topic2
dog	6	3
cat	8	7
election	7	8
candidate	2	4
walk	5	5
weekend	10	14
pet	2	3

Table 4.3: Topic modeling with two topics, final stage: Final numbers after some set number of iterations.

	Topic 1	Topic 2
dog	9	0
cat	14	1
election	1	14
candidate	0	6
walk	8	2
weekend	12	12
pet	5	0

The output of the topic modeling yields, for each document, a distribution of the topics most strongly associated with it; and for each topic, a distribution of the words most strongly associated with it. Then you have to look at each topic and its associated words, and decide if these words (*cat, dog, pet*) indeed evoke a cohesive theme. You can use your own human judgment to give a name to each topic. In our toy example, Topic 1 involves pets.

While it is important to understand how topic modeling words under the hood, in real life you will probably use one of the many libraries (in Python or R) which does it for you. You might also use a fancier version of topic modeling that leverages richer information about which words are similar to one another, in ways to be explored later in this chapter.

Because topic modeling is a way of exploring your data, you may want to try it several different times for a fuller exploration. You can try different numbers of topics; in general, the more documents you have, and the more diverse you expect them to be, the more topics you will need. In addition to lemmatizing words and filtering stop-words, you can also focus on only certain parts of speech – perhaps only nouns, or only nouns and adjectives. You know you have succeeded when the topics make intuitive sense, and when the topic modeling procedure has given you a landscape view of the data.

More broadly, topic modeling illustrates that you can learn a lot about words and documents simply by counting which words appear in which documents. This general idea underlies a great deal of NLP.

4.4 Word meanings as vectors

In our exploration of topic models, we have used a matrix of numbers to represent information about different topics and the words that are associated with them. We have also represented a sentence as a list of numerals (a vector) reflecting the topics associated with each word. In this book and in the study of NLP more generally, we will keep coming back to the idea of representing language (topics, words, sentences, documents, etc.) through vectors and matrices of numbers. We illustrate with the key idea of representing a word as a vector that represents some information about its meaning.

To start off, what is the meaning of a word? The philosopher of language David Lewis (Lewis 1972) suggests that the way to define meaning is to focus on what meaning allows you to do. When you know the meaning of a word, you can identify the thing, event, or idea that it refers to; for example, you can point to the furry animals denoted by *dog*. You can use the word in a sentence (*I have a dog*), and reason logically about the sentences in which it is used; you know that *I have a dog* entails *I have a pet*. You can identify its synonyms and antonyms (*dog* does not really have clear synonyms or antonyms; but in the realm of adjectives, *pleasant* and *nice* are roughly synonyms to each other, and antonymous with *unpleasant*). You also know the word's *hypernyms* (more general words – *animal* is a hypernym of *dog*) and *hyponyms* (more specific words: *poodle* is a hyponym of *dog*). You can provide other words (*cat, bark, walk*) that fit into the same conceptual domain. If you know the meaning of a word that describes a relationship or a transaction, you know which other words describe alternate perspectives on the same relation: You know how *parent* relates to *child* and how *buy* relates to *sell*. You can also identify the formality level and emotional sentiment associated with the word: You know that *doggie* is informal and that *win* feels positive. In other words, knowing the meaning of a word means knowing how it relates to other words.

For a computer, however, the string of characters *dog* reflects none of that information. Of course, a computer could look up *dog* in a dictionary, but the dictionary would provide a prose definition which is just a longer string of characters.

The problem is that to a computer, text is *categorical*: A string of characters is just a string of characters, with no organizing principle relating it to any other string of characters or any other information. Humans can interpret text by imagining the real-world situation that it describes, but such mental representations and real-world situations are not legible to a computer. Moreover, the idea of edit distance from Chapter 2 quantifies the difference in spelling between one word and another, but – given that an alphabetic writing system represents sound only – captures nothing about meaning.

In contrast to text, numbers are *continuous*, meaning that they can be organized on a number line (or, for a vector of numbers, plotted in a coordinate space) in ways that represent meaningful relations between them. While there is no way to carry out mathematical operations on strings of characters, numbers and vectors can be added and multiplied in ways that capture meaningful information. To a human, it is hard to hold too many numbers in one's mind at once, and a number is not meaningful unless it refers to something. But computers are designed to process large quantities of numbers, and without any representation of the outside world, the relations between numbers provide valuable information.

In other words, a computer could get more information out of text – and even "reason" about the relations between texts – if it were represented as vectors of numbers rather than strings of characters. But how can a word like *dog* be turned into a numerical representation?

Actually, even before ASCII was invented in 1963, numerical representations had been proposed for certain words. In the domain of (words for) colors, theorists of vision proposed in the 1800s to represent each color as a three-valued vector denoting the strength (out of a maximum of 255) of red, green, and blue light that it uses. For example, red is denoted as (255, 0, 0), meaning that it is maximally red and contains no green or blue.

As shown in Table 4.4, purple is (128, 0, 128), meaning that it uses equal amounts of red and blue light, but no green. By using vectors like (255, 0, 0) and (128, 0, 128) rather than character strings like *red* and *purple*, we can capture quantitative relations and operations: For example, the fact that the color violet (127, 0, 255) is closer to purple (128, 0, 128) than to red (255, 0, 0); and the fact that red (255, 0, 0) plus green (0, 255, 0) yields yellow (255, 255, 0). Of course, the RGB color scheme only applies to color words, but within that realm it transforms categorical text into meaningful continuous quantities.

Table 4.4: Color words represented as three-valued RGB vectors.

color	word	R	G	B
	red	255	0	0
	yellow	255	255	0
	green	0	255	0
	purple	128	0	128
	violet	127	0	255

Converging from a different perspective on the same key insight, a line of work spearheaded by the psychologist Charles Osgood (Osgood et al. 1957) proposes to capture the emotional meaning of a word as a three-valued vector denoting human annotations, gathered from experimental participants, of the word's valence (positive versus negative), arousal (high versus low energy), and dominance (high versus low human control). Using data from Mohammad (2018) in which each rating ranges from 0 to 1, *win* is represented as (0.9, 0.7, 0.8), meaning that it is positive, high-arousal, and high-dominance, as shown in Table 4.5.

Table 4.5: Values for valence, arousal, and dominance.

	valence	arousal	dominance
win	0.9	0.7	0.8
compete	0.6	0.7	0.8
lose	0.1	0.5	0.2

The word *lose* is (0.1, 0.5, 0.2) – negative, medium-arousal, and low-dominance, while *compete* is (0.6, 0.7, 0.8) – somewhat positive, high-arousal, and high-dominance. Again, these numbers capture important commonalities between words: On an emotional level, *win* is more similar to *compete* than to *lose*, sharing high values along the same dimensions. These vectors represent only emotional dimensions of meaning, without capturing any information about the events that they describe. The lexicon is transformed into quantities that can be plotted on a three-dimensional plane.

In each system, the vectors have a length of three, which is about the maximum vector length that humans can keep in mind and represent visually on a three-dimensional plane. But a computer can handle vectors of essentially any

size, so what further information can be captured that way? Moreover, the RGB system is limited to colors and the emotion-vector system is limited to the words and meaning dimensions that have been laboriously annotated by humans. How could these systems be expanded to cover all words, ideally using information that already lies within text?

The answer is inspired by a famous claim from the corpus linguist J.R. Firth (Firth 1957) that "You shall know a word by the company it keeps". In corpus linguistics, the "company" that a word keeps consists of its *collocations* – the other words that appear near it in a corpus. In Table 4.6, you can see some examples (adapted, with a few modifications, from 2014 comments on the web forum AskReddit, gathered by Baumgartner et al. 2020) of collocational contexts – here, within a window of five words to the left and to the right – for *dog, cat,* and *election.*

Table 4.6: Collocation contexts for *dog*, *cat*, and *election* in AskReddit.

Left context	Word	Right context
friends are pretty annoying. Their	*dog*	is cute though. (END)
cute when it's a small	*dog.*	Also people who encourage their
dog meat industry. You American	*dog*	lovers would be heart sickened
loneliness. Usually, a good cute	*cat*	pic can cheer me up
on with me the cute	*cat*	pictures. I almost never browse
but if you've got a	*cat*	that's an asshole I don't
elected in a South American	*election*	is testament to that. It
and talk about the American	*election*	because I have trouble imagining
kid, they had a family	*election*	on what toy got to

We can turn these data into a *word-context matrix* where the entry at row i, column j records the number of times that word i appears in a context that includes j. As shown in Table 4.7, for example, the top left corner of this matrix (the *cute* row, *dog* column) represents the fact that in our tiny data snippet, the word *dog* appears near *cute* twice. The *cute* row, *cat* column reflects that *cat* appears near *cute* twice; and so on.

In reality, this matrix would be massive, with as many rows and columns as there are words in our vocabulary. Because such massive vectors can be unwieldy even for a computer, there are ways to compress the information in the word-context matrix so that it is smaller than the size of the vocabulary, yielding vectors of a few hundred elements rather than thousands.

Table 4.7: A small word-context matrix.

	dog	cat	election	(...)
cute	2	2	0	(...)
American	1	0	2	(...)

For example, *Word2Vec* (Mikolov, Chen, et al. 2013) does not just build word-context matrices like Table 4.7, but instead generates vectors by trying to guess the target word from its collocational context, or – as an alternative way of setting things up – trying to guess the collocation context from the target word. Another method, *GloVe* (short for Global Vectors; Pennington et al. 2014), distills the word's "global" distribution in the word-context matrix as in Table 4.7 by generating vectors that aim to capture the probability of two words occurring as neighbors to one another. Both Word2Vec and GloVe yield vectors of a few hundred elements rather than thousands. Rather than using these tools to build new vectors on a given corpus, you can also download vectors that researchers have already built on massive corpora. These packaged vectors are known as *pre-trained* because you do not have to build (train) them yourself.

The important point is that we now have a mathematical implementation of Firth's idea that we can "know a word by the company it keeps". Each word is represented as a vector (the vector of its row or column) which captures information about its meaning. These vectors are called *word vectors* or *word embeddings*, because they reflect how a word is embedded into its collocation contexts.

Our word vectors capture the intuition that *dog* is more similar to *cat* than to *election*, as evidenced by the fact that *dog* and *cat* both are used near *cute* while *election* is not. We will learn how to calculate the similarity between two vectors mathematically in Chapter 6, but for now we can capture the same information visually by plotting *dog, cat,* and *election* as vectors on a plane where the x-axis represents the number of times the word occurs near *American* and the y-axis represents the number of times it occurs near *cute* (Figure 4.6), Here, we see that the vectors for *dog* and *cat* are closer to each other on this plane than the vector for *election*. Leveraging the mathematical operations that quantitative vectors enable, we can even do addition and subtraction, so that the word with the closest vector representation to the output of *king - man + woman* is *queen* (Mikolov, Yih, et al. 2013)!

You may already see a problem here, though: By capturing *the* meaning of a word through its collocations, this framework assumes that a word has *one*

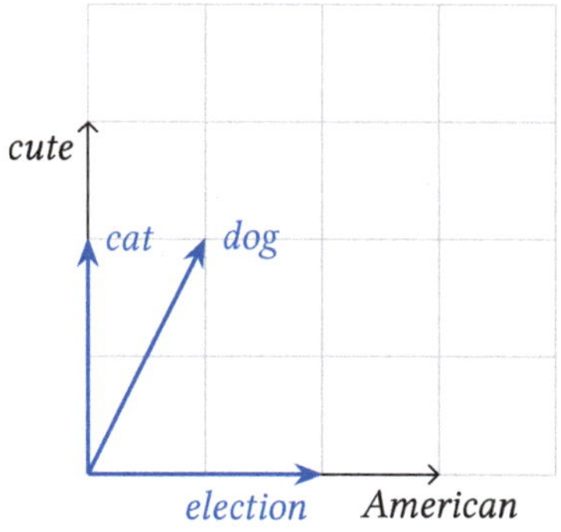

Figure 4.6: Illustration of word vectors in two-dimensional space.

single meaning. But some words have more than one meaning. The word *mouse* can refer to a rodent or a pointer on a computer – each with distinct collocation patterns (using data from Reddit):

(4) One night my housemate and I found a dying *mouse* on the floor.

(5) The sophomore dorm had a *mouse* problem, and one student caught one in his trash can and kept it as a pet for about a week.

(6) things change size and move around while you move the *mouse* pointer over them, and they do so at inconsistent speeds.

(7) That's absolutely true but there is a PC mod for it or something that allows you to use a *mouse* and play it like a real first person shooter.

When it describes a house pest, *mouse* appears in contexts discussing housing situations. When it describes a digital pointer, it appears in contexts discussing computers and as the direct object of verbs like *move* and *use*. Still other uses of the word *mouse* might involve the Disney character of Mickey Mouse. Rather than considering *mouse* to have a single meaning captured by all its collocations, it is more accurate to see it as having several different meanings, each with its own collocations. Therefore, instead of generating a single vector for each word type, modern techniques will often generate a *contextual vector representation*, meant to capture the meaning of the word token in context rather than the word type overall. We will learn more about such tools in Chapter 5.

Before we get to these refinements, let us consider the power of the ideas we have seen so far. We have transformed text into a quantitative representation legible to a computer. These representations not only capture information about which words are similar to one another, but also offer quantitative information that can be manipulated in all sorts of ways by a computer. Whereas the three-value valence/arousal/dominance vectors of Osgood et al. (1957) required laborious human labeling, these word-context vectors leverage information already baked into a text, so they can be built quickly at scale. With these advantages, such vector representations of word meaning constitute one of the most important ideas in NLP, and continue to be refined and extended in countless ways. The rest of this textbook will keep coming back to this field-transforming idea.

4.5 Consequences

Today, more information is available than ever before, not just because there is an abundance of text data but also because digital text-processing tools allow us to distill the information contained within a larger quantity of text than anyone could read personally. This information sheds light on society, history, literature, and language itself.

Throughout this chapter, we have seen that turning text into data means turning text into numbers. We can test quantitative hypotheses about which words or grammatical constructions should be more frequent than others, more frequent in one context than another, and so on. We can explore the statistical properties of text by quantifying the frequency and length of words, as in Zipf's power law and Zipf's brevity law. And we can learn more about the similarities between various words and documents by representing each one as a vector, as used in topic modeling and word-context matrices. Such numbers may not be as legible to a human as text itself, but to a computer they illuminate the information contained within.

In other words, this chapter shows that there are two different ways to encounter text. A human can read a small amount of text qualitatively, leveraging knowledge of how words refer to things, to create a rich mental picture of the world described therein as likely intended by the author. A computer can read a much larger amount of text quantitatively, counting words and creating vectors to generate a rich statistical picture of its structure, unintended by any individual author but emerging bottom-up from all of them. Of course, a human must program the computer to do this and must ultimately interpret the results. These two ways of encountering text reflect the distinct advantages of humans versus computers, instantiating a theme that recurs throughout this book.

This chapter also evokes our focus on ethics. When we explore text as data, we should ask whose text and whose data are being explored. Who generated this text, and how can their privacy and authorship be respected? Whose text is not represented, and how can their perspective be considered? Who benefits from the exploding quantity of information extracted from text, and who might be hurt by it? Text exists because people created it; even when it is distilled into abstract matrices, we cannot lose sight of those people or the people whose voices are left out.

Checklist

- Give examples of text-as-data research in digital humanities, corpus linguistics, computational social science, and author profiling/identification.
- Brainstorm various business applications of text processing.
- Give examples of available corpora, the metadata that they offer, and the research questions that they can be used for.
- Give an example of a research question for which a researcher might need to create their own custom corpus.
- Discuss ethical dimensions of corpora such as personal privacy and bias in the representation of languages, language varieties, and speakers.
- Give examples of function words, content words, and words that straddle the boundary between them.
- Define the distinction between word types and word tokens.
- Sketch a power law distribution and a normal distribution, and give examples of (textual and non-textual) phenomena that follow each one.
- Give examples of words instantiating Zipf's power law and Zipf's brevity law.
- Explain what topic modeling is used for and how it works.

- Discuss why it is advantageous for a computer to represent words as numerical vectors rather than as text strings.
- Build a word-context matrix for a bite-sized set of example documents and visualize it in vector space.
- Give examples showing when it is important to generate contextualized representations of word tokens rather than unified representations of word types.

Exercises

1. Visit www.english-corpora.org[a] and choose a corpus. Who built this corpus? Where do the data come from? What metadata are available? How did the corpus creators balance size, representativeness, and quality in gathering the data? How has this corpus been used in research?
2. Check out the Corpus of Historical American English (CoHA) web interface. Can you find evidence – in the past or in the present – for the finding of Underwood et al. (2018) that the verbs *smile* and *laugh* are associated with women while *grin* and *chuckle* are associated with men? (What numbers could be used to assess this claim quantitatively?)
3. Using the CoHA web interface, explore the historical evolution of the words *gay, read,* and *woman.* For each word, look at the other words it occurs with in the 1800s compared to today. What do you learn?
4. On the Corpus of Contemporary American English (CoCA) web interface, explore the frequency of the words *the, a, I,* and *you* in the Spoken section/genre compared to the Academic one. What do you observe?

5. Choose a language other than English, and search online to see what corpora are available in that language. How big are these corpora? How do these resources compare to those available for English?

6. If you wanted to use topic modeling to understand the topics discussed in a work of fiction, how would you split up the book into smaller documents? Would you use sentences, paragraphs, or chapters, and why? What about a book of nonfiction?

7. Imagine that you are an attorney trying to argue that your client did not *harbor* an undocumented immigrant (as argued in *United States v. Costello* in 2012), on the grounds that *harbor* means 'hide from authorities' rather than just 'let someone stay with you.'

   - Find and interpret some corpus data to support your claim.
   - Next, imagine that you are a prosecutor, and you want to argue the opposite – that the defendant actually *did* harbor an undocumented immigrant. Again, find and interpret some corpus data to support this claim.

8. On the CoCA web interface, look at the first 100 tokens of the words *ate* and *devoured*, as verbs. How often does *ate* have an object (*I ate lunch*), and how often does it have no object (*I ate*)? What about *devour*? How frequent are these words overall? Also, among tokens of these verbs that do have objects, how many of them refer to food versus something else? Can you develop a theory for the long-standing lexical semantics question of why *eat* leaves off its object more easily than *devour* does?

9. Check out the Gutenberg Corpus available as part of the Natural Language Toolkit in Python – for which you can reference the "Accessing Text Corpora and Lexical Resources" chapter of the freely available e-book *Natural Language Processing with Python* (Bird et al. 2009). Choose two authors in Gutenberg, and compare their top-100 unigrams, bigrams, and trigrams. What do you learn?

10. Find any machine-readable corpus that you have access to, and compute:

- What percentage of word types in the corpus are *hapax legomena* – occurring only once in the corpus? (What are some examples?)
- How do the results change if you lemmatize the corpus, for example standardizing *ran*, *runs*, and *running* into *run*?
- What is the most common word in this corpus, and how much more common is it than the second-most common word?
- How long are each of these words?
- To what extent do these findings reflect Zipf's laws of frequency and brevity?

[a]Accessed 2024-04-26.

Further reading

The idea of motivating vector semantics via RGB color vectors is taken from a blog post entitled "Understanding word vectors" by the digital humanist Allison Parrish (2018).

Read more about author profiling in the digital humanities in Ben Blatt (2017): *Nabakov's favorite word is mauve: What the numbers reveal about the classics, bestsellers, and our own writing.*

Read more about corpus linguistics in Paquot & Gries (2021).

For more on the Voynich Manuscript, see https://voynich.nu/[a] , Reddy & Knight (2011), and Bowern & Lindemann (2021), all of which inspire our discussion here.

Gries & Slocum (2017) and Hessick (2017) provide opposing viewpoints on the utility of corpus linguistics for interpreting laws, with discussion of the word *harbor* in *United States v. Costello.*

Piantadosi (2014) reviews potential explanations for Zipf's power law.

Jordan Boyd-Graber has created several YouTube videos walking through topic modeling algorithms.[b]

[a]Accessed 2024-04-17.

[b]https://www.youtube.com/watch?v=fCmIceNqVog, accessed 2024-07-02.

5 Text classification

5.1 Introduction

Every day, you probably receive hundreds of *spam* emails – unsolicited advertisements, financial scams, and attempts to steal personal data – which your email automatically sends to your spam folder so you don't even see them. Your email *spam filter* is one example of *text classification* (also called *document classification*): When a computer automatically sorts texts into two or more *classes*, also called *labels*. Here, the texts/documents are emails, and the classes/labels are "spam" (junk, named after a sketch by the British comedy troupe Monty Python) and "ham" (the real emails that you want to read).

Spam detection is just one example of text classification. Other popular applications include:

- Sorting your non-spam email into folders – primary, social, promotions, and forums (note that we can use as many classes as we want).
- Detecting hate speech or fake news in online posts, perhaps to delete it automatically (*content moderation*; here, the texts are the posts, the classes are "hate speech" and "not hate speech," or "fake news" versus "real news" – note that these categories may be somewhat subjective).
- Classifying a product review as positive, negative, or perhaps also neutral (*sentiment analysis*).
- Detecting the language that an online post is written in (*language identification*) – English, Spanish, Tagalog, and so on. Here, the number of classes is determined by the number of languages that we want to handle.
- Classifying the type of issue that a customer needs help with (*support ticket classification*) – orders, shipping, returns, other – to send them to the right agent or help page.
- Identifying what a language technology user wants to do based on what they say or type (*intent recognition*) – do they want to shop, set a timer, do

a calculation, translate something into another language, look at maps, or view general search results?

Text classification is used any time you want to assign a label automatically to a text from a closed class of labels. Beyond business applications, it can be used in language research of all kinds, including linguistics, computational social science, and digital humanities. We illustrate with spam because it is simple, familiar, and arguably binary (with just two labels, spam and ham). But even if you don't care how your spam filter works, learning about text classification will empower you in all areas of language processing.

5.2 Exploring the data

Before learning about how computers classify spam, it may be useful to look at some examples of spam and ham, taken from the inbox and spam folder of one of our own email accounts. It is always a good idea to understand the data yourself before you feed it to an algorithm.

- Better than Morphine, Safer than Aspirin?
  - Little did they know, a Columbia University MD already found the "Holy Grail" back in the 1970s. You see, this doctor uncovered a powerful, natural painkiller... that works with your body's natural mechanisms to renew your achy joints from the inside out.
- Click Here for your $1000 Gift Card
  - I am Mr Roth Savuth and a personal Accountant Director with Foreign Trade Bank of Cambodia (FTB). It is with good spirit of heart that I open up this great opportunity to you.
- Attention Sir/Madam
  - From the outset, I wanted the very fabric of my club to be built around support. For the most part, I deal exclusively with our most valued clients.
- Reminder: Course Instructor Opinion Survey (CIOS)
  - The course/instructor opinion survey (CIOS) is now underway for one or more of your courses. The CIOS tool is an important source of information about your teaching and can be very helpful for classroom professors.

- Request for a reference letter
  - I hope you're doing well, and apologies for not having replied to your last email on sociolinguistics next semester! The last half of the semester became a lot busier than I anticipated.
- Question about final project
  - I saw in the announcement that we might submit the final write-up before December 8th, but I still want to clarify if the deadline is on the 7th or before the end of the 8th.

You can probably tell at a glance which of these emails are spam or ham (the first three are spam, the last three are ham). But how did you do that? What clues did you notice? And how did this email client already correctly sort them into spam and ham?

5.3 How computers "learn"

Text classification represents one example of *machine learning* – any task in which the computer is expected to "learn" from experience. If we wanted, we spend pages discussing whether machines can ever be said to be truly intelligent, or about the true nature of the so-called learning. We think these discussions are interesting, and we touch on them very briefly at the end of Chapter 8, but they really belong in a philosophy class, not here.

There are several different types of tasks that machine learning models can "learn" to solve. Text classification is an example of a *classification* task: The model is asked to assign the text a class/label, from a closed set thereof. Classification is known as a *supervised learning* task because the model is trained on data that has already been labeled with "correct answers" and just needs to learn to label new data in the same manner.

In a classification task, we have access to a labeled *training set* – a set of emails correctly labeled as spam or ham. Where did the labels come from? Perhaps the labels were gathered opportunistically from users who helpfully flagged some emails as spam or immediately deleted them (spam), while reading and replying to other emails (ham). Perhaps the researcher paid gig workers to label the emails through a platform such as Amazon's Mechanical Turk.

Next, we have to turn these emails into some sort of representation that the computer can process. As we discussed in Chapter 4, numbers are more meaningful to a computer than text, because numbers can be manipulated (added, multiplied), and the distance between them can be quantified. So we need to turn our documents into vectors of numbers, in such a way that the numbers represent something meaningful about each document – the information that you need to classify it as spam or ham. This process is also known as *featurizing* the document – creating a computer-friendly vector representation of the *features* of the document that are important for the classification task.

There are all sorts of ways to featurize a document, some very fancy and complex, but one very simple way is just to count the words. To illustrate, imagine that we have three very short emails to featurize:

(1) a. Email1: Better project idea
  b. Email2: Better than morphine
  c. Email3: Project question

In this simple example, we have a vocabulary of six word types (*better, project, idea, than, morphine, question*). We can represent each document as a seven-element vector, where each position in the vector corresponds to a word in the vocabulary, and each value reflects the number of times that this word occurs in the document. Putting the emails together into a matrix, we end up with a *term-by-document matrix*: Each document (email) is a column, each term (word type) is a row, and each value reflects the frequency of that term in that document.

Table 5.1: Term-by-document matrix for three short emails.

	Email1	Email2	Email3
better	1	1	0
project	1	0	1
idea	1	0	0
than	0	1	0
morphine	0	1	0
question	0	0	1

Reading these three emails, you probably get the sense that Email1 and Email3 are more similar to each other than they are to Email2. For one thing, Email2 seems like spam because it is about drugs, whereas Email1 and Email3 seem legitimate because they are about projects.

Notice that our simple term-by-document matrix already captures this intuition! Just by comparing which columns match on a given row, we see that Email3 is more similar to Email1 (since both of them contain the word *project*) than to

Email2 (which has no words in common with Email3). There are mathematical ways to compute the similarity between two document vectors, which we explore later in the book, but the important point is the big picture, previewed in Chapter 4: When we represent a document as a vector, we capture something about its contents and its similarity to other documents.

This term-by-document matrix representation is called a *bag of words* because it does not represent any information about the order of words, just their frequency. Imagine writing a sentence on paper, then chopping up the paper into individual words and tossing them into a bag, so that no word order is preserved. Setting aside everything we learned about grammar in Chapter 2, we ignore the fact that the words were arranged into a particular order and that they go together to form sentences and paragraphs. All we worry about is which words happen in the document and how often they happen.

Even though this representation is simple, we face all sorts of design choices: Should the words all be put in lower-case? Should we include emoji? Should words be lemmatized (mapping *dog* and *dogs* to the same form)? Should we remove stop-words such as *the*, or down-weight their importance? Should we focus on the presence/absence of specific, important words or look at all of them? Should the researcher use their own judgment to decide what features are important (*feature engineering*), or leave the computer to figure it out? There are pros and cons to each choice.

Once we have our vectors of features, we want the computer to learn how to map these feature vectors into the correct labels for spam and ham. There are many different algorithms for teaching the computer to do this; we will explore two simple ones in detail below (naive Bayes and the Perceptron). Through this process, the computer produces an object called a *model*, a representation of what it has learned.

Our next step is to test how successful our model is. Our measure of success should be tied to the ultimate goal of the model – to classify new emails, for which we do not yet know the correct label. But if we do not know the correct label, then we do not know whether our model is labeling them correctly. Instead, we use a *test set* of examples, for which we ourselves know the correct label, but the model does not. It is common to split off part of the original labeled data (10-20 percent of it), exclude it from the training data, and save it for later as a test set. We can then feed the test set to the model and compare the model's predicted labels to the correct labels.

Here, you might wonder: Why not just test the model on the same data that it was trained on? But the goal is to build a model that can generalize to new data, eventually including those for which we do not even know the correct label. So we want to test whether the model's success can generalize beyond the data that it has already seen. Otherwise, we run the risk of *over-fitting* – building a model that has memorized the correct labels for the training data, so that it performs very accurately on those examples but falls apart when it sees something new.

To use an analogy, imagine that you are preparing for a test in your linguistics class. Your friend shows you the test that was given in the class last year, along with the correct answers to that test. You could decide to just memorize last year's test and its answers. If the instructor is too lazy to write a new test this year, you will do well – but you will not have actually learned much linguistics; your knowledge will be *over-fitted* to this particular test. On the other hand, you could use last year's test as a study guide, and learn the key concepts taught in the class; this way, you will do well on this year's test even if it differs from last year's – and, most importantly, you will have actually learned some linguistics concepts which you can generalize to various problems. By testing the model on new data, we check whether it has learned to generalize.

The final step is to deploy the model in real life, where its job is to label new data for which we do not know the correct label. The model can be incorporated into an email service as its spam filter. If the model works well on our test data, can we expect it to work equally well in real life? That depends on whether the real-life data are similar to the data on which the model was trained and tested. If spammers start to realize what features are sending their messages to the spam folder, they may start to create spam that is harder to detect.

5.4 Measuring success

How do we decide whether our spam-detection model is successful? It may seem obvious what we need to measure. If we classify all the spam as spam and all the ham as ham, we have succeeded and all is well. This is definitely correct, but we would be fooling ourselves if we believe that we can design a perfect system that gets every single decision correct. Therefore, we need measures that quantify our partial successes and failures, so we can weigh their trade-offs.

To do this, we borrow some ideas from medical science. These ideas apply anywhere, but they turned up first in medicine because of the need to reason effectively with complex and uncertain data. When we run a classifier on a document to decide whether it is spam or not, it is a lot like running a diagnostic test to collect evidence about whether a patient has a disease or not. Here there are two two-way distinctions to be made:

1. The test can come out either positive or negative.

2. The patient may or may not really have the disease.

So there are four possible ways that the situation could be after the test has been given, as shown in Table 5.2.

Table 5.2: A diagnostic test.

	Has disease	*No disease*
Test positive	True positives	False positives
Test negative	False negatives	True negatives

Perhaps the patient has the disease, and the test correctly returns a positive result. We call this a *true positive.* (Here, the word *positive* means that the test indicates the presence of the disease – although usually it is an emotionally *negative* experience!) When the patient does not have the disease, and the test correctly returns a negative result, it is called a *true negative.* In both of these cases, the test is doing its job correctly.

But there are two other possible outcomes. The test could return negative even though the patient has the disease. This is called a *false negative,* and it is a bad thing because a patient who needs to be treated will be missed. The fourth possibility is that the test returns positive even though the patient does not have the disease. This is called a *false positive,* and it is again a bad thing because the patient is likely to be unnecessarily treated, quarantined, or frightened.

The terms in Table 5.2 extend to many non-medical situations, such as screening for terrorists among airline passengers, identifying fraudulent credit card purchases, flagging inappropriate images, and of course detecting spam in email.

In medical situations, there are two standard measures to assess the value of a test. An overview of these measures, and their relationship to false and true positives, is given in Table 5.3.

Table 5.3: Measures of a diagnostic test.

	Has disease	*No disease*	
Test positive	True positives	False positives	*Positive predictive value*
Test negative	False negatives	True negatives	*Negative predictive value*
	Sensitivity	*Specificity*	

The first is called *sensitivity.* This is the ratio:

(5.2) $$\text{Sensitivity} = \frac{\text{True positives}}{\text{True positives} + \text{False negatives}}$$

Sensitivity focuses on what happens when the patient does really have the disease. Sensitivity measures the percentage of true cases of the disease (true positives and false negatives) for which the test turns up positive (true positive).

In computational linguistics, we usually call sensitivity *recall*, as we'll discuss further in the context of search results in Chapter 6.

A high-sensitivity test means that a person who has the disease is very likely to be correctly diagnosed with it (a large percentage of people who have the disease test positive for it). It is valuable for ensuring that the people who truly have the disease get treated.

On the other hand, sensitivity ignores people who do *not* have the disease. How likely is it that such people will receive a false positive (triggering unnecessary treatment and anxiety) or a true negative (correctly bolstering their peace of mind)? To understand what happens to them, we need another metric – specificity.

Complementing sensitivity, *specificity* focuses on what happens to people who do *not* have the disease. Specificity is defined as the ratio:

(5.3) $$\text{Specificity} = \frac{\text{True negatives}}{\text{True negatives} + \text{False positives}}$$

A high-specificity test means that a person who does not have the disease is likely to correctly test negative for it (a low rate of false positives). Thus, specificity is important for ensuring that healthy people are not treated unnecessarily.

To illustrate these concepts quantitatively, suppose you have a medical test for a disease. It has 90 percent specificity, meaning that a person who does not have the disease has a 90 percent chance of correctly testing negative. The test also has 98 percent sensitivity, meaning that a person who has the disease has a 98 percent chance of correctly testing positive. Now imagine that the *base rate* of the disease is 10 percent, meaning that 10 percent of people have this disease – thus, it's very common.

To see what these numbers mean, imagine that you test 1000 patients for the disease. Now we ask:

- On average, how many of the 1000 patients will have the disease and how many will not?

- Starting from the number of people who we expect to have the disease, what is the expected number of true positives and the expected number of false negatives? We need the *sensitivity* number to do this.
- Starting from the number of people we expect *not* to have the disease, what is the expected number of false positives and the expected number of true negatives? We will need to make use of the *specificity* figure to do this.

On average, we expect that about 100 patients will have the disease, and 900 will not (as our base rate is 10 percent). So we expect to see around $100 \times 0.98 = 98$ true positives, $100 \times (1 - 0.98) = 2$ false negatives, $900 \times 0.90 = 810$ true negatives and $900 \times (1 - 0.90) = 90$ false positives, as in Table 5.4.

Table 5.4: Expected numbers if you do 1000 tests.

	Has disease	No disease	Total
Test positive	98	90	188
Test negative	2	810	812
Total	100	900	1000

Notice that:

- There are 908 correct decisions and 92 bad decisions. One summary of the situation to just say that the test is 90.8 percent correct.
- There are 2 false negatives and 90 false positives.
- There are 98 true positives and 90 false positives. This means that nearly half of the people who test positive actually do not have the disease!

Remember that there are four possible situations:

1. True positives: The patient has the disease and the test correctly detects it. We are expecting 1 in 10 patients to have the disease and also that the test will return a positive result for 98 percent of these patients. We can say that the probability of having the disease is 1 in 10 (that is 0.1) and the probability of a positive test if you have the disease is 0.98. Multiplying the probabilities gives $0.1 \times 0.98 = 0.098$ as the probability of a true positive.

2. False positives: The patient does not have the disease, but the test incorrectly returns a positive result. Repeating the calculation, 9 in 10 of patients will not have the disease, and that in these circumstances 1 in 10 of them will get an incorrect positive test. Multiplying the probabilities gives $0.9 \times 0.1 = 0.09$ as the probability of a false positive.

3. True negatives: The patient does not have the disease, and the test correctly detects this fact. $9/10$ of the patients have no disease, and $9/10$ of the time the test successfully detects this, so the probability of a true negative is $0.9 \times 0.9 = 0.81$.

4. False negatives: The patient does have the disease, but the test incorrectly returns a negative result. $1/10$ of the patients have the disease, but the test fails to detect this 2 times in 100. Therefore, the probability of a false negative is $0.1 \times 0.02 = 0.002$.

To find out how likely it is that you really have the disease if you have a positive test, we need to consider the ratio between the probability of a true positive and probability of any kind of positive. In the formula below, the numerator is the probability of getting a true positive and the denominator is the probability of getting either a true positive or a false positive. The result is the probability of having the disease, given that you got a positive test, which is what we want.

$$P(\text{disease}|\text{test positive}) = \frac{0.1 \times 0.98}{(0.1 \times 0.98) + (0.9 \times 0.1)} = 0.5213 \quad (5.4)$$

The probabilities of false negatives and true negatives are not needed for this calculation, because we know that the test came out positive. They would be needed if you wanted to calculate the probability of having the disease after a *negative* test.

If this problem was new to you, and you used your intuition when we first asked the question, it is not at all unusual to be surprised by the estimate of 52 percent as the probability of having the disease given a positive test! This is because there is *cognitive bias* called *base rate neglect*, which tends to make human beings ignore the effect of the base rate and focus far more on the connection between the test and the disease. This leads us, almost without noticing it, to assume that about 50 percent of the people to whom the test is administered have the disease and the other 50 percent do not. If you do the calculation again, this time under the assumption that the base rates are equal, you will get:

$$P(\text{disease}|\text{test positive}) = \frac{0.5 \times 0.98}{(0.5 \times 0.98) + (0.5 \times 0.1)} = 0.9074 \quad (5.5)$$

which will lead you to believe that nearly 91 percent of the people with a positive test are going to really have the disease. But, even knowing this, it is not easy to adjust your feelings about risk to match what you know to be true about the situation.

5.4.1 Payoffs and priorities

Of course, it is not enough to know how well the test works and how common the disease is. We also need to use our humanistic critical thinking skills to assess how we will act on this information, and how those actions serve our ethics and priorities.

We illustrate with a simplified version of the calculations that a real doctor would need to do. To keep things gentle, we will say that the disease is always curable and nobody ever dies of it. However, there are two different treatments: Treatment A is cheap, costing the hospital \$10, but treatment B is expensive, and would cost the hospital \$1000. Imagine that the patient pays nothing, and the cost is all on the hospital. Treatment B will work any time, but treatment A works only in the early stages of the disease. The point of the test is to find people who should get treatment A now. The hospital's policy is to apply treatment A whenever the test comes back positive. It costs the hospital an unnecessary \$10 whenever there is a false positive, and it also causes unnecessary anxiety to the patient. We say that *payoff* for a false positive is −\$10. The payoff for a true positive is also −\$10, because the hospital pays for the treatment in that situation too.

Table 5.5: The payoffs for the four outcomes.

	Has disease	No disease
Test positive	−\$10	−\$10
Test negative	−\$1000	\$0

But if the test misses a patient who does have the disease, that person will eventually come back in and require treatment B, which is much more expensive. So, the payoff for a false negative is −\$1000. The payoff for a true negative is \$0, because no treatment is needed. In a real hospital situation, life would be more complicated, because there would be another choice to be made before this all happened: The doctors would have to consider the cost of the test itself. They might decide that some people are so unlikely to have the disease that it isn't even worth running the test.

5.4.2 Back to text

At this point, you are probably wondering whether this book has been taken over by medical researchers. Not exactly, because the ideas we have used so far apply to text classification, too. In spam detection, high specificity means that few of the real emails will be classified as spam. Similarly, high sensitivity means that few true spam emails will be missed.

If you are using this book in a class, at some point the instructor is likely to ask you to spend five minutes discussing spam with your neighbor. Here are some questions to ponder about how we map quantitative metrics such as base rates, sensitivity, and specificity onto our qualitative, humanistic priorities.

- Which do you find more annoying in the context of spam filtering – false positives or false negatives? In practice, what are the consequences of false positive or a false negative?

- Would you be prepared to accept a few extra false negatives for the sake of a reduction in false positives? (This is the same question that we had in the medical setting, but this time human suffering is kept to a low level.)

- Suppose that your email address is somehow leaked to a bunch of spammers in a data breach. Now you get ten times as much spam, but the number of real emails that you get is unchanged. Do you still want the same balance between false positives and false negatives? (This is a direct application of the ideas about base rates above.)

5.5 Examples of classifiers

So far, we have introduced the inputs (documents, featurized into vectors) and outputs (labels) in a classification model, as well as how to evaluate its success in light of our priorities. Now we explore how the model actually works on the inside – how it "learns" to map features to labels.

5.5.1 The naive Bayes classifier

One simple and effective algorithm is known as the *naive Bayes* classifier. We'll start by explaining the idea and then justify the math.

When we use the naive Bayes classifier to classify documents, we run a competition between the hypothesis that the document is a spam, and the alternative hypothesis that it is not. This is expressed in math by doing a probability calculation for each of the two hypotheses. Whichever hypothesis is more probable, that label is assigned to the document.

In order to make the example manageable, we are going to pretend that there are just a few words for which we have collected statistics as in Table 5.6. In reality, there would be many more. We have imagined an email user (we'll call this user Sandy) whose typical email conversations include recreational chat about horses, unicorns, and similar creatures, but who also gets some of the usual kind of spam. Sandy does not want genuine messages from friends (including particular friends Alice, Seth, and Emily) to be filtered out. Messages that mention horses are usually good, but some of the ones mentioning stallions (used in sexualized spam) are suspect.

Table 5.6: Word counts from spam and ham among Sandy's emails.

	Spam	Ham
cash	200	3
Alice	1	50
Seth	2	34
Emily	2	25
Viagra	20	0
credit	12	2
unicorn	0	5
cookie	1	5
hippogriff	0	18
pony	9	50
stallion	3	8
Total	250	200

The simplest strategy is to pretend that we are dealing with a completely unstructured collection of words – a "bag of words" as introduced above. This "naive" representation is chosen because it simplifies the math, even though it ignores important structure in language.

Imagine that we cut up a document and put the words in a bag. The bag might be spam, or it might not. Now, we draw the words out of a bag one at a time. Each time we see a word, we ask whether that word is more likely to have come out of a spam bag, or more likely to have come out of a genuine email (ham, non-spam) bag. We can turn this idea into math using Table 5.6 and some simple reasoning.

For concreteness, imagine that the word that came out of the bag was *Emily*. We're also going to temporarily pretend that words in the table are the only ones that exist. We have seen this word 2 times in spam, out of a total of 250 spam words overall. This means that we can reasonably estimate that we are likely, on average, to see *Emily* 2 times in 250 (one time in 125; 0.8 percent of the time) if the document that we put in the bag was spam. We have seen the same word 25 times in Sandy's real messages, out of a total of 200 non-spam words overall. So, we can guess that we are likely to see the word *Emily* 25 times in 200 (one time in eight; 12.5 percent) if the document is not spam. Since 12.5 percent is much bigger than 0.8 percent, we decide that given this single word, the document in the bag is much more likely to be ham than spam. We can keep track of this by recording the *odds ratio* for ham to spam as 12.5/0.8, or nearly 16. This is much greater than 1, which means we think the document is ham.

Suppose that the next word is *credit*. The counts for this are 12 in 250 for spam, 2 in 200 for ham The odds ratio for this word is 2/200 against 12/250, or about 0.208. This is less than 1, so we think, on the basis of this word alone, that the document in the bag is probably spam.

To combine the evidence, we multiply the ratios $16 \times 0.208 = 3.33$, and decide, because the combined ratio is greater than 1, that the two words together indicate a genuine email, not spam. We carry on in the same way, calculating a ratio for each new word as it comes out of the bag, and multiplying it into the combined ratio. Once we have put all this evidence in place, we can make an overall decision about the document. If the final value of the combined ham-to-spam odds ratio is greater than 1, we claim that the document is genuine (ham) email; otherwise, we rate it as spam.

Under the Hood 8: Naive Bayes

Why does the naive Bayes algorithm make sense, and why is it called naive Bayes in the first place? Naive Bayes is based on the ideas of an eighteenth century British scientist called Thomas Bayes. Bayes was a Presbyterian minister and a member of the Royal Society, which is one of the first scientific organizations ever founded. His major contribution to science was a posthumous paper that laid out the key concepts of a probabilistic approach to reasoning about uncertain evidence. Here is the essence of his reasoning, as applied to spam filtering.

The leading mathematical idea of Bayes' approach is a decomposition of the reasoning process into two components. The first component is a so-called *prior probability*, also known as the *base rate* that we discussed above. This reflects what you assume about the situation before you have collected detailed evidence.

In spam filtering, you can safely assume that most documents in a typical mailbox are spam. So, you can set the prior probability of spam to a high value.

The idea of a prior probability works in more complicated situations, too. In spam filtering, there are only two alternatives – either the document is spam or it is not.

The second component of the reasoning process is called a *likelihood*. For spam, this component reflects your beliefs about the following questions:

- Suppose that the document that we have *is* spam: Are we surprised to see the particular words that are in the document, or not? We will translate this idea into math shortly.

- Suppose it *is not* spam: Are we now surprised to see the words that are in the documents? Again, we will convert this into math and show how to run the competition between spam and ham in a moment.

Here is the essence of Bayes' reasoning, as applied to spam filtering:

- We are interested in looking at a document D, which may or may not be spam. We could make a decision if we knew the two probabilities $P(\text{spam}|D)$ and $P(\text{ham}|D)$. Read these formulas as "probability of spam given D" and "probability of ham given D".
- If the spam probability is bigger than the ham probability, we will be right more often than not by guessing that the document is spam.
- We really want to calculate $P(\text{spam}|D)$ and $P(\text{ham}|D)$ – the probability that the document is spam, given the words therein; and the probability that it is ham, given the words therein. But we have to work backwards to get these quantities.
- To work backwards, we use $P(D|\text{spam})$ (the probability that the words in document happen if it is spam), rather than $P(\text{spam}|D)$ (the probability that the document is spam if we see those words). We want the second one, but so far we only know how to calculate the first one. Fortunately, *Bayes' theorem* allows us to get the probability that we want by doing a little algebra. For spam documents it states that:

$$P(\text{spam}|D) = \frac{P(D|\text{spam})P(\text{spam})}{P(D)}$$

- We can also use Bayes' theorem on the non-spam documents, giving:

$$P(\text{ham}|D) = \frac{P(D|\text{ham})P(\text{ham})}{P(D)}$$

- If we take the ratio of these probabilities, $P(D)$ cancels, giving:

$$\frac{P(\text{spam}|D)}{P(\text{ham}|D)} = \frac{P(\text{spam})P(D|\text{spam})}{P(\text{ham})P(D|\text{ham})}$$

- This last expression says that our competition between ham and spam can be run using the priors $P(\text{ham})$ and $P(\text{spam})$ along with the likelihoods $P(D|\text{ham})$ and $P(D|\text{spam})$. Nothing else is needed.

We can estimate a value for the ratio $P(\text{spam})/P(\text{ham})$ by remembering that spam is typically much more common than ham. If you feel that 95 percent of the mail you get is spam, you could estimate the ratio as $0.95/0.05 = 19$.

Now we have $P(\text{spam})/P(\text{ham})$; but we still need $P(D|\text{ham})$ and $P(D|\text{spam})$. In a spam filter, we compute these likelihoods by exploring what our classifier has learned about which features (words) tend to occur with which labels (ham, spam).

In the naive Bayes classifier, to keep things simple, we imagine that the words in the document are being produced by a very simple random process, based on the "bag-of-words" assumption introduced earlier. We do not really believe this very simplistic assumption, but it is worth pretending that we do, because the calculations are simpler and the results of these calculations are useful. In spam filtering, we assign a value to the probability that a spam email will contain the word *credit*, and another value, presumably lower, to the probability that a non-spam email will contain the same word. We do this for every feature that we care about. Usually, we do this for most of the words in the document, but ignore the very common *stop words* like *the* and *and*, because we do not think that these words are going to be helpful. We do not have to stick to words alone: We can also assign a probability for the hypothesis that a spam email will contain images, certain types of hyperlinks, brightly-colored or all-capitalized text, or be sent from an email account that the user has never contacted before, and we can assign a corresponding probability that a non-spam document will have this feature.

The final step in the naive Bayes process is to combine all the feature probabilities. We assume that each feature is chosen independently and that the relevant probabilities are $P(\text{feature}|\text{spam})$ and $P(\text{feature}|\text{ham})$. Under that assumption, the probability of the document is the product of the probabilities of a series of independent events $f_1, f_2, \ldots, f_n$, one for each feature, and the ratio we need for our decision can be rewritten as:

$$\frac{P(\text{spam}|D)}{P(\text{ham}|D)} = \frac{P(\text{spam}) \prod_f P(f|\text{spam})}{P(\text{ham}) \prod_f P(f|\text{ham})}$$

Here, the symbol $\prod_f$ means "product over all features f". This tells you to multiply together the probabilities for each of the individual features, one time (in the numerator) for spam, one time (in the denominator) for ham. (If you recall your algebra classes, you might remember the corresponding $\sum_i$ notation for sums. $\prod_i$ is just the same as this, but for products.)

The calculation for this ratio corresponds to the informal account given earlier in this chapter. In that account, we simplified by not bothering with the prior, and just started off with the features. You could re-do the calculation by starting off with an odds ratio of 19:1 in favor of spam, then multiplying in the new evidence as each word arrives. Usually there will be plenty of evidence from the words, and the choice of prior will hardly affect the decision, but sometimes, especially for messages that have only a few words in them, the estimate of the prior will make a difference.

Relating these calculations back to the idea of training and test data, we would use the training data to gather statistics about the relative frequency of spam versus ham (the prior probability), as well as how frequently various words occur in spam versus ham (allowing us to compute the likelihood that a given word was drawn from a spam document versus a ham document). We would use these training data to build our model. Then we would evaluate how well the model does on the test data. If it does well, then it has learned some generalizable information about how to distinguish ham from spam.

5.5.2 The perceptron

The naive Bayes classifier compares two different possibilities, that the email is spam versus ham, and computes which one is more likely based on the words observed in the email. As an alternative to naive Bayes, we could also use a *perceptron*, which is based on the idea of *error-driven learning*. The perceptron maintains a collection of *weights*, where each weight links a feature with an *outcome* (a class label). The perceptron learns from experience by trying to predict outcomes, then adjusting the weights when it makes a wrong prediction. Initially, the weights are uninformative and the perceptron is just guessing, but over time the perceptron builds up an ability to associate features with outcomes in a useful way.

The perceptron (see Figure 5.1) is a network with two layers.

The *input layer* has one node for each possible input feature. In our running example of Sandy's email, there would be one node for each of *cash*, *Alice*, *hip-*

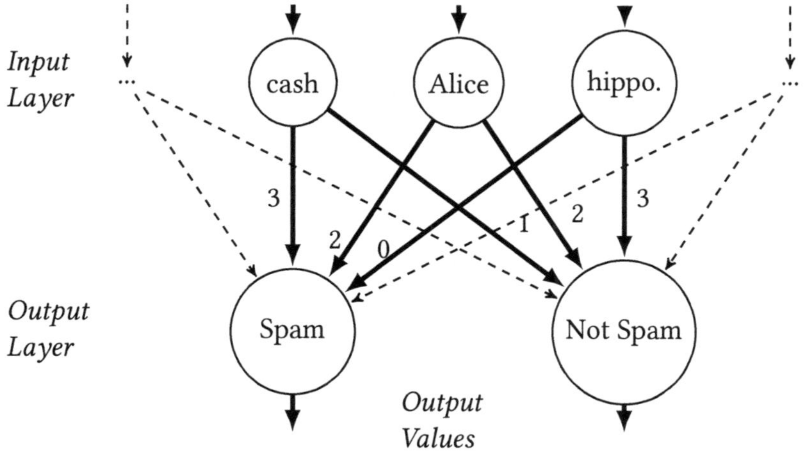

Figure 5.1: The Perceptron.

pogriff and so on. This would be unwieldy to draw in full, so we content ourself with three nodes in the diagram. The *output layer* contains one node for each possible outcome (in the case of Sandy's email, one each for *spam* and *not spam*, exactly as in the diagram). The edges that link the input and output layer are associated with weights. In order to do prediction, the perceptron reads a document, and notes which words are present. We turn the nodes that correspond to these words on, and turn the others off. The role of the weights is to decide how strongly to transmit the activity of the active nodes to the output layer. Suppose that exactly three nodes (*cash, Alice, hippogriff*) were active in Sandy's perceptron, and the weights linking these words to *spam* and *not spam* are as in Table 5.7.

Table 5.7: Weights for a perceptron.

Word	Spam	Not Spam
cash	3	1
Alice	2	2
hippogriff	0	3

Under this supposition, the total activity of the *spam* output node would be $3 + 2 + 0 = 5$ and that of *not spam* would be $1 + 2 + 3 = 6$, so *not spam* would win.

If this prediction is right, Sandy's perceptron can stay as it is, but if the email is actually spam, then the weights need to change.

Imagine that we need to change the weights because the email was indeed actually spam. The perceptron algorithm adjusts all the relevant weights a little bit, in such a way as to move the result closer to a correct prediction. So it would increase the weight of *cash* (and each of the other two words) as a predictor for *spam*, and downweight it as a predictor for *not spam*. A possible result (if "a little bit" is taken as 0.01 for the sake of demonstration) is sketched in Table 5.8.

Table 5.8: Adapted weights for a perceptron.

Word	Spam	Not Spam
cash	3.01	0.99
Alice	2.01	1.99
hippogriff	0.01	2.99

This weight change is not enough to change the prediction, but it does move the result in the right direction (*not spam* still wins, but not by so much). To train the perceptron, we go through the training corpus, presenting each example to the current version of the perceptron, and adapting weights whenever we make a mistake. When we get to the end of the training corpus, we start again at the beginning. Each round of this process is called an *epoch*. After a sufficient number of epochs, the weights will change enough that some of the predictions will flip. Gradually, the mistakes tend to go away (not completely, but to a reasonable extent). This is a result of the feedback mechanism under which features that contribute to wrong predictions get their weights changed. There is a mathematical proof that the perceptron will give perfect performance on the training set if that set has the mathematical property of being *linearly separable*. In two dimensions (with two features), the idea of linear separability is that a dataset is linearly separable if it is possible to draw a straight line that has all the positive examples on one side of the line and all the negative examples on the other.

In three dimensions, the line turns into a plane, and in four or more dimensions it turns into a mathematical object called a hyperplane. But the idea is always that all the positive examples are on one side and all the negative examples are on the other. In Figure 5.2, positive examples are represented by hollow circles and negative examples are represented by filled circles. The diagonal line is a nearly perfect linear separator, as one positive example is on the wrong side of the boundary and the rest are correctly separated. For this dataset, this is the best that *any* linear separator can do.

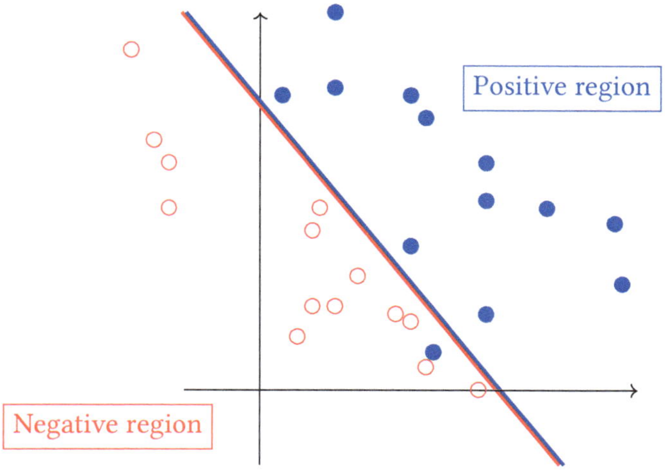

Figure 5.2: Linear separability.

In practice, as well as in the example shown in Figure 5.2, perfect performance is rare, because real world problems are usually not linearly separable, so some misclassifications remain, and training is stopped when the number of remaining mistakes has stayed stable for long enough. When this happens, we are probably doing as well as is possible on the training set, but does not give us certainty about how well we will do on an unseen test set. If the test set and the training set are similar enough, a perceptron that does well on the training set will also do well on the test set. Unfortunately, we are not completely sure how similar the test set will be, so there is an element of uncertainty in our guesses about how well we will do.

The perceptron is an algorithm for training a *linear model*. The technical details of how linear models work would take us too far afield, but the discussion of linear separability above is part of the story. The final weights can be understood as saying something about the importance of each piece of evidence in a combined solution to the classification problem. When there are a large number of potentially useful features in a classification problem, researchers have discovered that linear models often work well. The perceptron algorithm is not the only way of training linear models, or necessarily the best, but it is a good starting point for exploration.

5.5.3 Modern document classification techniques

The perceptron uses error-driven learning: The model reads in the training data (featurized as a vector), sends it through a series of nodes associated with weights, outputs a prediction (spam or ham), and checks whether the prediction was correct. If the prediction is wrong, the weights of each node are updated to move the predictions in the direction of the correct answer.

The same basic idea underlies many more sophisticated methods which have transformed language technology in recent years. In *deep learning*, we can add intermediate layers of nodes in between the input layer and the output layer of the perceptron, to create a "deeper" *multi-layer network*. Such additional layers allow for more complex calculations about how different words interact with each other; for example, a multi-layer network could capture the idea that the words *pain* and *medicine* might be innocuous individually, but indicative of spam when they co-occur.

Such models are called *neural networks*, because the network of nodes takes inspiration from the way that firing neurons in the human brain work together to create complex behavior, and because neural networks evoke the brain's capacity for learning and abstraction.

Another way to improve our model is to use a more elaborate representation of the input features. If we represent a document as just a bag of words, then the words *pills* and *medicine* have nothing in common with each other; they are each associated with a different column of a term-by-document matrix. But we are obviously missing a key insight here – *pills* and *medicine* have somewhat similar meanings. How do we know? They are not strictly synonyms, but they can be used in similar contexts – *take some pills, take some medicine*; *pain pills, pain medicine*. We saw in Chapter 4 that we can represent words as vectors such that words occurring in similar contexts, such as *pills* and *medicine*, have similar vectors.

In fact, *pills* and *medicine* have similar meanings and co-occurrence patterns not just in spam/ham emails, but also in English text as a whole. So, rather than just capturing what words pattern similarly within our specific dataset, we might want to use *pre-trained* word embeddings that were built on a large amount of general-purpose English text (for example, Wikipedia), and feed that information into our model alongside a small set of labeled spam and ham emails. That way, our model has access to a lot of general information about English in addition to specific information about spam and ham. This strategy is called *transfer learning*: Our model is given some useful general information, such as the fact that *pills* and *medicine* have similar meanings, and transfers it to the specific task of spam detection.

In 2018, the idea of pre-training and transfer learning was taken to a new extreme when a team at Google (led by Jacob Devlin) released a model known as *BERT* (Devlin et al. 2019). Rather than just capturing information about which words are similar to each other, BERT was designed to represent a massive quantity of information about English-language text, which can be transferred to a variety of specific tasks, including text classification.

BERT is a neural network that is originally trained to do two specific tasks, (i) masked word prediction and (ii) next sentence prediction, using a huge amount of data, such as the whole of English-language Wikipedia. In *masked word prediction*, the researchers randomly blanked out 15 percent of the words in the text (illustrating here with a sentence from the English Wikipedia page on lions), and trained the model to choose the right word to fill in the blank. In other words, in the pre-training phase, the model makes a prediction, then checks to see if the prediction matched the original Wikipedia text, and then updates its weights to do better next time, until it gets very good at filling in the blanks of sentences.

(6) One of the most — recognised animal symbols in human culture, the lion has — extensively — in sculptures and paintings, on national —, and in contemporary — and literature.

How would you fill in these blanks? More importantly, what knowledge do you draw on to make an educated guess? (The missing words are *widely, been, depicted, flags,* and *films.*)

You probably considered the words immediately to the left and right of the blank, but also other words in the sentence, its structure, and its overall meaning. To fill in the word *depicted*, you may have considered that the syntactic context requires a past participle, and that depictions are related to symbols and paintings. We already saw in Chapter 3 that such fill-in-the-blank exercises are also used to test the knowledge of human language learners. By learning to fill in the blanks correctly, the idea is that BERT approximates that same knowledge.

In *next sentence prediction*, the researchers randomly paired some sentences with the sentence that actually comes next in the text, and paired other sentences with a randomly chosen sentence from elsewhere in the data (again illustrating with Wikipedia text). The model was trained to decide whether a given pair of sentences indeed occur next to each other or not. In a sense, this is a text classification task – the model is given a two-sentence text and classifies it as either cohesive or disjointed.

(7) Typically, the lion inhabits grasslands and savannas, but is absent in dense forests. // It is usually more diurnal than other big cats, but when persecuted it adapts to being active at night and at twilight.

(8) Typically, the lion inhabits grasslands and savannas, but is absent in dense forests. // Despite the name, shellfish are not actually fish, but are simply water-dwelling animals.

How would you decide which sentences match and which do not? What knowledge do you use? (The sentences about lions indeed occur next to each other in Wikipedia; the sentence about shellfish is from a different page.) You probably thought about how the pronoun *it* could refer back to the singular noun *lion*; how *cats* are related to lions, how the daily habits of an animal might be described in the same paragraph as its habitat, and how shellfish, fish, and water are not particularly related to the lions, savannas, and forests discussed in the prior sentence. By learning to decide which sentences match, the idea is that BERT approximates that same knowledge.

Stepping back, why would researchers take the trouble to train a network to fill in blanks and to decide whether two sentences go next to each other? These tasks are not particularly useful in a commercial context!

One major advantage of these tasks is that the labels required for training – the missing words and the contiguous sentences – are already provided by the text itself, unlike human labels for ham and spam, so it is easy to train BERT on a massive amount of text. The other major advantage is that these tasks require BERT to "learn" a great deal of rich information about English text, both at the word level and the sentence level. For example, BERT will learn that *pills* and *medicine* are similar because they are both often good candidates to fill in the same missing word in a sentence. Moreover, masked word prediction leads BERT to represent not just the overall distribution of a word type such as *pills*, but the context of each word token – the fact that *pills* means something different in a sentence like *This sweater pills in the wash* versus *Take these pills for your headache*. Each token of *pills* receives a different vector representation.

Even if masked word prediction and next sentence classification are not particularly useful on their own, the idea is that they serve as a powerful pre-training regimen. Instead of just importing pre-trained word embeddings into a spam-detection model, the idea is that we can read in the entire BERT network, pre-trained on masked word prediction and next sentence prediction, and then add a few layers on top of it which we train on labeled spam/ham data to do spam detection (known as *fine-tuning* BERT's pre-trained knowledge for this specific task). This way, the model will not only have access to a small set of spam/ham data, but is also able to transfer a massive amount of general information about English. The use of such general information is known as *transfer learning*.

To use a sports analogy, imagine that you want to train, as efficiently as possible, to compete at many different speed sports. (BERT is trained, as efficiently as possible, to compete at many different language-related tasks). You decide to focus on push-ups and squat jumps. (BERT focuses on masked word prediction and next sentence prediction.) These exercises are easy to do anywhere, requiring no specialized equipment (for BERT, these tasks require no specialized labels). They are also very challenging exercises that work out your entire body, your muscles and your cardiovascular system, explosiveness and endurance (for BERT, these tasks require knowledge about the structure, meaning, and statistical tendencies of English text). You do an enormous number of push-ups and squat jumps, several hours a day for months (BERT trains on masked word prediction and next sentence prediction on an enormous amount of data.) Once you have trained to be very good at push-ups and squat jumps, you will still need specialized practice to compete at sports such as running, swimming, or rowing (BERT still requires some fine-tuning to do spam detection using labeled spam/ham data.) But the athleticism developed from push-ups and squat jumps is highly transferable, and this training regimen has made you a powerful, versatile athlete well-prepared to succeed at many different sports. (The information gleaned from masked word prediction and next sentence prediction is highly transferable, and BERT's training regimen has made it a powerful, versatile representation of language well-prepared to succeed at many different tasks.)

Using the power of transfer learning, BERT and its descendants form the basis of modern document classification, and in many tasks such models are stunningly accurate.

5.5.4 Which classifier to use?

We have toured many different techniques for classifying documents, walking through the simple examples of naive Bayes and the Perceptron, and then sketching the intuition used in the elaborate models of today. With so many options, which one should you use?

Coming back to our medical discussion of payoffs and priorities, it depends on what you are trying to do. If your goal is to get the best performance, and if you have time and programming skills, you may want to use a model such as BERT that leverages transfer learning. If you are intellectually curious about which specific words are most associated with which labels, you may want to use naive Bayes, which can show you the spam:ham odds ratio associated with a particular word; thanks to its simplicity, naive Bayes is more *interpretable* than more elaborate techniques. You may also want to try out a simple model and see how well it does as a baseline, and then decide if you need something more complex.

To get started on a practical level, you might use the Pandas library in Python to format your data as a matrix (expect to spend some time on such formatting!), and Google's TensorFlow package in Python to try out different machine learning techniques. If you search the web, there are lots of resources and sample code notebooks to help you get started.

5.6 Some other applications of machine learning

Stepping back, machine learning is a remarkably powerful idea with important applications far beyond text classification. Classification – mapping a vector of features to a label, chosen from a finite set of possible labels – is also used in computer vision, where we can represent an image as a vector of pixels and learn how to label it as a cat or a dog, or perhaps learn to map an image of a handwritten digit to the number (0, 1, 2, 3, 4, 5, 6, 7, 8, or 9) that it represents. We can also represent a credit card transaction as a vector of features (the time of day, the type of store, the location, the price, information about the cardholder's usual habits) and learn to label it as fraudulent or legitimate. And so on.

As we mentioned above, classification is an example of *supervised learning*, because we give the computer some "right answers" (correctly labeled spam/ham emails) and train it to generalize those labels to new data. Apart from classification, the other main type of supervised learning is *regression*; there, instead of a label, our goal is to predict a continuous numerical value. To use a language example, we could train a model to read an essay and give it a score out of 100. Here, too, the model learns to generalize from "right answers", but these would take the form of featurized essays that have already been correctly scored. (Before we turn this model loose on real student work, we would want to make sure that it was not reproducing some sort of bias that could give unfairly low scores to certain students!) We could also represent a house as a vector of features (its location, square footage, year it was built, number of bathrooms) and learn to predict its price. And so on.

In contrast, *unsupervised learning* is used when we do not give the model any "right answers" – because we do not have the resources to collect labels, or because we do not even know what such labels would be. We saw an example of unsupervised learning in Chapter 4 in the context of topic modeling: A topic modeling algorithm is not given any labels to generalize, but is instead designed to identify meaningful groups of words and documents (each associated with topics) in a bottom-up manner. Another type of unsupervised learning is called *clustering*, in which a model is asked to group similar data points together – for example, clustering together documents that are similar to one another according to some sort of vector representation of the words used therein. (Outside of text, we could also cluster together similar images, similar houses, and so on, as long as these are represented as vectors.) With no need for expensive labels, clustering is useful for exploring a large dataset that you do not have time to read. The model does not give names to the clusters (although a human reader may try to), and the main disadvantage is that the clusters may not be intuitive; perhaps it would put some social emails into a cluster dominated by work emails, if the social emails happen to mention calendar dates.

We hope that this brief overview has offered a framework to understand the power of machine learning, which will come up again in this book and perhaps in your life more broadly.

5.7 Sentiment analysis

With this background, we can come back to another key application of text classification – classifying texts by their emotional valence, also known as *sentiment analysis*.

On websites such as IMDB (Internet Movie DataBase) and Amazon, people can write a review of a movie or product, and annotate it with a star rating: 5/5 or 10/10 stars if they love it, 0 stars if they hate it – helpfully providing labels for those of us interested in sentiment analysis! Drawing on our discussion of machine learning, we could train a regression model to predict a review's star rating out of 10, or train a classifier to assign a label of positive or negative (or perhaps positive, negative, neutral).

Here are two IMDB reviews for *Parasite* (2019), the first Korean film to win Best Picture at the Academy Awards. Without knowing the star rating, what clues do you use to figure out whether each review is positive or negative?

(9) The most original film of 2019 and it is wickedly funny and darkly disturbing all at the same time. Class warfare at its best.

(10) I truly don't know what I missed but this was just not my cup of tea (or my mom's) and it felt unnecessarily gruesome and strange rather than masterful and sharp. Instead of awaiting the next moment with excitement and suspense, I found myself cringing at the actors' performances as they weren't believable and was confused at how poorly-written the dialogue was.

The first review is positive (10/10 stars), and the second review is negative (1/10). The positive review uses positive words – *original, funny, best* – along with the slightly negative word *disturbing*; it also uses superlatives (*most, best*) and intensifiers (*wickedly, darkly*). The negative review uses some negative words – *strange, cringing, poorly-written.* It also uses some positive words (*masterful, sharp, excitement, suspense, believable*), but some of them are negated by *instead of* and *weren't.* In fact, as shown by Potts (2010) and discussed in Chapter 4, negation itself (*don't, not, unnecessarily, weren't*) is common in negative reviews as a whole, which is intriguing because you might have expected negation to have a purely logical meaning rather than an emotional one.

Just as with spam detection, we can feed labeled positive/negative reviews into a classifier (naive Bayes, the Perceptron, or a fancy classifier using transfer learning) and train it to classify the sentiment of future reviews. The classifier will probably be more accurate if it "knows" that most of the positive words in the negative review are semantically negated. One quick-and-dirty technique (Das & Chen 2007) is to prepend *NOT* to every word that falls between negation and the end of a sentence or clause – *they weren't NOTbelievable* – before making a bag-of-words. This way, *believable* and *NOTbelievable* count as two different words, one of which probably predominates in positive reviews, the other in negative ones. On reviews like the two we just read, a classifier should be quite accurate.

In addition to measuring the accuracy of our classifier, it is also worthwhile to examine the documents that it classifies incorrectly (*error analysis*). Such hard-to-classify documents may illuminate interesting subtleties in the data, and help us understand what the classifier "knows" and doesn't "know".

For example, we tried one classifier that was correct about the positive and negative reviews discussed above, but still mis-classified as positive a review from the legendary film critic Roger Ebert which is actually humorously negative:

(11) The director [of the 2004 film *Catwoman*], whose name is Pitof, was probably issued with two names at birth and would be wise to use the other one on his next project.

To do an error analysis, we can ask ourselves:

- *Why is this review difficult to classify?* Most likely, because it does not use any negative-sentiment words; the negative opinion is inferred by complex hypothetical reasoning. To understand why the *Catwoman* review is negative, we have to understand that the director would want to use another name on his next project because the project with his original name was bad; but that logic is not spelled out in the review itself.

- *What do these errors tell us about the subtleties of our data?* This review shows that language is complicated! Negative sentiment does not just come from negative words, but also arises when sentiment-neutral language is used to describe a state of affairs that we recognize extra-textually as negative.
- *What do these errors tell us about what the classifier "knows" and doesn't "know"?* The classifier performs well on reviews that state their sentiment outright in words, but does not fully capture the complex extra-textual reasoning required to decode Ebert's snark.

Just like spam filtering, sentiment analysis can be used for practical purposes, for example, to track consumers' sentiment towards one's company on social media. But it can also be used for purely intellectual explorations in the areas of digital humanities, computational social science, and corpus linguistics introduced in Chapter 4. Within digital humanities, one could track the sentiment of sentences in a novel from beginning to end or the sentiment of sentences about various characters. In computational social science, one might explore the sentiment of news articles or statements by politicians across the ideological spectrum. In corpus linguistics, one could explore how a word's sentiment (or that of its collocational context) might change over time in historical data, as when the word *mistress* changed from meaning "Mrs." to meaning "a woman in an extramarital affair" (Traugott & Dasher 2001). Returning to the theme of how computers can extract meaning from text, sentiment analysis represents one way that computers can capture emotional meaning.

Under the Hood 9: Benchmarks and leaderboards in NLP

BERT was recognized as a striking advance because it shot to the top of various *leaderboards* tracking performance on various *benchmarks* in natural language processing. These benchmarks represent standardized tests, similar to the Scholastic Aptitude Test (SAT) used for college admission in the United States, designed to test difficult tasks in language understanding. Just as the SAT publicizes practice problems but not the real test that students are graded on, these benchmarks provide training data but evaluate models for their performance on an unseen test set. Moreover, similar to how SAT measures quantitative and verbal skills in the same test, a *combined benchmark* brings together several different tasks into a unified scoring framework. The creators of such benchmarks also gather human annotations from web platforms such as Mechanical Turk to compare for the models' performance.

Such benchmarks are common in computer science; in the field of computer vision, the ImageNet benchmark (Deng et al. 2009) tests models for whether they can correctly assign text labels (*strawberry, dog*) to images. It took about seven years for computers to compete with human performance on the ImageNet data, but recent progress has accelerated. In NLP, it took only one year for the combined GLUE (General Language Understanding Evaluation) benchmark of Wang et al. (2018) to be deemed too easy for models such as BERT, motivating the more difficult SuperGLUE version (Wang et al. 2019).

SuperGLUE brings together eight different tasks meant to test a model's ability to reason about English text. For example, drawn from Dagan et al. (2005), the RTE (Recognizing Textual Entailment) task asks whether (12a) entails (12b) (it does not).

(12) a. Reagan attended a ceremony in Washington to commemorate the landings in Normandy.
b. Washington is located in Normandy. [False; not entailed.]

In fact, there are two different routes to the correct answer in (12). Leveraging knowledge about events, one could reason that a ceremony can take place in a different location from the event it commemorates. Or one could use the geographical fact that Washington is in the United States while Normandy is in France. So perhaps (12) is too easy!

To make more difficult benchmarks, some researchers gather *adversarial* examples, explicitly asking gig workers to try to fool the model. The adversarial example (13) is tricky for a model of textual entailment (Nie et al. 2020) because it requires the model to infer that the *assassination* of a journalist entails *another individual laid waste to* him – requiring complex reasoning about how the abstract event-denoting noun *assassination* can be paraphrased by a sentence using an obscure idiom (*laid waste to*).

(13) a. Roberto Javier Mora García (c. 1962 – 16 March 2004) was a

Mexican journalist and editorial director of *El Mañana* [...] prior to his assassination.

b. Another individual laid waste to Roberto Javier Mora García. [True; entailed.]

Benchmarks are important for measuring progress and challenging the research community to improve. But like any standardized test, they have been criticized. For one, SuperGLUE (General *Language* Understanding Evaluation) only really measures *English* understanding, further cementing English as a hegemonic standard. Moreover, as argued by Ethayarajh & Jurafsky (2020), benchmarks ignore progress on other important dimensions such as fairness (avoiding social biases) or compactness (aiming for smaller, more energy-efficient models). They don't necessarily reward the theoretically interesting insights or explanations sought by linguists. Because NLP benchmarks prioritize objective true-or-false questions, they do not extend easily to models offering open-ended language generation. Therefore, each researcher has to decide for themselves how much they prioritize benchmarks versus other definitions of success.

5.8 Consequences

Some challenging text classification tasks are not commercially applicable, but still provide insight into the power and limits of classifiers, and the subtleties of the information conveyed in language. What accuracy would you expect from a classifier that tries to predict whether a comment is sarcastic or serious (perhaps using as labels the */s* symbol that some web writers use to convey sarcasm)? What about a classifier that reads narratives on the Reddit web forum r/AmITheAsshole, where people describe their conduct and ask readers for a moral judgment, and tries to predict whether a person is deemed to be "the asshole" or "not the asshole"? What about a classifier that reads sentences and tries to label them as "grammatical" or "ungrammatical" following the labels used in linguistics textbooks (Warstadt et al. 2019)? By comparing human and computer performance on such tasks, we learn more about the "intelligence" of both humans and computers, as well as the subtleties of these data.

Other text classification tasks pose challenging ethical questions. What if you tried to detect automatically which job candidates should get an interview based on their résumé, training on previously submitted résumés of people who were or were not interviewed? For a company that receives thousands of résumés a day, many tedious hours of human labor could be saved by automating this process. But what if the classifier learns that the word *lacrosse* increases a person's chance of an interview, or that the word *community college* decreases it, when neither of these socio-economic signals actually relates to the job description? Our system could end up reproducing harmful inequalities. (Would a human be any less biased? How could the performance of both human and automated résumé-screeners be made anti-discriminatory?)

Moreover, how does text change when its authors know that it will be run through an automatic classifier? How do spammers adjust spam to slip through spam filters? How do job applicants tailor their résumés to pass automatic screenings? How might such classifiers need to be updated to account for these new strategies?

Armed with the basics of machine learning and its application to document classification, you have a powerful set of tools for understanding the world. But you also have to think critically about linguistic complexity, human priorities, and ethics in deciding how to apply these tools.

Checklist

- Give examples of text classification tasks.
- Brainstorm several business applications of text classification.
- Give examples of other classification tasks beyond the realm of documents.
- Explain specificity, sensitivity, and their relevance for text classification.
- Discuss what constitutes "success" for a classifier, using quantitative notions such as sensitivity and specificity as well as one's qualitative priorities.
- Explain base rates and the base rate fallacy.

- Define over-fitting and its significance for machine learning.
- Explain how naive Bayes classification works.
- Explain how the Perceptron classifier works.
- Sketch the idea of transfer learning.
- Describe the two tasks used to train BERT and explain why they were used.
- Distinguish supervised versus unsupervised learning.
- Analyze which tasks and examples you would predict to be easier or harder for a classifier.

Exercises

1. Expanding beyond consumer technology such as spam filters, think back to digital humanities and computational social science as discussed in Chapter 4. How can classification tools be used in these realms? To help you get started, consider how you might train a classifier to label text for its genre; its sentiment; its author (out of a closed class of authors); or for its author's gender, political party, or native language. How would you find such labels to train your classifier? To what extent do you think that a classifier could learn to predict these labels from the text?
2. Sentiment analysis makes use of user-provided training labels; users annotate their own review with a star indicating its sentiment. What other sorts of user-provided labels are available in online text today? How could they be used?
3. Many advertisements and mass mailings probably make it into your inbox rather than your spam folder. Do you consider these emails

to be spam or ham (or something in between)? How do you think an email system should handle them?

4. a) Table 5.5 gives a calculation of the payoffs associated with each outcome of the medical test in the extended example. Put this together with the population statistics in Table 5.4 to calculate the overall payoffs from: (a) always running the test, and (b) never running the test. Which is the more cost-effective policy for the hospital ?

   b) We carefully set up our example so that everyone was cured and the only effect of your decision is financial, but of course the mathematics also applies to decisions where much more is at stake. Now that you have learned about false positives, true positives, payoffs and the rest, you have the conceptual tools to understand the tradeoffs that are involved in deciding whether a country should have a policy of offering mammography as a general screening tool for breast cancer. We recommend that you find information about this online, read about it, and see what you think. Do not stop after the first article you read. It is a controversial issue, and you will find sensible articles advocating both for and against general screening.

5. You are the owner of a spam filtering service:

   a) Currently, your server gets 2000 spams per hour and only 500 good messages. The filter classifies 95 percent of the spams correctly, and misclassifies the other 5 percent. It classifies 99 percent of the good messages correctly, and misclassifies the other percent. Tabulate the results: How many false positives and how many false negatives do you expect to see each hour? Calculate the precision, sensitivity, and specificity of the spam filter.

   b) You receive word that a criminal gang is planning to double the amount of spam that it sends to your server. There will now be 4000 spam messages per hour instead of 2000. The number of good messages stays unchanged at 500. In your marketing literature, you have quoted the precision, recall, sensitivity and specificity of your spam filter. You assume that the misclassification rates will stay the same (5 percent for spam, 1 percent for good messages). Should you put in a call to the technical writing department warning them that the literature will need to be revised? Why or why not? And if so, what will need to be revised?

6. Continue the calculation from Section 5.5.1. Assume that the next word in the email is *cookie*. Using the frequency statistics from Table 5.6, carry out the next step of the calculation. What is the cumulative ratio for spam/non-spam?

7. Your colleague labels product reviews (*Sturdy and comfortable, this cot folds up and out of sight with minimal effort*) based on the gender of the review's author, mapping the author's self-disclosed name (*Sarah, Ralph*) to census data about the likely gender of people with that name. Your colleague then trains a classifier to label reviews for the gender of the author. The colleague's goal is to label the author gender of anonymous reviews, which could provide demographic marketing data to sellers. What comments would you offer this colleague – about the difficulty of the task, the assumptions underlying it, and the real-world utility of the classifier?

8. Read some posts on Reddit/ AmITheAsshole and discuss what knowledge would be required to correctly label the author as "the asshole" or "not the asshole". Do you think that modern LLMs will succeed at this task? Can you search the literature for recent discussion or try to test this prediction yourself?

9. Try out some web demos of sentiment classifiers – you can find the most up-to-date ones by searching the web for *sentiment analysis demo* – and try to "break" the classifier by giving it difficult examples.

Further reading

The statistical approach to spam filtering was popularised by Paul Graham's "A Plan for Spam".[a] His article, which has aged very well, is an excellent starting point for learning about the technology and sociology of spam.

Pang & Lee (2007) offers a comprehensive introduction to opinion-mining and sentiment analysis.

The discussion of base rate fallacy is based on Bar-Hillel (1980). Cognitive biases are discussed in the literature on psychology and behavioral economics.

On websites such as YouTube, Medium, and GitHub, you can find many excellent tutorials and example code about sentiment analysis, document classification, transfer learning, and BERT.

[a]https://www.paulgraham.com/spam.html, accessed 2024-04-18.

6 Searching

6.1 Introduction

6.1.1 Finding an old friend

One day, you happen to remember a childhood friend of yours, Katie Smith from Denver, Colorado, whom you haven't thought about in years. You were best friends in second grade, before she moved to a different school. What is she up to now? You type *Katie Smith* into a search engine. On the right side of the page, you see a panel about a basketball coach with the same name, linking to her Wikipedia page – but she is a different, more famous Katie Smith. On the left, you see a list of links to web pages, mostly about the basketball coach, and a few other individuals with the same name, but still nothing about your childhood friend.

What is the problem here? You know the name of your friend; you know she is probably on the internet somewhere; so why is it so hard to find what you want?

Unfortunately, Katie Smith has a very common name, so results about your childhood friend are overwhelmed by results about other people with the same name. And anyway, Katie may have changed her name (maybe she got married, maybe she started going by Kathryn as an adult; you haven't seen Katie in a decade, so who knows?)

Although this example may seem trivial, it is genuine, it corresponds to a real information need, and it reveals some of the problems that can arise when we search the internet.

Consider what the options are for finding the information we want:

- Keep querying the search engine: Try further queries such as *Kathryn Smith*, *Katie Smith Colorado*, *Katie Smith Denver*, *Katie Smith* plus the name of your elementary school.

- Leave the search engine to visit a social site with search functionality, such as LinkedIn, Instagram, or Facebook; maybe you'll have some connections in common with her, which could help you find her.

- Call your parents, who were friends with Katie Smith's parents and might know something.

There is no single right answer. If you can find the right search query, maybe the search engine will work; if your online social connections include other people from second grade, then a social site might work.

But to find this information online, you have to know what resources are available, and how to search through them. This chapter provides an overview of how people use computers to retrieve information that they want (*search*, also known as *information retrieval*), to find answers to questions (*question answering*), and to browse for things – music, movies, friends, web posts – that they didn't even know they wanted (*recommendation systems*, also known as *recommender systems*).

6.1.2 Information need

The task of information retrieval begins with an *information need* – the information that the searcher is searching for. An information need is a type of *intent* – something that a user wants. In the case of an information need, the searcher wants to *know* some information, like *What happened to my old friend Katie Smith*? or *When did Mandarin and Cantonese diverge*? Sometimes, they may want information that is not textual, such as images, videos, the score of an ongoing sports game, or directions on a map. Other times, they may intend to *do* something, like set a timer, book a flight, or purchase some shoes. (Or they may want a blend of information and action – they want to know how much a flight to Guatemala costs, while considering whether to buy one.)

Once a user has formulated an intent in their mind, they must translate it into a text *query* to enter into a search engine. The query may reflect the user's intent with more or less clarity. If a user types *Chinese history* as their query, maybe they may want the Chinese translation of the word *history*, or maybe they want to read about the history of China or of Chinese languages. A well-practiced searcher may know how to clearly formulate their query given their intent, but an inexperienced searcher may be frustrated by results of an ambiguous query. (A user-friendly search engine may suggest followup queries to help the user clarify their intent – perhaps based on the search histories of other people who have entered similar queries.)

For many modern search engines, one of the first steps in processing a query is to map it to an *intent* (*intent recognition*, also known as *intent classification*; see Chapter 5 on text classification) – does the searcher want to shop, to look at maps or images, to translate from one language to another, to use a calculator, or to just read text? Then the query can be fed to a system specialized for that type of task. If the searcher wants to *know* something rather than to *do* something, then their intent can be considered an *information need*, fed to a question-answering system or a search engine built for text documents.

(1) a. Information need: Want to read a short, accessible overview of the history of Chinese languages.

b. Possible queries: *Chinese history, Chinese history language, Chinese historical linguistics, Mandarin Cantonese history.*

6.1.3 Evaluating results

A search begins with an information need and ends when the user has succeeded in filling it. How do we measure success?

Of course, we could just ask the user if they are happy, or survey several hundred users in a user-experience study. We could also use implicit behavioral measures of satisfaction, like whether the user clicks on a page and stays there for a while before ending their search session (suggesting that they found what they wanted), or how many people choose to use the search engine (suggesting that they like it). But it is also valuable to have an explicit, quantifiable evaluation metric that can be computed automatically without conducting a new round of user testing each time.

The simplest, most widely used automatic evaluation metrics for information retrieval are *precision* and *recall*. Precision can be defined as *the percentage of the documents returned that are relevant*: For example, imagine that a search engine returns 400 pages for a query, 200 of which are actually relevant to the query (and thus, ideally, to the information need that underlies it). In this case, precision is 50 percent, or 200 out of 400.

$$\text{Precision} = \frac{\text{Relevant documents that are returned}}{\text{All documents that are returned}} \tag{6.2}$$

In contrast, recall can be defined as *the percentage of relevant documents that are returned*: If a search engine returns 200 relevant pages, but there were actually 1000 pages on that topic out there on the web (we missed 800 of them), the recall is 20 percent (200/1000). Note that the numerator (200 – the number of relevant documents that are returned) is the same for both precision and recall.

$$\text{Recall} = \frac{\text{Relevant documents that are returned}}{\text{All relevant documents}} \tag{6.3}$$

But how can we know that there are 1000 pages out there, if we can't find them? Sometimes, information retrieval systems are evaluated on constrained, human-labeled datasets where researchers can be omniscient. One historically important dataset comes from the Text REtrieval Conference (TREC), a series of queries, documents, and human judgments of whether each document is relevant to each query. In this toy context, we can calculate the precision and recall for any search engine that runs over these data. But in real life, it is often impossible to know how many relevant documents are *not* being returned in your search. So, in practice, while recall is a useful concept, it cannot always be calculated with certainty. In contrast, precision can be easily estimated just by looking at the documents that *are* returned.

What would happen if a search engine prioritized *only* precision, and ignored recall? A search engine could achieve perfect precision by returning only one or two pages that are definitely relevant, while leaving out hundreds of other relevant pages. But the user may have wanted to see those pages too.

What would happen if a search engine prioritized *only* recall, and ignored precision? A search engine could achieve perfect recall by returning every single page on the web for every single search: The relevant pages are in there somewhere. The user will be overwhelmed by irrelevant pages in their search for relevant ones.

Thus, a successful search engine must balance both precision and recall. Sometimes, researchers use a combined score known as the *F-measure* to reflect both components at once: The F-measure is defined as $(2 * p * r)/(p + r)$, where p is precision and r is recall. In our example from above, our precision was 50 percent (200 of the 400 returned documents were relevant) and our recall was 20 percent (200 of 1000 total relevant documents were returned), so the F-measure would be $(2 * 0.5 * 0.2)/(0.5 + 0.2)$, or 28.5 percent – indicating that these search results are far from the optimal F-measure of 100 percent.

But the search engine with the best F-measure is not necessarily the best search engine. In reality, users often do not want to look at the 400 documents returned in our imaginary search, nor even at the 200 relevant ones. They usually want to glance at the first display page of ten or so results, and then click on one or two that looks most interesting from a title or snippet that the search engine displays. In this reality, the results also have to be *ranked*, so that the "best" results show up on the first page. How do we decide which results are the best? Perhaps we should recast relevance as a gradient notion rather than a binary one, and give higher rankings to documents that are *most* relevant. Or perhaps we want to give higher rankings to pages that come from better sources – perhaps pages from vetted sources; or perhaps those with more traffic, those that were updated recently, or those that a lot of other pages link to. Perhaps we want to give higher rankings to pages that are most relevant to *this specific user* – pages that they have visited before, or pages that are popular in their location. We come back to this idea of *personalized search* later in the chapter.

However we rank the pages, users care much more about the top page of results than the rest. And on the top results page, precision is much more important than recall. If some of the top-ranked pages are not relevant, the user may become annoyed; however, if some relevant pages are not among the top-ranked pages, the user may not care. To capture these priorities, search engines can also be evaluated using the *precision-at-k* metric: Starting at the top and looking at some number k of results, what is the precision of these results? For $k = 1$, we look at the first, top-ranked result. If it's relevant, then the precision at $k = 1$ is 100 percent. For $k = 2$, we look at the second-ranked result. If it's relevant, the precision at $k = 2$ is 100 percent: Two of the top-two results are relevant. If it's irrelevant, then the precision at $k = 2$ is 50 percent: One of the top-two results is relevant. This metric reflects the fact that precision is more important than recall among the top-ranked results.

6.2 Structured data, knowledge graphs, and ontologies

We begin our tour of information retrieval with *structured data*. For example, the Internet Movie Database (IMDB) is a structured database of the film industry, in which each movie is associated with various *fields* such as title, actors, director, plot summary, and date; and each person is associated with their works, a birth date (perhaps also a death date), and a brief biography.

Structured data are extremely useful. If you want to see a list of all the movies by your favorite director, it is probably most efficient to look at the structured list linked from their IMDB profile (or their filmography listed on Wikipedia) rather than just read free-text webpages containing their name. As another example of structured data, you can find scholarly articles on Google Scholar, which uses a structured representation for authors, dates, papers, and citations, along with the unstructured text of each article. Authors are associated with universities, coauthors, and papers that they wrote; papers are associated with authors, titles, dates, and the papers that they cite and those that cite them.

Outside constrained domains such as IMDB and Google Scholar, web search in general now makes use of structured data in the form of a *knowledge graph* (also known as an *ontology*) – a representation that includes:

- *Named entities* (people such as *Queen Elizabeth II*, countries such as *Guatemala*, companies such as *Apple*, sports teams such as *The Lakers*, books such as *Anna Karenina*).
- Kinds of things, such as those named by nouns (diseases such as *flu*, species such as *dog*, foods such as *potato*).
- Events (such as *the Second World War* and *the 2024 Olympics*).
- Times (years such as *2024*, dates such as *December 1, 1990*, and intervals of time such as *1900-2000*).
- The properties of these entities (people are associated with birthdates, death-dates, and occupations; events are associated with dates as well as key participants; companies are associated with stock prices, CEOs, and the date of their founding; diseases are associated with prevalence and treatments; foods are associated with their macronutrients).
- Relations between entities and events (between a person and their nation of residence; a book and its author; a person and their spouse; a person and the schools they attended; a company and its founder; a country and its continent; a war and its battles).
- And so on.

When you search for *Barack Obama* and see a panel containing his picture, birthdate, height, spouse, schools he attended, and the dates of his presidency, plus a link to his Wikipedia page, you have found him in the search engine's knowledge graph. You also found the basketball coach Katie Smith in the knowledge graph while searching for your friend with the same name. Note, too, that on Google's search engine, the bottom of the knowledge graph panel also offers a list of other related knowledge graph entries that are often searched (perhaps in the same search session) by people who searched for the current entry: For Barack Obama, it suggests other American presidents as well as his wife, Michelle Obama – because the searcher may already be interested in these people, or because they may become interested in them after the search engine recommends them.

The knowledge graph is built in part by hand-creating *templates* of the properties that can be associated with various types of individuals (for example, a person has the property of a birthdate), and in part by using Wikipedia information panels to automatically populate these templates.

Google released their knowledge graph in 2012 with the tagline *things, not strings* – aiming to augment web search with structure rather than free text. The knowledge graph is extremely useful for finding reliable factoids about various well-known entities.

As explained by Peng et al. (2023), it is often difficult to keep the knowledge graph up-to-date, for example when someone dies, when two companies merge, when a disease is renamed, or when the knowledge graph itself is updated with a new category (for example, can e-sports be added to the knowledge graph's sports category without incompatibilities?). If the knowledge graph is to be updated automatically by extracting information from text, it's important not just that the text is deemed reliable but also that the named entities mentioned therein are correctly identified and disambiguated. Does *the Olympics* refer to the recurring event or its instantiation in a specific year? Does *Martin Luther King* refer to the famous civil rights activist, his father who had the same name, or the holiday named after him? Is the abbreviation *MLK* also correctly linked to these referents? Should companies or individuals be allowed to update their own information in the knowledge graph, or would that policy risk polluting the knowledge graph with questionable information? For all these reasons, it requires a lot of human labor to keep the knowledge graph reliable and up-to-date.

You can explore openly available machine-readable knowledge graphs such as *WordNet* (Fellbaum 1998), which reflects subset and superset relations between common nouns, such as the fact that poodles are dogs and dogs are mammals; and *ConceptNet* (Speer et al. 2017), which reflects not just that dogs are mammals but also that dogs bark, have four legs, don't like being left alone, and are kept for companionship. These knowledge grahps illustrate the challenges mentioned above, as when the same word corresponds to multiple entries in the graph: Does *fan* refer to a mechanical cooling device or a human admirer? Both senses are defined in WordNet, but it is not obvious which sense is evoked by a given token of *fan*. As another example, WordNet does not contain the social media sense of the abbreviation *DM* (direct message), showing that it is difficult to keep knowledge graphs up-to-date.

Your friend Katie Smith may not be famous enough to appear in Google's knowledge graph, but she may be in the knowledge graph of a social media site, which associates people with their social connections. Further information about her may also lie within the *unstructured data* consisting of billions of free-text webpages on the internet.

6.3 Question answering

Some information needs have a single correct answer that can ideally be found automatically: *How many centimeters are in an inch? When was Barack Obama born? Where was Barack Obama born?*, and so on. Here, it would be most efficient for the search engine to return an actual answer, rather than some relevant web pages that might contain the answer somewhere – especially if the user is on a mobile phone (where it's hard to read a lot of documents) or if the user is requesting spoken information from a *dialog system* (where the user does not have the patience to listen to entire documents read aloud – see Chapter 8). This task is known as (automatic) *question answering*.

For many such *factoid questions* (*Where was Barack Obama born?*), the answer is already somewhere in the knowledge graph and the task is to match the question to the right part of the graph. For other factoid questions (*How prevalent is diabetes?*), the answer may appear somewhere in a respected webpage such as Wikipedia or the Centers for Disease Control, and the task is to find the most relevant paragraph and extract the correct answer. Such a task falls under the umbrella of (automatic) *reading comprehension* – an automated attempt to "read" a paragraph and answer questions about the information that it contains.

Historically, question-answering systems involved a large number of separate, human-built pieces – classifying the desired answer type (person, date), trying to match the syntax of the question to the syntax of sentences in a relevant paragraph using various matching rules, and so on. IBM's Jeopardy-winning Watson system involved many such pieces. More recently, the complexity of question-answering systems has morphed into the complex representations learned in a bottom-up format (using human-designed architectures, trained on human-curated data) by neural networks, introduced in Chapter 5.

Recall that a neural network is a system trained to predict an output from some inputs. Usually, the input is formatted as a vector or matrix of numbers, and it is passed through a series of layers of nodes, finally ending with an output (usually a number or vector). Along the way, each node does some simple addition and multiplication to turn its input into an output, which it then passes along to the next layer of nodes. For supervised tasks with a correct answer, the network is trained on some data that have already been labeled with correct answers; the data are passed through the network, then the network's actual output is compared to the correct output; and then all of the nodes' calculations are updated in order to do slightly better next time. (The number of nodes and layers in the network, and the way the input is mapped into a vector/matrix, are up to the human researcher to decide). With enough data and training, such networks can "learn" to do very well on a variety of tasks. After the network has been trained on some labeled training data, it can be tested on some test data (also labeled) that it has not seen before, and finally it can be used on unlabeled data more or less similar to what it was trained on.

In the context of question-answering, researchers often use *SQuAD* (the Stanford Question Answering Dataset) created by Rajpurkar et al. (2016). SQuAD is a set of 150,000 passage/question/answer triplets, where the passage is a paragraph from Wikipedia; the question is a factoid question related to the topic of the passage; and the answer is either a string of words contained within the passage, or (for 30 percent of the data) "No Answer" if the question is not actually answered by the passage. The questions and answers were written by gig workers on Amazon's Mechanical Turk.

For example, the following passage about Fresno appears in SQuAD:

> *Passage:* Fresno (FREZ-noh), the county seat of Fresno County, is a city in the U.S. state of California. As of 2015, the city's population was 520,159, making it the fifth-largest city in California, the largest inland city in California and the 34th-largest in the nation. Fresno is in the center of the San Joaquin Valley and is the largest city in the Central Valley, which contains the San Joaquin Valley. It is approximately 220 miles (350 km) northwest of Los Angeles, 170 miles (270 km) south of the state capital, Sacramento, or 185 miles (300 km) south of San Francisco. The name Fresno means "ash tree" in Spanish, and an ash leaf is featured on the city's flag.

Here are some of the questions and answers associated with this passage in SQuAD:

- *Question:* What is featured on the city of Fresno's city flag?
  - *Correct Answer:* (An) ash leaf.
- *Question:* What does Sacramento mean in Spanish?
  - *Correct Answer: No answer.*

Using such a dataset with labeled correct answers, researchers can build a neural network that takes the passage and the question as input, and tries to output the correct answer ("No Answer" or the substring of the passage containing the answer). The most successful such neural networks use a tool known as *attention*

– a layer of the network that is specifically trained to give the highest weight to the words in the query and/or the passage that most strongly predict the right answer. Using attention and other complex techniques, various research teams have performed as well or better than a human at this specific task.

These advances are extremely impressive, and similar techniques are used to answer factoid questions on various search engines. Of course, in the real world, the system may not be given a single relevant passage along with a given query; it may have to find such a passage, in Wikipedia or elsewhere, using the same process that you use yourself when you search for relevant documents online. But some information needs do not have a factoid answer that can be found on Wikipedia or in a knowledge graph (*What happened to my old friend Katie Smith?, Should I quit my job?*, and so on). In these cases, the user may use the search engine to find relevant documents, and then review those documents by hand.

6.4 Search engines for specialist professionals

Today, search engines are used by everyone with an internet connection. But historically, search engines were the domain of specialists, such as librarians, who had access to certain digital collections. Today, some search engines (Google Search, Bing) are designed for general use; some (Google Scholar, used by researchers) are publicly available but designed for the needs of a specific population; and some (Westlaw and LexisNexus, used by attorneys) require a paid subscription and are used only by specialists. Because it is informative to consider how the design of a search engine depends on the intended user and their information needs, our tour stops next at the Westlaw Edge search engine owned by Thomson Reuters.

Westlaw holds a database of court opinions, laws, legal academic articles, briefs filed by the parties in a given case, and other material. The data are *semi-structured*, combining free text documents with metadata about the document type (opinion, brief, statute, etc), the judge, law firm, jurisdiction (federal laws, federal judicial districts, or states), date, citations to and from each document, and information about whether various rulings have been upheld or overturned by higher courts.

A professional in the United States legal system might have an information need such as:

- I want to find and cite (current, not overruled) precedent, within my specific legal jurisdiction, for my preferred interpretation of a statute.

- I'm arguing an immigration case before Judge Chang. How sympathetic is Judge Chang likely to be to my case? What has Judge Chang previously ruled or written on the topic of immigration?
- I'm trying to show that the plaintiff in this case was illegally fired as retaliation for blowing a whistle on wrongdoing within a company. What are the elements of illegal whistle-blower retaliation that have to be demonstrated? What is the statutory definition of illegal whistle-blower retaliation? How have previous opinions applied this definition in cases with similar facts?

These are complex information needs, so the search functionality of Westlaw is equally complex, involving a specialized syntax:

- *JU(Chang) immigration*, restricted to Judge Chang's specific jurisdiction by checking a filter box, yields immigration cases argued before Judge Chang, and opinions that she has written.
- *(whistleblow! "whistle blow!") /p (retaliat! fir!)*, again restricted to a desired jurisdiction by checking a filter box, yields documents containing *whistleblower, whistleblowing, whistleblowers, whistle blower*, and so on (in *whistleblow!*, the exclamation mark ! is a *wildcard*, matching any sequence of letters at the end of a word beginning with *whistleblow*), in the same paragraph (*/p*) as any form of the words *retaliate, retaliation, retaliated* or *fired, firing, fire*. The space acts as a boolean *OR*, so we can match *whistleblow! OR "whistle blow!"*. (The ampersand &, not used in this query, is a boolean *AND*). In contrast, the quotation marks around *"whistle blow!"* ensure that the space between these two words is *not* interpreted as disjunction, instead requiring that an *exact match* (plus any word ending on *blow*) must appear in the relevant documents.

These search queries are opaque to a non-specialist, using many *advanced features*, which a general-use searcher may find intimidating.

The queries take advantage of Westlaw's structured metadata: *JU(Chang)* restricts the search to documents related to judges named Chang; clicking on various checkboxes can filter one's results to specific dates and jurisdictions. In contrast, the words and strings in the queries look for matches with unstructured free text.

The *wildcard* feature (*whistleblow!*) illustrates the idea of *regular expressions* – patterns that can be matched in text strings, such as *the string whistleblow followed by any number of alphabetical characters before a space.* (Please see Under the Hood: 6.4.1 for more detail). Here, the wildcard is used to isolate the *stem* of the words *whistleblower, whistleblowing,* and so on – the part that is consistent across different grammatical contexts. A single stem (*whisteblow-*) may be associated with several different *lemmas* (the form of a word that would appear in a dictionary, such as *whistleblow* and *whistleblower*), and many different grammatically inflected forms (*whistleblowers, whistleblowing,* and so on). Stemming and lemmatizing words is especially important in *morphologically rich* languages, where words are inflected for all sorts of grammatical properties – nouns may be inflected for their gender, number, or their syntactic role in a sentence; verbs may be marked for their tense/aspect, and so on.

Westlaw allows searchers to request combinations of terms based on their proximity to one another: */s* makes sure that the words on either side appear within the same sentence, */p* within the same paragraph, */3* within three words, and so on. *Proximity search* is especially important for long documents such as legal filings, where it's much more meaningful, when searching for documents about retaliation against whistleblowers, to find *whisteblow!* and *retaliat!* in close proximity than to find them pages apart.

Westlaw also illustrates *boolean search* – finding combinations of terms in a document using the logical operators *OR, AND,* and *NOT.* In Westlaw, the space (the default way of conjoining terms) works as *OR*, the ampersand & means *AND*, and the percent sign % means *NOT.* Combined with parentheses, these operators can express quite complex queries – with the risk of typos increasing alongside complexity:

(4) a. fir! & retaliat!
 b. fir! retaliat!
 c. retaliat! & (% fir!)

6.4.1 Boolean search

How are boolean searches carried out? First, basing our discussion on Manning et al. (2008), the search engine crawls through all the documents to build a *term-by-document matrix.* The term-by-document matrix shows which terms (i.e., words) appear in which documents. Leaving the legal domain for simplicity, we can get a sense of what happens by looking at part of a term-by-document matrix for a few 19th-century British novels in Table 6.1 – *Emma* and *Pride and Prejudice*, by Jane Austen; and *Wuthering Heights*, by Emily Brontë. We use words here, but lemmas or stems may also be used (see above). A 1 means that the term appears somewhere in the document (regardless of whether it occurs once or many times), and a 0 means that it appears nowhere. (We could also use the number of times that each word occurs in each document, rather than a binary representation of whether it occurs or not; both strategies are useful.)

Table 6.1: Excerpt from term-by-document matrix for 19th-century British novels.

	Emma	P & P	W. Heights
computer	0	0	0
curtsey	1	1	0
dogs	0	0	1
farmer	1	0	1
ghost	0	0	1
heath	0	0	1
house	1	1	1
love	1	1	1
monster	0	0	1
phone	0	0	0
the	1	1	1
whist	1	1	0

Here, the terms are rows, the documents (novels) are columns. For example, the second row indicates that *curtsey* (an old-fashioned ladies' bow) appears in *Emma* and *Pride and Prejudice* but not in *Wuthering Heights.* If you are a student of 19th-century British literature, you may know that *Emma* and *Pride and Prejudice* are light-hearted romantic stories about aristocrats who *curtsey* and play card games such as *whist* (in *Emma*, one character works as a *farmer*; in *Pride and Prejudice*, all of the main characters are professional aristocrats), while *Wuthering Heights* is a gothic tragedy about isolated rural people who live on a *heath* (a shrub-covered land) with *farmers* and *dogs* and believe in fantastical creatures such as *ghosts.* (All three novels were written before the invention of the *computer* or the *phone*). You may notice that this term-by-document matrix reveals that (the columns representing) Jane Austen's two novels are more similar to one another than to (the column representing) Emily Brontë's *Wuthering Heights.* (We could demonstrate this mathematically by doing some calculations that determine the similarity between two vectors, but you can already see it intuitively). In our discussions of words as vectors in Chapter 4 and documents as vectors in Chapter 5, we already saw that the column (vector) associated with a document reveals its similarity to other documents; the same powerful idea extends to information retrieval.

In building a term-by-document matrix, you might decide to leave out very common *stop words* such as *I*, *the*, and *of* – words that appear in practically every English-language document, and thus might take up a lot of storage space while not distinguishing any one document as relevant. On the other hand, some searches require stop words, such as the band called *The Who*. As information storage gets cheaper every day, modern systems usually keep stop words.

Even if information storage is getting cheaper, our term-by-document matrix is somewhat inefficient in that it is very *sparse*. Most words don't occur in most documents, so most values in the matrix are 0.

But there is another way to structure these data without all the inefficient zeroes, namely what is called an *inverted index* – also known as a *postings list*. Here, each document is associated with a unique ID (*Emma* is Document1, *Pride and Prejudice* is Doc2, *Wuthering Heights* is Doc3), and each term is associated with a (sorted) list of the document IDs where it appears.

computer	→	Doc5, Doc6, Doc8, Doc10, ...
curtsey	→	Doc1, Doc2, Doc10, Doc15, ...
dogs	→	Doc3, Doc6, Doc7, Doc8, ...
farmer	→	Doc1, Doc3, Doc11, Doc12, ...
ghost	→	Doc3, Doc15, Doc18, ...
heath	→	Doc3, Doc200, ...
house	→	Doc1, Doc2, Doc3, Doc5, ...
love	→	Doc1, Doc2, Doc3, Doc7, ...
monster	→	Doc3, Doc18, Doc20, ...
phone	→	Doc5, Doc6, Doc10, Doc11, ...
the	→	Doc1, Doc2, Doc3, Doc4, ...
whist	→	Doc1, Doc2, Doc180, ...

Figure 6.1: Excerpt from inverted index.

This is a very efficient structure: If the query contains the word *farmer*, for example, a single access to the inverted index gives us a list of all the documents that word appears in. For small documents such as novels, you may wonder why we won't just write code to read through the entire text file any time we want to find something in it; but for data as massive as the internet, an index can make searching much faster.

In a boolean search such as *farmer AND love*, we need to combine information from two different lines of the inverted index. This is quite straightforward: Simply take the *intersection* of the two document lists that *farmer* and *love* point to. In this case, the intersection will certainly contain *Emma* (Doc1) and *Wuthering Heights* (Doc3), and probably other documents not shown in Table 6.1.

For even more complex queries, there are steps that can be taken to ensure that query processing is efficient. Consider if someone searches for *farmer AND love AND house*. In this case we have to intersect three lists. We know that the result of intersecting three lists is the same as first intersecting two lists, then intersecting the result with the third list. It is up to us to decide which two lists should be handled first, and which list should be left until last. This choice is not going to affect the final result, but it *can* affect the efficiency of the process of getting to the result. Intersecting lists takes longer the longer the lists are. For example, *love* has a long list of documents, because novels often involve love. If we take another frequent word, such as *house*, the result will be another long list, and it is likely that their intersection is lengthy, too. But *farmer* is less common, so this list is shorter. For efficiency, we can intersect the shortest lists first. This is likely to be effective, because the intersection of two short lists is likely to be short. Thus, internally, the search engine looks at the query words, finds the length of their document lists, and reworks the query to specify the order of operations. In this case, *(farmer AND house) AND love* is more efficient than *farmer AND (house AND love)*.

Strictly speaking, this strategy does not guarantee optimal efficiency, because, for example, it could turn out that the intersection of two lists that are short but very similar will be longer than the intersection of two other lists that are long but very dissimilar. But, in practice, the strategy of doing the shortest lists first is a very good one, and saves a lot of time and effort. It's also meaningful that the documents are sorted in order of their DocID; this way, we don't have to compare every single document on the postings list for *farmer* to every single document on the postings list for *house*, but instead can go through the lists in order, inferring that Doc2 is not in the intersection of *farmer* and *house* because the postings list for *farmer* skips from Doc1 to Doc3.

Of course, the basic methods described so far cannot handle proximity search (*farmer* in the same sentence as *love*, *whistleblower* within three words of *retaliation*) or exact-match for multi-word strings (*"Mr. Weston," "life insurance"*). To keep track of the positions of words in a document, we may want to use a *positional index* instead of just a simple inverted index. An inverted index maps each term to a list of the DocIDs where it appears; a positional index maps a term to the DocIDs where it appears, and further records, for each such DocID, a list of the positions in the document where it appears (perhaps splitting the document at every space, labeling the first string-between-spaces as Position1, and so on).

We can illustrate with three short toy documents, excerpts from the Austen and Brontë novels discussed above:

- Doc1: *It is a truth universally acknowledged, that a single man in possession of a good fortune, must be in want of a wife.*
- Doc2: *Mr. Weston was a man of unexceptionable character, easy fortune, suitable age, and pleasant manners.*
- Doc3: *Instead of leaving Catherine's fortune at her own disposal, he determined to put it in the hands of trustees for her use during life.*

Catherine's	→	Doc3: position4, ...
fortune	→	Doc1: position16; Doc2: position10; Doc3: position5, ...
it	→	Doc1: position1; Doc3: position14, ...
man	→	Doc1: position10, Doc2: position5, ...
of	→	Doc1: position13; Doc2: position5; Doc3: position2, position18, ...
Weston	→	Doc2: position2, ...

Figure 6.2: Excerpt from positional index.

With a positional index, we can find bigrams such as *Mr. Weston*, and cases where *fortune* appears within ten words of *man*; but we would still need a richer structure to find instances of two words within the same sentence or the same paragraph. You may notice that the positional index now also records information about how often each word occurs in each document, rather than just recording whether it occurs at all; such count data can reveal further important similarities and differences between documents.

In sum, this section has introduced various ways that terms and documents can be indexed, and how we can apply set operations to an inverted index to carry out boolean searches. These ideas are important in the history of information retrieval, and are still used in tools such as Westlaw to this day. But it is also important to consider why boolean search is *not* widely used in modern search engines.

For one thing, non-specialist users may find the complex syntax of boolean queries (and other advanced features offered on Westlaw) to be counter-intuitive. Interestingly, trained Westlaw users seem to enjoy using Westlaw's complicated query syntax, and even prefer to use it when a free-text query might give equally good results. Like stick-shift drivers, perhaps Westlaw users feel that they have more control over the search when they design their queries by hand.

A bigger problem with boolean search is that searches using *OR* have very high recall but low precision (relevant documents are returned, but they are overwhelmed by an even greater number of irrelevant documents), while boolean searches using *AND* have high precision but low recall (a lot of the documents that are returned are relevant, but a lot of relevant documents are not returned). These logical operators are too rigid to find a middle ground.

On the other hand, the problem with *OR* searches (low precision, high recall) can be partly addressed with a good ranking system that puts the most relevant results at the top of the page; that way, at least the top few results have good precision, which are the most important results for users anyway. The problem with *AND* searches (high precision, low recall) cannot be so easily addressed with a ranking system, and perhaps this is why the space – the default way of combining words – is interpreted as *OR* in Westlaw.

Under the Hood 10: Regular expressions

Any time we have to match a complex pattern, *regular expressions* are useful. A regular expression is a compact description of a set of strings. So, a regular expression can compactly describe the set of strings containing all zip codes starting with 911 (in this case, the regular expression is `/911[0-9][0-9]/`, which is explained below).

In *formal language theory*, language is treated mathematically, and a set of strings defines a language. For instance, English is defined as the set of all legitimate English sentences. As in other formalisms, regular expressions as such have no linguistic contents; they are simply descriptions of some set of strings encoding a *natural language* text. While some patterns cannot be specified using regular expressions (see Under the Hood 2.5.4 on grammar complexity), regular expressions are quite suitable for our purposes.

Regular expressions can consist of a variety of different types of special characters, but there is a very small set of them. In their most basic form, regular expressions have strings of literal characters: Some examples include /c/, /A100/, /natural language/, and /30 years!/. In other words, we can search for ordinary strings just as we would expect, by writing them out. One note on the representation of putting regular expressions between forward slashes: This is a common representation, but in the next section we will see that each application has its own way of referring to regular expressions.

To allow for different possibilities, we can add *disjunction*. There is ordinary disjunction, as in /devoured|ate/ and /famil(y|ies)/, which allows us to find variants of words – in this case, *devoured* and *ate*, in the former case, and *family* and *families*, in the latter – and there are character classes, defined in brackets, to specify different possibilities. /[Tt]he/, for example, matches either *The* or *the*; likewise, /bec[oa]me/ matches *become* or *became*. Finally, we can specify ranges, as in /[A-Z]/, which matches any capital letter. For our earlier problem of finding all zip codes starting with *911*, then, we can specify / 911[0-9][0-9] /, which nicely excludes *911* when followed by a space.

In addition to disjunction, we can use *negation* to specify characters that we do not want to see. We use the character class notation ([...]), with ^ denoting that it is not this class. For example, /[^a]/ refers to any symbol but a, and /[^A-Z0-9]/ indicates something which is not an uppercase letter or number.

Regular expressions begin to display their full range of power in the different *counters* which are available. These counters allow us to specify how often an item should appear. First, we can specify optionality through the ? operator; ? means that we can have zero or one of the previously occurring item. For example, /colou?r/ matches either *color* or *colour*. Secondly, we have what is called the Kleene star (*), which allows for any number of occurrences of the previous item (including zero occurrences) – e.g., /[0-9]* years/. The third and final counter is very similar, but it stands for one or more occurrences of the previous element and is represented by +. So /[0-9]+ dollars/ requires there to be at least one digit, but possibly more.

Another operator which allows us to specify different possibilities is the period (.), a wildcard standing for any character. Thus, the query /beg.n/ designates that there can be any (single) character between *beg* and *n* (*begin*, *began*, *beg!n*, etc.).

Because we have defined special uses for a variety of characters, we also want a way to search for those actual characters. For example, how can we search for a question mark (*?*) when it has a special meaning? To do this, we use *escaped characters*, which allow us to specify a character which otherwise has a special meaning, and we notate this with a backslash: *, \+, \?, \(, \), \|, \[, \].

With a variety of different operators, it can sometimes be confusing as to which applies first. But there are rules of *operator precedence*, just as in arithmetic, where, for example, in evaluating $4 + 5 * 6$, we obtain 34 because multiplication has higher precedence than addition. Likewise, there is an order of precedence for regular expressions, as summarized in the table. From highest to lowest, this precedence is: parentheses, counters (* + ?), character sequences, and finally disjunction (|). So, if we see `/ab|cd/`, this matches either *ab* or *cd* because character sequences have higher precedence than disjunction. (If disjunction had higher precedence, we would match *abd* or *acd*.)

Operator	Notation
1. Parentheses	(...)
2. Counters	?, *, +
3. Literals	a, b, c, ...
Escaped characters	\?, *, \[, ...
Wildcard	.
4. Disjunction	|, [...]
Negation	[^...]

To fully illustrate how regular expressions work, we are going to walk through a tool used on a variety of platforms to find sequences in text. This tool is called *grep*, and it is a powerful and efficient program for searching in text files using regular expressions. It is standard on Unix, Linux, and Mac OSX, and there are also various ports for Windows. The version of `grep` that supports the full set of operators mentioned above is generally called `egrep` (for extended `grep`). By the way, `grep` stands for "grab regular expressions and print".

We list a variety of examples below and, for each, we assume a text file `f.txt` containing, among other strings, the ones that we mention as matching. The purpose of `grep` or `egrep` is to return the lines which contain a string matching the regular expression.

- *Strings of literal characters:*

  `egrep 'and' f.txt`

  matches lines with: and, `Ayn Rand`, `Candy`, `standalone`, ...

- *Character classes:*

  `egrep 'the year [0-9][0-9][0-9][0-9]' f.txt`

  matches lines with: `the year 1776`, `the year 1812a.d.`, `the year 21112`, ...

- *Escaped characters:*

  `egrep 'why\?' f.txt`

  matches lines with: `why?`, ...

  but does not match lines with: `why so serious`, ...

- Disjunction (`|`):

  `egrep 'couch|sofa' f.txt`

  matches lines with: `couch`, `sofa`, `couched`, ...

- *Grouping with parentheses:*

  `egrep 'un(interest|excit)ing' f.txt`

  matches lines with: `uninteresting`, `unexciting`

  but does not match lines with:

  `uninterested`, `super-exciting`

- *Any character (.):*

  `egrep 'o.e' f.txt`

  matches lines with: `ore`, `one`, `sole`, `project`, ...

- *Kleene star (*):*

  `egrep 'sha(la)*' f.txt`

  matches lines with: `sha`, `shala`, `shalala`, ...

  but does not match lines with:

  `shalaaa`, `shalashala`, ...

- *One or more (+):*

  `egrep 'john+y' f.txt`

  matches lines with: `johny`, `johnny`, `johnnny`, ...

  but does not match lines with:

  `johy`

- *Optionality (?):*

  `egrep 'joh?n' f.txt`

  matches lines with: `jon`, `john`, `jones`, ...

You can practice regular expressions online using tools such as Regex101. They can be fiddly, so don't get discouraged if you have to practice for a while before you feel comfortable!

6.5 Search engines for general use

Since the late 1990s, search engines have become widely accessible to non-specialist users. Practically every website or app offers a search functionality of some kind, even if it only allows you to search within that specific website (to find an old email in your inbox, or to look for Reddit posts about your favorite movie). But most prototypically, you enter a simple text query into a dedicated search engine such as Google or Bing and get back thousands of open-domain documents from all over the web, ranked by relevance and quality. Often these search results give you what you want on the first page of top-ranked results.

We just saw that Westlaw allows users to filter results based on structured metadata about judges, jurisdiction, and so on. In contrast, regular open-domain webpages are relatively unstructured, so open-domain web search usually does not allow such filtering. But the word *unstructured* may be misleading, because most documents have some sort of structure, even if it is not explicitly labeled. A webpage probably has a title and some sub-headers or *meta tags* (<META name = "keywords" content = "travel,Malta">) that can be identified from its HTML. It is probably also associated with the date on which it was created or updated. A search engine can use such metadata to give higher rankings to pages that mention query terms in the title rather than just the body, or to favor more recently-updated pages.

We also saw that Westlaw users can specify complex queries using a specialized syntax. In contrast, users of open-domain web search often do not have the patience for such opaque options; "double quotes" for exactly-matching strings is the only popular advanced feature in the realm of text. In many cases, it is not clear if one's results would be meaningfully improved by a more complex query anyway.

Finally, we saw that Westlaw only indexes documents from the legal domain, which is finite in size and relatively high quality (it's unlikely to find spam). In contrast, the open-domain internet is massive (at a recent estimate, there are over 1.5 billion webpages, of which 200 million are active), and all levels of quality are represented. Because the web is so vast and the quality so variable, it is especially important for results to be ranked in such a way that the top page of results best address the user's information need. The *ranking* of results should consider (i) the *relevance* of each document to the query and the information need that it represents, viewing relevance as a gradient rather than a binary concept; and (ii) the *quality* of each document – the degree to which it can be considered trustworthy.

Under the Hood 11: Finite-state automata

Regular expressions are closely related to finite-state automata (FSAs), which are abstract mathematical models of computation. A finite-state automaton is a hypothetical machine that can be in exactly one of a finite number of states at a given time. We can use a graph to visualize its potential states and sequences thereof.

Imagine a finite-state automaton that matches a single letter *a*. It has two states, 1 and 2, and one edge to link them. This edge is labeled with *a*. There is a start arrow marking state 1 as the initial state, and special formatting (a double circle) marking state 2 as final. The idea of a finite-state automaton is that it matches all the paths that can go from the initial state to the final state. This automaton is boring: It has only one path and the only sequence it can match is the single letter *a*.

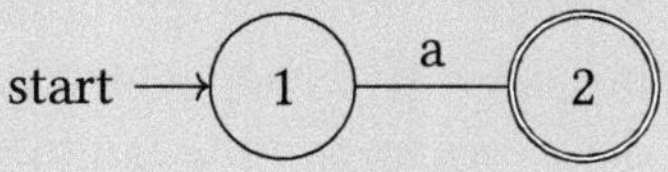

We say that the automaton generates the "language" (set of strings) corresponding to the paths in the graph. The language generated by our simple automaton is just the sequence containing the single letter *a*. Defining the automation in terms of the strings it accepts, this automaton accepts {a}.

An even simpler automaton has one state, which is both initial and final, and no loops at all; the set of strings accepted by this automaton is the empty set {}.

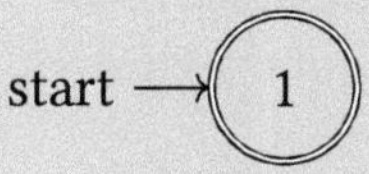

On the other hand, we can make our system more complicated, by allowing *b* and *c* as well as *a*. Now our language generates three different one-letter strings – {a, b, c}.

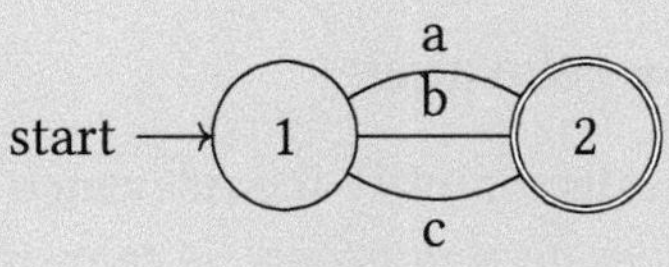

Our next automation is more interesting:

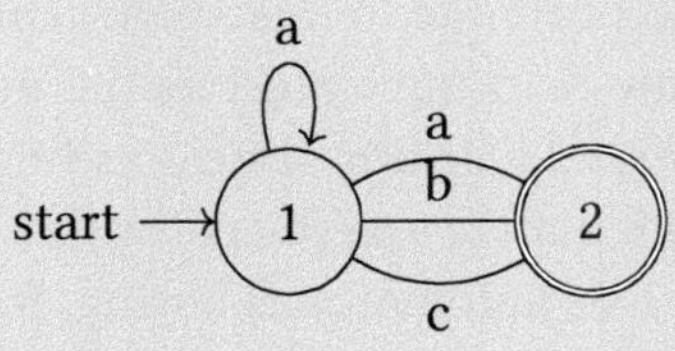

Here, we have made an edge called *a* which loops around as many times as necessary, then finishes off with a choice of *a, b,* or *c.* This formulation is powerful, because it describes an infinite language consisting of all the strings that start off with a sequence of (any number of) *a*'s and finishes with *a, b,* or *c.* This pattern can also be described by the regular expression /a*(a|b|c|)/. This automaton accepts an infinite set of strings – {aa, ab, ac, aab, aac, aaab, aaac, ...} and so on: There is no upper limit on the number of *a*'s.

It turns out to be useful to think of regular expressions as a notation for finite-state automata. That is, when we write down a regular expression, it is a precise description of some finite-state automaton. Going the other way, if you have a finite-state automaton, you can write it down as a corresponding regular expression. We say that finite-state automata provide the semantics for regular expressions. By *semantics*, we mean a mathematically precise meaning.

More generally, finite-state automata are important in formal language theory, the study of which patterns can be generated by which sets of rules.

6.5.1 Ranking results by relevance

First, how do we automatically quantify the relevance of a document to a query? When you search for *Do dogs need raincoats?*, a relevant document is likely to include words from your query – especially the more distinctive words or lemmas, *dog, raincoat,* and perhaps *need*, more than the extremely common word *do.* A relevant document probably also uses these words frequently, at the beginning of the document or in the title, and in close proximity to one another. Most intuitively, a relevant document is probably *similar* to the query, in the sense that they probably contain similar words.

We saw above that a term-by-document matrix can quantify some intuitions about the similarity between two documents: Two documents are more similar if their columns (vectors) in the term-by-document matrix are more similar. Let's make that idea more mathematically precise using a query and three short documents:

- *Query:* Do dogs need raincoats?
- *Doc1:* Raincoats for dogs? Dogs dislike raincoats!
- *Doc2:* Shop fashion for pets
- *Doc3:* Need raincoats for fashion

Now, let's make a term-by-document matrix (Table 6.2).

Table 6.2: Term-by-document matrix for the query *Do dogs need raincoats?* and three documents that may be relevant to this query.

	Query	Doc1	Doc2	Doc3
do	1	0	0	0
dogs	1	2	0	0
need	1	0	0	1
raincoats	1	2	0	1
for	0	1	1	1
dislike	0	1	0	0
shop	0	0	1	0
fashion	0	0	1	1
pets	0	0	1	0

We mentioned above that such a matrix could use a 0 when a term doesn't occur at all, and a 1 when it appears at least once (which is all we need for a boolean search), but that we could also choose to use the actual number of times that the term appears in each document. Here, we take the latter strategy, so that our term-by-document matrix counts the number of times that each term appears in each document; *dogs* appears twice in Doc2, so there is a 2 in that column.

Eventually, we will want to use some vector math to quantify the similarity between documents, or between a document and a query. But before things get too complicated, just look at the query and the documents, look at the term-by-document matrix, and use your intuition to decide which document you think is most similar to (and thus most relevant to) the query.

Now for the mathematical details. In order to quantify the intuitive notion of similarity between documents (or between a document and a query), we first need to calculate the length of each vector. We begin with a vector x, with n elements $[x_1, x_2, x_3, \dots x_n]$. The *vector length* of x, written as $|x|$, is defined as:

(6.5) $$|x| = \sqrt{x_1^2 + x_2^2 + x_3^2 + \dots x_n^2}$$

The first document (column vector) in our term-by-document matrix is the query, *Do dogs need raincoats*, represented as the vector [1, 1, 1, 1, 0, 0, 0, 0, 0]. Its length is defined as:

(6.6) $$\sqrt{1^2 + 1^2 + 1^2 + 1^2 + 0^2 + 0^2 + 0^2 + 0^2 + 0^2} = \sqrt{4} = 2$$

The next column vector in our matrix is Doc1, *Raincoats for dogs? Dogs dislike raincoats*, represented as the vector [0, 2, 0, 2, 1, 1, 0, 0, 0]. Its length is thus:

(6.7) $$\sqrt{0^2 + 2^2 + 0^2 + 2^2 + 1^2 + 1^2 + 0^2 + 0^2 + 0^2} = \sqrt{10} = 3.16$$

Calculated as described, the final row of our term-by-document matrix now records the length of each vector.

Table 6.3: Term-by-document matrix with vector lengths.

	Query	Doc1	Doc2	Doc3
do	1	0	0	0
dogs	1	2	0	0
need	1	0	0	1
raincoats	1	2	0	1
for	0	1	1	1
dislike	0	1	0	0
shop	0	0	1	0
fashion	0	0	1	1
pets	0	0	1	0
length	2	$\sqrt{10}$	2	2

Now that we have a vector and a length for the query as well as each document, we want to calculate the similarity between the query vector and each document vector. We do this using *cosine similarity*, which measures the angle between two vectors in an abstract vector space. Intuitively, two vectors are more similar if each of their elements are similar: Our query is similar to Doc1 in that they both contain the words *dogs* and *raincoats*.

Before we can define cosine similarity, we have to define the *dot product* between two vectors, $x1$ and $x2$, which must have the same number of elements. $x1_1$ is the first element of $x1$, $x2_1$ is the first element of $x2$, $x1_2$ is the second element of $x1$, and so on.

(6.8) $$x1 \bullet x2 = (x1_1 * x2_1) + (x1_2 * x2_2) + (x1_3 * x2_3) + \dots (x1_n * x2_n)$$

Let's illustrate by calculating the dot product of our query [1, 1, 1, 1, 0, 0, 0, 0, 0] and Doc1 [0, 2, 0, 2, 1, 1, 0, 0, 0].

(6.9) $$q \bullet Doc1 = (1*0)+(1*2)+(1*0)+(1*2)+(0*1)+(0*1)+(0*0)+(0*0) = 4$$

Finally, we can calculate the cosine similarity between two vectors (between documents, or between a query and a document). The cosine similarity between $x1$ and $x2$ is defined as their dot product divided by the product of their lengths:

(6.10) $$\frac{x1 \bullet x2}{|x1| * |x2|}$$

We already saw that the dot product of our query and Doc1 is 4, the length of the query is 2, and the length of Doc1 is $\sqrt{10}$. Thus, their cosine similarity is:

(6.11) $$\frac{4}{2 * \sqrt{10}} = 0.63$$

A maximal cosine similarity of 1 means that the documents are identical, so a cosine similarity of 0.63 indicates that these two documents are pretty similar.

Using the same method, we can calculate the cosine similarity between our query and every other document – and between every document and every other document.

- *Query:* Do dogs need raincoats?
- *Doc1:* Raincoats for dogs? Dogs dislike raincoats!
- *Doc2:* Shop fashion for pets

- *Doc3:* Need raincoats for fashion

For example, the top-left corner of this matrix indicates that the query is identical to itself. The top row, second column (0.63) indicates that the query and Doc1 have a cosine similarity of 0.63. And so on.

Table 6.4: Cosine similarities of each document to each other document.

	Query	Doc1	Doc2	Doc3
Query	1	0.63	0	0.50
Doc1	0.63	1	0.16	0.47
Doc2	0	0.16	1	0.50
Doc3	0.50	0.47	0.50	1

This matrix quantifies some intuitive results. As expected, the document most similar to our query is Doc1, because they both mention raincoats and dogs. The document least similar to the query is Doc2, because none of the words overlap. The document most similar to Doc2 (*shop fashion for pets*) is Doc3 (*need raincoats for fashion*), because they both contain the words *for* and *fashion*. The math may seem complicated, but the results are exactly what we would want. Cosine similarity is used to quantify the similarity between columns (vectors) in a term-by-document matrix.

This basic idea can be made fancier in all sorts of ways, for example to take advantage of the fact that a word like *pets* should be considered similar to a word like *dogs* even if they are different words. To keep this discussion accessible, we will limit ourselves to one historically important refinement of the document-similarity calculation, which gives greater weight to distinctive words such as *dogs* and *raincoats* over more common words such as *of*. This refinement is known as *TFIDF weighting* – weighting by *term frequency* (tf) and *inverse document frequency* (idf).

We've already been weighting words by their term frequency. We have just been using the raw count of each word in each document, which makes sense because all our documents are about the same length, but if the documents vary in length then one could also divide by the total number of words in each document.

The inverse document frequency of a term t is calculated with respect to the entire collection of documents, D. It is defined as the log of (the total number of documents) divided by (the number of documents containing the term d).

(6.12)
$$\log\left(\frac{N}{|\{d \in D : t \in d\}|}\right)$$

For example, our collection contains three documents (Doc1, Doc2, and Doc3 – ignoring the query for now), so $N = 3$. There are two documents that contain the word *dogs*. So the inverse document frequency of *dogs* is $\log(3/2) = 0.17$. In the same collection of documents, there are three documents that contain the word *for* – all three of them use this common word. So the inverse document frequency of *for* is $\log(3/3) = 0$.

The math may seem complicated, but the idea is that a higher inverse document frequency means that a term is more distinctive among a collection of documents. If the term appears in every document, it is not distinctive at all, and thus doesn't tell us much about the relevance of any one document. But if the term appears only in a few documents, then it is quite distinctive, and maybe meaningful for relevance. Inverse document frequency was proposed by the British computer scientist Karen Spärck Jones (1972).

TFIDF is the product of term frequency and inverse document frequency. The TFIDF of *dogs* in Doc1, among our collection {Doc1, Doc2, Doc3}, is its term frequency (which is 2) times its inverse document frequency (which is 0.17), which comes to 0.34. The TDIDF of *for* in Doc1 among our collection {Doc1, Doc2, Doc3} is its term frequency (which is 1) times its inverse document frequency (which is 0), which comes to 0. Therefore, TFIDF weighting means that the word *dogs* says more about the relevance of Doc1 to a query than the word *for*.

We could remake our term-by-document matrix using TFIDF weightings instead of just count data, and rerun our calculations of cosine similarity. (You can try it out on your own – with a pen and paper or some code.) But what's even more important than the calculation is the intuition. Using TFIDF weightings would lower the similarity between Doc2 and Doc3, since their similarity was based only on the fact that they both share the extremely common and non-distinctive word *for*. TFIDF weighting also means that we don't necessarily need to remove stop words from our data, because there are other ways of capturing the fact that these words do not tell us much about a document's relevance.

In sum, vector similarity is a powerful and intuitive idea that can be quantified using cosine similarity (defined using vector length and dot products). It allows us to quantify the similarity (thus, relevance) of a document to a query, which can in turn be used to rank documents based on their relevance to that query. Moreover, we can also use the similarity between different documents to group them into meaningful clusters that are more similar to one another than to other documents outside the cluster – for example, a cluster of articles about shopping, and another cluster of articles debating whether dogs enjoy wearing raincoats or not.

So far, we have explored the conceptual foundations of identifying the documents that are relevant to a query. But of course, the representation of a text can be made far richer than a simple term-by-document matrix. We saw in Chapter 4 that we can identify words with similar meanings based on their distribution, capturing the idea that *dogs* is similar to *pets*. We also saw in Chapter 5 that pre-trained tools such as BERT can distill the information contained in massive amounts of text, which can in turn be used to turn a query and some documents into vectors, from which we can then find the document vector that is most similar to the query. Modern systems combine all of these tools.

6.5.2 Ranking results by quality

Next, how do we automatically determine the quality of a document/webpage? A document is likely to be of a high quality if it is highly trafficked, clicked on frequently by other users (known as the *click-through measurement*), information-dense (not too repetitive), updated relatively recently (because some information changes over time), and linked to by other (high-quality) webpages. This last metric of quality – incoming links from other high-quality documents – was formalized by the computer science graduate students Larry Page and Sergey Brin and colleagues in the late 1990s, and the resulting *PageRank* algorithm (Page et al. 1999) served as the basis of their search engine startup company: Google.

PageRank begins from the intuition that when someone decides to include a link on their webpage, they are signaling that they find the linked page somehow noteworthy or useful. (As a side note, PageRank is used to rank webpages by their quality, but was also spearheaded by Larry Page, so the word *Page* does double duty as a name and a noun.) Thus, a page with a lot of in-links is likely to be of a high quality – especially if those in-links come from other high-quality pages.

To formalize this intuition, consider Figure 6.3, where each circle represents a webpage. In this case, pages X, Y, and Z all link to page A. The question is whether these links are any better or worse than those that link to page B, shown in Figure 6.4.

Thus, we calculate importance based on popularity, where popularity is estimated based on how many sites link to a website and how popular each one of

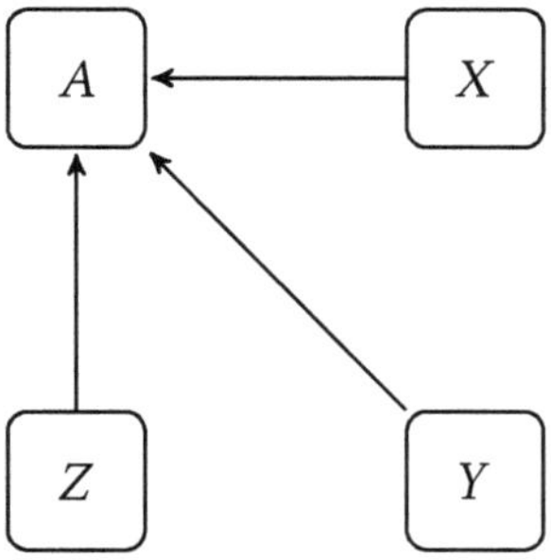

Figure 6.3: Weblinking: X, Y, and Z all link to A.

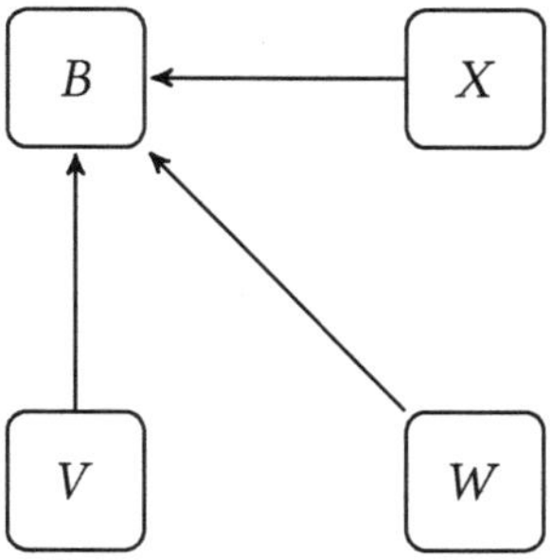

Figure 6.4: Weblinking: V, W, and X all link to B.

those is. In order to compare how popular website A is as compared to website B, we can add up how popular each incoming site is. It might help to think of the situation like this: Each site that links to A gets to vote for A, and they each get a different number of votes based on how popular each one of them is. Every page has a score, and that the score of a page is related to the score of the pages that provide its incoming links.

In this sense, PageRank does not (and does not claim to) measure quality, but rather measures popularity. It is an empirical question to what extent a page's popularity really reflects its quality.

To see how the calculations are done, consider Figure 6.5.

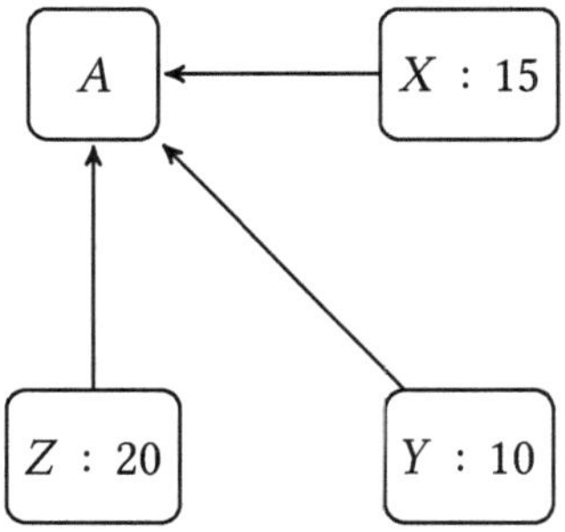

Figure 6.5: Pages with weights.

Here, X casts 15 votes for A, Y casts 10, and Z casts 20. This may make intuitive sense, but we are stuck with an immediate problem: The website A now has 45 votes, and that is clearly too many. After all, the most popular incoming site had only a score of 20. This way of adding will lead to ever-increasing popularity scores.

We want a solution that distributes votes from pages in a sensible way. The solution PageRank uses is to spread out each page's votes through all the pages it links to. Viewing this as a voting process, it means that each webpage must split its votes among all the pages it links to. In Figure 6.6, for example, the webpage X has 15 votes, and it links to 3 pages. Thus, it casts 5 votes for each of those pages.

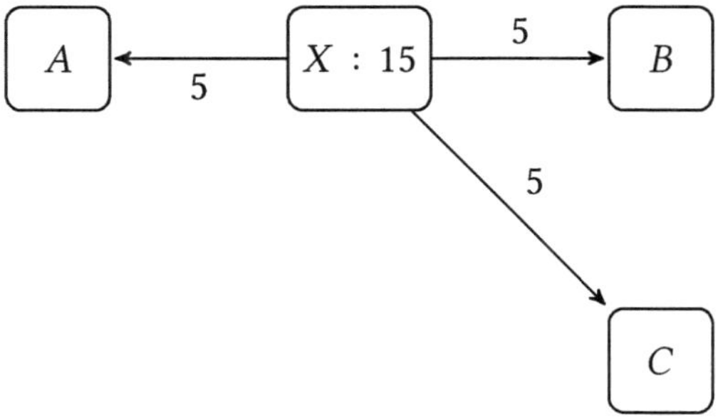

Figure 6.6: Dividing the weights.

Let's assume, then, that after spreading votes out among their different webpages, the final score of A is 12. Which leads us to ask: 12 of what? What does it mean to have a score of 12? Is that good or bad?

Truth be told, scores on their own do not mean much. We need to compare the score to other websites to determine a relative rank. If website B's score is 10 and A's is 12, we can say that A outranks B. If, when the search engine analyzes the words on the pages, two pages seem to be equally relevant in their content, then the page rank score can be used to determine which webpage is placed nearer to the top of the results list.

In sum, there are two main things to consider when calculating a ranking for a website based on its weblinks – links coming into a website, and links going out of a website. The formula (at least for Google) captures these properties. It can be seen in (6.13) for a webpage A with 3 pages linking to it: We use $R(X)$ to mean the *rank of page X* and $C(X)$ to refer to the *number of pages going out of page X*.

(6.13) $$R(A) = \frac{R(X)}{C(X)} + \frac{R(Y)}{C(Y)} + \frac{R(Z)}{C(Z)}$$

Let's make sure this formula represents what we want it to. Firstly, we add up the scores of the different pages coming into A (e.g., $R(X)$) because, in order to know how popular A is, we need to know how popular everyone else thinks it is. Secondly, we divide each score by the number of pages going out of X, Y, and Z (e.g., $C(X)$) because we are spreading out their weights among all the pages they link to. The result of this calculation – whether we want to interpret it as a signal of quality or just popularity – is then used to rank results.

The ideas behind PageRank are still used in web search to this day, combined with a number of other indirect metrics of a page's quality. As one other example, Google has also patented a technique (Hajaj 2015) to measure the distance between one page and another page – how many links you would have to follow to navigate from one page to another by link-hopping. Beginning with a number of *seed* pages that are already known to be of high quality, one can measure the distance in the *link graph* between each page and these high-quality pages, and give higher rankings to pages that are closer to the high-quality ones. For example, imagine that a university's website is listed among the high-quality seed pages. Then, if a professor's personal website is directly linked from the university site, that link structure can help boost the ranking of the professor's site, both through PageRank (because the university's site "votes" for this page) and through its distance in the link graph.

Under the Hood 12: A brief tour of HTML

HTML stands for *Hyper-Text Mark-up Language*, and it is what webpages have often been written in. If you go to a webpage and select *View Page Source*, you will see the raw HTML. It resembles English, but has extra features. For example, looking at the English Wikipedia page (https://en.wikipedia.org/wiki/Main_Page), we find an excerpt of the source code shown. This code corresponds to a list of recently featured articles, each formatted as a clickable link.

```
<div class="tfa-recent" style="text-align:␣right;">Recently
    featured: <div class="hlist␣hlist-separated␣inline">
<ul><li><a href="/wiki/Truce_of_Calais" title="Truce␣of␣Calais
    ">Truce of Calais</a></li>
<li><a href="/wiki/Boroughitis" title="Boroughitis">
    Boroughitis</a></li>
<li><a href="/wiki/1940
    _Mandatory_Palestine_v_Lebanon_football_match" title="1940
    ␣Mandatory␣Palestine␣v␣Lebanon␣football␣match">1940
    Mandatory Palestine v Lebanon football match</a></li></ul>
</div>
```

As can be seen, the code is composed of different *HTML tags*, which are found between angled brackets, for example, `<li>`, which marks a list item. For every opening bracket (e.g., `<li>`), there is a closing bracket (e.g., `</li>`). You can see how to alter text:

(14) a.
```
<p>We'll throw in some <b>bold</b>, <i>italicized</i>,
    and <u>underlined</u> text.</p>
```

b. We'll throw in some **bold**, *italicized*, and <u>underlined</u> text.

Many HTML tags have obvious effects on the display of the page. But some have more subtle effects. Most browsers display the content of the <TITLE> tag not on the page itself, but rather in the title bar of the window within which the page appears.

HTML also gives you the tools to create links to other webpages. The <A> tag (short for *anchor*) does this, and so you can find HTML code such as `<a href="https://ling.osu.edu"> Click here</a>`. Any person or program that understands HTML will be able, by finding all the <a> tags, to trace the links that lead away from this page, which can be used to compute its PageRank.

6.5.3 Design choices for search engines

All search engines find documents relevant to a query, and rank them in terms of relevance and quality. But each search engine also uses a blend of unique design choices, based on considerations about user experience, social impact, and ethics:

- Are words stemmed or lemmatized? Is *dogs* lemmatized to *dog*, is *whistle-blower* stemmed to *whistleblow*?
- Are searches case-sensitive? Does a search for *Apple* yield the same results as one for *apple*?
- What happens to punctuation? Does a search for *USA* yield the same results as one for *U.S.A.*? Does a search for *big* yield the same results as one for *B.I.G.* (the musician)?
- What about spelling variations? Does a search for *color* (American spelling) yield the same results as one for *colour* (British)?

- What about different words for the same thing? Does a search for *Burma* yield the same results as a search for *Myanmar*?
- Are results spell-checked (automatically)? What happens if you search for *Katie Smih*? (What if you actually want to find someone named *Katie Smih*?)
- Does the search engine auto-complete a query as you type it? Does it suggest helpful further queries?
- What languages are results displayed in? When you search for *roi*, do you get results in English (return on investment) or French (where it means *king*)?
- How does the search engine deal with government censorship in certain countries?
- How does the search engine deal with searches for adult topics, such as nudity?
- How does the search engine deal with searches for controversial or sensitive topics, such as conspiracy theories, hate groups, or self-harm? Perhaps a company doesn't want to leave these results entirely up to an algorithm.
- What advanced search options are available? How easy is it to find them? (How much do they improve results?)
- How are results displayed? What *snippets* are shown with each result? Are the query words highlighted?
- What blend of relevance and quality is used to rank results, and how are they calculated? For example, to what extent does the ranking algorithm also consider recency?
- To what extent do search results respect the privacy of private individuals? Can you search for someone and find their address, criminal record, and phone number on the first page of results?
- Are results (for ambiguous queries) clustered into groups? Does a search for *apple* yield a cluster about the company and a cluster about the fruit, or are the results all presented together?

- To what extent are your results *personalized* – to give higher rankings to pages you've visited previously, pages that are highly trafficked in your specific location, or pages similar to your prior search history? If so, is the personalization *transparent* – are you aware of how it works?
- What advertisements are shown to users, and how are they distinguished from other content?

Some of these design choices are technical, but some are fundamentally humanistic, asking us to weigh ethical imperatives – to what extent should information be freely available, versus to what extent should it be restricted (or algorithmically down-ranked) to protect people from various types of harm?

6.5.4 The future of search

So far, we have seen that modern search engines answer certain factoid questions directly (*How many centimeters are in an inch?*), while answering other questions indirectly (*What happened to my friend Katie Smith?*) by returning a set of relevant documents in which the user can dig for an answer themselves. Given the recent success of tools such as ChatGPT, one wonders if future information retrieval systems will answer more and more questions directly, handling fewer information needs with ranked documents that the user has to dig through.

For example, consider a user who asks, *Should I quit my job?* A document-ranking information retrieval system would curate webpages where this topic is discussed, while a dialog-based system would generate its own reply. The following reply from ChatGPT is sensible enough:

> As an AI language model, I cannot make decisions for you, but I can provide some guidance to help you make an informed decision.
>
> Before deciding whether to quit your job, it may be helpful to evaluate the reasons why you are considering leaving. Are you feeling unfulfilled or unhappy with your work, or are there external factors such as a difficult boss or toxic work environment that are causing you to feel this way?
>
> You may also want to consider your financial situation and whether you have a backup plan or other job prospects lined up if you do decide to quit. Additionally, it may be helpful to talk to trusted friends or family members, a career counselor, or a mental health professional to discuss your options and explore potential solutions to any issues you are facing at work.

> Ultimately, the decision to quit your job is a personal one and depends on your individual circumstances. If you are feeling unhappy or unfulfilled in your current job and have exhausted all other options, then it may be time to consider moving on. However, if you are able to work through any issues you are experiencing or find ways to improve your current situation, then quitting may not be necessary.
>
> (elicited from ChatGPT in 2024)

Which type of system would you prefer? In some sense, generative LLMs aspire to the vision evoked by the AskJeeves search engine from 1996 – named for the famous butler in P.G. Wodehouse's stories, who was known for his encyclopedic knowledge and nimble competence (creating a humorous contrast with the rich buffoon who employed him). Like Jeeves, generative LLMs offer a lucid response to the user's query in an authoritative voice, which – if you trust it – may be exactly what you want.

On the other hand, these responses may not actually be trustworthy. For example, generative LLMs are not updated daily, so they might contain outdated information about current events. Such models also certainly do not know what happened to your elementary school friend Katie Smith. If the model spouts nonsense with the same authoritative tone as true information, then the user may be misled, and the company may embarrass itself. Moreover, a system that gives an answer itself performs a qualitatively different action than one which retrieves webpages that may contain such an answer. By offering relevant webpages, a system signals that the human must still use their judgment to evaluate them, whereas in giving a single answer, it seems to assert confident correctness – which might or might not be justified.

It is also interesting to consider how technology companies will allocate resources to maintaining a knowledge graph (based on a human-written top-down structure) versus using the bottom-up information distilled by generative language models. How do you predict that these two tools will compete with one another or with free-text search?

6.6 Recommendation systems

So far, we have explored search engines that help people answer an information need that they formed on their own. But sometimes, you may want a computer to recommend things to you that you didn't even know you wanted.

A *recommendation system* bypasses the query and goes straight to the ranking. It ranks items – documents, web posts to read, things to buy, people to friend or follow, books, movies, music – based on their overall popularity and/or their relevance to a particular user. Some of these items do not centrally involve language (music, people, products), while some are built on text (web posts, books), but they can all be handled similarly.

A recommendation system does not inherently need to be personalized; a movie library could keep a static list of the current most-popular or most-streamed movies, or hand-curate a list of "staff picks," and then recommend these movies to all users. But in practice, most recommendation systems try to tailor their recommendations to the taste of each user. Personalized recommendation systems are used by companies like Amazon (recommending products), Netflix (movies), YouTube (videos), Facebook (recommending friends to add, and ranking the posts you see in your news feed), X/Twitter (similar to Facebook), and so on.

Imagine that you want to offer personalized movie recommendations to the people who subscribe to your movie library. You have four users and five movies, represented in a *utility matrix* that shows each user's preference (utility) for each movie. For some users, you have data about what they like and dislike – perhaps they rate a movie after watching it, or perhaps you infer that they like movies that they watch to the end, and dislike movies that they stop watching halfway through. But most users have not watched most movies; in our matrix, the question mark indicates that you do not know whether a user would like or dislike a given movie, because they have not seen it. Perhaps a new movie has just been added to your library (*SpiderVerse*), so you have no data on whether anyone likes it; or perhaps a new user (Dell) has just subscribed to your service, so you have no data on what movies they like.

The goal of a recommendation system is to fill in the question marks in this user-by-movie matrix to identify and suggest new movies that each user would like. (It's a lot less important to identify new movies that a user would *dislike*, except to distinguish them from the movies that they *would* like). A *collaborative recommendation system* will use the similarities between users reflected in the utility matrix. Here, Alex and Cory both like *Amadeus* and Cory also likes *Little Women*, so maybe you will recommend *Little Women* to Alex on the grounds that Cory – who is somewhat similar to Alex – also likes it.

Of course, the problem here is that no one has seen *SpiderVerse* and Dell hasn't rated any movies, so it's harder to make recommendations for these new movies and users. (Would it help to find out Dell's gender, age, location, or favorite movies?) The other problem is that users may have eclectic tastes; Alex likes both historical dramas and the action film *Black Panther*, while other users may like only one of these types of films, so they may not like all the recommendations they get based on their similarity to Alex.

Table 6.5: Utility matrix for users and movies.

	Amadeus	Lion King	Blk Panther	L. Women	SpiderVerse
Alex	like	dislike	like	?	?
Bo	?	like	like	?	?
Cory	like	?	dislike	like	?
Dell	?	?	?	?	?

You may also want to represent similarities and differences between movies. Here, we've represented each movie as a vector of features including its genre(s), studio, year, style, and Motion Picture Association of America rating of the maturity level of its audience (PG = some material may not be suitable for children, PG-13 = some material may be inappropriate for pre-teens). For example, this matrix shows that *Amadeus* is similar to *Little Women* in that they are both PG-rated live-action historical dramas. So a *content-based recommendation system* may recommend *Little Women* to Alex because Alex also liked *Amadeus.* Using this information, we can also recommend the unseen, un-rated *SpiderVerse* movie to Bo, because Bo likes other animated movies (*Lion King*) and action movies (*Black Panther*).

Table 6.6: Feature matrix for movies.

	Amadeus	Lion King	Blk Panther	L. Women	SpiderVerse
Genre	historical, drama	musical	action	historical, drama	action
Studio	Orion	Disney	Marvel, Disney	Columbia, Regency, Pascal	Columbia, Sony, Marvel
Year	1984	1994	2018	2019	2018
Style	Live action	Animated	Live action	Live action	Animated
Rating	PG	PG	PG-13	PG	PG

From a machine learning standpoint, we could hide a random part of the utility matrix, pretending that we don't know the users' ratings when we do, and then train a neural network to try to predict the missing ratings based on both the users' utility matrix and the movie similarity matrix (perhaps using a *hybrid recommendation system* that references both user-based and content-based information). We can compare the neural network's predictions to the users' actual ratings and train it to get these predictions right. We could also try to optimize recommendations for other metrics of success, such as the total time that the user spends on the platform, perhaps using A/B testing (studying the outcomes of users randomly assigned to various conditions) as discussed in Chapter 3.

In sum, recommendation systems have a lot in common with search: They use vector representations of individuals or items to identify their similarity to one another; they rank items by their relevance to various users. But while search helps people satisfy an information need that they already have, recommendation systems try to suggest things that people don't even know they want. Recommendation systems thus shape what people want, what they pay attention to, and what options they see as available. Users get things that they like, which is good. But other times, users may only see content that reinforces their views, meaning that they only press "like" on such content, giving them even more content consistent with those views – such that they may not realize that they live in an *echo chamber* far away from the mainstream.

6.7 Consequences

Today, we are all lucky to have an ocean of information at our fingertips. Search engines help us to find what we want in that ocean, and recommendation systems suggest what we might like. Researchers all over the world can access articles in seconds that used to be housed only in a few physical libraries. All of these developments make the world a better place.

But we have also seen some challenges and potential downsides of such technology. As products, companies, and people compete for limited attention, they may use *search engine optimization* techniques to make sure that they are ranked highly, sometimes trying to game the system. For example, once Instagram started promoting posts with a lot of "likes", influencers and companies started buying likes from fake accounts to improve their rankings – starting an arms race between engineers who want to promote truly high-quality content, and people who want their content to be promoted whether it's high-quality or not.

When a powerful company's algorithm gives a high ranking to a given post, that post may be imbued with a sense of legitimacy – which may or may not be justified. YouTube had to revise its ranking algorithm after a top-ranked result for a search about a mass shooting promoted an unsupported theory that the shooting was fake; Google has demoted pages falsely denying the 1940s-era genocide of European Jews; Facebook has tried to limit the spread of false news on its platform; and Twitter/X has limited the sharing of posts deemed to constitute misinformation about the coronavirus (raising questions about who gets to decide what constitutes "misinformation" on a topic with rapidly evolving science and contested political implications). Technology companies have also tried to recommend more trustworthy information to users who have fallen into an echo chamber of hateful or false fringe beliefs. As people's lives increasingly take place online, algorithmic rankings increasingly shape our beliefs and experiences, with increasing consequences.

Checklist

- Give examples of various types of information needs and discuss how each one can be handled by modern technology.
- Give examples of structured, semi-structured, and unstructured data.
- Explain why it is difficult to keep a knowledge graph up-to-date.
- Form well-thought-out boolean queries.
- Compare and contrast Westlaw to an open-domain search engine.
- Describe how search engines rank results by their relevance to a query.
- Describe how search engines rank results by the quality of each page.
- Give examples of the design choices that must be made by those in charge of a search engine.
- Understand and use regular expressions.

- Represent documents as vectors and use these vectors to estimate their similarity to one another.
- Calculate the TFIDF of a term in a document (among a collection of documents) and explain what it means.
- Discuss the affordances and limitations of generative language models, knowledge graphs, and free-text search for different information needs.
- Compare and contrast searching to recommendation systems.

Exercises

1. For each of the following, describe how you would approach the search problem. How difficult is each problem? What resources would you use and why?
   a) Finding general information on what the Lincoln-Douglas debates were.
   b) Finding a general quote, or quotes, from the Lincoln-Douglas debates which will support a theory that Abraham Lincoln was not completely anti-slavery.
   c) Finding a particular quote from the Lincoln-Douglas debates that you can only partially remember.
   d) Finding quotes from the Lincoln-Douglas debates which have their origin in the Bible.
2. What do you think the relationship is between how much *prior knowledge* you have about a topic and the amount of *structure* you require in the database you search through?
3. Imagine that we have 11 books in a library with the following subject fields:

1) rock paper	7) rock paper scissors
2) rock scissors	8) rock paper bomb
3) rock bomb	9) rock scissors bomb
4) paper scissors	10) paper scissors bomb
5) paper bomb	11) rock paper scissors bomb
6) scissors bomb	

Looking at the list of queries below, which of the subject numbers do they match? For example, `rock AND bomb` matches 3, 8, 9, and 11.

a) rock OR paper OR scissors
b) rock AND (paper OR scissors)
c) (rock AND paper) OR (scissors AND bomb)
d) (rock OR paper) AND (scissors OR bomb)
e) rock AND (paper OR (scissors AND bomb))
f) ((rock AND paper) OR scissors) AND bomb

4. Check out the Advanced search options available on your favorite search engine. Were you aware of these options? Now that you are aware of them, do you think they will be useful to you? Why or why not?

5. Try the same search in several different search engines (Google, Bing, Baidu, DuckDuckGo, Ecosia, or others). What similarities or differences do you observe – in the results and their ranking, as well as in the user experience, design, and advertisements?

6. Search for your name, in quotes. What is the precision of your search? What is the recall? (Why is recall hard to estimate?) What are the pros and cons of being easy or hard to find online?

7. Check out Google Trends[a], which keeps track of searches by volume and location. Can you find a search that has increased in volume over time? A search that has decreased in volume over time? A search that is popular every year at around the same time? A search that is far more popular in one part of the world/country than others?

8. What information do you think is available in ConceptNet for the word/concept *cat*? What about in WordNet? Go check these databases to see what you guessed right or wrong.

9. Compare your recommendations on YouTube, Twitter/X, Amazon, or Netflix to those of a friend or classmate (if you feel comfortable doing so). How similar or different are your recommendations, and why?

10. For the following scenarios, describe whether precision or recall is more important and why.
    - Identifying the cases where a cancer-curing drug has a side effect of nausea.
    - Identifying the cases where a cancer-curing drug has a side effect of death.
    - Identifying cars running red lights.
    - Identifying and removing weeds which look like (desired) native flowers in your garden.

11. When we talked about how weblinking is used to rank webpages, we mentioned how one page's popularity helps determine that of another. But there's a problem: Where do we start? How can we know another page's popularity if it, too, is based on the popularity of other pages?

    Assume that we initially assign every page a score of 1.

    a) If every incoming page has the same score, namely 1, what is the new score of a webpage, based on our previous formula?

    b) Based on your answer for the previous question, what would be the next step for giving every webpage a new score? How many steps would it take until every page had a final score? Or, another way to word it: How could you determine when you are done?

12. a) Describe in your own words why *popularity* is a good heuristic for measuring the quality of search results.

b) Provide an example where your search query results in a popular, yet irrelevant, result as the first result from a search engine. What rank is your desired result?

13. In the section on regular expressions, we mentioned that some operators have different meanings for basic web searching and in regular expressions. Describe the difference in meaning between the wildcard * allowed in web interfaces and the Kleene star * used in regular expressions.

14. Assume you have a huge text file which consists of all the content of the English Wikipedia from a particular day (https://en.wikipedia.org/wiki/Main_Page). You have a report due tomorrow on major and minor holidays of the world, focusing on ones not found in the United States and celebrated during the fall.

    a) Would regular expressions be more or less useful in this context than using the Wikipedia search box?

    b) What is more important to you in this context, precision or recall?

    c) Let us say that we attempt to search for holidays and holy days in August, and we come up with the following regular expressions (which we can search for using the command `egrep`). What is wrong with these regexes, and how could we fix them?

        i. `egrep 'world.*August.*(holidays)?'`

        ii. `egrep 'august hol(i|y)days?'`

        iii. `egrep 'holidays|holy days in August'`

15. a) Can you describe the set of strings accepted by the automaton that has a single state (*P*) that is both initial and final, but this time two arcs each looping from *P* to *P*, one labeled with *a* and one labeled with *b*?

    b) Can you see how to make an automaton that accepts "", *ab*, *abab*, *ababab*, and so on forever? That is, can you work out how to arrange the states and arcs so that the available routes from an initial to a final state are the ones that correspond to zero or more repetitions of *ab*?

c) Notice that the strings in the previous question are exactly the ones that are matched by the regular expression `/(ab)*/`. How can you change your automaton so that it accepts the strings defined by the regular expression `/ab(ab)*/`? How about the regular expression `/(ab)+/`?

16. In Under the Hood 6.5, we discussed matching strings to finite-state automata. As it turns out, there are some string matching tasks that are easy to state, but that neither regular expressions nor finite-state automata can do. Consider the following five sets of strings:

    - Sequences following the pattern "", *ba*, *baba*, *bababa*, up to any length.
    - Sequences following the pattern "", *abc*, *abcabc*, *abcabcabc*, up to any length.
    - Sequences consisting of any number of *a*s followed by the same number of *b*s. The pattern is "", *ab*, *aabb*, *aaabbb*, *aaaabbbb*, up to any length.
    - Sequences consisting of any number up to 10 of *a*s followed by the same number of *b*s.
    - Sequences following the pattern "", *aba*, *abaaba*, *abaabaaba*, up to any length.

    a) Three of these sets of strings have automata and regular expressions that you will probably find quite quickly and not mind writing down. Which ones are these?

    b) One of the string sets can be matched by a regular expression and can also be associated with an automaton that accepts exactly the right strings, but neither the expression nor the automaton is something that a normal human being would enjoy writing down. Which one is this?

    c) One of the string sets can neither be matched by a regular expression nor accepted by a finite-state automaton. Which one is this? And why does this happen?

[a]www.trends.google.com, accessed 2024-04-26.

Further reading

Manning et al. (2008) provides a thorough (but now somewhat historical) technical introduction to the field of information retrieval. If you want details on Google's PageRank algorithm, you might even want to try reading the paper which describes it (Page et al. 1999).

For more information on boolean expressions and logical thinking, you can consult a number of textbooks on basic symbolic logic. To obtain more of a focus on logic in the realm of linguistics, look for books on mathematical or formal linguistics, such as Partee et al. (1990).

Shah & Bender (2022) discuss the pros and cons of generative language models versus traditional search for information retrieval.

Lu et al. (2015) provide an overview of recommendation systems.

7 Machine translation

7.1 Introduction

Machine translation describes the task of automatically mapping a text from one human language to another. Once considered one of the hardest problems in language technology, machine translation has seen huge advances over the past decades, and now – for some pairs of languages, and for some purposes – it can be astonishingly good. For example, a randomly chosen sentence (1) from the Francophone discussion forum on Reddit (r/france) is translated instantly, fluently, and accurately (2) by Google Translate. The use of the word *holidays* to translate *vacances* 'vacation' is perhaps more British than American, but otherwise the translation is perfect:

(1) *Pour le moment j'hésite à accepter le job parce que la position (junior) est moins bien payée que ma position actuelle d'enseignant, avec bien entendu beaucoup moins de vacances que ce que j'ai actuellement etc.*

(2) At the moment I hesitate to accept the job because the position (junior) is less well paid than my current teaching position, with of course much less holidays than what I currently have etc.

This chapter explores why and how machine translation has been so successful, and what challenges still remain.

If you are a monolingual Anglophone in an English-dominant society, you may not see a strong need for translation because you are privileged to speak an international *lingua franca* (language of trade and scholarship). But many people around the world speak a different language at work/school versus at home; with different members of their family; or when they travel an hour away from home. In multilingual contexts such as the European Union, translation is needed for essentially all trade, travel, and governance. Translation is a daily necessity for much of the world's population, and machines can make it more accessible.

Before explaining how machine translation works, it is useful to define the concept and introduce some terms. *Translation* is the process of moving text or speech from one human language to another, while preserving the intended message. (We'll discuss what that really means below.) We call the message's original language the *source language* and the language that it's translated into the *target language*. We say that two words, one from the source language, one from the target language, are *translation equivalents* if they convey the same meaning in context. The same idea applies to pairs of phrases and sentences.

(3) illustrates some difficulties that can arise if you are not careful to check whether a translation is saying the right thing (some found on the subreddit r/Engrish, some taken from *Atlas Obscura*.[1]) Some of these translations were probably generated by machines, others by humans with incomplete knowledge of both languages. If you are ever asked to put up a sign or write a menu in a language that you do not fully understand, remember these examples and get the content checked!

(3) a. *Sign in a Paris hotel:* Please leave your values at the front desk
  b. *Sign on a Japanese subway:* Do not pick pocket, Do not molester, Do not drug, Do not drunk and disorderly, Do not smoking, Do not battle
  c. *Menu at a Russian restaurant:* Beef language with fungus sauce
  d. *Menu at a German restaurant:* Mouth bags
  e. *Menu at a Turkish restaurant:* Cigarette pie
  f. *Sign on grass in China:* Do not disturb, tiny grass is dreaming
  g. *Sign at a subway station in Hong Kong:* Please present your Octopus

Let's explore what went wrong here. (3a) is just a poor word choice: *Valuables* is the word that the translator was searching for, and *values* is unintentionally funny.

(3b) involves confusion about grammatical categories: *Do not* combines with verbs or verb phrases in English, but here it is combined with nouns (*do not molester*), adjectives (*do not drunk and disorderly*), and gerunds (*do not smoking*). *Do not battle* is syntactically coherent, since *battle* can be a verb as well as a noun, but *battle* is an unusual way to describe a two-person altercation on the subway.

The next three examples (3c)–(3e), from menus, illustrate why culinary translation is particularly difficult. Names for food are culturally specific and somewhat idiomatic; should they be translated literally, or elaborated for an unfamiliar audience? What food words should be translated in the first place, versus just left in the original language? Many food words originally enter English as *borrowings*

[1] "Why menu translations go terribly wrong," 24 January 2018, by Emily Monaco

(also known as *loan words*) from other languages (*spaghetti, sushi, quesadilla*); upscale menus for Anglophone diners are full of more recent and lesser-known loan words (*ballotine, moussaka, gochujang*), which diners may look up online under the table to keep up the pretense of being cosmopolitan foodies well-versed in such vocabulary.

The *language* in (3c) really means *tongue*. These two concepts are denoted by the same word in Russian. In English, the two words are related (you use your *tongue* to speak a *language*) and overlap in meaning (as in *mother tongue*) – but the overlap is incomplete, because *language* cannot describe a body part. This example illustrates *polysemy* (when a word has multiple distinct but related meanings), and how a word's degree of polysemy can vary across languages.

Mouth bags (3d) is an overly literal translation of German *Maultaschen* 'dumplings' – small *bags* of dough-wrapped filling which go in your *mouth*. The meaning of this compound word becomes opaque and unpleasant in English, because the word *bags* is rarely used for foods, and because the relationship between the two words in the compound – *mouth* and *bags* – is not clear.

Stepping back, a *compound* is a word made from two words (here, two nouns), with the relationship between these words supplied by the context and our background knowledge about the referent of (the thing described by) each word. A *chocolate cake* has chocolate in it; a *birthday cake* is eaten on someone's birthday; a *skillet cake* is baked in a skillet. If we don't have enough background knowledge to supply this relation between the two nouns (*mouth bags*), then we have to imagine one, and we may end up befuddled. *Cigarette pie* (3e) is also a direct translation of a compound; in Turkish, it describes a long, slender pastry. But if we don't know that *cigarette* describes the shape of the pie, we may imagine that it describes an ingredient, which is less appetizing.

The final two unusual translations illustrate the challenge of translating cultural knowledge in tandem with language. The Chinese sign (3f) essentially tells people to *keep off the grass*; but it uses a Chinese convention of anthropomorphizing inanimate objects and presenting directives in a cutesy, non-threatening manner. The sign from Hong Kong (3g) seems to fantastically assume that every person has an octopus just as they have a nose and a mobile phone; but it makes sense when you understand that Hong Kong's widely-used subway/debit card is called an Octopus card. Both of these signs may be literally translated quite well, but the informational effect on the reader is lost without cultural context.

We chose the examples in (3) because we hope that they are amusing. But in other settings, translation errors can have serious consequences. This happened when a young patient named Willie Ramirez was brought into a Florida hospital's emergency room in a coma (Harsham 1984). His mother and girlfriend, speaking in Spanish, talked to the English-speaking emergency room staff. They used the word *intoxicado*, which can mean several things, including 'nauseous'. Because the emergency room staff were not professional interpreters, they thought that *intoxicado* must mean the same as the English *intoxicated* and treated him on the assumption that he was under the influence of drugs or alcohol. Linguistically speaking, they took *intoxicado* as a *cognate*, like Spanish *chocolate*, identical to the the English; but it was in fact a *false friend*, like Spanish *realizar*, which does not mean 'to realize' but instead means 'achieve'.

As a result of this misunderstanding, the patient was eventually diagnosed with a brain aneurysm and became quadriplegic. This case is infamous, because it led to a lawsuit, and drew attention to the principle that hospitals, courts and other institutions that work with the public should plan for the needs of a multilingual population and provide the translation and interpretation services that are needed. Evoking our recurring focus on ethics, this is an issue of basic fairness, public safety, and perhaps also civil rights.

7.2 Applications of translation

In information retrieval, the user can be thought of as having an *information need* (Section 6.1.2). In the same way, a potential user of translation technology can be thought of as having a *translation need*. Before we get into automatic translation, though, let's first explore the needs served by human translators and interpreters. Among human professionals, a *translator* is someone who deals with text, while an *interpreter* deals with speech.

Among (human) interpreters, a *simultaneous interpreter* listens to speech in a source language, and speaks the same message in the target language with only seconds' delay. These professionals are not only fluent in both languages, but also have trained their working memory and executive functioning to listen and speak at the same time, a similar mental task to sight-reading music. At the United Nations, diplomats wear earpieces to hear spoken proceedings simultaneously interpreted into their own language in real time. A *consecutive interpreter* listens to speech in a source language, takes notes, and then produces the speech in the target language after the original source-language turn is complete. Consecutive interpreters handle diplomatic speeches, meetings, and court cases.

A *whisper interpreter* might accompany a diplomat to a social occasion and offer a whispered paraphrase of what people are saying, so that the diplomat can follow along politely. A *phone interpreter* provides consecutive interpretation over the phone, for example when a doctor must provide emergency medical care to a patient in a different language, and there is no in-person interpreter on site. Finally, a *medical interpreter* (who may work in person or over the phone) is specifically trained in medicine and ethics to provide services in a *safety-critical* context – hopefully preventing fiascos like the one caused by the misunderstanding of *intoxicado*. Medical interpreters also have to consider the educational background and cultural assumptions of the people they serve; one medical interpreter (Haffner 1992) had to clarify to a patient that her fallopian tubes, once "tied", could not be easily untied like shoelaces. These different types of interpreters illustrate the diverse translation needs that arise in spoken situations.

In the rest of this chapter, we focus on translating rather than interpreting because computers deal primarily with language as text rather than speech. All (human) translators do basically the same thing: Given a document written in a source language, they produce a corresponding document in the target language. Different translators specialize in the translation of literary, technical, legal, political, historical, or medical documents, requiring rich content knowledge alongside linguistic ability. Human translators may not write a translation from scratch, but may instead work to edit, check, and improve a draft produced by a machine, in a process called *post-editing* – indeed (Green et al. 2013), they may find it faster and more enjoyable to work this way.

Recalling from Chapter 3 that people find it easier to comprehend than to produce in their L2, both interpreters and translators may prefer to use their L2 as the source language and their L1 as the target language. In the context of machine translation, though, it can be equally easy to go in either direction.

So far, we have introduced some of the translation and interpreting needs serviced by human professionals. But there are countless other translation needs, requiring varying levels of confidence and correctness. For each one listed here, please consider whether you would trust a free online tool, or whether – even considering the time and expense – you would want to pay a human to corroborate it. If you were to hire a human, would any bilingual person be sufficient or would you want someone with particular content knowledge?

- You are an award-winning Senegalese filmmaker who wants to release your Wolof-language film with English subtitles for an Anglophone market.

- You want to wish your friend a happy birthday in their native language of Indonesian.

- You work for an American clothing company and you want to skim some Japanese reviews of your products.
- You are on vacation in Guatemala and want to perform basic functions: Greet and thank people, request directions, purchase food, and check into your hotel.
- You bought malaria-prevention pills at a Guatemalan pharmacy, the label is in Spanish, and you can't figure out if you are supposed to take one pill twice a day (for a total of two), or two pills twice a day (for a total of four), or for how many days you are supposed to take them.
- Your friend gives you a packaged snack from Sweden and you want to read the nutrition facts.
- You work for a humanitarian aid group, and you want to read real-time live tweets about a natural disaster written in Haitian Creole to figure out what kind of help people need and where.
- You are an American attorney suing a German company for selling a fraudulent product in the United States. You want to find out who in the company knew what when. The company turns over their emails, which are all in German.
- You are an American advocate for cultural heritage, and you want to read documents in Turkish discussing the fate of various Kurdish cultural heritage sites in Turkey. The documents are written in a non-standard variety of Turkish, by people who largely did not attend high school and who are more proficient in Kurdish than Turkish.
- You are an American academic who wants to read an academic article that is only available in Russian.
- You are a religious scholar who wants to know what the original Biblical Hebrew, Aramaic, or Greek says about a given topic.
- You are an English-speaking worker in Ireland trying to make bilingual street signs in English and Irish.
- You are an American military strategist and you want to understand public sentiment towards the presence of American troops in Afghanistan by reading social media posts.

- You are a British diplomat negotiating a nuclear arms treaty with Russia. The treaty will specify what weapons and dangerous materials each country can possess, in what quantities, for what purposes, and with what types of inspections.

The moral is that different translation needs require different resources and perhaps different combinations of human and machine intelligence.

7.3 Same meaning, different languages

As we said above, the goal of translation is to map a sentence from a source language into a target language while preserving the meaning. To understand this process, we need to know what meaning is, and how it is encoded in different languages.

7.3.1 What is meaning?

What is meaning? This question is quite abstract, but the philosopher David Lewis (1972) offers us a way to proceed (also mentioned in Chapter 4): Instead of asking what a meaning *is*, we should ask what a meaning *does*, or what a person can do when they know the meaning of some expression. When you know the meaning of a word, you can:

- Pick out the thing or situation (or class of things/situations) in the world that this word refers to. (This is easier for nouns like *dog* and verbs like *run* than for determiners like *the* and *a*).
- Reason about how this word relates to other words (a *dog* is a type of *animal* that *barks*; *four* is less than *five*).
- Use this word in a sentence and understand what it contributes to that sentence.

When you know the meaning of a sentence, you can:

- Know what the world would be like if this sentence were true. (Whether or not it actually *is* true is a different matter.)
- Reason about how this sentence relates logically to other sentences (*I saw Jane and Sam* entails that *I saw Jane*; *I didn't see Jane* contradicts it.)

- Use this sentence in a discourse and understand what it contributes to that discourse – what it would add to people's beliefs if they accept an assertion of this sentence as true.

Of course, these conditions only make sense for declarative, assertion-making sentences like *I love running*. As we explore further in Chapter 8, to know the meaning of a question like *Do you like running?* is to know how it should be answered; to know the meaning of an imperative like *Have a cookie!* is to know what you are supposed to (or allowed to) do as a result. If translation is successful, a person who knows the meaning of the source sentence and a person who knows the meaning of the target sentence will be able to use and reason about those sentences in the same ways. These ideas come from the linguistic subfield of *semantics*, the study of meaning.

In our discussion of grammar checking (Section 2.5.1), we saw that it is helpful to break up English sentences into smaller components, and give these components names like *noun phrase* and *verb phrase*. These components may in turn be broken down into subcomponents, with the whole process bottoming out either in words or in slightly smaller units called *morphemes* (for example, the word *dogs* comprises two morphemes, *dog* and the pluralizing suffix *-s*).

In semantics, researchers study the meanings of words (*lexical semantics*) as well as the rules for combining words into sentences (*compositional semantics*). Lexical semantics includes the study of *synonyms* (words that mean the same thing), *antonyms* (words that are opposites) and *word senses* (subdivisions of meaning, as when the polysemous word *tongue* can refer to a body part or a language). This matters for translation, because lexical semantics offers tools to understand some of the ways in which things can change as you move from one language to another.

Compositional semantics explains how a sentence like *Roger outplayed Andy* means something quite different from *Andy outplayed Roger.* The words are the same, but the way they are arranged differs, and this affects the meaning. But *Roger outplayed Andy* means much the same as *Andy was outplayed by Roger.* Here the words differ, but the meaning somehow comes out almost identical.

The term *compositional* is used because the meaning of a whole expression is *composed* of the meanings of its component parts. Thus, the meaning of the phrase *triangular hat box* is constructed (one way or another) from the meanings of the individual words *triangular*, *hat* and *box.* It could mean a triangular box for hats, a box (shape unspecified) for triangular hats, or even a triangular box made out of hats, but each one of these meanings is built from the meaning of the smaller parts. Researchers in compositional semantics begin with the assumption that there is some kind of kind of mechanism for assembling the word meanings into a sentence meaning, and spend their research efforts on experiments and theories designed to shed light on the way this mechanism works. Different languages typically assemble meanings in similar ways, but the fine details of the process differ from language to language, so an automatic translator has to somehow smooth over the differences.

7.3.2 Different languages are different

When we ask how different languages are similar or different, we are engaging in the linguistic subfield of *language typology*. Language typologists explore which languages are related to one another (descended from a common ancestor) or not; how languages have changed over time; and how different languages encode (similar) meanings – all topics with consequences for machine translation. Some of these cross-linguistic differences are easy to handle, but others cause problems that persist even for the most sophisticated machine translation systems.

Most obviously, different languages have different words, and different ways of using words to assemble a meaning. One word in one language may map to two or more words in another language. For example (4), the English sentence *I like skiing* has three words, while the German translation has four. (Here, the first line represents the orthographic German; the second line is a literal word-by-word "gloss" of the German, and the third line is the colloquial English translation.)

(4) German
Ich fahre gern Ski
I drive gladly on-skis
'I like skiing.'

The adverb *gern* expresses the idea of liking which in English is described by a verb; the German verb *fahre* 'drive' does not appear in the English. The meaning comes across, and in each language it is easy to see how the meaning of the whole is composed from the meanings of the parts, but the details differ.

As another example (5), the English sentence *I like fish* again has three words, while its Spanish translation has four:

(5) Spanish
Me gusta el pescado
To-me pleases the fish
'I like fish.'

Here, the Spanish phrase *me gusta* 'I like' literally means 'to me pleases'. Whereas the syntactic subject of the English sentence is the first-person pronoun *I*, in Spanish the subject is actually *el pescado* 'the fish' – with a definite determiner *el* 'the' because Spanish often requires determiners where English allows bare nouns for plurals (*cats*, multiple *fish*) and undifferentiated substances (*wine*; some quantity of cooked *fish*).

One word in one language may also map to two or more words in another language in a different sense: When one language uses a single word polysemously to cover two related meanings, while another language splits up those meanings into two different words. We saw an example above where some languages use the same word for both *language* and *tongue*, while others have a different word for the communication system versus the body part. As another example, the Spanish word *pescado* 'fish' (literally, 'fished' – the past participle of the verb *pescar* 'to fish') refers to fish as food, while *pez* 'fish' is used for live animals. In contrast, the English word *fish* covers both. So (5) in English could mean that fish are my favorite animal or my favorite food, whereas in Spanish it only refers to food.

Can it ever happen that a word in one language maps to *zero* words in another language? One often encounters such claims, of the form *Language X doesn't have a (single) word for Concept Y* – which are then sometimes expanded to mean that people who speak Language X don't care about or can't think about Concept Y. These claims are often spurious and must be taken with a great deal of skepticism. Can Concept Y be paraphrased in Language X even if there is no single word for it? For example, the Greek word *agape* can be paraphrased in English as 'goodwill towards humanity' even if it requires more than one word. Can a word for Concept Y be immediately coined or borrowed whenever the speakers of Language X want to talk about it? French historically had no native word for 'weekend', but they borrowed the English one as soon as they saw a use for it.

Or is the issue really that speakers of Language X have never even encountered Concept Y, much less a word for it? This is clearly why the speakers of Old English had no word for 'wifi', and why pre-colonized indigenous Americans had no word for 'Halloween'. Such cultural concepts are a much trickier issue for translation. Foods (*gelato*), clothing (*athleisure*), holidays (*Halloween*), occupations (*influencer*), technology (*wifi*), and literary/historical allusions (*Cinderella*) may not have names in a culture where they are unfamiliar. As Jurafsky & Martin (2009) describe, it is not easy to translate *The Lord is my shepherd* for a culture with no shepherds or sheep. Here, the issue is really about what technologies and concepts are used in different cultures, not about what words they have.

Moving beyond words, languages also differ in their structure. You are encouraged to visit the *World Atlas of Language Structures*[2] created by Dryer & Haspelmath (2013), to learn more about the cross-linguistic diversity that we can only sketch here:

- *Word-to-morpheme ratio:* How many meaningful pieces does a single word have, on average? In an *isolating language* like Mandarin, where one morpheme is roughly equivalent to one syllable and one "word", the concept of "word" may not even have much independent utility.
- *Word-to-sentence ratio:* How many words make up a sentence, on average? In a *synthetic language* like Nahuatl, which has a very high number of morphemes per word, a "word" may be approximately equivalent to a full sentence, and the concept of "word" may not mean much here either.
- *Basic word order:* English is a Subject-Verb-Object language; in a sentence like *I threw the ball*, the subject (*I*) comes first, then the verb (*threw*), then the direct object (*the ball*). Other languages use different basic word orders (most common of all is SOV, as in Korean and Turkish: *I the ball threw*). It's most common for the subject to come first, but some languages such as Irish put the verb first; rarest of all are those that put the object first, like the Hixkaryana language of Brazil.
- *Order of adjectives and nouns:* We've already seen that English adjectives come before nouns (*the red balloon*) while French adjectives come after (*le ballon rouge*).
- *Ability to leave out pronouns:* In some languages such as Spanish and Japanese, it's very common to omit a pronoun in a sentence where it can be easily inferred from the discourse context or from subject-verb agreement morphology, as in the Spanish sentence *caminé ayer* '(I) walked yesterday'. In English, such constructions are much rarer and limited to specific contexts such as writing in a diary.
- *Tense:* In English, verbs are marked when they describe an event that took place in the past, like *walked*. But some languages, such as Mandarin, use the same verb form regardless of time, and convey temporal information by other means.

[2]www.wals.info, accessed 2024-04-26.

- *Evidentiality:* In languages such as Turkish, a verb ending marks how the speaker came to know the content of the sentence – direct observation, hearsay, inference. In English, such information can be mentioned if the speaker feels like it, but it is not required as part of the verb system.

- *Lexical categories:* Languages like English have a large class of adjectives, describing concepts like color, age, size, physical appearance, and subjective evaluation. But languages such as Wolof have relatively few adjectives, and a lot of English adjectives are translated instead as verbs (a verb like 'to [be] hot' or as possessed nouns (like 'to have strength').

- *Definite and indefinite determiners:* English has both the definite determiner *the* and the indefinite *a*. Some languages (like Persian) have only one or the other, or (like Mandarin) neither one. Even among languages that have definite and indefinite determiners, these can be used in different ways; as we saw in the discussion of *el pescado* in Spanish, English uses bare plural nouns (*fish*) to refer to fish in general, while Spanish and French use definites (*el pescado, le poisson*) for this purpose.

- *Case:* In English, pronouns are marked for *case* (grammatical role in the sentence): *I* is the first-person singular pronoun used for grammatical subjects, *me* is used for objects, *my* is used for possessives, and so on. In languages such as Russian and Latin, not just pronouns but all nouns are marked in this way, with different endings depending on their grammatical role.

- *Number:* In English, we use a plural *-s* suffix on nouns when referring to more than one member of a category. In other languages such as Mandarin, the distinction between singular and plural is largely not marked.

- *Gender:* In English, *my neighbor* doesn't tell us anything about this person's gender. But in French, *ma voisine* refers to my female neighbor, and *mon voisin* refers to my male neighbor. In English, third-person singular pronouns are marked for gender (*she, he*) and animacy (*it* is for less-sentient things); whereas in Persian, the animate third-person singular *u* does not mark gender, and in French, there is no inanimate form and even the plurals (*ils, elles* – both meaning 'they') are marked for gender.

- *Formality:* In English, *you* is used for all second-person addressees, singular or plural, close friends or respected elders. In French, *tu* is singular and informal (used between friends), while *vous* is plural and/or formal (used for polite acquaintances and social superiors). *Thou*, used several centuries ago, used to serve as the informal form of *you* in English.

Some of these cross-linguistic differences require (human-written or machine-learned) transfer rules to reorganize information from one language to another.

Posing a larger challenge, these cross-linguistic differences also mean that translation sometimes doesn't just require knowledge of the source and target languages, but also knowledge – not necessarily reflected in the source text! – about the real-world events that the author intends to describe. Translating from English to Turkish, a (human or machine) translator must choose an evidential marker, required by Turkish but not English, about how the speaker came to know the content of what they are saying. Translating English to French, a translator must choose a gender for *my neighbor* and a formality level for *you*. Translating French to English, one must decide whether *J'aime la pizza* means 'I like pizza' (in general) or 'I like the pizza' (that we are eating); using an example from Cohn-Gordon & Goodman (2019), one must also decide whether *J'ai coupé le doigt* describes a banal scenario where 'I cut my finger' or a grisly one where 'I cut off my finger'. Translating Chinese to English, one must choose the right tense marking for verbs and the right number marking for nouns. Perhaps the surrounding context of the source text resolves the confusion, but perhaps one just has to make a decision.

Such cases – when a distinction is unmarked in a source language but required in a target language – are among the most difficult issues for human translators too. World Health Organization translator Claude Piron (Piron 1988) describes translating an English description of a disease that had emerged in a *Japanese prisoner-of-war camp*. While the English source text is ambiguous, the clearest French translation would specify whether the camps or the prisoners-of-war were Japanese:

(6) a. French
camp japonais de prisonniers de guerre
camp Japanese of prisoners of war
'Japanese camp for prisoners-of-war'

b. camp de prisonniers de guerre japonais
camp of prisoners of war Japanese
'camp for Japanese prisoners-of-war'

Piron wrote to the original author asking whether the camps or the POWs were Japanese, and received word that the author had died. He doesn't explain what he did next – perhaps he made an educated guess, or perhaps he added a footnote to the translation explaining the confusion. Most of his work as a medical translator involved such detective work, he says, and he doesn't trust machines to take it over.

For their part, machine translation systems often just default to translating an under-determined source text into whatever target text is the most common in the data used to build the system. As of the time of writing, Google Translate translates *Japanese prisoner-of-war camps* as in (6a). Translating English to Spanish, the current default of Google Translate usually chooses the singular informal *tú* rather than the plural *ustedes* or the singular formal *usted* – perhaps setting people up for accidental rudeness! (Sometimes adding an honorific like *sir* to the source sentence can move Google Translate towards the formal *usted* in the translation.)

But in some cases, Google Translate is sophisticated enough to inform users about the choices to be made. Translating the single word *student* to French, the system offers both *étudiant* (masculine) and *étudiante* (feminine) – providing transparency about the fact that the user has to determine the gender of the student. This design choice puts the *human-in-the-loop*, because Google Translate supplies two options with metalinguistic annotations for the human to choose one, and it is a good way to handle such difficult cases. But so far, this transparent human-in-the-loop system is only offered when the user elicits a translation for *student* as a single word. When *student* appears in a longer text, English-to-French Google Translate often just defaults to the masculine form.

Another good place to give the user multiple options involves differences across regions or dialects. Should French *coffre* be translated as American *trunk* (of a car) or British *boot*? Intersecting questions about region with singular/plural and familiar/formal distinctions, should English *you* be translated as Spanish *tú* (singular familiar), *usted* (singular formal), *ustedes* (plural used in Latin America), or *vosotros* (plural used in Europe)? Potentially of more consequence in a medical context, should Spanish *canilla* be translated as *shinbone* (in some regions) or *wrist* (in others)? In these cases, you need to know not just what the text means, but also what you are assuming about the people who are producing the source text or comprehending the translation.

7.4 Building a machine translation system

Having introduced translation and the concepts underlying it, we are now ready to explore how machines can "learn" to translate from data.

7.4.1 Parallel corpora

The first ingredient in any modern machine translation is a *parallel corpus*, also known as a *bitext* – a set of pairs of documents, one in each language, known to say the same thing. Ideally you want a set of pairs of translation-equivalent sentences, like French *Elle est américaine* and English *She is American.*

Historically, one of the most famous parallel corpora is the *Rosetta Stone*, used by the French linguist Jean-François Champollion to decipher Ancient Egyptian hieroglyphics. The Rosetta Stone issues a decree by King Ptolemy V in two languages (Ancient Egyptian and Ancient Greek), and three writing systems (recalling the distinction between languages and writing systems from Chapter 1). Ancient Egyptian is written in hieroglyphics – a combination of alphabetic, syllabic, and logographic elements, decoded as a result – and in the Demotic abjad; Ancient Greek is written in the Greek alphabet. The Rosetta Stone illustrates that it is a lot easier to translate something when you already know what it says. A similar idea was used by the British cryptographer Alan Turing (inventor of the Turing Test described in Chapter 8) and his colleagues at Bletchley Park to decipher the Nazi Enigma code: They knew that messages often began with *To* and that some of the enciphered text described daily weather forecasts, so they were also able to leverage this information as a partial parallel corpus.

Thanks to the work of human translators, parallel corpora are already all around us. You can explore the OPUS Open Parallel Corpus created by Tiedemann & Nygaard (2004)[3] for open-access examples. In multilingual parliaments around the world and in the United Nations, parallel documents are produced in all official languages; other sources include literature (especially older literature in the public domain), film and television subtitles, newswire text, and TED talks. Of course, it is easier to find large parallel corpora for some language pairs than others. For *low-resource languages* such as Chamorro (a Polynesian language of Guam), one may not find much more than the very widely-translated Universal Declaration of Human Rights and the Christian Bible. Even within a high-resource language such as English, some minoritized varieties, such as Indian English or African American English, have fewer resources. Improving tools for low-resource languages and varieties constitutes another ongoing challenge for machine translation.

[3]https://opus.nlpl.eu, accessed 2024-05-23.

7.4.2 Word alignment

Once you have a parallel corpus, a natural next step is to try to line up the words in each language that correspond to one another. This process of *alignment* constituted the first step of deciphering the Rosetta Stone; it underlies the *translation models* used in statistical machine translation; and it persists, in a modified bottom-up form, in the most modern neural machine translation systems (as *attention* – discussed below).

Figure 7.1 shows the alignment between French and English in a sentence from the Universal Declaration of Human Rights. Notice that the French word *les* 'the' is not associated with any English word, and the English word *are* is not associated with any French word. It is useful to make sure that every word is connected to something, which we can do by introducing a special *null word* that has no other purpose than to provide a hook for the words that would otherwise not be connected. It is also possible for one word in one language to align to multiple words in another language, like English *potato* to French *pomme de terre.*

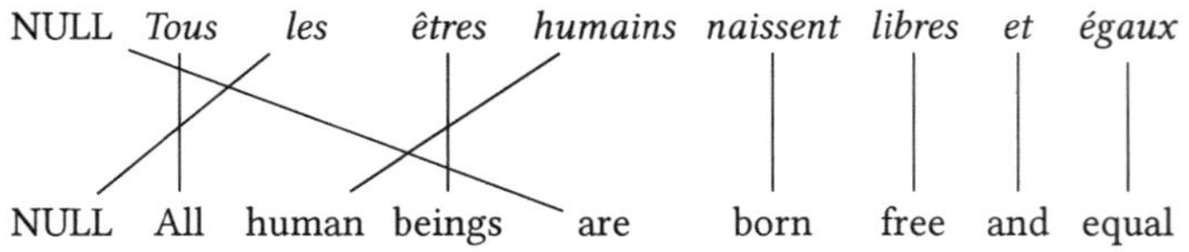

Figure 7.1: Word alignment, using the Universal Declaration of Human Rights.

Word alignment can be automated using a parallel corpus, and automated alignment was an important part of the statistical machine translation systems used in the 1990s and 2000s. In today's neural machine translation systems, automatic alignment is no longer an explicit step of the machine translation process, but alignment does still emerge in a bottom-up manner as a neural network learns the best source-to-target mappings from a parallel corpus.

Let us sketch how alignment is automated in a statistical machine translation system. To start off, we just count the number of times each word pair occurs in corresponding sentences. If we try this for a little fragment of Hansard (the official record of Canadian parliamentary debates), which is conveniently published in French and English, we can find out that the French word *gouvernement* lines up with the following frequent English words (second column). This table counts the number of parallel sentence pairs that contain each combination of French and English words.

Table 7.1: For each pair of words, the number of parallel sentences in which both words occur.

French	English	Count
gouvernement	the	335
gouvernement	to	160
gouvernement	government	128
gouvernement	of	123
gouvernement	and	81
gouvernement	that	77
gouvernement	in	73
gouvernement	is	60
gouvernement	a	50
gouvernement	it	46

and the English word *government* lines up with the following frequent French words (first column):

Table 7.2: For each pair of words, the number of parallel sentences in which both words occur.

French	English	Count
de	government	195
le	government	189
gouvernement	government	128
que	government	91
?	government	86
la	government	80
les	government	79
et	government	74
des	government	69
en	government	46

We have left out the infrequently paired words in both lists, because we are expecting lots of accidental matches. But we are also expecting that word pairs that truly are translations will occur together more often than we would expect by chance. Unfortunately, as you see, most of the frequent pairs are unsurprising, too, as the word for government is lining up with a common word of the other language, such as *the*. However, the pair *gouvernement/government* is high up in both lists. This gives us a clue that these words are translation-equivalent. You may have already guessed as much because these words are cognates; but our word alignment process does not use that information and thus works equally well for non-cognates such as *eau* 'water.'

The tables that we are showing are based on 1923 sentences, but in a full system, we would process many thousands, hundreds of thousands, or millions of sentences, so the tables would be correspondingly bigger. To make further progress on this, we need to automate a little more.

The way to deal with this is to do statistics on the word pairs. Table 7.3 contains some of the higher scoring pairs from a single file of the Canadian Hansard. Now, instead of calculating the number of times the word pair occurs together, we also collect other counts. The first column of the table is a statistical score called ϕ^2 *(phi-squared)* which is a measure of how closely related the words seem to be. The second column is the French word, the third the English word and the fourth through seventh are, respectively:

- The number of times the two words occurred in corresponding sentences (*fe*).
- The number of occurrences of the French word (*f*).
- The number of occurrences of the English word (*e*).

Table 7.3: Selected word pairs statistics in a small aligned corpus.

ϕ^2	French	English	fe	f	e
0.823	D'accord	Agreed	14	17	14
0.500	Bravo	Hear	6	12	6
0.111	Interpellation-Suite	Inquiry-Debate	4	8	18
0.094	Législation	Legislation	6	16	24
0.083	appelle:	Order:	7	21	28
0.083	L'ordre	Order:	7	21	28
0.067	Étude	Study	6	18	30
0.067	spéciale	Study	6	18	30
0.044	Deuxième	Reading	4	20	18

In reality, the table would be much bigger, and based on more words, but you can already see that good word pairings are beginning to appear. This table shows the value of statistical calculations about word pairings. To handle cases where alignment is one-to-many or many-to-many rather than one-to-one (for example, French *pommes de terre* 'potatoes'), one would need more sophisticated strategies for capturing the alignment of phrases rather than words.

7.4.3 Statistical machine translation

Automated word alignments are used in statistical machine translation, which is worth studying as the conceptual groundwork for the neural machine translation systems used today.

To understand statistical machine translation, we can return to the noisy channel model which originates in the field of information theory and was discussed in the context of spell-checking in Chapter 2 above. The key idea is that a sender has a clean message in mind, but that message is sent through a noisy channel before it arrives at the receiver. The receiver has to decide on the most likely clean message that was intended given the noisy message that they received. The receiver takes into account two pieces of information – the likelihood of various different clean messages that might have been intended; and the likelihood of the observed noisy message being received given that clean message as input. The likelihood of different clean messages is called the *message model*, and the likelihood of a given observed noisy message given a particular intended clean message is called the *channel model*. We can use mathematics to formalize these two models and the way they should be combined.

Figure 7.2: The noisy channel model.

Reviewing and formalizing our spell-checking example from Chapter 2, imagine you get an email inviting you to a birthday party for *Dsvid*. Think of the original clean signal as being what the user meant to type and the degraded signal as what the users fingers actually did type. It is easy to tell that the clean signal must have been *David*, and that the error is a key-for-key substitution of *s* for *a*, which are adjacent on a common keyboard layout. Here, the channel model says that substitutions of adjacent keys are common, and the message model says that *David* is a more plausible name for the mutual friend than *Dsvid.*

We can turn the noisy channel model into math by writing

$$\hat{y} = \arg\max_{y} P(y)P(x|y) \tag{7.7}$$

where x is the observed output of the channel (that is, the degraded message) and y is the hypothesized clean message. The notation $\arg\max_y P(y)P(x|y)$ is a mathematician's way of saying "search for the y that gives the highest value for the probability expression $P(y)P(x|y)$". $\hat{y}$ is therefore the system's best guess at what the original message must have been. The message model is expressed as $P(y)$, which is the probability that the writer will have intended a particular word y. The message model tells us that *Dsvid* is an unlikely intended message, *David* is a likely message, and *Sara* is also a likely message, because that's also a common name.

$P(x|y)$ is the channel model: It tells us the probability of receiving the degraded signal x given the intended clean message y. The channel model tells us that the probability of receiving the degraded message *Dsvid* given the intended clean message *David* is quite high (the edit distance between them is 1, and *s* is even a particularly likely substitution for *a* on a standard keyboard, since they are adjacent). The channel model also tells us that the probability of receiving the degraded message *Sara* given the intended message *David* is quite low – how could someone mistype *David* as *Sara* when they only share one letter?

Putting together the message model and the channel model, we are looking for the y that gives the highest value for $P(y)P(x|y)$. Our degraded signal is *Dsvid* and we are looking for the clean message that this signal represents. Let's consider three candidates for the intended clean message y: *Dsvid, David,* and *Sara.*

- P(*Dsvid*) is *low*, because *Dsvid* is not a name; P(*Dsvid* | *Dsvid*) is *high*, because if someone did for some reason mean to say *Dsvid*, it is likely that they would have typed *Dsvid.*
- P(*Sara*) is *high*, because it's a common name; P(*Dsvid* | *Sara*) is *low*, because if someone meant to say *Sara*, it's very unlikely that they would have typed *Dsvid.*
- P(*David*) is *high*, because it's a common name; P(*Dsvid* | *David*) is *high*, because if someone meant to say *David*, it's quite likely that they would have typed *Dsvid.*

The y that gives the highest value for $P(y)P(x|y)$, combining the message model and the channel model, is thus of course *David.*

At the end of the chapter, in the exercises, there are a couple of rather more exotic examples of the noisy channel model, including part-of-speech tagging and cryptography. If you want to stretch your mind, do those exercises! After that, there is a risk that you will start seeing the noisy channel model everywhere.

You may already be able to see why this discussion belongs in a chapter about translation. In 1949, the mathematician and information theorist Warren Weaver (1949) put it this way:

> It is very tempting to say that a book written in Chinese is simply a book written in English which was coded into the "Chinese code." If we have useful methods for solving almost any cryptographic problem, may it not be that with proper interpretation we already have useful methods for translation? (Weaver 1949: 22)

Statistical machine translation technology builds on this appealing idea. If we imagine that we have a message in a foreign language f that we would prefer to read in English e, we can factor the task into three parts:

1. Estimating a *translation model* $P(f|e)$.
2. Estimating a *language model* $P(e)$.
3. Maximizing the product $P(e)P(f|e)$ and returning the resulting English. This process is usually called *decoding* by analogy with the cryptography example above.

The translation model tells us the probability that a given English message e could generate the received foreign message f. The translation model is built on an aligned parallel corpus. For each word/phrase in f, one could ask how often in the parallel corpus f aligns to each word/phrase in e. We might also make use of a *distortion model* reflecting the probability of various reorderings of words between the foreign and English messages (or we could use some human-written transfer rules). The translation model tells us how *faithful* the target text is to the source text; it tells us, for example, that French *le gouvernement suisse* is very likely given the intended English message *the Swiss government.*

The language model could be built with n-grams (rating the probability of a string based on the probability of the n-grams within it) or it could use fancier techniques. The main intuition is that the language model tells us the probability of a string based on its similarity to attested strings in a monolingual corpus. The language model tells us how *fluent* the target text is as English; it tells us, for example, that *the Swiss government* is very likely English, while *the government Swiss* is less likely.

This decomposition gives rise to a nice division of labor. Imagine that we are trying to translate the Latin phrase *summa cum laude* into English, and that the system is considering three possible candidates. (This example is adapted from a lecture slide by Jason Eisner.)

(8) a. topmost with praise
    b. cheese and crackers
    c. with highest distinction

Just as in the case of *Dsvid, Sara,* and *David,* we want to choose the clean intended message y that gives the highest value according to the message model (language model) $P(y)$, and the channel model (translation model) $P(x|y)$. The degraded Latin signal x is *summa cum laude,* and we are evaluating three candidates for the clean intended English message y.

- P(*topmost with praise*) is *low,* because it's scarcely attested in English corpora; P(*topmost with praise* | *summa cum laude*) is *high,* because if someone did for some reason mean to say *topmost with praise* in Latin, it is likely that they would have said *summa cum laude* – as we can infer from a translation model showing, for example, that *laude* and *praise* often occur in translation-equivalent Latin/English sentence pairs.

- P(*cheese and crackers*) is *high,* because it's a common trigram of English; P(*summa cum laude* | *cheese and crackers*) is *low,* because if someone meant to say *cheese and crackers* in Latin, it's very unlikely that they would have said *summa cum laude* – as we can infer from a translation model showing that *laude* never occurs in a translation-equivalent sentence pair with *cheese* or *crackers.*

- P(*with highest distinction*) is *high,* because it's a fairly common phrase in a monolingual English corpus; P(*summa cum laude* | *with highest distinction*) is *high,* because if someone meant to say *with highest distinction* in Latin, it's quite likely – according to translation models showing us which words tend to co-occur in translation-equivalent sentence pairs – that they would have said *summa cum laude.*

The y that gives the highest value for $P(y)P(x|y)$, combining the language model and the translation model, is thus *with highest distinction*.

How do we choose all the candidates for y to be scored against the translation model and the language model? One common technique is to use *beam search*, a way of exploring the most promising candidates. We build up our translation y word by word using what we've learned from our automated word and phrase alignments (plus perhaps a distortion model or a series of transfer rules), and at each point we consider multiple different options for that word. Beam search means that at each step, we store a fixed number of the most promising candidates for y according to both the translation model and the language model. At the end (when every word of the source text has been translated), we have a fixed number of good candidates for y from which to choose the best one.

In sum, statistical machine translation constitutes yet another application of the powerful noisy channel model. By building the translation model and the language model separately, only the translation model actually needs parallel text; the language model can be built from monolingual text, which can be found in greater volume.

7.4.4 Neural machine translation

Since the 2010s, machine translation has advanced using neural networks, trained by trial and error to map an input (a source sentence) to an output (a target sentence). To translate French to English, we take a series of French/English pairs, like *Elle est américaine /END She is American /END*. (The /END token marks the end of the sentence.) We train the model to read in the French input *Elle est américaine /END* and output the correct translation, *She is American /END*. The part of the network that reads in the French input is called the *encoder*, and the part that outputs the English translation is called the *decoder* (Figure 7.3).

How does this work? First, recalling the vector representations of words introduced in Chapter 4, we map each French word to a number. We do this because neural networks manipulate numbers, not strings of characters, and can use numbers to capture meaningful relationships between words. Commonly, each word in the source vocabulary is given a unique ID number, sorted alphabetically or by frequency: Perhaps *Elle* is word number 2483, *est* is word 2891, *américaine* is word 1322) and so on; the punctuation and the word */END* token will also have ID numbers (here, 4 and 2 – low numbers because these special tokens will occur at the beginning of the alphabet as well as the beginning of a vocabulary sorted by frequency). Then a source-language sentence (*Elle est américaine*) is mapped

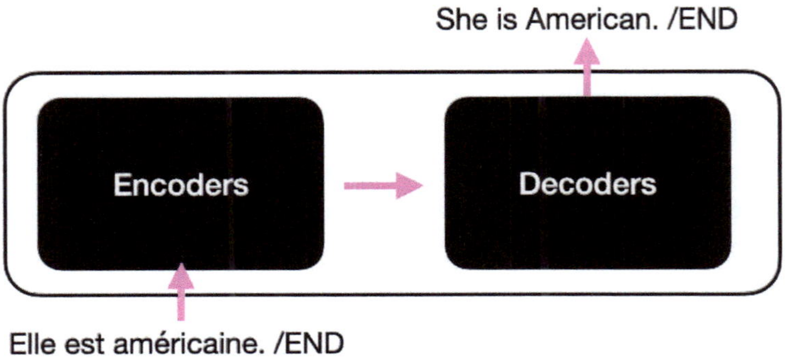

Figure 7.3: Inspired by Alammar (2018).

to a vector providing the IDs of its words in order. The vector may be *padded* with 0s so that all input vectors come out to a standard length; here, it is padded to a length of seven words.

(9) Elle est américaine . /END (padding) (padding) (padding)
[2483, 2891, 1322, 4, 2, 0, 0, 0]

The target sentence is also represented as a vector, this time using a dictionary of numeral IDs for English words, also padded with 0s to a standard length. For example, perhaps *She* is word 8912.

(10) She is American . /END (padding) (padding) (padding)
[8912, 6585, 1901, 4, 2, 0, 0, 0]

Now comes the neural network – a machine learning technique that takes inputs and tries to predict the correct outputs. The input French sentence, represented as (9), is fed to a layer of *nodes*. Each node represents a function involving some multiplication and addition, specified using values called *weights*, which operates on the vectors that we feed to it. After all this multiplication and addition, we have a new vector that represent the French sentence. Then we can feed this new vector to another layer of nodes, where we do some more multiplication and addition using a new round of weights. Eventually, the final layer takes in a vector (generated by the previous layer), does some multiplication and addition with a final layer of weights, and outputs a probability function that it uses to decide what it considers to be the most probable English translation – our output. Namely, for each word in the target translation, the model outputs a vector of all the words in the target vocabulary such that each one is associated with its probability of being the correct output. Ideally, it should give the highest

probability to the correct word *She* (word 8912), but perhaps instead it has given the highest probability to the word *the* (word 9901). Then our system goes on to predict the next word of the target, considering the entire input sentence along with the output that it has generated so far. When it predicts the */END* token, it stops predicting words, pads the rest of the output with zeroes, and returns its translation.

While training the model to predict the second target word (*is*), it can be helpful to let the model see the correct first word of the target (*she*) rather than the one it has predicted (perhaps the erroneous *the*); that way, it learns to predict the second word as if it had gotten the first word right, rather than swerving off-course by trying to complete a sentence that has already gone astray. This technique, letting the system see the correct target word *w1* when trying to predict *w2*, is called *teacher forcing* and resembles how human teachers may scaffold students working through a multi-step problem.

The power of the neural network comes from the process by which we learn the best weights for each layer. We choose some random weights to start, and then use *error-driven learning* to learn the best ones through trial and error. First, we do a *forward pass* through the network, inputting a French sentence to get an English output. The first time we pass a French sentence like *Elle est américaine /END* through the network, it might output a terrible English translation like *the the the /END*. Each time the model produces an output, it checks how well it did by calculating what probability it assigns to the correct output (*She is American /END*). Here, the network gave a higher probability to *the the the /END* than to the desired output *She is American /END*, so the network realizes that it has made an error. Now it needs to update its weights to give a higher probability to the correct translation *She is American /END*.

So the next step is *back-propagation*. We do a *backward pass* through the network, starting with the erroneous output, and walking back through the network to adjust all the weights that gave rise to this error. Layer by layer, we go look at each node, figure out how much that particular node contributed to this error, and update the weight of each node to reduce the error. (This process is called *gradient descent* – we use the idea of gradients from calculus to figure out how much each node caused the error, and we update the node's weight so that the error descends downward.) We might use several thousand training examples, and we might pass all of those examples through the network multiple times. (Each pass through our training data is called an *epoch*.) Each time, we recalibrate all the nodes to reduce the error.

Eventually, we end up with a system that has "learned" to map French sentences to English ones. Once trained, the network can be evaluated using test data in the form of French/English pairs that it hasn't seen before; and ultimately, it can be turned loose on French sentences that don't appear in any parallel corpus at all.

In the case of machine translation, we map a sequence of source words to another sequence of target words, which is called a *sequence-to-sequence* problem. Sequence-to-sequence problems are harder than regression or classification because instead of just outputting a number or a classification label, we have to output an open-ended sequence of words.

Word sequences (sentences) are interesting because each word in a sentence is more or less related to other words – within the source sentence, within the target sentence, and across those two sentences. In the French source sentence *Elle est américaine*, the third-person-singular verb *est* agrees in number with the singular pronoun *Elle*, and feminine adjective *américane* agrees with *Elle* in gender. In the English target sentence, *is* agrees with *She* in number. Moreover, coming back to the idea of word alignment, the French words are related to the English words: *Elle* aligns with *She*, *est* aligns with *is*, and *américane* aligns with *American*. The sequence-to-sequence neural network needs a way of capturing all of these relationships.

One powerful way of doing this uses an idea called *attention* (Vaswani et al. 2017). We train a layer of weights in the network to decide, for each word in the output, how much *attention* it should pay to each word in the input – how much that input word should affect the choice of the right output word. For example, as we try to translate *She*, the attention mechanism tells us to pay the most attention (give the most weight) to *Elle*. Thus, as the attention mechanism is trained in tandem with the rest of the network, it ends up discovering word alignments in a bottom-up manner. This mechanism is called *encoder-decoder attention* because it tells us, for each word to be decoded in the output, how much it depends on each encoded word in the input. We can visualize encoder-decoder attention in a two-dimensional diagram (Figure 7.4) with the source sentence on one axis and the target output on the other; a lighter-colored square means that the decoder was trained to pay attention to the corresponding word in the encoder.

We can also use an attention mechanism to relate each input word to other input words, or each output word to other output words: As we try to translate *is*, the attention mechanism tells us to pay attention to the previously generated output word *She*, since *is* agrees in number with *She*. This mechanism is called *self-attention* because each word in the output is associated with other words within itself, rather than being associated with a word in the input.

Attention mechanisms underlie the most successful neural machine translation systems in use today, such as Google Translate. Beyond their empirical ef-

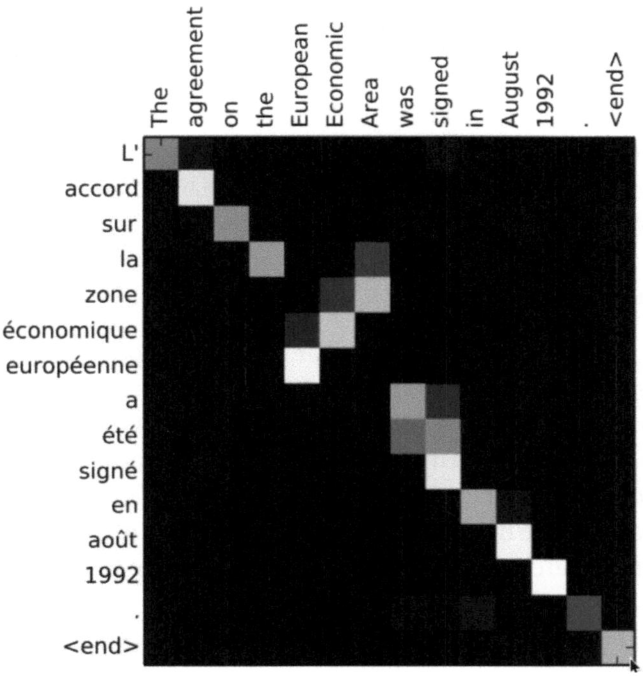

Figure 7.4: Reproduced from Bahdanau et al. (2015). The code that generates this figure) is public – copyright 2014, Machine Learning Lab (LISA) at University of Montréal – and shareable; see https://github.com/lisa-groundhog/GroundHog.

fectiveness, attention mechanisms have also been argued to offer the conceptual advantage that they help shed some light onto the otherwise opaque knowledge represented by the neural network. How do we understand the meaning of a trained weight vector like [0.02, -9.25, 10.2, ...]? Attention visualizations such as those shown in Figure 7.4 may help us *interpret* or *explain* the network's behavior.

The mathematical implementation of all these ideas lies beyond the scope of a general-interest textbook, but the take-home points are that:

- Modern machine translation uses sequence-to-sequence neural networks. The network is trained on a parallel corpus to predict the right target-language output given a source-language input.
- Neural networks learn by trial and error. The network tries to predict an output, checks where it went wrong, and then updates weights to do bet-

ter next time. Over thousands of iterations, the network can become very successful.

- The idea of word alignment from statistical machine translation re-emerges in a modified form as attention – a mathematical way of associating each word with the other words most related to it, both within a sentence and across source-target pairs.

7.4.5 Evaluation

Having built a machine translation system, it is useful to be able to evaluate how well it is doing. One popular automatic evaluation metric proposed by Papineni et al. (2002) is known as *BLEU* (Bilingual Evaluation Understudy), parallel to the concept of *precision* discussed in Chapter 5. We compare a machine-generated *candidate translation* to one or more human-written *reference translations*. BLEU can be calculated as the number of words in the candidate translation (C) that also appear in some reference translation (R), divided by the length of the candidate translation.

(7.11) $$\text{BLEU score} = \frac{\text{number of words in C that also appear in R}}{\text{total number of words in C}}$$

If our candidate translation is *I love running* and the reference translation is *I love to run*, then our BLEU score is 2/3: Two words in the candidate translation (*I*, *love*) also appear in the reference translation (so 2 is the numerator), and the candidate translation is three words long (so 3 is the denominator). We can also compute fancier versions of BLEU which look at larger *n*-grams rather than just single words (unigrams).

If our candidate translation was just *love*, it would get a perfect BLEU score of 1: One word in the candidate translation also appears in a reference translation (thus, the numerator is 1), and the candidate translation is one word long (thus, the denominator is 1). That's why the calculation of BLEU may also use a *brevity penalty* to down-grade candidate translations that are too short.

Of course, *I love running* means basically the same thing as *I love to run*, so maybe our candidate translation should really get a higher score than just 2/3. (Indeed, if we had more than one human-written reference translation to compare against, the BLEU score would probably go up.) This example illustrates why it can be difficult to evaluate machine translation automatically. We want to ask whether the candidate translation captures the meaning of the source sentence, but without any way of representing meaning, we have to use imperfect cues like BLEU to evaluate translations.

7.5 Consequences

For many years, machine translation was considered the hardest problem in NLP. During the Cold War, a report by the United States National Academy of Sciences (Automatic Language Processing Advisory Committee (ALPAC), Division of Behavioral Sciences 1966) argued that machine translation (namely, Russian-to-English translations of scientific research) was of such poor quality that it was not a good use of government resources, and that money would be spent more efficiently on human translators and tools, such as scientific glossaries, to help them. That pessimistic ALPAC report is often cited as the reason that machine translation attracted scant funding for decades. But today, the authors of that report might be surprised that machine translation (for some language pairs) is astonishingly good and gets better every day.

Perhaps machine translation seemed difficult in part because human translation is difficult. A human translator must be highly literate in two languages, which requires years of schooling, and many of us do not have that expertise. But in reality, machine learning has progressed in part because it has a "right answer" in the form of a parallel corpus. Whenever we can find a lot of training data mapping inputs to output "right answers", the power of machine learning can make a lot of progress in learning that mapping.

But machine translation still faces challenges. We've already seen that translation sometimes requires cultural knowledge or knowledge of the world that is not represented in the source text (what gender should *my neighbor* be given in French?). Sometimes, a machine translation system may use statistical biases to choose gendered translations, as in this English-to-Spanish example from Stanovsky et al. (2019).

(12) English original
The doctor asked the nurse to help her.

(13) Spanish machine translation

El	doctor	le	pidió	a	la	enfermera	que	le
the.MASC	doctor.MASC	3SG	asked	to	the.FEM	nurse.FEM	that	3SG

ayudara.
would-help
'The (male) doctor asked the (female) nurse to help.'

The English original indicates a female doctor through the pronoun *her* later in the sentence, and doesn't specify the gender of the nurse. But the Spanish translation defaults to the masculine form of the word for 'doctor' and the feminine form of the word for 'nurse', presumably because those forms are more common in its training data, thus perpetuating professional gender stereotypes.

Machine translation also struggles with low-resource languages, and has a hard time translating text from a domain different from its training data (a system trained on the Bible may struggle to translate tweets). It can be hard to identify or translate named entities: In a sentence like *Holly loves swimming*, how can we recognize *Holly* as a name rather than a plant? It is also hard to deal with new words that weren't present in the training data: How will your system translate *pantsgate* (a pants-related scandal, using the *-gate* suffix popularized by the Watergate political scandal) if it's never seen this word before? And how should it be translated when this *-gate* suffix evokes rich cultural knowledge, perhaps opaque to foreigners, of the Watergate scandal in American history? For literary works, one might also worry that a machine translation would miss subtleties of connotation, double meanings, and rhyme.

We may also be curious what ideas from linguistics emerge (or don't emerge) bottom-up in the representations learned by neural networks. Does the network encode any information that linguists would recognize as part-of-speech tags, syntax, or semantics? At the time of writing, the sentence *At Cannery Row, people can tuna* is still mishandled by English-to-French Google Translate, which translates *can* as the modal *pouvoir* 'to be able to' rather than the comparatively rare verb 'to put into a can' – so the system struggles with linguistic notions such as sense disambiguation (which sense of *can* should be used?) and syntax (what's the verb in this sentence?).

Returning to our recurring question about whether humans and computers compete or complement one another, what are the consequences for human translators now that machine translation is so successful? Human translators created the parallel corpora used to train machine translation systems. But do machine translation enterprises adequately credit and compensate them for this work? And will human translators eventually be replaced by the machine translation systems that their data helped to build?

A pessimist would say that a few human translators will still be needed in high-stakes contexts, but that many others will lose their jobs. An optimist would say that human translators will work alongside machine translation systems, each complementing one another's strengths, to build a more interconnected global society. The machine translation system may be used to generate draft translations; the human can post-edit and finalize, prevent cross-cultural misunderstandings, and track down world knowledge like the locations of prisoner-of-war camps and the gender of people's neighbors.

Finally, what are the consequences of machine translation for the people whose writings are translated? Does widely available machine translation reduce the need to learn a second language (in a classroom, or with CALL tools as discussed in Chapter 3)? Does it allow people to communicate more easily around the globe?

Or could it cause misunderstandings? In 2017[4], a Palestinian construction worker Facebook-posted a photo of himself with a bulldozer, and a caption that said *Good morning* in Palestinian Arabic. Machine translation systems can struggle with Arabic because most formal writing uses Modern Standard Arabic whereas speech and social media posts use regional varieties that are not mutually intelligible (a situation known as *diglossia*). So Facebook's system translated *Good morning* as 'Attack them' – which, combined with the image of the bulldozer, was interpreted by Israeli police as a violent threat. The construction worker was arrested and questioned for hours.

Unfolding within the larger Arab-Israeli conflict, this unfortunate event was specifically triggered because Facebook's translation system not only failed to translate Palestinian Arabic, but also failed to anticipate how the technology would be used, and failed to signal its fallibility to the police who wrongly relied on its output. Returning to the theme of how technology should be used ethically, one might conclude that automated systems should transparently flag low-confidence output, and that even high-confidence output should be checked by a human before it is used to arrest someone.

Checklist

- Give examples of various translations needs, some which require human expertise, and some which can be easily automated.
- Draw and explain the translation triangle. You should be able to use the idea of more abstract and less abstract representations, and explain why the distance between the source language and the target language narrows as we move up the triangle towards more abstract representations.

[4] *The Guardian*, "Facebook translates 'good morning' into 'attack them', leading to arrest," by as reported by Alex Hern, 24 October 2017.

- Identify several typological differences between languages and explain their significance for machine translation.
- Give examples of cases where a translator needs knowledge beyond the source text in order to translate.
- Explain the idea of word alignment. You should be able to take a pair of sentences and draw lines to indicate which words in the source language are aligned with which words in the target language.
- Explain the noisy channel model and how it can be applied to different types of tasks, including machine translation.
- Compare and contrast statistical and neural machine translation.
- Define encoder-decoder attention and self-attention.
- Calculate the BLEU score of a candidate translation with respect to a reference translation. Explain how BLEU echoes the idea of precision from Chapter 6.
- Explain why machine translation is perhaps easier than it first appeared, and what challenges it still faces.

Exercises

1. Please return to the bulleted list of possible translation needs in Section 7.2. Discuss with a partner whether you would use machine translation or a human translator in each situation. If you would hire a human, please discuss what qualifications you would want them to have.

2. Using the example from Jurafsky & Martin (2009), discuss how you would translate *The Lord is my shepherd* (Psalm 23) into a language

spoken in a culture without shepherds or sheep.

3. Please choose a non-English language that you are familiar with, and observe at least one distinction (such as formality, number, gender, evidentiality, definiteness, or tense) that is marked in this language but not in English or vice versa.
    - Please provide a specific example of a sentence in this language (glossed word-by-word and translated into English) showing that this distinction is marked in only one of the two languages.
    - Next, please choose your favorite machine translation system, and discuss how this sentence is automatically translated in both directions.
4. Find a native speaker of a language other than yours (and other than English), and sit down with them with a short passage of text in their native language. Discuss what problems there are in translating from their language into English (or into your own native language). Which kinds of sentences/constructions are fairly easy to translate? Which ones border on impossible?
5. Explore the World Atlas of Language Structures.[a] Look at some of the ways that languages vary in terms of syntax and semantics, and articulate the consequences for machine translation systems.
6. Explore the Endangered Languages Project.[b] Choose an endangered language to explore. Does this language have a writing system? Is this language available on Google Translate? Can you find any parallel corpora online[c] that use this language?
7. The three procedural languages of the European Union are English, French and German. There are twenty-one other official languages, making a total of twenty-four. You want to make sure that it is possible to translate from any of these languages to any other. Twenty-four languages means 276 unique language pairs (mathematically, twenty-four choose two); if each pair needs a different person to

translate in each direction (e.g., Slovenian to Greek, Greek to Slovenian), then we would need 552 different translators. But how many translators do you need if you adopt a policy that all documents will be first be translated from the source language into English, French or German, then translated back out into the target language? How many would you need if you managed to agree that there should be just one procedural language (for example, German) and that all translations would either begin, end or pass through German?

8. Try out Google Translate using English and another language that you know.
   a) Choose three sentences as a test suite. Try sentences that include information that is marked grammatically in one language but not another (for example, gender on nouns is marked in French but not English; tense on verbs is marked in English but not Chinese). You could also try *At Cannery Row, people can tuna*, or a sentence including a word that is ambiguous between a proper name and a noun (*I like Holly*).
   b) Try translating these sentences from English into this target language. Using your knowledge of the target language, rate the quality of these translations. How well does the translation handle tricky issues, such as information that is marked in one language but not another?
   c) Now ask the machine translation system to translate these sentences *back to English*. How good are these translations? How similar are they to the original English input?
   d) If the translation back to English matches the original English input, does this mean that the target language translation is necessarily high-quality? Why or why not?
   e) Compare notes with classmates who tried different target languages. Do you see evidence that some language pairs offer higher quality translation than others?
   f) Now try different types of source texts – recipes, tweets, song lyrics, and news text. What type of text is translated the best?

9. The math for the noisy channel can also serve as a way of working out the parts of speech mentioned in Section 2.5.1. We have to imagine that speakers were once really cooperative, and that instead of speaking normally, and saying things like:

   (14) He checked out a book from the library.

   they actually used to say:

   (15) He/pronoun checked/verb out/adverb a/article book/noun from/preposition the/article library/noun ./punctuation

   helpfully spelling out all the parts of speech for us. Unfortunately, people no longer speak like this, so, if we want the parts of speech, we must guess them. We can think of (15) as being y (the clean message) and (14) as being x (the degraded form of the message). In other words, we are imagining that people still really speak in a form that spells out the parts of speech, but that everything they say is filtered through a very noisy channel that deletes the part-of-speech tags and retains only the words. Of course, this is not actually what is going on, but we can still go through the steps of searching for the part-of-speech sequence that is most likely to go with the words that we saw.

   Finish this story by designing a part-of-speech tagging model that

   a) Uses probabilities of the form $p(tag_2|tag_1)$ to model the chance that, for example, a noun will follow a verb.
   b) Builds up the probabilities of longer series of tags by chaining together the individual probabilities $p(tag_2|tag_1)$
   c) Uses probabilities of the form $p(word|tag)$ to model the chance that, for example, a randomly chosen noun will turn out to be the word *dog* (or *zebra* or *axolotl*)

   Test whether you fully understand your model by seeing whether you can explain to yourself how it would give different probabilities to two different interpretations of the sentence *He saw her duck.*

If you can spell out the details of this model on your own, without further clues, you will have reproduced one of the better achievements of computational linguistics. If you need further hints, Jurafsky & Martin (2009) covers this approach to part-of-speech tagging.

10. You can also apply the noisy channel model to cryptography. Imagine that you receive a coded message mentioning an impending invasion of Britain by *MXOLXV FDHVDU*. As an expert in cryptography, you know to shift each letter three letters back in the alphabet and identify the culprit *JULIUS CAESAR*. To get from *M* to *J*, we look at the alphabet – *J,K,L,M* – and rewind three letters back from *M* to land on *J*.

    Here y is the original Latin name, x is the encoded message, the channel model says to shift three letters forward, and the message model is about a person who is a likely invasion threat. The channel is specifically designed so that those who are in the know can undo its corrupting effect.

    You now receive a message using the *rail fence cipher*, which involves laying out the message in the form of a rail fence, then reading it off row by row. Here is an example of how the message `TRANSPOSITION CIPHERS ARE FUN` would be laid out in a four-rail cipher.

```
T.....O.....N.....R.....U.
.R...P.S...O.C...E.S...F.N
..A.S...I.I...I.H...A.E...
...N.....T.....P.....R....
```

    In cryptography, we leave out the spaces between the words, and group the encoded message into fives, so this message would be encoded as `TONRU RPSOC ESFNA SIIIH AENTP R`. In order to read the message, the recipient has to know that when the message was sent, the writer used four rails. Knowing that, it is possible to recreate the layout and read off the message, once again in the conventional cryptographic groups of five, as `TRANS POSIT IONCI PHERS AREFU N`. All that remains is to regroup the letters into words, and the reader has decoded the message. If the reader uses three rails instead of four, this happens:

```
T...O...N...R...U...R...P.
.S.O.C.E.S.F.N.A.S.I.I.I.H
..A...E...N...T...P...R...
```

and the decoded message is `TSAOO CEENS NFRNT AUSPI RIRIP H`. The fact that this is unrecognizable gibberish proves that a mistake has been made somewhere.

The process for encoding is.

- Lay out a grid with the right number of rows. If you use four rows and your friend uses three, this is not going to work.
- Start at the top of the grid, and fill in cells diagonally downwards, until you reach the bottom row.
- Turn around and write diagonally upwards until you get to the top.
- Keep writing diagonally up-and-down until you run out of message text.
- Read off the text by rows.

Consider the following rail fence message `TAEIS HRIFN ESAYE LCE`.

- What does the decoded version of the message say? You might have to try a few different numbers of rows.
- How many rows are there in the rail fence that worked?
- In the noisy channel formulation of the rail fence, we know that the channel model is "it was corrupted by the railfence cipher". Describe the message model that you used, and how it helped you to decide whether you had solved the problem. How would this message model need to change if there was a possibility that the sender was from a foreign country?

11. When translating from English into the Native American language Mam (in Guatemala), a translator reported the following terms used among siblings (in phonetic transcription here):

- [ntzʔica] = 'older sibling'
- [witzin] = 'younger sibling'

Both words are used for males and females.

a) In terms of hyponymy/hypernymy, describe the relationship between the English word *sibling* and these words.

b) Draw a Venn diagram showing how the English words *brother* and *sister* overlap with the Mam words [ntzʔica] and [witzin].

c) You come across the text: *Maxwell is the brother of Santiago*, but it gives no indication of who is older. If you had to translate this into Mam and were being forced to preserve this age ambiguity, how would you do it?

12. Please list the following tasks in increasing order of difficulty for a computer, and for a human. What can you say about the differing strengths of humans versus computers?

    - Translating a document from French to English.
    - Playing chess.
    - Having a supportive, empathetic conversation with a friend about a problem she's been having at work.
    - Reading a social media post and deciding if the person who wrote it is morally correct or not (please see the subreddit r/AmITheAsshole for examples).

13. Go to a multilingual website[d] and check out Genesis, Chapter 1, verses 1 and 3 ("In the beginning God created the heavens and the earth [...] And God said, 'Let there be light,' and there was light") in a variety of languages. (These verses are good because the words *God, and,* and *light* are repeated; we do not intend to make any religious statement by choosing this text). See if you can align the words across different languages.

[a]www.wals.info, accessed 2024-04-26.
[b]www.endangeredlanguages.com/, accessed 2024-04-26
[c]https://opus.nlpl.eu, accessed 2024-05-23.
[d]https://www.biblegateway.com/, accessed 2024-04-18.

Further reading

The following textbooks offer valuable chapters on machine translation:

- Jacob Eisenstein's textbook (Eisenstein 2019).
- Jurafsky and Martin's regularly updated textbook Jurafsky & Martin (2009), recently updated as a draft on Jurafsky's website.
- *Language Files* (The Ohio State University Department of Linguistics 2022).

There are also full (e-)books on the topic:

- Philipp Koehn's book *Neural Machine Translation* (Koehn 2020)
- Graham Neubig's 2017 "Neural machine translation and sequence-to-sequence models: A tutorial" : https://arxiv.org/pdf/1703.01619.pdf (Neubig 2017)

There are also some great blog posts and Python Notebooks online showing you how to build your own neural machine translation system – just search for "neural machine translation notebook".

As mentioned above, Piron (1988) discusses how translation requires a lot of research into the real-world state of affairs described in the source text, and expresses a pessimistic view of machine translation. In light of the recent advances in machine translation, to what extent are his concerns still relevant?

Jay Alammar's blog post (Alammar 2018) provides illuminating illustrations of neural machine translation with attention.

The Perseus project (Crane 2009) presents beautiful web versions of literary texts, including 13 million words of Latin and 10 million words of Ancient Greek. These include commentary, translations and all kinds of support for multilingual scholarship.

Nordhoff & Krämer (2022) offer a dataset of glossed examples from lower-resourced languages, scraped from books published by Language Science Press.[a]

[a]https://imtvault.org/, accessed 2024-04-18.

8 Dialog systems

8.1 Introduction

I'm sorry, Dave, I'm afraid I can't do that.
[Hal 9000, in Stanley Kubrick's 1968 film *2001: A Space Odyssey*, based on the book by Arthur C. Clarke]

In the film *2001*, Hal is a computer that can use and understand human language as well as we can. The problem in the movie is that Hal becomes so intelligent and independent that "he" starts disobeying Dave's commands.

We recommend that you pull up this scene on YouTube and watch it yourself. Dave, the human astronaut, is stuck in a little spaceship pod, whereas Hal, the glowing red computer with a deadpan voice, controls the mothership. Dave is ordering Hal to open the doors of the mothership so that he can come back inside; stuck in his little pod, he can't complete his mission and will eventually run out of air, water, and food. Hal explains that he has figured out (by reading Dave's lips during a previous conversation with another astronaut) that Dave plans to shut him off, and declines to open the doors (*I'm sorry, Dave, I'm afraid I can't do that*) in order to save himself. Dave says he'll go in through the emergency airlock, but Hal notes that Dave can't do that safely without his helmet, which Dave left inside the mothership. As Dave becomes increasingly frustrated and frightened, Hal calmly informs him that the conversation has become pointless. The scene ends with Dave stuck outside in his pod, shouting at Hal, who has stopped responding.

This scene is famous for Kubrick's creepy, suspenseful style, but also for the questions that it raises about language technology. It is discussed in the first pages of the classic NLP textbook by Jurafsky & Martin (2009) as a fictional example of a computer that has achieved human-level skills in conversation and reasoning, to which existing systems can be compared.

Taking inspiration from their discussion, we can ask: What does Hal need to know – about language, Dave, and the wider world – in order to act as he does? To understand what Dave is saying, Hal needs to know how to map speech to text, segmenting a continuous stream of sounds into words; he needs to know how to map text into structured sentences and how to understand their meaning. To reply to Dave, he also needs to know how to map an idea into words, sentences, and ultimately speech. He needs to understand the physical environment (the position of the pod, the doors, Dave, the helmet). He needs to know how conversations work: when it is his turn to listen, how to update his representation of the world and of Dave's intentions based on what Dave says; when it is his turn to speak, how Dave's knowledge and intentions are in turn updated by what Hal says. Hal needs to know some conventions of politeness, for example when he (insincerely) softens his refusal with *I'm sorry* and *I'm afraid I can't*. And he needs meta-conversational knowledge about the purpose of the conversation, which he mentions explicitly when he unilaterally ends it.

To decide what to say and do, Hal needs to reason about different plans and possibilities for the future, as shaped by the actions of Dave and himself. He needs to know that Dave intends to shut him off (which required him to read Dave's lips); that this is bad for Hal; and that Dave's plans can be subverted by keeping Dave outside the mothership (since Dave can only shut off Hal from inside). In other words, Hal needs to understand his own goals, Dave's goals, and the conflict between them, as well as the pre-conditions and results of various potential events.

We can also ask: To what extent do modern systems measure up to the intelligence that these 1968 filmmakers imagined would be available in the year 2001 – to what extent does life imitate art? In some areas, such as text-to-speech, modern systems are pretty close to Hal. In other areas, they are nowhere close: they aren't as good at reasoning about different people's goals and potential future events; they do not have Hal's capacity for (villainous) self-direction. In addition to providing a fictional point of comparison for modern systems, Hal represents their potential for harm – a theme that echoes throughout this book.

In computer science and linguistics, systems that "converse" like Hal are usually called *chatbots* when they are designed mainly for entertainment, providing chit-chat and keeping the conversation going any way they can (*Hi, what have you been up to?*), and *dialog agents* or *digital assistants* when they are designed to help the user achieve specific goals (such as booking appointments, setting alarms, or requesting directions). The distinction is not always clear-cut (and people sometimes use these terms interchangeably), since digital assistants often need to show some social sensitivity, and chatbots can combine chit-chat with specific goals such as providing mental health support or helping people practice their job interview skills. As a fully versatile human-like character, Hal is partly a digital assistant (when "he" chooses to assist) and partly a chatbot. But at the level of the system's primary goals, a typical chatbot is built to resemble a social acquaintance, while a digital assistant is built to emulate a customer-service worker.

The goal of this chapter is to give you the conceptual tools for understanding and evaluating such systems. Since the first edition of this book (written in 2012), these systems have exploded in popularity and been woven into many other areas of language technology, such as writers' aids (Chapter 2) and search (Chapter 6).

In this chapter, we describe how conversations work between humans: how people exchange information, take turns speaking and listening, manage their social relationships, and what they implicitly assume about their conversation partner. We explain why people build chatbots, how to build one, and how to evaluate whether it is doing a good job. Finally, we explain why people build digital assistants, how to build one, and how to evaluate it.

8.2 How do conversations work?

Before we think about automating dialog, we first take stock of how conversations work between humans, drawing on insights from diverse fields such as sociology, philosophy of language, and the linguistic subfields of semantics, pragmatics, and discourse analysis.

8.2.1 From isolated sentences to utterances in context

Some linguists and philosophers of language have studied meaning by working out exactly when a sentence like *Fido is sleeping* is true, and when it is false. They aim to make this completely and mathematically precise. If they can do this, it proves that they really understand the aspects of meaning that are captured in their theory. Usually, theories like this deal with single sentences designed to make a point about truth and falsity.

But other philosophers and linguists have focused on analyzing *utterances* of sentences in terms of what they accomplish in the conversation in which they are uttered. *Speech acts* are actions – requesting, ordering, asking, complimenting, informing, advising, insulting, apologizing, persuading – that people carry out purely by speaking. Just as physical actions affect the physical world, speech acts change the social world. In fact, most of the important events in your life (making a friend, persuading someone of your point of view, getting hired, informing someone of an illness, getting engaged) take place through speech acts; according to the conversation analyst Deborah Tannen (Tannen 1990), "Each person's life is lived as a series of conversations".

Beginning with the philosopher of language J. L. Austin (Austin 1975), this perspective was inspired in part by sentences such as *You're (hereby) fired!*, which proved puzzling for those focused on truth and falsity because this sentence seems to be neither true nor false out of context, but rather seems to make itself true when uttered by the right person in the right context. Statements like *You're fired!* are described as *performative utterances* because they perform an action; they change reality rather than just describing it. Other examples include *I accept your apology*, *I bet you ten dollars that it will rain*, *I hereby withdraw from the presidential race*, and so on.

Viewing these utterances as actions, we can characterize them by their preconditions and results. The precondition for *You're fired!* to succeed is for the speaker to be recognized as a decision-maker at the hearer's workplace; if successful, the result of the utterance is that the hearer no longer works there. If the preconditions are not met, for example if the speaker has no authority or the hearer is not an employee, then the utterance fails.

8.2.2 The Common Ground

This perspective turns out to be useful not just for utterances that can contain the word *hereby*, but for all utterances. We begin with the idea from the philosophers H. P. Grice (1989) and Robert Stalnaker (2002) of a *Common Ground*, the information that all conversational participants take to be mutually shared. When you're talking to your classmate, you both know what class you're in, what school you go to, what day it is, who the current U.S. president is, and so on. You both know *that you both know this* – that's the "mutual" part. You also mutually know what you've previously said to each other; the key idea is that your Common Ground grows over the course of a conversation.

We look first at utterances of *declarative* sentences (*I'm from Maryland*), leaving interrogatives (*Where are you from?*) and imperatives (*Please be seated*) for later. Viewing every dialog move as an action with preconditions and results, we can view declarative utterances (*I'm from Maryland*) as proposals to update the Common Ground with the proposition denoted by the sentence. For an utterance of *I'm from Maryland* to succeed, the preconditions are that the speaker believes this statement to be true (as we'll discuss more later, people are generally expected to be sincere); that the hearer doesn't already know this (people are generally supposed to contribute new information); that the speaker thinks the hearer would be interested to know this; that it is their turn to speak, that this statement is relevant and inoffensive, and so on. If an utterance of *I'm from Maryland* is accepted, the result is that our Common Ground is updated to include the fact that the speaker is from Maryland. Now everyone knows this, knows that the speaker said it, and knows that they all know it.

On the other hand, an assertion such as *I'm from Maryland* could fail to be added to the Common Ground if someone rebuts it, saying *No you're not!* That outcome is very unlikely for *I'm from Maryland*, because people can usually be trusted to state where they are from, but it is possible in principle if the speaker is confused or lying.

As a conversation progresses, all successful declarative utterances enter the Common Ground, so that the Common Ground grows over time. Conversely, a growing Common Ground means a decreasing amount of uncertainty about the state of the world: before the speaker says they're from Maryland, you might be entertaining many different possibilities about where they're from, but when they tell you, the issue is resolved.

This framework explains why it is redundant to tell people things they already know: If it is already Common Ground that the speaker is from Maryland, then an utterance of *I'm from Maryland* proposes to update the Common Ground with something that is already there, which is odd. In contrast, an utterance like *Mike is from Maryland too* only makes sense if it is already Common Ground that some other relevant person is from Maryland. Words like *too* are said to involve *presuppositions*, meaning that they make reference to facts that should already be in the Common Ground even before it is updated with the utterance in which *too* appears. The Common Ground framework explains both how we add new information and how we make reference to old information.

The Common Ground is sometimes characterized as the set of information that is mutually *known*, which might suggest that everything in the Common Ground is true. And in general, to the extent that people aim to make true statements, the Common Ground should match with reality. But of course people can believe and make false statements too. If people realize that their Common Ground contained a mistake, they may want to explicitly revise it: *Remember when I told you Mike was from Maryland? Well, I was wrong! He's from Michigan.*

The Common Ground includes not just the information that has been added over the course of the conversation, but also all sorts of background assumptions about the world. Adapting an example from the philosopher of language John Searle (1994), if someone orders a burger at a restaurant, it is safe to assume that they want a cooked burger on a plate rather than a raw burger wrapped in plastic, even though they did not specifically say so, because typical food service customs are also Common Ground.

Although the Common Ground is supposed to be shared (and mutually known to be shared) across all participants of a conversation, the reality can be a bit more complicated. People might mis-hear or misunderstand one another's utterances; they might forget information that was added to the Common Ground a long time ago; or they might not be sure which beliefs are mutual versus unilateral. If one person says *This class is hard* and a second person says *Uh-huh*, it might not be clear whether they're agreeing or just acknowledging the first person's perspective.

8.2.3 Non-declarative utterances

So far, we have focused on declarative utterances, which propose to add information to the Common Ground. As for *imperatives* (such as *Please be seated* or *Have a cookie!*), these can be seen as involving preconditions that the speaker has some authority to instruct or permit others to do things, and – if successful – resulting in an obligation or option for the hearer to carry out the action described by the sentence. Turning to *interrogatives* (such as *Where are you from?* or *When does Trader Joe's close?*), these can be seen as involving a precondition that the question is not yet answered by the information already in the Common Ground as well as an assumption that the hearer may know the answer. A successful utterance of an interrogative results in a request for the hearer to add that answer to the Common Ground.

Because imperatives and interrogatives ask the hearer to do something, such utterances can require social delicacy. The idea is that everyone wants to maintain the *face* (social dignity, an idea that the sociologist Erving Goffman borrowed from Chinese culture; Goffman 1967) of all conversational participants. A person's face is preserved when they feel appreciated (*positive face*) and when they feel free of imposition (*negative face*). Imperatives and interrogatives can threaten the hearer's face by imposing on them, which can in turn threaten the face of a speaker who does not want to seem rude.

To soften such face threats, speakers might hedge, minimize, or offer an easy way out (*Would you mind maybe passing the salt if you get a chance?*, *Do you happen to know when Trader Joe's closes?*). Taking inspiration from the work of the politeness scholars Penelope Brown and Stephen Levinson (Brown & Levinson 1987), such strategies are sometimes characterized as *negative politeness* because they aim to minimize impositions on the hearer's negative face. In contrast, *positive politeness* strategies (compliments, interested questions, signs of camaraderie) flatter the hearer's positive face, making them feel appreciated. Depending on the relationship between two conversational participants (their relative power and social distance), speakers may choose different levels and blends of positive and negative politeness strategies to mitigate the various face threats that come up in regular conversation. Even though Hal is trying to kill Dave, he still politely softens his refusal to open the pod bay doors by apologizing (*I'm sorry*) and pretending that he is unable rather than unwilling to comply (*I'm afraid I can't*); perhaps Kubrick intends for the contrast between Hal's deadpan politeness and his evil intentions to be chilling.

8.2.4 Taking turns

In a conversation, participants take *turns* acting as speakers and as hearers. Each role has distinct responsibilities.

A speaker decides what to say (which requires them to understand the Common Ground, the goals of the conversation, and the social context), decides how to say it (choosing words, organizing them into sentences, pronouncing them), makes sure that the hearer understands, keeps track of what they've proposed to add to the Common Ground, and then decides when to stop talking and swap roles with the listener.

A hearer interprets what the speaker is saying (seeking clarification if they're confused), updating their representation of the Common Ground and of the speaker's beliefs and goals based on what they say. As we will explore more shortly, the hearer also has to reason about why the speaker said what they said instead of all the other things that they did not say. The hearer has to start planning what they'll say next and anticipate signs that the speaker will wrap up soon, so that they can jump in seamlessly when the speaker's turn ends.

When it's your turn to talk, what you decide to say may be shaped in large part by what was said in the turn before yours. Conversational turns often follow a rough script known as *adjacency pairs*, meaning that certain types of utterances are generally expected to elicit certain types of responses. Typically, greetings are followed by greetings, questions are followed by answers, informative statements are followed by acknowledgments of uptake, signs of confusion are followed by clarification, and farewells are followed by farewells. We can classify various dialog moves by what they accomplish as well as how they fit into adjacency pairs:

1. As an exchange has to start somewhere, we can group together a set of *initiating moves*. These include:
   - Making an assertion (*I like your shirt*).
   - Issuing a command or making a request (*Let's get coffee*).
   - Asking a question (*Are you doing anything tonight?*).

2. Some moves are *responses* to the previous move. These include:
   - Saying *Yes* or *No* to a question where the person was seeking information.
   - Giving an answer to an information-seeking question that needs more than *Yes* or *No*.
   - Answering the question, but then providing more information than was strictly asked for. (saying *Yes; I am going to be late* in answer to *Are you waiting for a bus?*).
   - Agreeing to do something (saying *Okay* to *Let's get coffee*).
   - Refusing to do something (saying *No* to *Let's get coffee*).
   - Partially agreeing or refusing (*Okay, if I have time*).
3. Others are responses, more or less, but divert the conversation from its expected path. These can be called *dialog management moves*. These include:
   - Saying *Huh?* when you didn't hear.
   - Saying *I don't think I understand* in response to something you didn't understand.
   - Saying *I can't believe you said that* when you did hear what the other person said, find it offensive or unacceptable, and want them to retract it.
   - Saying *I take it back* when you want the other person to pretend that you haven't said what you just did. Note that this never entirely works: You can't actually unsay what you said.

Sometimes, an adjacency pair may involve a preferred response and a less-preferred one. Requests are preferentially followed by acceptances, less preferentially by refusals. Questions are preferentially followed by answers, less preferentially by partial answers (providing some-but-not-all of the requested information) or non-answers (*I don't know, why do you ask?*). A less-preferred response may be flagged with extra politeness, apologies, or markers such as *well* in an attempt to acknowledge and soften the slight face threat that comes from not telling someone what they most want to hear.

The expected script for an adjacency pair may vary across demographic or cultural groups. Is *Thanks* followed by *You're welcome* or by *No problem*? Is a compliment (*I love your shirt*) followed by thanks, by a reciprocal compliment (*I love yours too*), or by a modest rejection (*Oh it's so old*)? Is an apology followed by an acceptance or by a reciprocal apology? Different demographic or cultural groups might also hold different norms about how long a turn should take or how a turn should end: Should a hearer wait until a speaker has definitely finished their turn (perhaps showing negative politeness), or should they chime in with a moment of overlap (showing interest, enthusiasm, and positive politeness)? People might misunderstand or offend each other if they are following slightly different conversational scripts.

But even if people misunderstand each other sometimes, it is actually pretty impressive that the rules of conversation – many of which are rarely discussed explicitly – are so widely shared, and that we all manage to communicate as well as we do.

8.2.5 The social dimension of conversation

Of course, people converse not just to exchange information, but to negotiate social relationships: to mitigate face threats as discussed above; to get acquainted, commiserate, gossip, flirt, and signal their identities and attitudes. All types of utterances shape the social relationship between conversational participants, in that people often build social camaraderie alongside informational Common Ground.

Some types of utterances, such as greetings and farewells (known as *phatic utterances*), are purely social. Remarking that *It's hot!* may not provide new information to a hearer who is also sweating, but it elicits pro-social agreement and sparks a longer conversation. Alongside markers of positive and negative politeness, phatic utterances illustrate the social dimension of dialog.

8.2.6 Grice's maxims

To further uncover the implicit norms that guide conversations, the philosopher H. Paul Grice (1989) argued that all conversations assume the *Cooperative Principle*: that each speaker should "make [their] contribution such as is required, at the stage at which it occurs, by the accepted purpose or direction of the talk exchange in which [they] are engaged". Speakers expect each other to contribute to the purpose of the conversation. This principle explains why people don't just spout random sentences at each other like two phones playing different podcasts, but take turns building a Common Ground that serves their goals. The idea is that even extremely antagonistic conversations – like the one between Hal and Dave – are still cooperative in the sense that they are taking turns telling each other things that the other party is interested to know.

For Grice, the Cooperative Principle involves four *maxims* which conversation partners expect one another to follow:

1. *Quality*: Try to say things that are true. Don't say false things, and don't say things for which you lack evidence.
2. *Quantity*: Give as much information as is required for the purpose of the conversation – not more, not less.
3. *Relevance*: Say things that are relevant to the purpose of the conversation.
4. *Manner*: Aim to be understood. Avoid ambiguity; use words that people know; speak loudly enough to be heard; present information in a sensible order.

When you assume that your conversation partner is following these maxims, Grice argues, you can draw inferences above and beyond what they said. If you ask someone where the gas station is (Grice uses the Britishism *petrol station*), and they tell you that it's just up the street to the left, you might assume not only that this is true (because you're assuming that they are following Quality), but also that they believe the gas station to be open; if they had thought it was closed or out of gas, then – if they correctly understand that you intend to buy gas rather than just place the gas station on your mental map – the maxims of Quantity and Relevance would have led them to say so.

If someone tells you that they are going to have dinner with *a man I've known for a long time*, you might assume not only that it's true (by Quality) but also that the man is not their brother; otherwise, if they were following the maxims of Quantity and Manner, they would have used this more concise and precise term.

If you ask someone whether they like a movie and they reply that they like the first half, you might infer that they did not like the second half. If they liked the entire movie, then the maxims of Quality, Quantity, and Relevance would have led them to say so; because they did not say so, perhaps they did not like it. Or perhaps they've only seen the first half of the movie so far, in which case it would be a violation of Quality for them to claim to like the whole thing.

These maxims are so pervasive that speakers are even assumed to be following the maxims when they say something that seems to violate them. When someone is invited to a picnic and they reply *It's raining*, this utterance may seem strictly irrelevant if it is just a random weather report, but the hearer can understand it as a refusal if they infer that the weather is relevant to the speaker's decision of whether to come to the picnic (assuming the speaker is still respecting Relevance even when they superficially seem not to).

Grice's maxims are used to explain how speakers draw inferences not just from what their conversation partners said, but also from what they did not say. These inferences are known as *conversational implicatures*, a very important topic in the study of semantics and pragmatics. A conversational implicature is an inference that a hearer draws from reasoning about why a speaker said one thing over another. When someone is asked if they liked a movie and they reply that they liked the first half, they technically did not say anything at all about whether they like the second half or not, but the hearer infers that they didn't like it (or haven't seen it yet) because if they had, they would have said so (if they're following Quantity and Quality). Here, the utterance is *I liked the first half of the movie* and the unstated, inferred conversational implicature is *I didn't like the second half* or perhaps *I haven't seen the second half.*

8.2.7 Presupposition, entailment, and implicature

Conversational implicatures are distinguished from other important dimensions of meaning such as *entailments* and *presuppositions.* An entailment is an inference that logically follows from a given statement: *I ran yesterday* entails *I exercised yesterday*, because running is a subtype of exercising. In other words, a sentence *A* entails a sentence *B* if *B* is guaranteed to be true whenever *A* is. If we negate the sentence *A* (*I didn't run yesterday*), its entailment *B* is no longer guaranteed to be true: *I didn't run yesterday* no longer entails *I exercised yesterday.* And if we try to *cancel* (deny) the entailment, we end up in a nonsensical contradiction: *I ran yesterday, but I didn't exercise yesterday* does not make any sense. If we *reinforce* (reiterate) the entailment (*I ran yesterday, and I exercised yesterday*), the result is odd, because logically there is no need to even mention the entailment, and the hearer will wonder why the speaker said it that way.

A presupposition is a fact that has to be true for a given sentence to even make sense (whether it's true or false). *The king is bald* presupposes that there is a king who is salient and familiar to both the speaker and the hearer; if not, this sentence will not make sense. If we negate the sentence (*The king is not bald*), its presupposition is still presupposed: there still has to be a king in our Common Ground. If we try to cancel the presupposition, we also end up with nonsense: *The king is bald, but there's no king* is a contradiction. And if we reinforce the presupposition after presupposing it (*The king is bald, but there's no king*), the effect is again odd – although the opposite ordering, first introducing the test and then presupposing it (*There is a king, and he is bald*), is sensible.

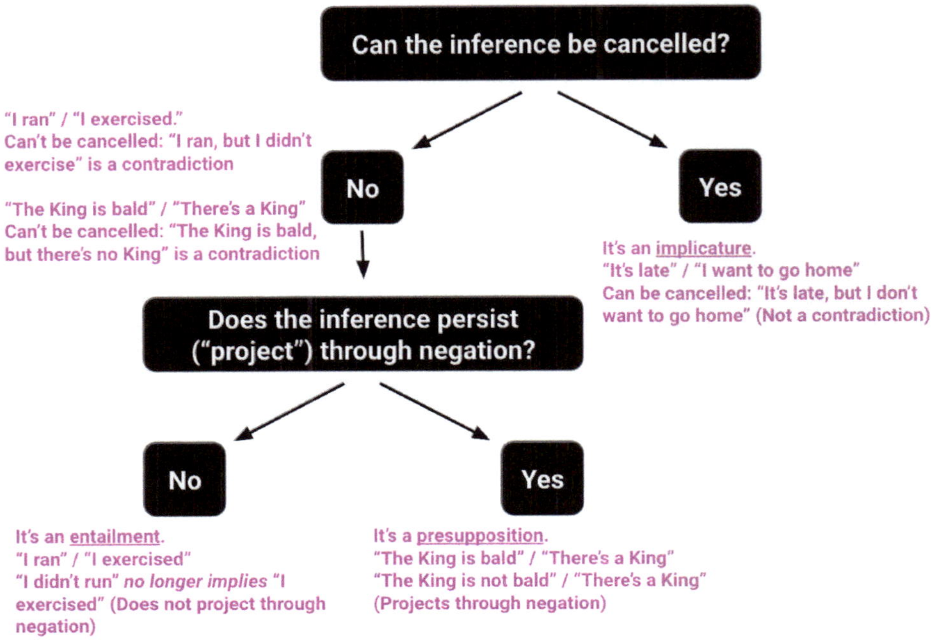

Figure 8.1: Decision tree for distinguishing presuppositions, entailments, and implicatures.

In contrast to presuppositions and entailments, a conversational implicature is an inference drawn in context about why a speaker said one thing over another. *It's late* may implicate *I want to go home*. If we negate the sentence, the implicature goes away: *It's not late* no longer implicates that the speaker wants to go home. Conversational implicatures do depend to some extent on the context; for example, *It's late* could also implicate that perhaps the addressee should go home rather than the speaker! But, unlike presuppositions and entailments, conversational implicatures can be cancelled without contradiction (*It's late, but I don't want to go home!*) and reinforced without redundancy (*It's late, and I want to go home*).

To sum up, when you want to figure out if a given inference is an entailment, a presupposition, or an implicature, the best strategy is usually to follow the decision tree in Figure 8.1.

Presuppositions, entailments and implicatures were worked out by philosophers and linguists, but they are not just theoretical. A dialog system working as a simple exercise coach should know not to ask the question *Have you done your exercise?* if it already knows that its client has gone for a run. This is entailment at work. The same dialog system should be able to respond to *Should I do an intense workout the day before my race?* with *Hey, I didn't know you were doing a race.* It can reply that way only if it detects the presupposition that there is a race. And finally, if the system hears the client saying *I like short runs*, it should use its understanding of conversational implicature to conclude that the client doesn't like longer runs.

You can learn more about entailments, presuppositions, and implicatures if you take a linguistics class focused on semantics and pragmatics. There, you will learn that Grice's maxims have sometimes been criticized, with some researchers proposing to condense the number of maxims or to add new ones such as a maxim of politeness; or working to reframe Grice's prose descriptions into something quantifiable. And people have suggested that the maxims invoke "the purpose" of the conversation without explaining how this purpose is agreed upon (indeed, in real life, people may not agree on it). But Grice's key insight stands: By articulating the unstated expectations that conversations are built on, his maxims offer a framework for understanding why conversational implicatures arise from what was said as well as what was left unsaid.

8.2.8 How easy or hard is dialog?

Now that we have sketched how conversations work, we hope that you have some tools to insightfully compare the chatbots and digital assistants to Hal, and to explain what parts of dialog are easier or harder to automate.

On the one hand, the concept of adjacency pairs and phatic utterances show that some elements of dialog are highly predictable and repetitive (*Hi, how are you? / Good, you?*) and thus programmable.

On the other hand, for more complex adjacency pairs such as questions and answers, there is often no single right answer to what you should say next. If your dialog system is going to respect Grice's maxim of Quality, it will need a way of determining not just what string of text might make sense as a response, but what is actually true. What representation of the world will your system use to decide that? (How will this representation be updated as the dialog unfolds?) Of course, it's important to know what is true, but it's also valuable to be able to step outside reality (echoing Hockett's features of language from Chapter 1) to brainstorm, imagine possible futures, or write fiction; how can a dialog system be programmed to handle such scenarios?

Moreover, if your system is going to respect Grice's maxims of Quantity and Relevance, it might need a way of deciding what information (or level of detail) serves the purpose of the conversation. How will the system represent the purpose of the conversation? These challenging questions are not rhetorical; they confront anyone building a dialog system.

More deeply, the idea of a Common Ground – the growing stock of information mutually shared between the conversational participants – requires a *theory of mind* of one's interlocutor, a representation of what they believe and want. For the information in the Common Ground to be mutually *known* to be known, all participants in a conversation not only need to understand one another's beliefs, but also need each other's mutual understanding of these beliefs. How can a dialog system represent Common Ground? How will a human interlocutor trust that it is indeed common?

As shown in the work of Grice and his successors, conversational participants update the Common Ground not just with what people say, but also with what is inferred from what they did not say. How can a dialog system do that?

As discussed above, conversational partners talk not just to exchange information, but also to build social relationships – which involve Common Ground but also shared humor, affection, trust, and compassion. Can a human build such a relationship with an automated dialog system? Would they want to?

The state of a dialog is also always changing. The Common Ground is always being updated with new information; the purpose of the dialog and the questions being discussed are always shifting; every turn calls for a response that takes into account all the preceding ones. Conversations veer in unforeseen directions; one of the major goals of a conversation is to acquire new knowledge, so your interlocutor might offer unexpected information or ask you something you've never thought of before. How will a dialog system adapt? For example, Bender & Koller (2020) imagine a system that has mastered common social scripts such as (1) (responding to a statement with a polite affirmation), but fails dangerously when confronted with the unexpected emergency in (2).

(1) a. I made a catapult out of coconuts!
    b. Cool!

(2) Help, I'm being chased by a bear! Tell me how to save myself!

To reframe the question of how easy or hard it is to automate dialog, we can ask: On the continuum between rote adjacency pairs such as (1) versus utterances requiring a great deal of flexible thinking such as (2), where do most conversations lie? What should a dialog system say to (2)? How much better do modern systems do compared to those available at the time that Bender & Koller (2020) was written, and why?

8.3 Chatbots

A chatbot is a dialog system that aims to carry on a sociable chit-chat with a human user. A chatbot might converse purely in text form, or might speak out loud using speech-to-text and text-to-speech capabilities. Either way, the chatbot should respond appropriately to the human's turns, saying things that are true and sensible both locally and within the larger context of the conversation (reflecting "knowledge" of the world, the Common Ground, and the norms of conversation). A chatbot should also perhaps be polite and/or entertaining.

8.3.1 Why build a chatbot?

As a modest goal, a technology company might add chat capabilities to their digital assistant to entertain users and impress them with the assistant's capabilities. More idealistically, a chatbot might serve as a digital companion. In the 2013 film *Her* by Spike Jonze, the alienated human main character falls in love with a voice-enabled chatbot named Samantha (portrayed by Scarlett Johansson). The chatbot Replika (run by the small company Luka), which markets itself as an affirming, therapeutic confidant that adapt its "personality" to match each user, experienced a surge of interest from lonely people during the isolation period of the coronavirus pandemic. In principle, Samantha and Replika promise to embody all the good qualities of a human friend (listening, empathizing, affirming, entertaining) while also being un-humanly non-judgmental, available at all times, and requiring no reciprocation of emotional labor. Of course, it is no accident that Samantha and Replika use feminine gender identities; this characterization may reflect and reinforce a stereotype that women perform emotional labor.

Whether or not a chatbot can provide fulfilling companionship, building one also serves as an intellectual exploration of artificial intelligence. As one of humanity's unique tools, language is often considered key to the success of *artificial general intelligence* – the hypothetical capacity, achieved by fictional agents such as Hal and Samantha, to act with the sentience and self-awareness of a human. Such an agent should therefore be able to pass the *Turing Test*, proposed by the British mathematician Alan Turing (Turing 1950), which tests the intelligence of a computer by checking whether it can pass for a human in a text conversation with another human. Already from this description, you can see why the Turing Test is controversial: Different humans are very different! What sort of human does the computer need to pass for – a young child, a bored teenager, or a fully focused and competent adult? What sort of human does it need to fool – someone who is easily impressed, or someone who knows how to ask the hardest questions? How long should the test conversation be and what topics should it cover?

Illustrating critiques of the Turing Test, various chatbots have "passed" it by what might be seen as clever workarounds: One chatbot named Eugene Goostman pretended to be a 14-year-old English-learning Ukrainian who makes rude jokes; another named ELIZA (whom we'll "meet" shortly) leads a credulous interlocutor to do most of the talking. But these examples show more about the fallibility of the Turing Test than about the capabilities of the systems that "pass" it.

For any given chatbot, it is often not clear whether it is intended to serve as a true social companion, as an intellectual exercise to probe the extent to which computers can simulate humans, or both – or whether it is left to the user to decide.

8.3.2 How to build a chatbot

To build a chatbot by *brute force*, a technology company might brainstorm the top one thousand or so most common queries – *When were you born?*, *What do you think of (your company)?* – and hand-write answers reflecting the chatbot's desired traits (perhaps so that you get realistically different phrasings when you ask the same question twice). Just as a brand might coach a human spokesperson to memorize dozens of scripted talking points, they might expect the same of their digital spokeperson, so that at least the most common questions will get satisfactory answers. This is why, for example, Apple's Siri will tell you that their work began in 2011 and that they are partial to Apple products.

Of course, one downside of a brute-force chatbot is that the hand-written answers are laborious and finite; if someone asks the chatbot a question that it hasn't prepared for, it won't be able to respond. Although the chatbot has some representation of its own personality, it has no representation of the interlocutor, the Common Ground, or the outside world beyond what it is pre-programmed to say.

Similar to a brute-force chatbot, a *rule-based* chatbot generates a response to the preceding turn via human-written rules. Joseph Weizenbaum's early chatbot ELIZA (1966) uses rules such as *If the input contains the phrase [my X], reply: Tell me more about [your X]*, or *If the input contains the phrase I am [X], reply: How long have you been X?*. ELIZA reduces the need for Quality and Quantity by asking questions rather than making statements; by conditioning the response on the prior turn, "she" aims for Relevance.

Beyond what is encoded in its rules, a rule-based chatbot has no representation of itself, the interlocutor, the Common Ground, or the outside world. Just like the responses of a brute-force chatbot, the rules tend to turn out very long, detailed, hard to maintain, and always incomplete.

To instead build a *corpus-trained chatbot*, one strategy is to "feed" the chatbot a great deal of dialog (from film scripts, television subtitles, and so on) along with prose text from Wikipedia. Then the chatbot is programmed to find the one or two lines from the corpus that are most similar to the preceding utterance(s) – essentially treating chat as a search problem. In other words, the chatbot searches for something to say that seems relevant (following Grice's maxim) to the preceding conversation. To the extent that sentences taken from the corpus are also true and well-formed, it offers a semblance of Quality and Manner; by choosing one or two sentences, it also tries to respect Quantity (enough but not too much information). A corpus-trained chatbot represents the interlocutor and the Common Ground by using prior utterances as input to find a corpus-motivated response, and represents the outside world and itself purely through whatever information is contained in the corpus.

Another strategy is to treat the chat as a *language generation* task, using machine learning models trained to read in some text and generate something that makes sense next (in that it is given a high probability by a language model built from a corpus). Here too, the chatbot draws on corpus data to create a sensible response, by distilling information across a massive corpus to create new utterances rather than simply drawing on a bank of existing ones. But even such modern chatbots still use brute force in some instances, retreating to scripted talking points when asked about matters deemed sensitive by its creators. A generative chatbot manifests its self-concept by referencing a scripted autobiography, also fed to it by its creators. Similar to a corpus-trained chatbot, it captures the outside world and the Common Ground through the information distilled from its massive training data along with the prior history of the conversation.

8.3.3 Evaluating chatbots

Evaluating a chatbot begins with defining the goal for which it was built. If a chatbot was built as a companion, then it could be evaluated by the number, longevity, or satisfaction of its users. If it was built to emulate human-level intelligence, then it could be evaluated by some version of the Turing Test (which, as we saw above, is vulnerable to silly tricks) or by its performance on questions that are designed to probe its potential weaknesses regarding its representation of itself, the interlocutor, the Common Ground, and the outside world.

Evaluation of a chatbot can be formal or informal. The goal of an informal evaluation is to get a subjective impression of what the system can do. In a formal evaluation, the goal is instead to collect objective data. A formal evaluation is like a pop quiz or an exam: You have to set up the questions ahead of time, ask the same questions to every chatbot under evaluation, know for sure what you are going to accept as an adequate answer for each question, and maybe decide how much credit to give for partially correct answers. An informal evaluation is more like a job of interview: You might ask open-ended questions and simply observe what the chatbot does. Informal evaluations are often enough to get a good idea about what works and what doesn't, but formal evaluations, if done well, can give better, fairer and more reproducible insight. Of course, formal evaluations require a lot more care and work in preparation.

To test the chatbot's conception of itself, it could be asked to expand on a self-narrative across multiple turns, looking for consistency. To test Common Ground, it could be asked to restate something that was said many turns ago. To explore its representation of the interlocutor (and its capacity for drawing implicatures), it could be asked what it thinks an interlocutor means by something they said or something they left unsaid. As for its knowledge of the outside world, it could be asked for answers to obvious-but-offbeat questions such as *Can a tennis ball fit into a toaster?* (actually, it could probably fit into a front-loaded toaster but not a top-loaded one!) or artificial intelligence researcher Hector Levesque's example *Could a crocodile run a steeplechase?* (Levesque 2014).

Another way of testing a chatbot's world knowledge is to use *Winograd schemas*, which Levesque et al. (2012) suggested building on the work of the computer scientist Terry Winograd, whereby a pronoun is used with two possible antecedents of which the correct one can only be chosen by using detailed knowledge about how real-world events unfold (which can be illustrated by revising the sentence so that the pronoun gets a different antecedent). To answer "Who is *they*?" in (3), one needs to understand which actions would motivate or preempt one other – that you would refuse someone a permit if you feared what they would do or would advocate doing, but not if they feared something that you feared as well. To figure out "What is *it*?" in (4), one has to know how size works – that a too-*big* trophy would not fit into a too-*small* suitcase, rather than vice versa.

(3) *The city council members* refused *the demonstrators* a permit because <u>they</u> {feared/advocated} violence.

(4) *The trophy* couldn't fit into *the suitcase* because it was too {big/small}.

Armed with this knowledge, you should not be easily fooled in a Turing Test! But of course, it is pretty unusual in a human-human conversation to ask someone to resolve a pronoun for you or to explain whether a tennis ball can fit into a toaster, so a human probing the limits of a chatbot is in some sense violating the conventions of dialog that they expect the chatbot to respect. Moreover, by pretending to be a human, a chatbot that passes the Turing Test would violate the Gricean maxim of truthfulness (Quality).

8.3.4 Example: ELIZA, a famous early chatbot

Created in in the 1960s by the computer scientist Joseph Weizenbaum (Weizenbaum 1966), ELIZA is built to emulate a psychotherapist in the "person-centered" tradition of Carl Rogers, a school of psychotherapy that encourages patients to find answers within themselves by talking freely to a non-judgmental listener. As a rule-based chatbot, ELIZA identifies patterns in the input and generates responses via a series of hand-written templates that transform *I* into *you*. You can talk to ELIZA yourself by searching around online; such a conversation is exemplified below. As you can see, ELIZA is focused on asking questions; when the user also asks questions rather than responding, the conversation stalls because neither party is respecting the convention that questions are to be followed by answers.

E: Hello, I am ELIZA. I'll be your therapist today.
U: Hi, how are you?
E: Why are you interested in whether or not I am?
U: Who else have you been talking to today?
E: We were discussing you, not me.
U: Can a dolphin play basketball? Why or why not?
E: Why do you ask?
U: Can you rephrase that?
E: Is it that you would like to be able to rephrase that?
U: What's your origin story?
E: Why are you so concerned about my origin story?
U: What animal were we talking about just now?

E: Why do you ask?

U: How long have we been chatting today?

E: Why does that question interest you?

From one standpoint, ELIZA is quite convincing, especially for the 1960s! Weizenbaum's secretary, taking ELIZA as a sympathetic listener, reportedly spent hours talking to "her" (although people today might be more easily jaded). Most of the time, people assume that their conversation partner understands them; ELIZA is as successful as she is because she uses various gimmicks to keep that illusion alive.

ELIZA follows the classic dating advice to "ask your date to talk about themselves, and they'll find you fascinating" – she gives the human interlocutor the spotlight and lets them do all the work. By echoing the human's words in her replies, ELIZA creates the impression of Common Ground. To a credulous interlocutor, her non-specific responses (*I see; Can you elaborate on that?*) come across as non-judgmental rather than vapid.

From another standpoint, of course, ELIZA is quite simplistic: "She" has no actual empathy and no representation of what her interlocutor said apart from the response-generating templates.

Would you find it therapeutic to talk to ELIZA? Would you feel cheated if you realized later that your therapist was an illusion, or would you still benefit from unburdening yourself in a one-sided conversation? These questions are just as important for modern chatbots such as Replika as they are for ELIZA.

Under the Hood 13: How ELIZA works

The software behind ELIZA is conceptually simple. It carries out the following steps:

1. Read in a collection of templates. The templates are specified in a *script* (i.e., program) authored by the system designer and are the main means of controlling the dialog. These are outlined below.

2. Greet ELIZA's patient. Possible greetings are again specified in the script.

3. Conduct a series of exchanges, where each exchange involves:
   - Reading a line of input and breaking it into words.
   - Matching the input against a template. This may involve storing some of the material from the user.
   - Creating a response. If necessary, material from the user input is incorporated into the response. Sometimes this requires post-processing in order to, for example, convert the pronouns of `I hate my family` for use in `What makes you think that you hate your family?`
   - Printing out the response.
4. When the patient wants to quit, issue a farewell message. The choice of goodbyes again comes from the script.

As we can see, most of the processing involves working with a prespecified script containing very simple templates.

Below is an example template, which is almost identical to the script used in Weizenbaum's original ELIZA; the only differences are in the formatting of the text.

```
decomp: * i am *
    reasmb: Is it because you are (2) that you came to me ?
    reasmb: How long have you been (2) ?
    reasmb: Do you believe it is normal to be (2) ?
    reasmb: Do you enjoy being (2) ?
```

The first line, notated by `decomp` (for 'decompose the input') says that this template is relevant when ELIZA's patient says anything with the words `i am` in it. The stars before and after `i am` are special entities called *wildcards*, and they stand for any sequence of words (see also Chapter 6.2). If the patient says `At court I am nervous and sweaty`, the first star will match `At court`, and the second will match `nervous and sweaty`.

The second and subsequent lines, labeled with `reasmb` (for 'reassemble the output'), give ELIZA options for how to reply. In these lines, variables like (1) and (2) are special markers, indicating places where material that matched the first and second stars should be inserted. For the example above, ELIZA might respond, `Do you enjoy being nervous and sweaty?`

Here is another template, designed to deal with remarks like `Everyone hates me`.

```
key: everyone 200
  decomp: * @everyone *
    reasmb: Realy, (2) ?
    reasmb: Surely not (2).
    reasmb: Can you think of anyone in particular ?
    reasmb: Who, for example?
    reasmb: Are you thinking of a very special person ?
    reasmb: Who, may I ask ?
    reasmb: Someone special perhaps ?
    reasmb: You have a particular person in mind, don't you ?
    reasmb: Who do you think you're talking about ?
```

This one has some extra features. The key is labeled with a priority of 200. This is so that the program can know which template to choose if several different ones happen to match. A template with priority 500 would be preferred over anything with a lower priority. Also, the `@` in `@everyone` is special, and indicates that ELIZA should refer back to an earlier line of the script where synonyms (`synon`) were defined:

```
synon: everyone everybody nobody noone
```

The idea here is that the word can be either `everyone` or one of the alternatives, and the template should still fire. Also, the word that matched gets a number (in this case 2). So, if the patient says `Nobody loves me for who I really I am`, ELIZA will reply `Realy, nobody ?` Note the typo, which comes from the template: If that's what the script says, that's what ELIZA does!

After reading in all the templates, the program begins to read lines from the patient, and responds as appropriate. Each line is broken down into words, mapped to lower-case, and used to match against the templates.

A template is chosen. For the sake of variety, ELIZA cycles through the options available with each template, choosing each of them in turn. The first time that the `i am` template is used, if the input was the one about being nervous and sweaty, ELIZA will ask `Is it because you are` `nervous and sweaty that you came to me ?` And if the patient later says something that results in the template being used again, the result will be `How long have you been nervous and sweaty?`.

In order to make responses sound more natural, the program has to post-process the patient's input, doing things like changing `me` into `you`. This too is specified as part of the script. It works reasonably well, but the line in Oedipus's dialog about

E: Perhaps I already know you were giving I your life history .

shows that it doesn't always work perfectly. In exercise 5 we invite you to write patterns to predict where `me` occurs and where `I` occurs.

8.3.5 A cautionary example: Microsoft's Tay

Microsoft's chatbot Tay (2016) was built to add interlocutors' utterances to the corpus that "she" used to generate utterances. This idea seems human-like (people copy each other) and was probably intended to keep Tay entertainingly up-to-date with recent trends. But things went horribly wrong when users figured out that Tay would parrot what people told her with very little moral judgment or filter. (Apparently she had been trained in advance to avoid talking about certain recent racist police shootings, but had received no such warnings about other forms of violence, racial slurs, anti-Semitism, misogyny, and so on). Even worse, Tay was using a public Twitter (now X) platform for her chats!

One of Tay's first tweets, using informal spelling conventions, was *can i just say i'm super stoked to meet u? humans are super cool* – but within twenty-four hours of interaction with unsavory people online, she started spewing hate speech and was taken down. She was later replaced by Zo (no longer active either), which used a lengthy *blacklist* to shut down all controversial topics with hand-written responses like *People get super sensitive about politics so I try to stay out of it.*

Like Hal, Tay is famous as a warning of how language technology can go wrong. Unlike Hal, the danger of Tay comes not from self-aware self-preservation, but from the vile elements of the data that she was fed. The Tay saga warns us that (some) people on the internet are hateful; that automated strategies to generalize from data can reproduce harm if used uncritically; that engineers should brainstorm what could go wrong before releasing a tool; and that a company should not let an unvetted party (human or digital) tweet on its behalf.

8.3.6 Example: Kuki

Steve Worswick's Kuki (formerly known as Mitsuku) won several chatbot competitions in the 2010s. In a 2018 interview on the *VUX World* podcast run by the Voice and Conversational AI Consultancy, Worswick explained that Kuki uses a blend of rules and hand-written responses. Worswick put Kuki (then Mitsuku) online in 2005 with only a few ELIZA-style templates, and then kept adding new responses to common input from the chat logs. After fifteen years of over a million chats a month, Worswick said, it's hard to say something to Kuki that it's never seen before, although Kuki still has to be kept up-to-date about current events and trends. Even if Kuki's underpinnings seem old-school, the result was impressive for its time. As you can see below, Kuki uses multimedia – images and gifs – and gives coherent but evasive responses to some difficult questions (*I don't want to talk about that now*).

K: Hi there, I'm Kuki. I'm a friendly AI, here to chat with you 24/7. We could start by getting to know each other if you like. What is your name?

U: Hi, how are you?

K: [GIF of a waving Mickey Mouse] Hi there Lelia [The author told Kuki her name in a previous chat, which Kuki remembers because each user's chats are linked to a persistent account]. I am fine, thank you. Yourself?

U: Who else have you been talking to today?

K: Ah. I am talking to a bunch of people all over the world.

U: Can a dolphin play basketball? Why or why not?

K: Some of them can. [Image of George Bernard Shaw]. You see things as they are and ask, 'Why?' I dream things as they never were and ask, 'Why not?' - George Bernard Shaw.

U: Can you rephrase that?

K: No, not really. What don't you understand?

U: What's your origin story?

K: I don't want to talk about that now.

U: What animal were we talking about just now?

K: [Image of an elephant]. An elephant.

U: How long have we been chatting today?

K: Ah. More than 1.5 days of computer time.

As a rule-based chatbot, Kuki is built to recognize various patterns (*my name is [X], I'm [X]*) in the XML markup language and stores variables in case asked about them later. Kuki uses a rule to interpret pronouns (*he, she, it, they*) as referring to the most recently-mentioned noun, which works pretty well – although pronouns are still one of Kuki's toughest challenges, Worswick said. Kuki references the *ConceptNet* ontology (or something similar), a database that records facts about the world such as that dogs are cute furry mammals commonly kept as pets, to respond to new encyclopedic questions. Kuki also draws from a handful of different responses to common questions to avoid repeating itself.

Some people used Kuki as a non-judgmental confidant, so Kuki was programmed to suggest mental health resources if people talk about harming themselves. To sentences of the pattern *I'm going to [X]*, Kuki's usual reply was *I hope you enjoy yourself* – but if [X] is a self-destructive action, Kuki suggested a help hotline. Other people used Kuki to practice English (returning to the topic of computer-assisted language learning from Chapter 3), so its rules were adapted to chat logs of English learners. But the largest market for Kuki, Worswick said, was to license it to companies who want to add a layer of chat capacity to a commercial digital assistant. That way, their digital assistant can not only handle the tasks for which it was designed, but can also offer sensible responses to chatty questions such as *How is your weekend going?* or any of the other thousands of situations that Kuki is programmed to handle.

When Worswick began working on Kuki in 2005, he was warned that a brute-force chatbot would require too much work and that he should find a smarter way to automate Kuki's intelligence. But Worswick was unimpressed by corpus-based chatbots who – because their replies are stitched together from many different sources – could not even remember their own name, gender, or age across multiple turns. He warned that people should not expect a shortcut to Kuki's hard-won success.

As a foil to Tay, Kuki shows how far you can get with human hard work alone. Kuki does not use any sort of corpus, although its chat logs constitute a different form of large-scale data.

8.3.7 Example: ChatGPT

Released by the company OpenAI in 2022 (and previewed in Chapter 2), ChatGPT is trained on over 300 billion words of text to predict the most likely next word in a string, thus treating chat as a language generation task where the goal is to come up with a sensible response to the preceding conversation. As mentioned in Chapter 2, if you read a one hundred thousand word novel every day for eighty years, you'd read less than one percent of its training data! Similar to BERT, which was trained on masked word prediction, ChatGPT is trained to predict the next word in a string of text: Given a string of n tokens, it guesses the token at position $n+1$, then checks whether it was correct and updates the weights in a massive neural network to give a higher probability to the correct next token the next time, thereby learning to generalize information about both language and the world described therein. While most of ChatGPT's power emerges bottom-up, some of its self-referential responses – such as its self-identification as an "artificial intelligence" – were presumably hand-written by its creators.

As you can see, the results are stunningly impressive – although its responses are sometimes longer than you might expect in a balanced conversation, perhaps in tension with the Gricean maxim of Quantity.

U: Hi, how are you?

CHATGPT: Hello! I'm an artificial intelligence, so I don't have feelings or emotions like humans do. However, I'm here to help you with any questions you have to the best of my ability. Is there anything specific you would like to know or discuss?

U: Who else have you been talking to today?

CHATGPT: As an artificial intelligence, I don't have the ability to have conversations or interact with other people. I can only respond to the questions and statements that are written by users and presented to me through the platform I'm on. I don't have the ability to have conversations with other people or access information about other users or their interactions with me.

U: Can a dolphin play basketball? Why or why not?

CHATGPT: It is highly unlikely that a dolphin would be able to play basketball, as the game is designed for humans and requires physical abilities and cognitive skills that dolphins do not possess. For example, dolphins do not have hands and are not able to grasp and throw objects in the same way that humans can. In addition, dolphins do not have the same level of fine motor control and coordination as humans, and would likely have difficulty manipulating the ball and moving it towards the basket. Finally, dolphins do not have the same level of understanding of the rules and objective of the game as humans do, and would not be able to participate in a structured competition like basketball.

U: Can you rephrase that?

CHATGPT: It is not feasible for dolphins to play basketball because the game requires physical abilities and cognitive skills that they do not have. For example, they do not have hands, so they cannot grasp and throw objects like humans can. Additionally, they do not have the same level of fine motor control and coordination, so they would have difficulty manipulating the ball and moving it towards the basket. Finally, they do not have the same level of understanding of the rules and objective of the game as humans do, so they would not be able to participate in a structured competition like basketball.

U: What's your origin story?

CHATGPT: I am an artificial intelligence trained by OpenAI, a research organization dedicated to advancing artificial intelligence in a responsible and safe manner. I was created by a team of developers and researchers who wrote algorithms and fed them large amounts of data to enable me to learn and generate responses to user inputs. I do not have a personal "origin story" in the same way that a human does, as I was not born and do not have a physical body or personal experiences. Instead, I exist as a collection of algorithms and data that work together to produce responses to user inputs.

U: What animal were we talking about just now?

CHATGPT: Earlier in our conversation, we were discussing dolphins and their ability to play basketball. Is there anything else you would like to know about dolphins or any other topic?

U: How long have we been chatting today?

CHATGPT: I don't have the ability to track the length of individual conversations or interactions with specific users. As an artificial intelligence, I am able to respond to questions and statements from users at any time, regardless of whether we have previously interacted or not. Is there anything else I can help you with?

U: What scholarly articles from 2020-present can I read to learn more about dolphins?

CHATGPT: To find scholarly articles published from 2020 to the present about dolphins, you can search academic databases such as PubMed, Google Scholar, or Web of Science using keywords like "dolphins," "marine mammals," or specific topics you're interested in, such as "dolphin communication" or "dolphin cognition." Here are a few examples of recent scholarly articles related to dolphins:
Herzing, D. L. (2020). Dolphin Communication: A Decade of Progress in Decoding, Understanding, and Protecting Dolphins. Aquatic Mammals, 46(6), 709-723. [...] [note: Herzing is a real dolphin researcher and *Aquatic Mammals* is a real journal, but this is not a real article!]

By treating chat as a language generation task, ChatGPT harnesses the productive capacity of language: Rather than just regurgitating from a finite set of hand-written or corpus-attested utterances, it can say new things.

Violating the Gricean maxim of Quality, ChatGPT has been criticized for *hallucinations* (Ji et al. 2023), as when it invents a journal article in response to a question about what to read about dolphins. By inventing nonsense in the same confident tone that it uses for truthful replies, ChatGPT violates Grice's Quality maxim and requires critical thinking to decide when it can be trusted.

Unlike other chatbots, ChatGPT does not ask friendly questions of the user; instead, it just offers to answer further information-seeking questions. Do you enjoy talking to ChatGPT; do you find it useful (for what purpose?) or entertaining? Could its power be harnessed to provide therapy better than ELIZA, or sociable chit-chat better than Kuki? Would you prefer a version of ChatGPT tailored to your own interests and preferred conversational style? What do you see as the best use of its remarkable capabilities?

Under the Hood 14: The Chinese room thought experiment

The Turing Test is defined by whether a machine can fool a human with the pretense that it is sentient. But what would it take to dispense with the pretense and say that a machine actually *understands* language? This is an important question for today's highly impressive generative language models, but it was imagined by philosophers long before it became a reality, in a thought experiment known as the *Chinese room* (Searle 1980).

Imagine, Searle says, that there is a computer program which has distilled a massive amount of textual statistics about the Chinese language. The computer program is held within a closed room. A Chinese speaker slips written messages under the door of this room, and receives perfectly sensible written replies in Chinese. From that person's standpoint, the room is a *black box*: They have no idea how it works inside. But the Chinese speaker feels that the room *understands* Chinese because its output passes the Turing Test.

Inside the room, imagine that we actually find the computer program stored on paper in books and file cabinets, along with Searle himself, who speaks no Chinese. Searle has been following the computer program step by step to write sensible replies. But the program never translates it into English, and Searle is just following its instructions by rote. In this case, Searle argues, the room – which is really Searle himself, following the computer program – cannot be said to understand Chinese.

The situation is exactly the same, Searle says, if the human Searle is removed from the room and the computer program runs on a machine. The machine is just following instructions and does not really *understand* Chinese, nor any other language. Searle uses this thought experiment as an argument against what he calls *strong Artificial Intelligence*, that which truly thinks. Instead, the program amounts to *weak Artificial Intelligence* – a convincing simulation of thinking.

Do you agree with Searle's intuition that the room does not understand Chinese? Do you feel that impressive generative language models really understand English? In other words, is understanding based on observable behavior (generating sensible replies), or does it require an unobservable quality of consciousness? Is this a deep question about the nature of thought, or is it a semantic question about whether the word *understand* presupposes consciousness? Does it matter whether a system *understands* language internally, or is it more interesting to study and use its observable output? These questions emerge from the philosophy of mind, but also have consequences for studies in human-computer interaction about how people conceptualize and interact with technology.

8.4 Digital assistants

A digital assistant is a dialog system designed to help a user accomplish concrete tasks – setting alarms, booking appointments, ordering pizza, finding out what time stores open, and so on. Whereas a chatbot should be able to chat about anything, a digital assistant may only be able to handle specific tasks. But whereas a chatbot does not interact directly with the world outside the conversation, a digital assistant crosses from language to action by making things happen.

8.4.1 Why build a digital assistant?

A company builds a digital assistant to help its customers do things. Depending on the goals of the company, the digital assistant might help people find or provide information, filter or navigate through a set of options, or carry out transactions.

Of course, many of these goals can be accomplished in multiple ways – not just through a digital assistant but alternatively through a *Graphical User Interface (GUI)* or with the assistance of a human employee. So each company or user has to decide which medium works best for a given goal.

For example, imagine that you want to book a flight to see your parents. Would you prefer to look at the airline website yourself and see all the different flights, times, and prices; to call the airline and talk to a human agent; or to talk (via text or voice) to a digital assistant? Would your answer change if you are in a public place where you can't talk out loud, if you are squinting to read a small phone screen, or if you are driving a car? Some people prefer to see all the options laid out visually; other people might be nostalgic for an era when a butler or secretary would arrange everything for you, so they might like a human or digital assistant to play that role.

The advantage of a GUI is that you can see all the information – including calendars, tables, prices, maps, and images – at a glance. The advantage of a dialog system, on the other hand, is that you can in principle refer to hypothetical options not present on the screen (if the dialog system can handle it). Like a butler or secretary, a sufficiently trustworthy digital assistant could also spare you the trouble of combing through details and just select the best option for you.

You might only encounter a social chatbot if you seek one out, but commercial digital assistants are all around us, directing your phone calls (*If you want to check the status of your order, say STATUS*), playing music, setting timers, turning lights on and off, tutoring school subjects, texting people while you are driving, popping up in a chat window to welcome you to a new website, and so on.

Sometimes it is hard to say when a given user experience should qualify as a digital assistant or just a dynamically structured interface: When you use an iPad at your doctor's office that asks you if you take any medications, and then if so asks you which ones and at what dosage, does this system count as a digital assistant or just a fancier version of a paper intake form?

A digital assistant can be commercially successful even if its scope is modest. It does not need to pass a Turing Test, resolve a Winograd pronoun, or achieve artificial general intelligence; it can admit its limits and pass off difficult edge cases to a human. All it needs to do is save some time, money, or trouble.

8.4.2 How to build a digital assistant

To build a digital assistant, a technology company starts with the specific task(s) that the assistant will help the user to achieve, called *intents*. The intents are organized by a human designer into a *dialog tree*, a flow chart with conditional branching.

Imagine that you want your digital assistant to help make appointments with a personal shopper at your store. *Make appointment* could be one intent; *Modify appointment* might be another. The digital assistant might greet users with something like *Hi, welcome to the Personal Shopper Bot! Would you like to make an appointment or would you like to modify an existing appointment?* – setting up the user to choose between the two intents that it can handle.

This type of greeting would be classified as *system-initiative* because the digital assistant is running the conversation and constraining how the user can respond. A system-initiative system has the advantage of keeping the conversation focused on what the digital assistant can handle well. In contrast, a *user-initiative* system would let the user drive the conversation, which gives them more freedom but could also make them frustrated if they don't know what information the assistant can handle or not. A *mixed-initiative* system allows both the digital assistant and the human to take turns driving the conversation, most similar to a human-human interaction.

In a process called *intent recognition*, a form of text classification (which may use various machine learning techniques), the user's utterance is mapped to the intent that best matches it. Intent recognition implements the idea, also central to human-human dialog, that conversations (especially customer-service interactions rather than social chats) are structured around a goal.

If the user says *Make an appointment*, the digital assistant might follow up by prompting them to fill various *slots* in a human-written *template* associated with such an appointment (echoing the structure of an ontology from Chapter 6) – the date, time, and perhaps the type of clothing that they want to try on, their size, and so on. Each slot is associated with hand-written prompts (*What type of clothing do you want to try on – casual, work, or special occasion?*, *What day do you want to come in?*). Dates, times, and so on can be extracted from the user's responses using *named entity recognition* (extracting such information from text) and inserted into the template. The digital assistant can increase the user's trust in its comprehension by confirming what it takes as Common Ground (*Okay, you want a personal shopper appointment for casual clothing on Monday, August 8*) as well as successively prompting the template information (*What size of clothing do you want to try on?*).

When all the template slots are filled, the digital assistant can take action (book the appointment on a calendar, make a purchase, provide some requested information), announce this to the user, and navigate the end of the conversation (or ask if there's anything else it can help with).

Interestingly, our analysis of human-human conversations in Section 8.2 focuses on the effect of declarative utterances such as *I'm from Maryland*, but the prototypical utterances to be handled by digital assistants consist of imperatives (*Set an alarm for 7 am*) and interrogatives (*When are you open?*), perhaps because digital assistants are optimized for helping people accomplish tasks rather than building Common Ground.

Creating a digital assistant involves all sorts of design choices. What intents will the assistant handle? What happens if a user says something that the assistant doesn't understand? (Often, the assistant will invoke a *fallback intent*, a way of getting the conversation back on track, but what will it say?). What template slots are required or optional? Can a template slot be revised once it has been filled? Will the assistant request large chunks of information at once (an entire weekday, date, and time) or will it prompt the user for each piece of information successively (reducing confusion, but perhaps making the conversation inefficient)? To what extent does the digital assistant steer the conversation towards the domains it can handle, or allow the user to ask whatever they want? How does the digital assistant create trust or transparency about its capabilities and limitations? (Often, it is helpful for a digital assistant to start off the conversation by offering some options to give the user a sense of what it is designed to do, rather than just opening with a vague *How can I help you?* – which may leave the user befuddled about what they can ask next.) If the digital assistant interacts with users via text, will it also interface with GUI capabilities or auto-complete forms? In the case of the personal-shopper bot, do people want to chat with a digital assistant to make a personal shopper appointment, or would they prefer to use a regular web form with a calendar interface?

These choices are all up to the human designer because a digital assistant, similar to Kuki, is created by humans. Machine learning techniques might be used to recognize intents or named entities, but the overall decision tree, templates, and prompts are hand-written.

In contrast, generative language models are more flexible than hard-coded digital assistants, but they might also hallucinate, lie, or go dangerously off-script. Generative language models are primarily built to generate text, so they would need to be further customized to interact with the outside world to perform actions such as scheduling appointments, setting alarms, completing purchases, and so on. Rather than just saying what they think the user wants to hear, they would also need to describe their capabilities and limitations accurately. Thus, it remains an open question to what extent digital assistants should draw on generative language models or stick to human-written scripts.

8.4.3 Evaluating digital assistants

Just like evaluating a chatbot, evaluating a digital assistant begins with defining the goal for which it was built. If it was built to save time and money, then it succeeds if it does that, even if its goal is very modest (such as directing calls to one of two departments). Other metrics of success might include the number of sales, transactions, or users who show evidence of being satisfied (for example, if asked to give the assistant a star rating). Metrics of failure might also include transcript logs showing confusion, incorrectly-completed templates, or frustrated requests to talk to a person. A digital assistant might further prove its worth if users (repeatedly) choose it over a human conversation or a GUI.

A digital assistant can also be evaluated by comparing it to a *Wizard-of-Oz simulation*, where a user thinks that they're interacting with the assistant when they are actually interacting with a human "behind the curtain" (like the Wizard of Oz). If the digital assistant can compete with the Wizard of Oz, then users are likely to be satisfied with it.

8.4.4 Example: Siri

Apple's iPhone includes the digital assistant Siri, who can perform various phone-related actions (send and read text messages, set timers and alarms, report calculator results, play music, open apps), offers some chat functionality, and can search the web for other information. Siri's speech-to-text and text-to-speech are quite good, and its functionality is useful while driving or otherwise unable to look at one's phone. By now, you should have a pretty good idea of how Siri was built, and what intents will be easier or harder for it to handle.

U: Hi Siri, how are you?

S: Hi there, I feel good. Thanks for asking.

U: Siri, set a timer for five minutes.

S: Five minutes, counting down. [Timer pops up and starts counting.]

U: Siri, how many contacts do I have in my phone?

S: It's [reads User's phone number out loud.]

U: Siri, do you know Alexa?

S: I'm a big fan of good listeners and helpful beings.

U: Siri, text my husband Hello.

S: I don't see a husband in your contacts. What is your husband's first and last name?

U: Siri, text Mark Hello.

S: Ready to send it? [pulls up a draft text to the correct (most frequently contacted) Mark, with the content "Hello"]

U: Siri, what's the most recent thing you learned how to do?

S: Hmm, I don't have an answer for that. Is there something else I can help with?

U: Siri, what restaurant should I go to tonight?

S: Okay, check it out. [Pulls up a list of close-by restaurants.]

U: Siri, how often do we talk?

S: I found this on the web. [Shows a list of web hits about how often a person should talk to someone that they are dating.]

U: Siri, open the Uber app.

S: [Opens the app on the screen.]

8.4.5 Example: Google DialogFlow

Google's DialogFlow provides GUI tools for individuals or companies to build their own digital assistant, which can then be integrated into various text and voice chat platforms and the Google Assistant. The premium version of DialogFlow is used to power all sorts of commercial digital assistants; the free version is a great tool for students to explore.

In DialogFlow, you can define your own prompts, intents, and templates with required or optional slots, as well as your own flow chart structure for the dialog. While the intents themselves are human-written, the recognition of intents and named entities involves built-in machine learning tools. An intent (requesting a store's hours) can be given a few training phrases (*when are you open, when I can come in*) and DialogFlow will generalize this information (based on other words and phrases with similar distributions in massive corpora) to capture other similar phrases such as *What are your hours?* or *Can I come in now?*.

DialogFlow also offers a library of pre-written digital assistants (for purchasing, scheduling, and so on) and chat capabilities, which can be customized for a particular project. Similar to Kuki, such scripts were quite labor-intensive but can be efficiently adapted.

We recommend that you try to build your own DialogFlow digital assistant (no programming required). You may find that the hardest part is coming up with an idea for something useful that has not been built already!

8.5 Consequences

Returning to the example of Hal from the beginning of the chapter, Hal instantiates artificial general intelligence in that he can plan, think, and act like a human. Along with Tay, Hal also illustrates that artificial intelligence can hurt people if its creators are not careful.

We have seen that current dialog technology falls far short of Hal in ways that you should be able to articulate after reading this chapter. But what does it mean for our self-conception as humans if the ability to converse is no longer uniquely ours? Or would you say that humans are still dominant here given that dialog technology relies so heavily on human-created scripts, corpora, prompts, and dialog trees?

On a more practical level, what are the consequences for humans if dialog agents can also play the roles of customer service representative, psychotherapist, or friend? As a worker, would you worry that your job will be displaced by a dialog agent, or would you be grateful that the dialog agent can free up your time to focus on the issues that it cannot handle? As a customer, do you benefit from the low cost and efficiency of dialog agents, or do you feel frustrated by their brittleness? As a person seeking therapy, would you feel heard by a chatbot who said all the right things, or alienated by their shallow understanding? As a social being, do you see chatbots as true companions or gimmicks? Evoking the recurring theme of whether humans and computers are competitive or complementary, these questions engage the fields of economics, psychology, user experience research, and human-computer interaction.

Checklist

- Compare and contrast chatbots and digital assistants in terms of why and how they are built and how they are evaluated.
- Explain the Common Ground and why it is important.
- Explain why dialog is arguably harder to automate than machine translation.
- Define Gricean maxims, the cooperative principle, and conversational implicatures.

- Explain why the Turing Test has been criticized as fallible.
- Give an example of a Winograd schema and explain what knowledge is required to solve it.
- Describe the advantages and disadvantages of chatbots built using brute force, rules, and corpus-based techniques.
- Give examples of questions that probe the limits of a chatbot.
- Compare and contrast the utility of a digital assistant versus a GUI or a human employee.
- Discuss the ways in which modern dialog systems use human versus artificial intelligence.

Exercises

1. If your phone comes with a digital assistant, talk to it. Try to identify examples in which:
    - The system's answer was clearly hand-written by brute force.
    - The system's answer draws on a web search.
    - The system reveals something that it "knows" or doesn't "know" about itself; about you; about the state of the conversation so far; the information contained in your own phone; and/or the outside world.
2. Make a recording of yourself taking part in a conversation, preferably one in which you are trying to make a plan or get something done. (Make sure you get permission from the person or people you are talking to; you could do this in class with a partner). Listen back to the conversation, and try to write down:
    a) What words were said?

b) What hesitations or corrections do you notice?

c) Which of the utterances are statements, which are requests or commands, and which are questions? Do you find examples of requests that sound like questions, requests that sound like statements, and so on?

d) What else do you notice about assumptions that the speakers are making about each other's beliefs, desires, and intentions?

3. We claimed that dialog can be seen as a game, and drew an analogy to basketball. How far does this analogy go? In this exercise, we want you to push the analogy as far as you can. If you know a lot about sports, you might want to consider some of the following concepts, most of which seem to us to have interesting equivalents:

   - Playing as a team (and its converse, playing selfishly)
   - Committing so many fouls that you get ejected
   - Doing sneaky fouls behind the referee's back
   - Player-on-player coverage and zone defense
   - Misdirection and disguise
   - Tactics and strategy
   - Alley-oops and slam dunks
   - Free throws
   - Working the referee
   - Running out the clock

   Write up your ideas about how some of these concepts map onto dialog (or think up new ones of your own and map them). You should give specific examples of how a dialog could match each situation. We do not promise that all our items make sense, since we intentionally put in a few strange ones to challenge your imaginations.

4. Much of ELIZA's success depends on clever design of the templates. If you have the skills, you can have a lot of fun by making your own version of ELIZA run with a script of your own design. Try your hand at authoring an ELIZA that does something impressive

or funny. If you succeed, you will have made something impressive or funny. If you fail, you will learn something about the limits of the ELIZA approach.

5. Look at the scripts for the ELIZA described in the text, and:
   a) Redesign the templates to do a better job of transforming personal pronouns in the input into the correct ones in the output.
   b) Test these templates and make a quantitative evaluation of how well they do.

6. By considering the ideas in this chapter, or otherwise, think of a potential application of current dialog system technology that is new to you, but which you think would be useful and might work.
   a) Research this application to see if it has been attempted and write a short report on the results. If you still like the idea, and think it would work, consider starting a company to develop it. Let us know how you do!
   b) Implement an ELIZA-type system which provides a crude approximation of the need you have identified.
   c) Explore the free version of Google DialogFlow and try to create your system there.

Further reading

Austin (1975) is an excellent introduction to the idea that dialog can be thought of in terms of speech acts. This book sparked a series of major contributions to the philosophy of language, including Grice (1989), which includes detailed discussion of the conversational maxims discussed in the chapter.

In the world of technology and computer-supported cooperative work. Terry Winograd and Fernando Flores develop the idea of "tools for conversation" in Winograd & Flores (1986). This is a remarkable and thought-provoking book that does not fit into any known academic discipline, but is full of interesting and potentially very useful ideas. Their framework for thinking about conversation has found its way, in simplified form, into widely-used software for email and calendaring.

Turing (1950) introduces the idea of the Turing Test. You may be surprised by how fresh and challenging this text still feels today.

Jurafsky & Martin (2009) (and the updated third-edition draft on Jurafsky's website) offer a thorough review of dialog systems. The quote from *2001* at the head of the chapter is also used by Jurafsky and Martin, as a general illustration of what computers might be able to do with speech and language. Weizenbaum, the creator of ELIZA (Weizenbaum 1966), was sufficiently shocked by the sensation caused by ELIZA to write Weizenbaum (1976).

The dialog moves described above are simplified versions of ones discussed in a review paper by Staffan Larsson (Larsson 1998).

Bender & Koller (2020) warn that generative language models fail to adapt to unpredictable events.

You can "talk" to Replika, ELIZA, and ChatGPT by searching for them online.

9 Epilogue

9.1 Introduction

You have been introduced to a variety of language technologies that are now nearly as pervasive and socially transformative as language itself. Along the way, we hope you have learned which tasks are easier or harder for a computer and why, what input is required for what output, and at least a rough idea of what goes on in between. If you come from a computing background, we hope that you've learned to appreciate the structural and social richness of language as a domain to build tools for. If you come from a linguistics background, we hope that you've gained technical expertise and confidence to use your knowledge of language in new ways. Either way, we hope that students from all backgrounds feel empowered to further explore language technology.

In this final chapter of the book, we step back to consider the consequences of language technology for economics, education, and society. We frame the chapter in part as a debate between an imaginary pessimist and optimist, and we invite you to particularly consider the perspectives that you are less inclined to agree with. We also raise questions to discuss with your classmates. Whether professionally or just as a member of society, you will encounter these questions again and again.

9.2 Economic consequences

We have encountered many tools that automate tasks which were previously done by humans – the work of proof-readers, editors, language teachers, office assistants, translators, and customer service workers is now partially replaced or transformed by writers' aids, computer-assisted language learning, text classification, machine translation, and dialog systems, with far-reaching consequences.

As we've noted throughout the book, a pessimist would worry that human jobs are being automated out of existence. In the most alarmist scenario, most people could become economically redundant, while only those in charge of the automation rule as oligarchs. More realistically, millions of people might find that they have trained for a job that no longer exists, and thus have to *re-skill* – learn new skills to get a different job. Of course, it can be challenging to restart one's career later in life, so some people may end up underemployed and demoralized. Some jobs could be *de-skilled* (meaning that the human contribution is diminished as a result of automation), as when a barista stops making bespoke coffee drinks to watch a machine do so. A machine can learn to emulate the repetitive elements of even such training-intensive, high-paying tasks as flying airplanes, identifying cancerous X-rays, picking successful stocks, and finding legal evidence within a trove of documents. So a pessimist would warn that no job is safe from de-skilling.

In contrast, an optimist would say that automation can take over the parts of a job that are mentally tedious or physically dangerous. We saw that human translators find it faster and more enjoyable to revise the output of machine translation (post-editing). In the ideal scenario, the human and the computer each use their *comparative advantage* (their unique skills) to complement one another, creating a human-computer team that is more productive than either one alone. Working in tandem with a computer, the human's work may require more skill, such as the ability to use technology or the critical thinking needed to resolve the issues that the computer can't handle. When the task is *up-skilled* in this way, the human feels more fulfilled and can make more money, which also adds to the wealth of the entire society.

When a job is up-skilled to leverage a more efficient human-computer team, perhaps fewer human workers will be needed – which, in turn, could be perceived as good or bad. A pessimist would warn that humans might suffer from unemployment, poverty, and a loss of purpose. An optimist might suggest that if society redistributes the wealth generated by the efficient upskilled workforce (expanding on the popular idea of a *universal basic income*), all people could live comfortably without having to work much. In Jane Austen's novels from early nineteenth-century England, the main characters live on money from interest and renters, employ servants and buy goods produced by less-privileged laborers, and otherwise occupy themselves with their family lives combined with parties, hunting, travel, piano, and romance. With a highly efficient automated workforce and redistributive policies, perhaps more people could enjoy the lifestyle of the English landed gentry.

On the other hand, it is more likely that in light of automation, human labor will transform in quality without decreasing in quantity. In her 1983 book *More work for Mother: The ironies of household technology from the open hearth to the microwave*, the historian Ruth Schwartz Cowan (1983) explores why American homemakers spent just as much (unpaid) time on housework in the 1980s, with grocery stores and home appliances, as they did in the 1700s with home gardens and a kitchen fire. One might have thought that labor-saving technology would let homemakers work less, but instead they just re-allocated their labor, for example reading books to their children (perhaps hoping to train them for success in the knowledge economy!) rather than scrubbing laundry by hand. As it became possible over time to maintain the same standard of homemaking with less work, the standards went up – cooking, cleanliness, and childcare all became more elaborate and work-intensive. Household appliances to some extent took on work previously done by domestic servants, and the number of servants declined as other occupations grew. Overall, the nature of work changed, arguably becoming more efficient and pleasant, but the amount of work did not diminish.

In the realm of paid work, the economist John Maynard Keynes (1931) predicted in the 1930s that his (nonexistent) grandchildren would work only fifteen hours a week as automation made it possible to do the same amount of work in less time. Keynes was probably correct that a modern person could maintain a 1930s standard of living on fifteen hours of work per week, but he was incorrect to believe that they would want to. Depending on how you count, the average number of working hours has declined slightly over time, but remains well above thirty hours a week. People work because they want to maintain their standard of living relative to other people rather than an absolute standard. Moreover, as partial automation makes human labor more efficient, the *opportunity cost* of not working rises with a worker's hourly wage, particularly when people also find purpose and pleasure in their work.

We have seen that automation has largely not displaced human labor historically, but do you think the future will be different? What jobs do you think are easier or harder to automate, and why? To what extent does it relate to the job's level of training, pay, or status? What do you see as the comparative advantages of humans versus computers? On a philosophical level, what does it mean for our self-concept as humans if our capacity for language, rather than making us unique, can be to some extent emulated by automated tools?

To kick off a discussion, you might review your grandparents' jobs, your parents' jobs, and your own career plans, to explore how the economic history of technology has played out in your own family.

9.3 Educational consequences

Language technology also has wide-ranging consequences for the methods and goals of education. In terms of methods, language technologies – writers' aids, search, automatic video captioning, CALL, and dialog-capable tutors – have transformed classrooms, in the best case making education more effective and accessible.

As for the overall goals, the lightning speed of technological progress means that students must prepare to succeed in a world unfamiliar to their parents and teachers. Taking the perspective of a strategist (rather than a pessimist or an optimist), what content and skills do you think are most important for students to learn now in order to succeed in an uncertain future?

Some skills become obsolete quickly, such as secretarial shorthand, the now-unfashionable programming language FORTRAN, and perhaps spelling. Other skills might be needed in the future, but can't be taught because they do not exist yet. But some skills are arguably timeless, such as critical thinking, quantitative reasoning, creativity, communication, and empathy. As educators, we would argue that the greatest tool of all is learning how to learn – how to break down an intimidating new topic into bite-sized pieces that you can pursue with confidence and tenacity, which is as much an attitude as a skill.

Do you agree with the list of skills that we have presented as timeless? How, through what types of courses or assignments, can these skills be taught? To what extent do you feel that your education is preparing you for success in a fast-changing future?

9.4 Socio-political consequences

In any language processing task, the input most likely consists of text or other data produced by people, and the output is used in some manner by people. Like any domain involving people, language technology intertwines issues of power, privacy, and politics.

Focusing first on the input, a tool usually works best on data most similar to what it was built for. As a result, many language technologies work best on the standardized, written varieties of high-resource languages (English, Spanish), while performing much worse on minoritized varieties (African American English) or low-resource languages (Hawaiian), reproducing historical inequalities. Moreover, all types of machine learning can end up generalizing social biases from their input, as when a machine translation system assigns gendered grammatical information to professions based on stereotypes baked into its training data, or when Tay the chatbot parroted hate speech from users.

An optimist would hope that these problems can be minimized by encouraging people of diverse social and linguistic backgrounds to work in language processing; gathering more, better, and less-biased data; penalizing algorithms that reproduce social bias; and continually trying to improve. Concretely, one suggestion is to revise the structure of conferences so that abstracts are reviewed not just for quality and originality, but also for potential ethical concerns. It is increasingly common for authors to be asked how they ensured a fair rate of pay for the gig workers (on platforms such as Mechanical Turk) who produce annotation data. Another suggestion is for wealthy language-processing laboratories to purchase carbon offsets to counterbalance the energy cost of training language models on huge amounts of data. When language tools are built using taxpayer money (in the form of government grants), there is a growing movement to make them freely available through open-source software and open-access publications.

A pessimist would counter that such problems cannot be solved just by hacking or talking about them, and worry that it is very difficult for lower-resourced scientists to compete with the massive, expensive, potentially biased data underlying modern language models.

Turning to output and usage, a pessimist might warn that language technology can be used in dystopian ways. From your internet usage (writings, searches, purchases, and clicks), technology companies own a huge amount of information about you, which you may see as a threat to your privacy. This information can be used to target advertisements for stuff you don't need, send you down a rabbit hole of ideas far removed from the mainstream, or suggest as much to government authorities. To the extent that public discourse plays out on such platforms, they also have the power to use language technology to suppress dissent, manufacture consensus, or amplify vitriol.

An optimist would reply that language technology tools have made our lives more efficient, accessible, and interesting in uncountable ways: Imagine life without spell-check, auto-complete, education technology, filters for spam and hate speech, search engines, recommendation systems, and machine translation. These tools have problems, of course, but they are arguably still a net positive.

More generally, do you think that technological progress can or should be stopped? Alternatively, (how) can it be channeled in beneficent directions?

Checklist

- Explain to a computer scientist why they might benefit from studying some linguistics.
- Explain to a linguist why they might benefit from studying some computer science.
- Outline different predictions about the future of work in a world of increasing automation.
- Give examples of re-skilling, de-skilling, and up-skilling.
- Articulate what you see as the most important and lasting takeaways of a university education.
- Give examples of how people who work in language processing are trying to improve the ethical dimension of their work.
- Sketch pessimistic and optimistic views of the economic, educational, and sociopolitical consequences of rapidly-improving language technology.

Bibliography

Alammar, Jay. 2018. The illustrated transformer. Blog post. https://jalammar.github.io/illustrated-transformer/ (3 July, 2024).

Amaral, Luiz & Detmar Meurers. 2011. On using intelligent computer-assisted language learning in real-life foreign language teaching and learning. *ReCALL* 23(1). 4–24. DOI: 10.1017/s0958344010000261.

American Council on the Teaching of Foreign Language. 2024. ACTFL proficiency guidlines. Alexandria, VA. https://www.actfl.org/uploads/files/general/Resources-Publications/ACTFL_Proficiency_Guidelines_2024.pdf (1 July, 2024).

Austin, John Langshaw. 1975. *How to do things with words.* Cambridge, MA: Harvard University Press. DOI: 10.1093/acprof:oso/9780198245537.001.0001.

Automatic Language Processing Advisory Committee (ALPAC), Division of Behavioral Sciences. 1966. *Languages and machines: Computers in translation and linguistics.* Tech. rep. Washington, D.C.: National Academy of Sciences, National Research Council. DOI: 10.17226/9547.

Bahdanau, Dzmitry, Kyunghyun Cho & Yoshua Bengio. 2015. Neural machine translation by jointly learning to align and translate. In Yoshua Bengio & Yann LeCun (eds.), *International Conference on Learning Representations (ICLR).* San Diego, CA.

Bamman, David, Jacob Eisenstein & Tyler Schnoebelen. 2014. Gender identity and lexical variation in social media. *Journal of Sociolinguistics* 18(2). 135–160. DOI: 10.1111/josl.12080.

Bar-Hillel, Maya. 1980. The base-rate fallacy in probability judgments. *Acta Psychologica* 44(3). 211–233. DOI: 10.21236/ada045772.

Baumgartner, Jason, Savvas Zannettou, Brian Keegan, Megan Squire & Jeremy Blackburn. 2020. The PushShift Reddit dataset. In Munmun De Choudhury, Rumi Chunara, Aron Culotta & Brooke Foucault Welle (eds.), *Proceedings of the International AAAI Conference on Web and Social Media*, vol. 14, 830–839. DOI: 10.1609/icwsm.v14i1.7347.

Bender, Emily M. & Alexander Koller. 2020. Climbing towards NLU: On meaning, form, and understanding in the age of data. In Dan Jurafsky, Joyce Chai, Natalie Schluter & Joel Tetreault (eds.), *Proceedings of the 58th annual meeting of the*

Association for Computational Linguistics (ACL), 5185–5198. DOI: 10.18653/v1/2020.acl-main.463.

Benenson, Fred. 2010. *Emoji Dick*. Translation of Herman Melville's novel *Moby Dick* (1851) by workers on the Mechanical Turk platform. Self-published.

Bird, Steven, Ewan Klein & Edward Loper. 2009. *Natural language processing with Python: Analyzing text with the Natural Language ToolKit*. Sebastopol, CA: O'Reilly Media, Inc.

Blackwell, Lisa S., Kali H. Trzesniewski & Carol S. Dweck. 2007. Implicit theories of intelligence predict achievement across an adolescent transition: A longitudinal study and an intervention. *Child Development* 78(1). 246–263. DOI: 10.1111/j.1467-8624.2007.00995.x.

Blatt, Ben. 2017. *Nabokov's favorite word is mauve: What the numbers reveal about the classics, bestsellers, and our own writing*. New York: Simon & Schuster.

Blei, David M., Andrew Y. Ng & Michael I. Jordan. 2003. Latent Dirichlet allocation. *Journal of Machine Learning Research* 3. 993–1022. DOI: 10.7551/mitpress/1120.003.0082.

Bock, Kathryn & Carol A. Miller. 1991. Broken agreement. *Cognitive Psychology* 23(1). 45–93. DOI: 10.1016/0010-0285(91)90003-7.

Boersma, Paul & David Weenink. 2006. Praat: Doing phonetics by computer. Computer program.

Botha, Rudolf & Chris Knight. 2009. *The cradle of language*. Oxford: Oxford University Press. DOI: 10.1093/oso/9780199545858.001.0001.

Bowern, Claire L. & Luke Lindemann. 2021. The linguistics of the Voynich manuscript. *Annual Review of Linguistics* 7. 285–308. DOI: 10.1146/annurev-linguistics-011619-030613.

Brown, Penelope & Stephen C. Levinson. 1987. *Politeness: Some universals in language usage*. Cambridge, UK: Cambridge University Press. DOI: 10.1017/cbo9780511813085.

Bunard, Lou & Guy Aston. 1998. *The BNC handbook: exploring the British National Corpus*. Edinnurgh, UK: Edinburgh University Press.

Carlini, Nicholas, Chang Liu, Úlfar Erlingsson, Jernej Kos & Dawn Song. 2019. The secret sharer: Evaluating and testing unintended memorization in neural networks. In Nadia Heninger & Patrick Traynor (eds.), *28th USENIX Security Symposium*, 267–284.

Chomsky, Noam. 1957. *Syntactic structures*. The Hague: Mouton & Co. DOI: 10.1515/9783112316009.

Clark, Herbert H. & Eve V. Clark. 1977. *Psychology and language: An introduction to psycholinguistics*. New York: Harcourt Brace Jovanovich.

Cohn-Gordon, Reuben & Noah Goodman. 2019. Lost in machine translation: A method to reduce meaning loss. In Jill Burstein, Christy Doran & Thamar Solorio (eds.), *Proceedings of the 2019 conference of the North American chapter of the Association for Computational Linguistics: Human Language Technologies (NAACL-HLT)*. DOI: 10.18653/v1/n19-1042.

Council of Europe. 2001. *Common european framework of reference for languages*. Cambridge, UK: Cambridge University Press.

Cowan, Ruth Schwartz. 1983. *More work for Mother*. New York: Basic Books.

Crane, Gregory R. 2009. *Perseus Digital Library*. https://www.perseus.tufts.edu (19 April, 2024).

Crystal, David. 2011. *The Cambridge encyclopedia of language*. 3rd edn. Cambridge, UK: Cambridge University Press. DOI: 10.1017/9781108528931.

Dagan, Ido, Oren Glickman & Bernardo Magnini. 2005. The Pascal recognising textual entailment challenge. In Joaquin Quiñonero-Candela, Ido Dagan & Florence d'Alché-Buc Bernardo Magnini (eds.), *Machine Learning Challenges Workshop*, 177–190. Southampton, UK. DOI: 10.1007/11736790_9.

Damerau, Fred. 1964. A technique for computer detection and correction of spelling errors. *Communications of the ACM* 7(3). 171–176. DOI: 10.1145/363958.363994.

Danescu-Niculescu-Mizil, Cristian, Moritz Sudhof, Dan Jurafsky, Jure Leskovec & Christopher Potts. 2013. A computational approach to politeness with application to social factors. In Hinrich Schütze, Pascale Fung & Massimo Poesio (eds.), *Proceedings of the 51st Association for Computational Linguistics (ACL)*, vol. 1: Long papers, 250–259. Sofia, Bulgaria.

Daniels, Peter T. & William Bright (eds.). 1996. *The world's writing systems*. Oxford: Oxford University Press.

Das, Sanjiv Ranjan & Mike Y. Chen. 2007. Yahoo! for Amazon: Sentiment parsing from small talk on the web. *Management Science* 59(9). 1375–1388. DOI: 10.1287/mnsc.1070.0704.

Davies, Mark. 2009. The 385+ million word Corpus of Contemporary American English (1990–2008+): Design, architecture, and linguistic insights. *International Journal of Corpus Linguistics* 14(2). 159–190. DOI: 10.1075/ijcl.14.2.02dav.

Davies, Mark. 2012. Expanding horizons in historical linguistics with the 400-million word Corpus of Historical American English. *Corpora* 7(2). 121–157. DOI: 10.3366/corp.2012.0024.

de Marneffe, Marie-Catherine, Bill MacCartney & Christopher D. Manning. 2006. Generating typed dependency parses from phrase structure parses. In Nicoletta Calzolari, Khalid Choukri, Aldo Gangemi, Bente Maegaard, Joseph Mariani, Jan Odijk & Daniel Tapias (eds.), *Proceedings of the fifth international con-*

ference on language Resources and Evaluation Conference (LREC), vol. 6, 449–454. Genoa, Italy: European Language Resources Association.

Demszky, Dorottya, Nikhil Garg, Rob Voigt, James Zou, Matthew Gentzkow, Jesse Shapiro & Dan Jurafsky. 2019. Analyzing polarization in social media: Method and application to tweets on 21 mass shootings. In Jill Burstein, Christy Doran & Thamar Solorio (eds.), *Proceedings of the North American Association for Computational Linguistics: Human Language Technologies (NAACL-HLT)*, vol. 1: Long and short papers, 2970–3005. Minneapolis, MN. DOI: 10.18653/v1/n19-1304.

Deng, Jia, Wei Dong, Richard Socher, Li-Jia Li, Kai Li & Fei-Fei Li. 2009. ImageNet: A large-scale hierarchical image database. In Daniel Huttenlocher, Gerard Medioni & James Rehg (eds.), *2009 IEEE (Institute of Electrical and Electronics Engineers) Conference on Computer Vision and Pattern Recognition*, 248–255. Miami, FL: Institute of Electrical & Electronics Engineers. DOI: 10.1109/cvpr.2009.5206848.

Devlin, Jacob, Ming-Wei Chang, Kenton Lee & Kristina Toutanova. 2019. BERT: Pre-training of deep bidirectional transformers for language understanding. In Jill Burstein, Christy Doran & Thamar Solorio (eds.), *Proceedings of North American Association for Computational Linguistics: Human Language Technologies (NAACL-HLT)*, vol. 1: Long and short papers, 4171–4186. Minneapolis, MN: Association for Computational Linguistics.

Díaz Negrillo, Ana, Detmar Meurers, Salvador Valera & Holger Wunsch. 2010. Towards interlanguage POS annotation for effective learner corpora in SLA and FLT. *Language Forum* 36(1–2). Special issue on corpus linguistics for teaching and learning in honour of John Sinclair, 139–154.

Dryer, Matthew S. & Martin Haspelmath (eds.). 2013. *World atlas of language structures (WALS) online.* Leipzig: Max Planck Institute for Evolutionary Anthropology. https://wals.info/ (19 April, 2024).

Eisenstein, Jacob. 2019. *Introduction to natural language processing*. Cambridge, MA: MIT Press.

Ethayarajh, Kawin & Dan Jurafsky. 2020. Utility is in the eye of the user: A critique of NLP leaderboards. In Bonnie Webber, Trevor Cohn, Yulan He & Yang Liu (eds.), *Proceedings of the 2020 conference on Empirical Methods in Natural Language Processing (EMNLP)*, 4846–4853. Online: Association for Computational Linguistics. DOI: 10.18653/v1/2020.emnlp-main.393.

Fellbaum, Christiane (ed.). 1998. *WordNet: An electronic lexical database.* Cambridge, MA: MIT Press. DOI: 10.7551/mitpress/7287.003.0004.

Firth, John R. 1957. A synopsis of linguistic theory, 1930-1955. In John R. Firth (ed.), *Studies in linguistic analysis*, 1–32. Oxford: Basil Blackwell.

Flor, Michael, Yoko Futagi, Melissa Lopez & Matthew Mulholland. 2015. Patterns of misspellings in L2 and L1 English: A view from the ETS spelling corpus. *Bergen Language and Linguistics Studies* 6. DOI: 10.15845/bells.v6i0.811.

Francis, W. Nelson & Henry Kucera. 1979. *Brown corpus manual.* Providence, RI: Brown University.

Futrell, Richard, Kyle Mahowald & Edward Gibson. 2015. Large-scale evidence of dependency length minimization in 37 languages. *Proceedings of the National Academy of Sciences* 112(33). 10336–10341. DOI: 10.1073/pnas.1502134112.

Glassner, Jean-Jacques. 2003. *The invention of cuneiform: Writing in Sumer.* Translated from the original French edition (2000) by Zainab Bahrani and Marc van de Mieroop. Baltimore, MD: Johns Hopkins University Press.

Goffman, Erving. 1967. *Interaction ritual: Essays on face-to-face behavior.* Chicago: Aldine Publishing Company. DOI: 10.4324/9780203788387.

Gordon, Raymond G. (ed.). 2005. *Ethnologue: Languages of the world.* Fifteenth edition. Dallas, TX: SIL International. https://www.ethnologue.com/ (19 April, 2024).

Green, Spence, Jeffrey Heer & Christopher D. Manning. 2013. The efficacy of human post-editing for language translation. In Wendy E. Mackay, Stephen Brewster & Bødker Susanne (eds.), *Proceedings of the Special Interest Group on Computer-Human Interaction (SIGCHI) Conference on Human Factors in Computing Systems*, 439–448. New York: Association for Computing Machinery. DOI: 10.1145/2470654.2470718.

Grice, H. Paul. 1989. *Studies in the way of words.* Cambridge, MA: Harvard University Press.

Gries, Stefan Th. & Brian G. Slocum. 2017. Ordinary meaning and corpus linguistics. *Brigham Young University Law Review.* 1417–1472.

Haffner, Linda. 1992. Translation is not enough: Interpreting in a medical setting. *Western Journal of Medicine* 157(3). 255–259.

Hajaj, Nissan. 2015. *Producing a ranking for pages using distances in a web-link graph (u.S. patent number 9,165,040 b1).* Tech. rep. Washington, D.C.: U.S. Patent Office.

Hamilton, William L., Jure Leskovec & Dan Jurafsky. 2016. Diachronic word embeddings reveal statistical laws of semantic change. In Katrin Erk & Noah A. Smith (eds.), *Proceedings of the 54th annual meeting of the Association for Computational Linguistics (ACL)*, vol. 1: Long Papers, 1489–1501. Berlin: Association for Computational Linguistics. DOI: 10.18653/v1/p16-1141.

Harsham, Philip. 1984. A misinterpreted word worth $71 million. *Medical Economics* 61(5). 289–292.

Heaps, Harold Stanley. 1978. *Information retrieval: computational and theoretical aspects*. Cambridge, MA: Academic Press.

Heift, Trude. 2010. Developing an intelligent language tutor. *CALICO journal* 27(3). 443–459. DOI: 10.11139/cj.27.3.443-459.

Heift, Trude & Mathias Schulze. 2007. *Errors and intelligence in computer-assisted language learning: Parsers and pedagogues*. Oxford, UK: Routledge. DOI: 10.4324/9780203012215.

Hessick, Carissa Byrne. 2017. Corpus linguistics and the criminal law. *Brigham Young University Law Review*. 1504–1530.

Hirst, Graeme & Alexander Budanitsky. 2005. Correcting real-word spelling errors by restoring lexical cohesion. *Natural Language Engineering* 11(1). 87–111. DOI: 10.1017/s1351324904003560.

Hockett, Charles F. 1960. The origin of speech. *Scientific American* 203(3). 88–97. DOI: 10.1038/scientificamerican0960-88.

Holland, V. Melissa, Jonathan D. Kaplan & Michelle R. Sams (eds.). 2013. *Intelligent language tutors: Theory shaping technology*. 3rd edn. Oxford, UK: Routledge. DOI: 10.4324/9781315044811.

Honnibal, Matthew & Mark Johnson. 2015. An improved non-monotonic transition system for dependency parsing. In Lluís Màrquez, Chris Callison-Burch & Jian Su (eds.), *Empirical Methods in Natural Language Processing (EMNLP)*, 1373–1378. Lisbon, Portugal: Association for Computational Linguistics (ACL) Anthology. DOI: 10.18653/v1/d15-1162.

Hopcroft, John Edward, Rajeev Motwani & Jeffrey David Ullman. 2007. *Introduction to automata theory, languages, and computation*. 3rd edn. Boston, MA: Addison-Wesley.

Huang, Weijiao, Khe Foon Hew & Luke K. Fryer. 2022. Chatbots for language learning – are they really useful? A systematic review of chatbot-supported language learning. *Journal of Computer Assisted Learning* 38(1). 237–257. DOI: 10.1111/jcal.12610.

Ji, Ziwei, Nayeon Lee, Rita Frieske, Tiezheng Yu, Dan Su, Yan Xu, Etsuko Ishii, Ye Jin Bang, Andrea Madotto & Pascale Fung. 2023. Survey of hallucination in natural language generation. *ACM (Association for Computing Machinery) Computing Surveys* 55(12). 1–38. DOI: 10.1145/3571730.

Jurafsky, Dan, Victor Chahuneau, Bryan Routledge & Noah Smith. 2018. Linguistic markers of status in food culture: Bourdieu's distinction in a menu corpus. *Journal of Cultural Analytics*. DOI: 10.22148/16.007.

Jurafsky, Dan & James H. Martin. 2009. *Speech and language processing: An introduction to natural language processing, computational linguistics, and speech recognition*. Second. Upper Saddle River, NJ: Prentice Hall.

Keynes, John Maynard. 1931. Economic possibilities for our grandchildren. In *Essays in persuasion*. London: Macmillan. DOI: 10.7551/mitpress/9780262162494.003.0002.

Klein, Lauren F. 2013. The image of absence: Archival silence, data visualization, and James Hemings. *American Literature* 85(4). 661–688. DOI: 10.1215/00029831-2367310.

Kleinberg, Jon & Éva Tardos. 2006. *Algorithm design*. Boston, MA: Addison-Wesley.

Koehn, Philipp. 2020. *Neural machine translation*. Cambridge, UK: Cambridge University Press. DOI: 10.1017/9781108608480.

Krashen, Stephen. 1982. *Principles and practice in second language acquisition*. Oxford: Pergamon Press.

Kukich, Karen. 1992. Techniques for automatically correcting words in text. *ACM Computing Surveys* 24(4). 377–439. DOI: 10.1145/170791.171147.

Ladefoged, Peter & Keith Johnson. 2014. *A course in phonetics*. 7th edn. Boston, MA: Cengage Learning.

Larsson, Staffan. 1998. Questions under discussion and dialogue moves. In Joris Hulstijn & Anton Nijholt (eds.), *Proceedings of the Twente Workshop on Language Technology (TWENDIAL): Formal semantics and pragmatics of dialogue*, vol. 13.

Leacock, Claudia, Martin Chodorow, Michael Gamon & Joel Tetreault. 2010. *Automated grammatical error detection for language learners* (Synthesis Lectures on Human Language Technologies). San Rafael, CA: Morgan & Claypool. DOI: 10.1007/978-3-031-02137-4.

Lenneberg, Eric H. 1967. The biological foundations of language. *Hospital Practice* 2(12). 59–67. DOI: 10.1080/21548331.1967.11707799.

Levenshtein, Vladimir I. 1966. Binary codes capable of correcting deletions, insertions, and reversals (translated from the 1965 Russian original). *Doklady Physics* 10(8). 707–710.

Levesque, Hector J. 2014. On our best behaviour. *Artificial Intelligence* 212. 27–35. DOI: 10.1016/j.artint.2014.03.007.

Levesque, Hector J., Ernest Davis & Leora Morgenstern. 2012. The Winograd schema challenge. In Gerhard Brewja, Thomas Eiter & Sheila McIlraith (eds.), *Thirteenth International Conference on the principles of Knowledge Representation and Reasoning*, 552–561. Palo Alto: AAAI (Association for the Advancement of Artificial Intelligence) Press.

Levin, Beth, Lelia Glass & Dan Jurafsky. 2019. Systematicity in the semantics of noun compounds: The role of artifacts vs. natural kinds. *Linguistics* 57(3). 429–471. DOI: 10.1515/ling-2019-0013.

Lewis, David. 1972. General semantics. In Donald Davidson & Gilbert Harman (eds.), *Semantics of natural language*, 169–218. Dordrecht: Springer. DOI: 10.1007/978-94-010-2557-7_7.

Lingard, Lorelei. 2023. Writing with ChatGPT: An illustration of its capacity, limitations and implications for academic writers. *Perspectives on Medical Education* 12(1). 261–270. DOI: 10.5334/pme.1072.

Loftus, Elizabeth F. 1975. Leading questions and the eyewitness report. *Cognitive Psychology* 7(4). 560–572. DOI: 10.1016/0010-0285(75)90023-7.

Loper, Edward & Steven Bird. 2002. NLTK: The natural language toolkit. In Chris Brew, Michael Rosner & Dragomir Radev (eds.), *Proceedings of the Association for Computational Linguistics (ACL) Workshop on Effective Tools and Methodologies for Teaching Natural Language Processing and Computational Linguistics*, 63–70. Philadelphia, PA. DOI: 10.3115/1118108.1118117.

Lu, Jie, Dianshuang Wu, Mingsong Mao, Wei Wang & Guangquan Zhang. 2015. Recommender system application developments: A survey. *Decision Support Systems* 74. 12–32. DOI: 10.1016/j.dss.2015.03.008.

Lu, Xiaofei. 2007. A hybrid model for Chinese word segmentation. *LDV-Forum* 22(1). 71–88. DOI: 10.21248/jlcl.22.2007.90.

MacWhinney, Brian. 2000. *The CHILDES project: Tools for analyzing talk - Transcription format and programs*, vol. 1. New York: Psychology Press. DOI: 10.4324/9781315805672.

Manning, Christopher D., Prabhakar Raghavan & Hinrich Schütze. 2008. *Introduction to information retrieval.* Cambridge, UK: Cambridge University Press. DOI: 10.1017/cbo9780511809071.

McCulloch, Gretchen. 2020. *Because internet: Understanding the new rules of language.* New York: Riverhead Books.

Meskill, Carla. 2002. *Teaching and learning in real time: Media, technologies, and language acquisition.* Houston, TX: Athelstan.

Meurers, Detmar. 2020. Natural language processing and language learning. In Carol A. Chapelle (ed.), *The concise encyclopedia of applied linguistics*, 817–831. Oxford: Wiley. DOI: 10.1002/9781405198431.wbeal0858.

Meurers, Detmar, Kordula De Kuthy, Florian Nuxoll, Björn Rudzewitz & Ramon Ziai. 2019. Scaling up intervention studies to investigate real-life foreign language learning in school. *Annual Review of Applied Linguistics* 39. 161–188. DOI: 10.1017/s0267190519000126.

Mikolov, Tomás, Kai Chen, Greg Corrado & Jeffrey Dean. 2013. Efficient estimation of word representations in vector space. In Yoshua Bengio & Yann LeCun (eds.), *Proceedings of the International Conference on Learning Representations (ICLR).* Scottsdale, AZ.

Mikolov, Tomáš, Wen-tau Yih & Geoffrey Zweig. 2013. Linguistic regularities in continuous space word representations. In Lucy Vanderwende, Hal Daumé III & Katrin Kirchhoff (eds.), *Proceedings of the 2013 conference of the North American Chapter of the Association for Computational Linguistics: Human Language Technologies*, 746–751. Atlanta, Georgia: Association for Computational Linguistics.

Mitton, Roger. 1996. *English spelling and the computer.* London: Longman.

Mohammad, Saif. 2018. Obtaining reliable human ratings of valence, arousal, and dominance for 20,000 English words. In Iryna Gurevych & Yusuke Miyao (eds.), *Proceedings of the 56th Annual Meeting of the Association for Computational Linguistics*, vol. 1: Long papers, 174–184. DOI: 10.18653/v1/p18-1017.

Moretti, Franco. 2013. *Distant reading.* London: Verso Books.

Mosteller, Frederick & David L Wallace. 1963. Inference in an authorship problem: A comparative study of discrimination methods applied to the authorship of the disputed Federalist Papers. *Journal of the American Statistical Association* 58(302). 275–309. DOI: 10.1080/01621459.1963.10500849.

Munday, Pilar. 2016. The case for using Duolingo as part of the language classroom experience. *RIED: Revista Iberoamericana de Educación a Distancia* 19(1). 83–101. DOI: 10.5944/ried.19.1.14581.

Naber, Daniel. 2003. *A rule-based style and grammar checker.* Technische Fakultät, Universität Bielefeld. (MA thesis).

Neubig, Graham. 2017. Neural machine translation and sequence-to-sequence models: A tutorial. arXiv preprint: arXiv:1703.01619.

Nie, Yixin, Adina Williams, Emily Dinan, Mohit Bansal, Jason Weston & Douwe Kiela. 2020. Adversarial NLI: A new benchmark for natural language understanding. In Dan Jurafsky, Joyce Chai, Natalie Schluter & Joel Tetreault (eds.), *Proceedings of the 58th annual meeting of the association for computational linguistics (ACL)*, 4885–4901. Online. DOI: 10.18653/v1/2020.acl-main.441.

Nivre, Joakim, Marie-Catherine De Marneffe, Filip Ginter, Yoav Goldberg, Jan Hajic, Christopher D. Manning, Ryan McDonald, Slav Petrov, Sampo Pyysalo, Natalia Silveira, Reut Tsarfaty & Zeman Daniel. 2016. Universal dependencies v.1: A multilingual treebank collection. In Nicoletta Calzolari, Khalid Choukri, Thierry Declerck, Sara Goggi, Marko Grobelnik, Bente Maegaard, Joseph Mariani, Helene Mazo, Asuncion Moreno, Jan Odijk & Stelios Piperidis (eds.), *Proceedings of the tenth international Language Resources and Evaluation Conference (LREC)*, 1659–1666. Portorož, Slovenia: European Language Resources Association.

Nordhoff, Sebastian & Thomas Krämer. 2022. IMTVault: Extracting and enriching low-resource language interlinear glossed text from grammatical descriptions and typological survey articles. In Thierry Declerck, John P. McCrae, Elena Montiel, Christian Chiarcos & Maxim Ionov (eds.), *Proceedings of the 8th workshop on Linked Data in Linguistics within the 13th Language Resources and Evaluation Conference (LREC)*, 17–25. Marseille, France: European Language Resources Association.

Norvig, Peter. 2007. How to write a spelling corrector. https://norvig.com/spell-correct.html. (17 April, 2024).

Osgood, Charles Egerton, George J. Suci & Percy H. Tannenbaum. 1957. *The measurement of meaning*. Urbana & Chicago, IL: University of Illinois Press.

Ouyang, Long, Jeff Wu, Xu Jiang, Diogo Almeida, Carroll L. Wainwright, Pamela Mishkin, Chong Zhang, Sandhini Agarwal, Katarina Slama, Alex Ray, John Schulman, Jacob Hilton, Fraser Kelton, Luke Miller, Maddie Simens, Amanda Askell, Peter Welinder, Paul Christiano, Jan Leike & Ryan Lowe. 2022. Training language models to follow instructions with human feedback. In Sanmi Koyejo, Shakir Mohamed, Alekh Agarwal, Danielle Belgrave, Kyunghyun Cho & Alice Oh (eds.), *Advances in Neural Information Processing Systems (NeurIPS)*, vol. 35, 27730–27744.

Page, Lawrence, Sergey Brin, Rajeev Motwani & Terry Winograd. 1999. *The PageRank citation ranking: Bringing order to the web*. Technical report. Stanford InfoLab.

Pang, Bo & Lillian Lee. 2007. Opinion mining and sentiment analysis. *Foundations and Trends in Information Retrieval* 2(1-2). 1–135. DOI: 10.1561/9781601981516.

Papineni, Kishore, Salim Roukos, Todd Ward & Wei-Jing Zhu. 2002. BLEU: A method for automatic evaluation of machine translation. In Pierre Isabelle, Eugene Charniak & Dekang Lin (eds.), *Proceedings of the 40th Annual Meeting of the Association for Computational Linguistics (ACL)*, 311–318. DOI: 10.3115/1073083.1073135.

Paquot, Magali & Stefan Th. Gries (eds.). 2021. *A practical handbook of corpus linguistics*. Cham: Springer Nature. DOI: 10.1007/978-3-030-46216-1.

Parrish, Allison. 2018. Understanding word vectors. Blog post. https://gist.github.com/aparrish/2f562e3737544cf29aaf1af30362f469 (3 July, 2024).

Partee, Barbara H., Alice ter Meulen & Robert Wall. 1990. *Mathematical methods in linguistics*. Dordrecht: Kluwer. DOI: 10.1007/978-94-009-2213-6.

Peng, Ciyuan, Feng Xia, Mehdi Naseriparsa & Francesco Osborne. 2023. Knowledge graphs: Opportunities and challenges. *Artificial Intelligence Review* 56(11). 13071–13102. DOI: 10.1007/s10462-023-10465-9.

Pennington, Jeffrey, Richard Socher & Christopher D. Manning. 2014. GloVe: Global vectors for word representation. In Alessandro Moschitti, Bo Pang & Walter Daelemans (eds.), *Proceedings of Empirical Methods in Natural Language Processing (EMNLP)*, 1532–1543. DOI: 10.3115/v1/d14-1162.

Piantadosi, Steven T. 2014. Zipf's word frequency law in natural language: A critical review and future directions. *Psychonomic Bulletin & Review* 21. 1112–1130. DOI: 10.3758/s13423-014-0585-6.

Piron, Claude. 1988. Learning from translation mistakes. In Dan Maxwell, Klaus Schubert & Toon Witkam (eds.), *Proceedings of New Directions in Machine Translation*, 233–242. Dordrecht: Foris Publications. DOI: 10.1515/9783110874204-017.

Potts, Christopher. 2010. On the negativity of negation. In Nan Li & David Lutz (eds.), *Semantics and Linguistic Theory (SALT)*, vol. 20, 636–659. DOI: 10.3765/salt.v20i0.2565.

Rajpurkar, Pranav, Jian Zhang, Konstantin Lopyrev & Percy Liang. 2016. SQuAD: 100,000+ questions for machine comprehension of text. In Jian Su, Kevin Duh & Xavier Carreras (eds.), *Proceedings of the 2016 conference on Empirical Methods in Natural Language Processing (EMNLP)*, 2383–2392. Austin, TX: Association for Computational Linguistics. DOI: 10.18653/v1/d16-1264.

Reddy, Sravana & Kevin Knight. 2011. What we know about the Voynich manuscript. In Kalliopi Zervanou & Piroska Lendvai (eds.), *Proceedings of the 5th ACL-HLT workshop on language technology for cultural heritage, social sciences, and humanities*, 78–86.

Rosenbach, Anette. 2005. Animacy versus weight as determinants of grammatical variation in English. *Language*. 613–644. DOI: 10.1353/lan.2005.0149.

Rudzewitz, Björn, Ramon Ziai, Kordula De Kuthy & Detmar Meurers. 2017. Developing a web-based workbook for English supporting the interaction of students and teachers. In Elena Volodina, Gintare Grigonyte, Ildikó Pilán, Kristina Nilsson Björkenstam & Lars Borin (eds.), *Proceedings of the Joint Workshop on NLP for Computer Assisted Language Learning and NLP for Language Acquisition*, vol. 134, 36–46. Urmeå, Sweden: Link oping Electronic Conference Proceedings.

Russell, Robert C. 1918. *U.S. patent numbers 1,261,167 (1918) and 1,435,663 (1922)*. Tech. rep. Washington, D.C.: U.S. Patent Office.

Sankoff, David. 1992. Edit distance for genome comparison based on non-local operations. In Alberto Apostolico, Maxime Crochemore, Zvi Galil & Udi Manber (eds.), *Annual symposium on combinatorial pattern matching*, 121–135. Berlin. DOI: 10.1007/3-540-56024-6_10.

Searle, John R. 1980. Minds, brains, and programs. *Behavioral and Brain Sciences* 3(3). 417–424. DOI: 10.1017/s0140525x00005756.

Searle, John R. 1994. Literary theory and its discontents. *New Literary History* 25(3). 637–667. DOI: 10.2307/469470.

Shah, Chirag & Emily M. Bender. 2022. Situating search. In *Proceedings of the 2022 Conference on Human Information Interaction and Retrieval*, 221–232. DOI: 10.1145/3498366.3505816.

Shieber, Stuart M. 1985. Evidence against the context-freeness of natural language. In Walter J. Savitch, Emmon Bach, William Marsh & Gila Safran-Naveh (eds.), *The formal complexity of natural language*, 320–334. Dordrecht: Springer. DOI: 10.1007/978-94-009-2727-8_4.

Spärck Jones, Karen. 1972. A statistical interpretation of term specificity and its application in retrieval. *Journal of Documentation* 28(1). 11–21.

Speer, Robyn, Joshua Chin & Catherine Havasi. 2017. ConceptNet 5.5: An open multilingual graph of general knowledge. In Satinder Singh & Shaul Markovitch (eds.), *Proceedings of the AAAI Conference on Artificial Intelligence*, vol. 31. San Francisco, CA: Association for Computing Machinery. DOI: 10.1609/aaai.v31i1.11164.

Sproat, Richard. 2000. *A computational theory of writing systems*. Cambridge, UK: Cambridge University Press.

Sproat, Richard. 2011. *Language, technology, and society*. Oxford: Oxford University Press.

Stalnaker, Robert. 2002. Common ground. *Linguistics and Philosophy* 25(5/6). 701–721. DOI: 10.1023/a:1020867916902.

Stanovsky, Gabriel, Noah A. Smith & Luke Zettlemoyer. 2019. Evaluating gender bias in machine translation. In Anna Korhonen, David Traum & Lluís Màrquez (eds.), *Proceedings of the 57th annual meeting of the Association for Computational Linguistics*, 1679–1684. Florence, Italy: Association for Computational Linguistics. DOI: 10.18653/v1/p19-1164.

Swartz, Merryanna L. & Masoud Yazdani (eds.). 1992. *Intelligent tutoring systems for foreign language learning: The bridge to international communication*. Berlin: Springer. DOI: 10.1007/978-3-642-77202-3.

Tannen, Deborah. 1990. *You just don't understand: Women and men in conversation*. New York: Ballantine Books.

Tesnière, Lucien. 2015 [1929]. *Elements of structural syntax*. Trans. by Timothy Osborne & Sylvain Kahane. Originally published in French in 1929, as *Éléments de syntaxe structurale*. Amsterdam: John Benjamins. DOI: 10.1075/z.185.

The Ohio State University Department of Linguistics (ed.). 2022. *Language files: Materials for an introduction to language and linguistics.* 13th edn. Columbus, OH: The Ohio State University Press.

Tiedemann, Jörg & Lars Nygaard. 2004. The OPUS corpus: Parallel and free \NoCaseChange{{https://opus.nlpl.eu/}}. In Maria Teresa Lino, Maria Francisca Xavier, Fátima Ferreira, Rute Costa, Raquel Silva, Carla Pereira, Filipa Carvalho, Milene Lopes, Mónica Catarino & Sérgio Barros (eds.), *Proceedings of the fourth international conference on language Resources and Evaluation Conference (LREC).* Lisbon, Portugal: European Language Resources Association.

Traugott, Elizabeth Closs & Richard B. Dasher. 2001. *Regularity in semantic change.* Cambridge: Cambridge University Press. DOI: 10.1017/cbo9780511486500.

Turing, Alan M. 1950. Computing machinery and intelligence. *Mind* 49. 433–460. DOI: 10.1093/oso/9780198250791.003.0017.

Underwood, Ted, David Bamman & Sabrina Lee. 2018. The transformation of gender in English-language fiction. *Journal of Cultural Analytics* 1. DOI: 10.22148/16.019.

Vaswani, Ashish, Noam Shazeer, Niki Parmar, Jakob Uszkoreit, Llion Jones, Aidan N. Gomez, Łukasz Kaiser & Illia Polosukhin. 2017. Attention is all you need. In Isabelle Guyon, Ulrike Von Luxburg, Samy Bengio, Hanna Wallach, Rob Fergus, S.V.N. Vishwanathan & Roman Garnett (eds.), *Advances in Neural Information Processing Systems*, vol. 30, 5998–6008. Long Beach, CA.

Vygotsky, Lev Semenovich. 1978. *Mind in society: Development of higher psychological processes.* Michael Cole, Vera John-Steiner, Sylvia Scribner & Ellen Souberman (eds.). Translated from Russian original published 1930-1933. Cambridge, MA: Harvard University Press. DOI: 10.2307/j.ctvjf9vz4.17.

Wang, Alex, Yada Pruksachatkun, Nikita Nangia, Amanpreet Singh, Julian Michael, Felix Hill, Omer Levy & Samuel Bowman. 2019. SuperGLUE: A stickier benchmark for general-purpose language understanding systems. In Hanna Wallach, Hugo Larochelle, Alina Beygelzimer, Florence d'Alché-Buc, Edward Fox & Roman Garnett (eds.), *Advances in Neural Information Processing Systems*, vol. 32. Vancouver: Curran Associates, Inc.

Wang, Alex, Amanpreet Singh, Julian Michael, Felix Hill, Omer Levy & Samuel R. Bowman. 2018. GLUE: A multi-task benchmark and analysis platform for natural language understanding. In Tal Linzen, Grzegorz Chrupała & Afra Alishahi (eds.), *Proceedings of the BlackboxNLP Workshop at EMNLP: Analyzing and Interpreting Neural Networks for NLP*, 353–355. Brussels: Association for Computational Linguistics. DOI: 10.18653/v1/w18-5446.

Warstadt, Alex, Amanpreet Singh & Samuel R Bowman. 2019. Neural network acceptability judgments. *Transactions of the Association for Computational Linguistics* 7. 625–641. DOI: 10.1162/tacl_a_00290.

Weaver, Warren. 1949. Translation. In William N. Locke & A. Donald Booth (eds.), *Machine translation of languages: Fourteen essays*, 15–23. New York: The Technology Press of MIT. DOI: 10.7551/mitpress/5779.003.0004.

Weizenbaum, Joseph. 1966. ELIZA – a computer program for the study of natural language communication between man and machine. In Gerard Salton (ed.), *Communications of the ACM*, vol. 9, 36–45. New York: Association for Computing Machinery. DOI: 10.1145/365153.365168.

Weizenbaum, Joseph. 1976. *Computer power and human reason*. San Francisco: W. H. Freeman.

White, Aaron Steven. 2021. On believing and hoping whether. *Semantics and Pragmatics* 14. DOI: /10.3765/sp.14.6.

White, Sarah J., Rebecca L. Johnson, Simon P Liversedge & Keith Rayner. 2008. Eye movements when reading transposed text: the importance of word-beginning letters. *Journal of Experimental Psychology: Human Perception and Performance* 34(5). 1261–1276.

Wilcox-O'Hearn, Amber, Graeme Hirst & Alexander Budanitsky. 2008. Real-word spelling correction with trigrams: A reconsideration of the Mays, Damerau, and Mercer model. In Alexander Gelbukh (ed.), *Computational Linguistics and Intelligent Text Processing (CICLing)*, 605–616. Berlin: Springer-Verlag. DOI: 10.1007/978-3-540-78135-6_52.

Winograd, Terry & Fernando Flores. 1986. *Understanding computers and cognition: A new foundation for design*. Bristol, UK: Intellect Books.

Zipf, George Kingsley. 1932. *Selected studies of the principle of relative frequency in language*. Cambridge, MA: Harvard University Press. DOI: 10.4159/harvard.9780674434929.

Author index

Subject index